SUPERPOWER SHOWDOWN

SUPERPOWER SHOWDOWN

HARPER
BUSINESS

An Imprint of HarperCollinsPublishers

How the Battle Between Trump and
Xi Threatens a New Cold War

BOB DAVIS AND
LINGLING WEI

FIRST EDITION

Designed by Nancy Singer

Cover Images: © CSA Images/Getty Images (eagle);
© Kevin5017/Shutterstock (dragon)

Library of Congress Cataloging-in-Publication Data
Names: Davis, Bob, author. | Wei, Lingling, author.
Title: Superpower showdown : how the battle between Trump and Xi threatens a new cold war / Bob Davis and Lingling Wei.
Description: First edition. | New York : Harper Business, [2020] | Includes bibliographical references and index. | Summary: "Wall Street Journal reporters Davis and Wei tell the inside story of the US-China trade war, examining how relations between China and the US, between Trump and Xi, have risen and fallen in the battle to become the world's sole economic and political superpower" Provided by publisher.
Identifiers: LCCN 2020008253 (print) | LCCN 2020008254 (ebook) | ISBN 9780062953056 (hardcover) | ISBN 9780062953049 (paperback) | ISBN 9780062953063 (ebook)
Subjects: LCSH: China—Foreign relations—United States. | China—Foreign economic relations—United States. | United States—Foreign relations—China. | United States—Foreign economic relations—China.
Classification: LCC DS779.47 .D388 2020 (print) | LCC DS779.47 (ebook) | DDC 382.0973/051—dc23
LC record available at https://lccn.loc.gov/2020008253
LC ebook record available at https://lccn.loc.gov/2020008254

---

20 21 22 23 24 LSC 10 9 8 7 6 5 4 3 2 1

DEDICATIONS

From Bob:
To Mike and Doris Davis, and Debra Bruno,
who have filled my life with love.

From Lingling:
To Zhong Guang, and to Zhong Lina and Wei Gengfu,
for never giving up.

CONTENTS

A NOTE TO READERS

This book is based primarily on hundreds of interviews in Washington, D.C., and Beijing over the past three years with government officials, former government officials, and the outsiders they ask for advice. Covering government officials in the two capitals is different in many ways, reflecting the different political systems. But in one big way it's similar: officials and other participants rarely are willing to talk candidly on the record.

To get to the truth we had to assure anonymity. Under the ground rules we established, we could use information from the interviews, but we couldn't say who provided it. Journalists and officials use different terms for this arrangement—usually "deep background" or "off-the-record." There is no precise meaning for either term. To try to avoid misunderstanding, we explained to those we interviewed that we planned to use the information they provided although we wouldn't say who revealed the scenes and information we describe.

If we were doing a story for the *Wall Street Journal* based on these interviews, we would have attributed many of the anecdotes to "people familiar with the events" or to "senior government officials," depending on who told us what. We dispense with those attributions in this book.

A journalist we both greatly admire, the *Washington Post*'s Bob Woodward, uses a similar arrangement in his many books about Washington. We generally followed that approach but modified it.

Readers rightly complain that it is difficult to judge the authenticity of works of journalism because sources aren't identified. But, as we say, to get the truth, we often had to agree to anonymity. If sources are identified in Washington, they could lose their jobs or standing. In Beijing, the punishment could be much worse.

There are times, however, when sources will allow themselves to be quoted on the record. Even if those quotes are sometimes anodyne, we think they help readers judge whether to trust the account. When participants in the events agreed to go on the record, we note it by putting the quote in present tense and generally adding a modifier like, "says in an interview." We also note the interview in the endnotes.

That doesn't mean that other times the person is cited or quoted in a scene that the person is the source of the information. Rather the material comes from a combination of government officials, former officials, and the people they talk to, sometimes bolstered by contemporaneous notes.

We realize this isn't a perfect solution. But we hope that the arrangement gives readers additional assurance of our efforts to get the story right.

SUPERPOWER SHOWDOWN

THREAT OF WAR, DECEMBER 2018

A month after the 2018 midterm elections, chief executives of seventy-five of the nation's leading manufacturing, technology, and financial firms gathered at the Four Seasons Hotel in the George-town section of Washington, D.C., to hear from top Trump adminis-tration officials. It was a chilly day and a gloomy time for the White House.

Republicans had come up short in the elections, losing control of the House of Representatives. The stock market was deep into a fall swoon. White House turmoil was deepening, as the chief of staff was about to resign. On that December 4, Washington was also pre-paring for the funeral the following day of President George H. W. Bush, who seemed like a leader from some Paleolithic period when politicians spoke civilly and soap-opera drama was reserved for TV.

The CEOs had a different concern on their minds: China. How badly were U.S.-China relations deteriorating? Was the trade war between the two nations spinning out of control? Should they re-make their business strategies and assume that tariffs, sanctions, and indictments would permanently limit trade and investment be-tween the two nations?

The group was part of what the *Wall Street Journal* calls its CEO Council—about two hundred companies that pay $24,800 a year to have senior executives join sessions in Washington and elsewhere around the world with policy makers. Sitting on a conference room stage, *Wall Street Journal* reporters and editors pepper administration officials with questions. The audience gets to vote on a question chosen by the editor, with the results displayed on an electronic screen at the front of the room.

The *Wall Street Journal*'s editor-at-large, Gerard Baker, an acerbic Brit, faced off with John Bolton, who was then the administration's national security advisor. The formal topic was "American Business in the World," but Baker moved immediately to China.

President Donald Trump and Chinese President Xi Jinping had met for dinner three days earlier in Buenos Aires, Baker reminded the audience. The two leaders had reached a ninety-day truce during which the United States promised to suspend its plans to raise tariffs.

"President Trump has certainly described [the meeting] in almost a 1938 Neville Chamberlain–type way. 'Peace in our time,'" Baker said, egging on Bolton, who had sat in on the Argentina dinner.

"I wouldn't say that," Bolton responded, laughing.

In quick succession, the blunt-speaking Bolton accused China of stealing U.S. intellectual property, forcing companies to give up technology against their will to their Chinese partners, and spying on U.S. firms. Sure, China was talking about buying more U.S. soybeans, he continued, and that was fine. But it was hardly enough to get the United States to back off.

"We don't see the American future being a Third World country supplying natural resources and agricultural products to China," Bolton said. "We need to see some major changes in their behavior. Structural issues, if you will."

Without these changes, he continued, there would be more punishment. "How about a rule that says there will be no imports into the United States of any products or services that are based on the theft of American intellectual property?" he said. What Bolton left unsaid was just as important. Who would determine whether Chinese imports were based on theft? Obviously, some U.S. agency. How would it decide? Anyone's guess. That could give the U.S. government authority to ban any import at any time—an enormous expansion of U.S. punitive power aimed at Beijing.

"Is that something the president and the administration's proposing?" Baker asked.

"We may have some authority in that area already," Bolton said. "We may need additional legislation. But this is what we're talking about."

The United States clearly had misread China's rise, he went on. "American policy was based on the assumption of bringing China into the WTO [World Trade Organization] would increase pressure to conform to international norms in trade and business areas. That has obviously not happened. We had decades of people who said the modernization and economic growth of China would produce increased political freedom and more representative government. That hasn't happened, either."

Baker then posed a question to the audience: "Will the U.S. and China find themselves at war sometime in the next twenty years?" That is, a real war, between two nuclear-armed nations that account for 40 percent of the world's gross domestic product (GDP), not simply a trade war. U.S. soldiers firing on Chinese soldiers; Chinese missiles raining down on U.S. aircraft carriers.

Half those voting in the audience—CEOs and other senior executives of companies whose predecessors had lobbied for China to join the WTO and who had counted on the kinds of political change in China that Bolton was deriding—said yes, the two nations were bound for war.

"I mean, actually, how do you respond to that?" Baker asked Bolton.

"Well, obviously, our strong desire is to avoid it," the national security advisor responded. "But I don't think it rests with us. I think it rests with China." In the final vote tally, about one-third of the executives said the two nations were headed for war, still an astoundingly high percentage, considering the audience.

How had it come to this moment? Not long before, ties between the United States and China were so promising that the two nations seemed wrapped in a permanent embrace. "Chimerica," academics called it. In Beijing, officials told Americans that their two nations were like an old married couple who needed each other, even though they might bicker. Now a senior U.S. official was threatening to cripple China by banning imports and blustered about the prospects of a shooting war. And U.S. CEOs had become so discouraged about the relationship that many of them figured war was in the offing.

Surely Donald Trump is part of the answer. Trump had made what he called China's "rape" of the U.S. economy one of his go-to riffs during campaign rallies. As president, he had put half of what China sold to the United States under tariffs by the day of the CEO Conference, and was threatening levies on the rest of Chinese imports. Various parts of the government were also working on sanctions of Chinese firms for espionage and other misdeeds. No president had taken measures anywhere near this extreme with a major trading partner since the 1930s.

"Trade wars are good and easy to win," the president tweeted in March 2018, as he announced tariffs on steel and aluminum imports aimed at pressuring China to shut down steel mills and smelters, a claim he repeated regularly afterward.

But Trump isn't the entire answer. The trade and economic battle didn't start with Trump and won't end with him. Relations were souring before he took office. Chinese leaders also deserve a big share of the blame, as do U.S. business leaders, who for decades acted as Beijing's lobbyists in Washington. Chinese President Xi Jinping was as swaggering about the outcome of a trade war as President Trump was. "In the West, you have the notion that if somebody hits you on the left cheek, you turn the other cheek," Xi told visiting U.S., European, and Australian chief executives in Beijing, three months after the Trump trade war tweet. "In our culture, we punch back."

This book explains how U.S.-China relations have sunk as low as they have and looks at where the United States and China are headed. Think of this as a romance gone bad. We tell the story from both capitals with insider detail gleaned from hundreds of interviews with government and business officials in both nations over the years the two of us have worked together. We started collaborating on U.S.-China stories when we both were posted in Beijing from 2011 to 2014. After one of us, Bob, returned to Washington, D.C., at the end of 2014, we continued to work together in a kind of binational arrangement. Lingling might get a tip in Beijing, work on it during her day, and then hand it off to Bob to continue pressing his sources during workday hours in Washington.

Our family stories blended with our journalistic interests and the economic saga we have tried to tell. In different ways, the two of us have been deeply affected by the changes we describe in the book. Lingling comes from a Chinese military family in a farm province in southeastern China, whose family prides itself on being part of the Communist Party's "red roots," because of her grandfather's connection to Chairman Mao.

Zhong Fuchang joined the Chinese Workers' and Peasants' Red Army in 1932 when he was just thirteen years old. Obedient and studious, he soon became a member of Mao's health detail and was by his side during the entire Long March, the six-thousand-mile trek by the Communists that established Mao as the undisputed party leader. Mao taught the young soldier how to read and write, and true to the proletarian values of the party, Mao changed Zhong's name Fuchang—or "wealth and prosperity"—to Guang, which means light. Zhong Guang was the name he used for the rest of his life.

After the founding of the People's Republic of China in 1949,

Mao offered Zhong Guang a senior government position in Beijing, but Zhong wanted to return home to Jiangxi, a province of shimmering rice fields whose capital city, Nanchang, is known as the "Red City" because the People's Liberation Army was founded there. But his party standing didn't save him during the Cultural Revolution of the late 1960s when Red Guards interrogated him because of his party-arranged marriage many years earlier to a North Korean woman who had fled to China during the Japanese occupation. The Guards suspected him of being a spy. He was only saved when Mao made a trip to Jiangxi, heard about his old aide's predicament, and declared to the province's Communist Party secretary, "Zhong Guang is a good comrade."

The story of Mao's intervention spread and became part of local lore. When Lingling's primary school and high school classes visited the mausoleums of Communist martyrs during spring breaks, her teachers would make sure to stop by her grandfather's tombstone for the students to pay their respects.

Lingling's family changed along with China. In the early 1990s, her father was discharged from the military after China drastically downsized its army, while her mother, Zhong Guang's daughter, stayed on as a military doctor.

Lingling's father, Wei Gengfu, became part of the new China that was opening up to the West. At first, he worked at a government agency promoting trade and attracting foreign investment. He helped local farms display their rice and oranges at the annual trade show held in the southern export hub of Guangzhou, known as the Canton Fair. He also spent a lot of time vetting proposed investments from Taiwan, a renegade province in the eyes of Beijing but a major source of overseas capital and capitalist know-how for the mainland. After his retirement in 2010, he became a consultant for private property developers and manufacturers looking to export overseas and stay in the good graces of the government.

For Lingling, her family history taught her about the enormous power of the party and its leader. But she started down a different path, as did many other Chinese youths who went to college in the early 1990s. China then was both opening up economically and keeping a close watch on students in the aftermath of the 1989 government crackdown on student democracy protests in Tiananmen Square and throughout the country.

Following her mother's dream of becoming a writer, Lingling chose a career in journalism. But it didn't take her long to realize how tightly the government controlled reporting. She attended journalism school at one of China's elite universities, Shanghai's Fudan University, which required months of military training before freshmen started classes. Mostly that involved learning how to march in goose step, studying Marxism-Leninism, and singing "Unity Is Strength," a propaganda piece of the party. But on some days, she was handed firearms and dispatched to a shooting range for target practice. "Imagine the target is an American," an instructor once told her.

The heavy-handed instruction pushed her in the opposite direction. Along with some of her classmates, she would stay up late listening to BBC and Voice of America on shortwave radio, trying to learn as much English as she could and imagining a life in a land of freedom. After graduation, she worked for the state-owned *Shanghai Star* writing about the frenzied efforts to turn former farmland in a section of the city called Pudong into a business and financial hub. Filling those pages was mostly a political exercise; over time, her desire to report more freely grew stronger.

After marrying a scientist in China, she and her husband moved to New York. Lingling went from a graduate degree at New York University in 2000 to an internship at the *Wall Street Journal* to full-time work at the newspaper. Along the way, she and her husband became U.S. citizens. Because of Chinese law barring dual citizenships, she had to give up her red Chinese passport.

In New York, she reported how once-obscure Chinese institutions and companies were gaining wealth and buying stakes in such marquee American financial firms as Morgan Stanley and Black-stone Group. She learned from Chinese officials how a glamorous real estate tycoon named Donald Trump donned a tuxedo to greet the chairman of China's largest state-owned bank when he leased an entire floor of Trump Tower. A line in the essay she wrote to get the *Wall Street Journal* internship stuck with her. "By coming here to study, I hoped to get beyond the limits imposed by my government," she wrote.

Still, her roots and her family are in China, a connection that pulled her back to Beijing in 2011 for a job in the *Journal*'s Beijing bureau. Since then, she has written stories critical of the government's handling of the economy and its secretive decision-making process. Time and again, some Chinese authorities complained that her coverage was hurting China. Although her parents often remind her of her red roots, they remain broadly supportive of her work. The support didn't fade when Lingling was ordered to leave China by Xi Jinping's government in March 2020, along with other American reporters from the *Journal*, the *New York Times*, and the *Washington Post*. That was the biggest expulsion of Western journalists from China since the Mao era, as the coronavirus pandemic deepened tensions between the two nations. Relations were already strained by the trade war.

Lingling's family roots didn't save her, though some officials lobbied to give her extra time before she had to leave. The expulsion marked an abrupt end to her China dream of reporting from her country. She thought about quitting to remain with her parents, who are both in their seventies, but they rejected that idea as soon as she raised it. "Don't give up," her mother told her.

Bob's family history traces a different side of the U.S.-China story—the impact of foreign competition on U.S. companies and workers, in this case the luggage industry in New York City.

Bob's father, Michael Davis, was a factory man and inventor, who wound up with a half-dozen patents to his name. In 1953, he patented a soft-sided garment bag that kept suits less wrinkled. The clothing hung on plastic hangers in the inside of the suitcase, which folded in half. He wasn't the only one to come up with the idea for a suit bag. It was an improvement on the garment bags used by servicemen like him during World War II.

Still, it was enough of an innovation to find partners, form a company, Crescent Mayfab Luggage, and set up a factory in the Bedford-Stuyvesant part of Brooklyn. Back then, well before the neighborhood's hipster days, Bed-Stuy was populated by immigrants from Puerto Rico and blacks from the South. Mike Davis ran the factory, which consisted of rows of sewing machines and ancient equipment that used steam to bend wood frames. His partner handled sales. He paid workers about ten cents more than minimum wage, which he felt was enough to keep the union off his back.

His timing in the 1950s was impeccable. Business travel was expanding, powered by the postwar boom, the construction of the Interstate Highway System, and the growth of jet travel. Traveling salesmen and executives needed to keep their suits looking crisp. The family moved to a modest garden apartment complex in Queens, called Deepdale Gardens, where the mothers were housewives and the fathers worked as salesmen, factory hands, and shopkeepers.

There, Mike Davis stood out. He was Big Mike, the rakish factory owner, who flaunted his newfound prosperity and partied in Manhattan after work. Every two years, he bought a new Cadillac or Lincoln Continental—always a convertible—while most everyone else in the neighborhood drove Chevys. Sometimes he would flip the keys to a teenage boy he knew and tell him to park the car for him, knowing how much the kids wanted to get behind the wheel of the most expensive car in the neighborhood. To them, he was Mad Mike.

But by the mid-1960s, his timing was off. Imports from Hong Kong, Taiwan, and South Korea were making deep inroads into the luggage industry, especially in the soft-sided bags he made. Bob's father told him he could handle the competition. How could dirt-poor countries make goods that competed with made-in-the-USA quality? That was a miscalculation made by many of his generation. In retrospect, Crescent Mayfab had no manufacturing advantage over Asia. It relied on low-cost labor to run old-fashioned technology to make mass-produced goods. Those same goods could be produced thousands of miles away by sewing machine operators who earned a tiny fraction of the U.S. minimum wage, and shipped to the United States at a price Mike Davis couldn't match. Although luggage imports faced high tariffs, that wasn't enough to protect the U.S. industry.

He tried making higher-end goods. In 1964, he moved into the golf bag business, creating "Gary Player Pro-Line" bags, endorsed by the great South African golfer. The bags, made of "pinseal Kangaroo" leather, retailed for $185. (One of Deepdale's most memorable evenings during those years was when Gary Player stopped by the small Davis apartment, as scores of neighborhood kids stood outside, hoping to get a glimpse of the golfer. Player, an exercise fanatic, did push-ups on the living room floor.) Five years later, he tried fashion luggage, introducing a line he called DaVinci. B. Altman & Company advertised the bags as "a new name in luxurious luggage" and sold them for as much as $110 each.

None of it worked and all of it came at an awful time, when his wife, Bob's mother, was dying agonizingly of cancer. Bob transferred from Syracuse University to Queens College, which was then tuition-free, to save money. His father's drinking, always a problem, worsened.

By 1972, Mike Davis sold the company for a song and was out of a job. With the luggage world suddenly globalized, he was recruited to run a luggage factory in northern Mexico. He turned that down. Too distant; too foreign. He wound up in Ellwood City, Pennsylvania—a kind of exile for him—designing and making luggage for

Airway Industries Inc. His new firm had started importing luggage from South Korea in addition to producing suitcases in its Pennsylvania factories.

With Airway, he took his first trips to South Korea to see the factories that had put him out of business. He told his son that he was impressed by the work ethic, quality, and cutthroat business practices of the managers there who quickly sized up the American importers. The Koreans didn't want Americans nosing around. "Their motto is, 'Get them in, get them laid, get them out,'" he said.

By the time he left Airway and retired to Florida in the mid-1980s, China was following the export-heavy development path pioneered by the Asian Tigers and had already grabbed the largest share of the luggage import market. As a consultant, Mike Davis designed suitcases for companies that manufactured in China, including Airway. The firm opened a factory in Hangzhou, about 450 miles east of Lingling's hometown in Jiangxi, before it went bankrupt in 2006. His garage was like a luggage museum, with samples of the different bags he had made over the years and those of competitors, which he dissected to see how they were made.

He said he wasn't bitter about China or other Asian exporters, even though the competition had wrecked his business and killed the entry-level jobs filled by migrants and unskilled workers in places like Brooklyn. But he was probably unusual in that regard among his generation of businessmen. He enjoyed the irony that his son was covering for the *Journal* the same competition he had experienced firsthand in business. For Bob, his father's business life was a lesson in grit and timing and facing reality.

Mike Davis died in March 1998. A year later, Chinese Premier Zhu Rongji—Boss Zhu, as he was known in China—arrived in Washington to cut a deal for his country to join the World Trade Organization, a move that would eventually turn China into the world's biggest trader and leave the United States wondering whether it had made the right choice in helping China prosper.

1

MISCALCULATIONS, APRIL–MAY 2019

After a year of pressure on Beijing, including levying tariffs on half of everything China sold to the United States, the American trade team thought it was closing in on a deal in late April 2019 to remake relations between the world's two economic superpowers.

U.S. tariffs hurt China more than its leader, Xi Jinping, publicly acknowledged. Electronics exporters in Dongguan and other coastal cities were losing American customers. Both government-controlled and privately owned businesses were delaying or canceling investment plans. Big U.S. companies were accelerating their decisions to move production from China to Vietnam, Malaysia, and other countries far from the trade war.

Chinese retaliatory tariffs were hitting their mark too, more than the U.S. leader, Donald Trump, would say. Soybean and other farmers in the rural areas crucial to Trump's reelection saw their Chinese market evaporating. Already the United States had spent about $10 billion compensating them. Looking to forestall a stock market plunge, Trump officials worked overtime to convince investors that the talks were on track by hyping positive news. Trump had staked his reelection bid on a strong economy and a surging stock market.

Now the economic outlook was deteriorating. In April, the manufacturing sector of Greece, racked by a decade of fiscal crisis, was growing faster than the manufacturing sectors of either China or America, according to surveys of industrial purchasing managers around the world conducted by the research firm IHS Markit. In May, purchasing manager surveys aggregated together showed that global manufacturing was in an outright recession.

American and Chinese officials hoped an end to their battle would help head off hard times. Since the two leaders had a friendly dinner in Buenos Aires at a Group of 20 (G-20) summit in December 2018, U.S. and Chinese negotiators had talked regularly by videoconference and flown across the Pacific a number of times to put together an agreement. The vibes were good, negotiators believed.

The two sides were working on a 150-page agreement covering many American complaints against China: pressure on U.S. companies to transfer technology, weak intellectual property protection, closed financial services markets, currency devaluation that helped Chinese exporters, and insufficient purchases of U.S. goods and services. Each chapter of the text started with a general commitment by China, followed by the specific laws and regulations China would amend to carry out its pledges. By some counts, the text required China to make at least sixty specific changes in its legal system. The Chinese propaganda machine portrayed offers to open up the domestic market as steps the country needed to make to keep the economy humming, not as concessions to America.

China still hadn't agreed to many U.S. demands, especially those requiring China to give up the industrial policies and subsidies it provides to firms in favored sectors. Those demands were seen as a threat to the Communist Party's rule and could undermine an economic system that had turned China from an economic backwater into the world's second-largest economy.

To enforce the deal, the two sides discussed a process where disputes were handled at increasingly senior levels. If no agreement was reached, each side had the right to reimpose tariffs. The United States was even pressing China to agree not to retaliate if the United States resorted to levies. This was one of the final issues to be resolved, the U.S. side believed. The two sides had already started discussions about where to hold a signing ceremony. Trump's Mar-a-Lago estate in Florida? Washington, D.C.?

But the U.S. side was naively optimistic and made several miscalculations about the power of the United States to force China to change. First, U.S. Trade Representative Robert Lighthizer continued to insist that Washington wouldn't remove any of its crippling tariffs when Beijing signed a deal. The tall, blunt negotiator thought that China would relent in the face of sustained U.S. pressure, a view he shared with his boss, the president. Lighthizer wanted to keep the levies in place until China demonstrated that it was carrying out its pledges. Although Trump's senior advisers had debated whether to remove tariffs as a good-faith gesture, so far Lighthizer hadn't budged. For Xi Jinping, though, eliminating the tariffs was a bottom-line demand, which he had made clear at the outset of negotiations. On this, he wouldn't bend. If he couldn't get the tariffs lifted, a deal wasn't worth much.

Second, the Americans misread the influence of the lead Chinese negotiator, Vice Premier Liu He, who was an ally and childhood friend of Xi's. Simply because Liu hadn't said no to U.S. proposals didn't mean Beijing had said yes. Although Liu regularly briefed Xi on the terms of the deal, the Chinese leadership hadn't signed on to the agreement, especially one that seemed so one-sided in America's favor. Unknown to U.S. negotiators, something entirely different was happening in the inner sanctums of power back in Beijing.

• • •

The view of the talks in Beijing was decidedly gloomier than the one in Washington. As Lighthizer and Treasury Secretary Steven

Mnuchin prepared to fly to Beijing in late April for talks they hoped could help sew up a deal, Xi thought it was time to loop in the other six members of the Politburo Standing Committee, the country's ruling body. Xi had maneuvered to become China's paramount leader. He had sidelined many of his rivals in an anticorruption campaign and eliminated the two-term limit on his role as president. His power, as general secretary of the Communist Party, nearly equaled that of Chinese leader Deng Xiaoping and even Mao Zedong. But Deng and Mao didn't have absolute power and had to deal with rivals, as did Xi.

Chinese politics is different from American politics, but Chinese leaders still face constraints. Especially since the death of Mao, party chiefs seek a consensus of the Politburo Standing Committee before taking dramatic actions. Xi had angered so many senior party officials, bureaucrats, and influential former officials with his anticorruption drive that he had enemies waiting to take him down a notch. He couldn't afford to be seen as weak in dealing with Americans, especially ahead of the October 1 celebration of the seventieth anniversary of the founding of Communist China.

At a late April meeting in the gated Zhongnanhai leadership compound, close to the Forbidden City, the onetime home of China's emperors, Xi asked his colleagues to review the details of the negotiations. Their answers were hardly reassuring; they signaled a much stronger resistance to proceeding than anyone on the U.S. side understood.

Three of the six spoke out immediately against a deal unless China could get a firm commitment from the United States to remove tariffs on all $250 billion of Chinese exports then burdened with levies.

Li Zhanshu, head of the National People's Congress, China's lawmaking body, objected strenuously to U.S. demands that China change specific laws by certain dates or face tariffs. China is a sovereign nation, Li argued. No country has the right to tell China what laws it must amend.

Wang Huning, a party ideologue focused on reclaiming China's prominent place in the world, was another firm no. Wang, who makes a point of not meeting with Westerners and rarely speaking in public, said many Chinese might view the proposed deal as a sellout, similar to the unfair treaties imposed upon China by Western forces in the nineteenth and early twentieth centuries.

Han Zheng, the most senior of China's four vice premiers, was the most surprising of the opponents. For years he had run Shanghai, a metropolis known for East-meets-West glamour. American businesses considered him an ally who supported foreign investment. But he also thought the tentative deal was too one-sided.

The three other standing committee members—Premier Li Keqiang, anti-graft czar Zhao Leji, and veteran political leader Wang Yang, who had negotiated for years with Americans on trade—weren't as vehement. They shared their colleagues' concerns, though they broadly supported a deal with the United States.

Faced with, at best, tepid support, Xi—himself an ardent nationalist—decided that Beijing needed to toughen its stance in negotiations. Here, Xi too made a series of miscalculations, which combined with those on the American side would eliminate the chance of a deal anytime soon, embitter both sides, and deepen the economic cost of the trade war so much that it threatened to drive the global economy into recession.

Time was on China's side, Xi believed. Trump's tough talk masked a fear about the American economy. Trump was constantly hectoring Federal Reserve chairman Jerome Powell to cut interest rates. That would only be necessary, the Chinese leader thought, if the U.S. economy was slowing precipitously. China's economy, on the other hand, had stabilized, and Beijing could start counting on allies in its trade battle, he believed. Some forty heads of state and government ignored a U.S. boycott and attended an April conference in Beijing on Xi's signature Belt and Road Initiative. The vast infrastructure lending and construction program was designed to put Beijing at the heart of trade from Southeast Asia to Europe.

Some advisers had been encouraging Trump to make allies of his European trade partners in the confrontation with China. Instead, he confronted them too, calling countries like Germany worse trade offenders than China. Xi tried to capitalize on Trump's belligerence. A March tour by Xi of Italy and France also gave him a sense that more countries would line up with China. European officials indicated they were worried that a deal to buy more U.S. goods would mean China would buy less from Europe. They needed China's vast market to bolster their economies and were wary of American intentions.

Be firmer with the Americans, Xi instructed Liu, the Chinese negotiator.

At a welcome dinner in the Forbidden City for the American negotiators on April 30, Liu hinted that he was having problems convincing his superiors to take the deal they had negotiated. On the same day, during a private meeting with Lighthizer and Mnuchin, Liu said the leadership strongly objected to specifying the laws China needed to change. This was more than the give-and-take of prior rounds, he made clear. He didn't have a mandate to cut a final deal. Beijing was still willing to change some legislation to honor its commitment to better protect U.S. intellectual property, among other U.S. demands, Liu said, but it would have to do so without seeming to yield to American pressure.

Detailed requirements, which started with the phrase "China shall," would have to be dropped from the text, even though that wording was crucial to the Americans who wanted ironclad guarantees that China would make the changes. China would rather meet U.S. demands by modifying certain regulations as part of a newly passed foreign investment law that promised to help U.S. companies compete more fairly in China, Liu said.

While the difference between changing laws instead of regulations may seem small, especially in China with a legislature widely considered toothless, to Lighthizer it was freighted with significance. The Obama administration had managed to get China to make administrative changes, but that hadn't noticeably reduced the problems U.S. companies faced in China. And the Trump administration was obsessed with not settling for anything Obama settled for. Lighthizer insisted that the National People's Congress approve changes. That would signal a deeper commitment by Beijing and make it tougher for Chinese judges to use phony reasoning to rule against U.S. companies. He also knew that changes requiring legislative approval are standard in international trade agreements. But his insistence was too much for a Chinese leadership protective, perhaps overly so, of Xi's strongman image when national sentiment against foreign pressure was rising.

The Americans weren't looking to compromise. They were looking for more concessions. During negotiations in the leafy campus of the Diaoyutai State Guesthouse, the U.S. side presented a detailed proposal on how China should open up its fast-growing cloud computing sector to companies like Microsoft and Amazon. To do business in China, foreign firms had to form joint operations and license their technology to local partners. Alibaba Group Holding Ltd. and other Chinese firms didn't face those restrictions in the United States.

Liu offered to issue more licenses and allow U.S. firms to control joint ventures for certain cloud services, instead of being limited to a 50 percent stake. But the United States wanted more. The Americans raised questions about a notice published in 2016 by China's Ministry of Industry and Information Technology that seemed to put restrictions on foreign cloud operators. If enacted, Americans could be blocked from the market even if they obtained licenses. The Chinese balked at rescinding the notice.

The Americans also wanted China to bump up its target for purchasing U.S. goods and services by roughly 50 percent to about $2 trillion over six years from $1.2 trillion. Chinese officials had proposed $1.2 trillion in "additional purchases" at Buenos Aires, according to Mnuchin. Even that target seemed wildly ambitious and caused some Trump advisers to roll their eyes at its improbability.

Meeting the $1.2 trillion goal would require about a 30 percent annual increase in U.S. merchandise exports to China from the $130 billion in 2017, before the trade war started. Since 2001, when China joined the World Trade Organization and became a major global trader, U.S. annual goods exports to China increased at a 30 percent pace only twice. Goods exports fell in four years. Now the United States wanted China to buy at an even a faster clip.

To Lighthizer, the increased target was part of the haggling involved in cutting a final deal. To the Chinese negotiators, though, this was an indication that Americans weren't bargaining in good faith.

Liu made it clear that China's leaders couldn't accept the draft as it was written. Okay, Lighthizer responded. Show me what you mean. Pick any of the seven chapters in the agreement and mark it up. Make as few changes as you can, consistent with your new instructions, and send it to me, he told the Chinese negotiator. Maybe the changes won't be as radical as you're suggesting and negotiations could continue as before. Lighthizer had come to trust and respect Liu as a committed reformer.

Liu picked the chapter on intellectual property, which was nearly completed. It called for changes in Chinese law, including criminal penalties—jail time—for those who repeatedly stole technology secrets or copied them. Lighthizer's goal was to make IP protection in China as tough as it was in the United States or Britain. While the United States was willing to give China the time it needed to rewrite the laws, the Americans insisted that tariffs stay in place to make sure Beijing would carry out its pledges.

China was moving in a different direction. On May 1, the social media account Taoran Notes, which often reflects the views of senior Chinese officials, posted this warning: "If one party only considers its demands and thinks it can use extreme pressure to force the other party to submit and ignore fairness, then there's not any other possibility than breaking up."

• • •

On Friday, May 3, the Americans received a formal response. Chinese negotiators emailed to Washington a Microsoft Word version of the tentative agreement, with about one-third of the intellectual property section crossed out in red, including requirements that China change its laws. Beijing also continued to hedge on whether it would bar currency devaluations aimed at helping Chinese exporters compete better, and disclose when China's central bank bought or sold foreign exchange so its activities could be more closely monitored.

The reluctance to accept changes in currency practices was particularly galling. China had already committed to refrain from competitive devaluation in multilateral agreements. Now it was balking at making essentially the same pledge to Americans. Treasury Secretary Mnuchin, the most dovish member of the administration on China, had negotiated that section. Beijing was embarrassing him and turning him into an opponent, too.

To Beijing, the changes were just another step in ongoing negotiations—yet another of the serious miscalculations made by both sides. The Chinese had backed away from other parts of the deal before, with no repercussions. Officials on both sides would stew, but continue to negotiate. During an exchange in February 2019, Lighthizer "read them the riot act" before the Chinese started negotiating in earnest, White House economic adviser Larry Kudlow told reporters at the time.

But Washington viewed the breadth of the changes this time as more than a tactical move; it was bad faith on the Chinese part. In Washington's eyes, China had broken its word.

Outraged, Trump wanted to retaliate immediately. China at the time faced 25 percent tariffs on $50 billion of goods and 10 percent tariffs on another $200 billion. Trump wanted to increase the tariffs on the latter amount to 25 percent, which would be enough to shut out those imports, and threaten to hit the rest of Chinese imports with levies. Lighthizer helped talk him out of acting rashly. Markets were bound to react badly to the news, he argued. Wait until the weekend to act, which would give traders more time to digest the news, and give him more time to try to figure out what happened.

Trump also took out his frustration on Mnuchin, who just a few days earlier had said the talks were in their final stages. But the Treasury secretary wasn't the only one caught flat-footed. Trump had told the press earlier that talks would be wrapped up shortly, as had Lighthizer.

The trade representative, who had joined the administration mainly to confront China, wanted to give Liu more time to sort out his political problems back home. No one in the White House understood the events in Beijing that led to the retrenchment. Many thought Xi had faced deepening opposition as more officials learned what was in the tentative deal. "Who is China's Peter Navarro?" asked some aides—referring to the White House trade adviser who implacably opposed any deal with China. Who were China's rejectionists? The Trump team didn't realize that Xi himself had lined up with the opponents.

Early Sunday morning, May 5, Trump tweeted his threats. On Friday, May 10, tariffs on the $200 billion of goods would increase to 25 percent, and the rest of Chinese imports would soon face the same levy. "Trade deal with China continues, but too slowly, as they attempt to renegotiate," the president tweeted. "No!"

The outburst caught Beijing by surprise. Liu He was due in

Washington on May 8 to continue negotiations, only two days before Trump's tariff deadline. Some of his team were scheduled to
arrive earlier. They had booked tickets on Air China for May 6.
How could they go if Trump was threatening a massive escalation?
The negotiators received an urgent message: stay put until further
notice. "Looks like we're not going," one of them said, early in the
morning on May 6.

Now it was Chinese officials who didn't understand what was
happening on the other side of the Pacific. They combed through
a transcript of a rare press conference that Mnuchin and Lighthizer held on May 6 to explain the president's actions. Lighthizer
sounded sympathetic about the political constraints facing Liu and
other negotiators. "We tried to accommodate changes that China
would ask in the text that we thought were needed for their own
purposes," Lighthizer told reporters. "But these are substantial and
substantive changes. And really I would use the word, sort of reneg-
ing on prior commitments."

Mnuchin added that he, Navarro, and Kudlow, who also attended the briefing, backed the president's decision to raise tariffs
"if we are not able to conclude a deal by the end of the week." In
other words, Beijing shouldn't look to Mnuchin to try to get the
president to ease off, as it had done before. For once, the U.S. economic team was united.

Still, the United States invited further negotiations. "We're not
breaking off talks at this point," Lighthizer said. In a nod to Liu, he
said, "We have a trusted relationship."

Inside the Beijing leadership compound, officials tried to figure
out how to reduce the hit to Chinese markets that was sure to follow Trump's tweets. On the morning of May 6, China's central bank
sped up a plan to release more funds for banks to lend. State-backed
investment funds were also instructed to buy shares to prevent a
market free fall. China's Foreign Ministry spokesman released a
statement saying the Chinese delegation would travel to the United

States, which often reassured markets, though the ministry didn't say when or provide any other details.

The Chinese effort didn't work. The benchmark Shanghai Composite Index fell 5.6 percent while its counterpart in Shenzhen tumbled 7.4 percent—their biggest single-day declines since 2016.

On May 7, a group of midlevel officials, including Finance Vice Minister Liao Min, a trusted aide to Liu, and Commerce Vice Minister Wang Shouwen, huddled to analyze the Lighthizer-Mnuchin press conference. Their conclusion: the Chinese side should try to keep the dialogue open to avoid a rupture that would be difficult to repair. Xi Jinping signed off on the recommendation the following day, May 8. Liu would travel with a pared-down staff, not the team of one hundred he had earlier planned to bring to finish negotiations. Neither the Chinese nor the Americans expected a breakthrough, let alone a completed deal.

"The goal was simply to keep the talks going, and to show China is a responsible party," said a senior Chinese official at the time. Beijing also sent a letter from Xi to Trump, which stressed the importance of the bilateral relationship and China's need to be treated as an equal.

Liu arrived in Washington on May 9 and plunged into talks with Lighthizer and Mnuchin. The pair took Liu for a working dinner at the tony Metropolitan Club, a Lighthizer haunt close to the trade representative's office. They met again on the morning of May 10. Separately, Trump complimented Xi's "beautiful letter" and said he would probably speak to the Chinese leader by phone. (He didn't.)

But the two sides made little substantive progress. Liu tried to convince Lighthizer that regulatory decrees issued by the State Council, the Chinese government's top decision-making body, were as good as the legal changes sought by Washington. Lighthizer didn't buy it.

On May 10, while Liu and his team were still in Washington, the Trump administration made good on its threats and ratcheted up the trade war by raising tariffs. Lighthizer also started the legal procedures to assess 25 percent tariffs on the remaining $300 billion or so of Chinese imports. Around that time, President Trump told a campaign rally in Panama City Beach, Florida, that the Chinese "had broke the deal." Now they would pay.

Before Liu flew back to China, he called together Chinese reporters covering his visit. He denied that China had reneged on its commitments. The United States didn't fully appreciate China's bottom line, he countered. Tariffs must be lifted; demands to boost U.S. imports higher than China's original offer must be dropped; and the agreement had to be "balanced" to ensure the dignity of both nations.

"We are very clear that we cannot make concessions on matters of principle," Liu said. "We hope our U.S. colleagues understand this."

• • •

Trump's anger at the Chinese actions had another important consequence that Beijing didn't foresee.

With Trump looking for ways to pressure China, John Bolton, the hawkish national security advisor, laid out a course of action that would truly rattle Beijing. He planned to try to cripple China's leading company, Huawei Technologies Company. Bolton was more of a hard-liner on China than Trump and understood better how to use government processes to get the outcomes he sought. Now that Trump was outraged by Beijing, Bolton had the president's ear. (Later, Trump's disagreement with Bolton on Afghanistan, North Korea, and other issues led the president to fire him.)

For months, the United States and China had been at loggerheads over Huawei. The Americans suspected that the telecommunications company was a tool of the Chinese military, which could tap Huawei's equipment and spy on the company's customers around the world, a charge Huawei vehemently denied. The United States also accused Huawei of breaking its sanctions laws by shipping products with U.S.-made components to Iran. The U.S. government had stopped buying Huawei equipment and was pressuring other governments to do the same, with limited success.

To Beijing, Huawei was a crown jewel. It was a Chinese firm that could outcompete Western rivals and become a global technology leader. The company was essential to China's ambition to dominate future technologies, especially the next-generation mobile communications network, known as 5G. Bolton believed that Huawei must be stopped. The United States wouldn't have trusted telecommunications to a Moscow telephone company during the Cold War, he argued. It was crazy to trust China now.

Bolton reminded Trump that the Commerce Department had been spending months weighing whether to put Huawei on what it called its "entity list"—a group of companies whose U.S. purchases were severely limited. Only firms that obtained a Commerce license could sell to the listed companies, and at that point Commerce had never announced a grant of any waivers. In bureaucratic language, there was a "presumption of denial" when it came to licenses, unless the company could provide a compelling reason to continue shipments.

Huawei relied on U.S. semiconductors and other electronic components for its advanced technology. Putting the company on the entity list could strangle the company, or at least halt its advance while it sought to build the technology itself or find other suppliers. Trump liked the idea and encouraged Bolton to move ahead. With Trump, "it makes sense to seize on the low moments and come in with a stack of papers that advance your goal," says a senior U.S. security official.

Bolton lined up allies among intelligence agencies, the State Department, and Pentagon who were deeply suspicious of Huawei. Then he sought out Lighthizer, who raised objections about the timing. An entity listing was bound to make it even harder to strike a trade deal. Mnuchin was even more emphatically opposed.

The blacklisting would hurt Huawei's U.S. suppliers and could lead to unintended consequences. But neither man was going to make a public stand against an idea that Trump had endorsed.

Commerce got the message and sped up the legal work needed for an entity listing. Commerce Secretary Wilbur Ross briefed the president about the department's progress on May 13. Two days later, Trump's most senior officials gathered in the Oval Office around 3:30 p.m. to ratify the decision. The president was so enamored of the sanction that he wanted the action announced that day, leaving little time to notify allies and the Chinese embassy, and prepare talking points for the press and supporters. The short notice made the decision making look amateurish.

To make sure the public understood the significance of what was happening, Commerce briefed a Reuters reporter before it published the press release, figuring the news service would explain clearly the complicated proceedings. Huawei had engaged in activities "contrary to U.S. national security," Commerce concluded, including violating U.S. sanctions against Iran. Huawei responded by saying it would work with the U.S. government "to come up with effective measures to ensure product security."

Bolton was exultant. "The shackles are off," he told his senior staff. Move ahead aggressively. In later months, Bolton would threaten to move intermediate-range missiles into Asia and redouble his efforts to sell advanced tanks and F-16 fighter jets to Taiwan. Senator Tom Cotton, an Arkansas Republican who was a fierce China opponent, tweeted: "@Huawei 5G, RIP."

In Beijing, officials were surprised and angered. Trump had miscalculated that targeting Huawei was just another pressure point. To Chinese officials, the move reinforced the idea that the United States didn't simply want a trade deal; it wanted to stifle China and keep it from ever challenging America. China's censors ramped up nationalist propaganda, including airing old movies glorifying the Chinese fighting Americans during the Korean War.

State media labeled those advocating a deal with the United States as "capitulators."

Xi Jinping also looked for ways to strike back. Five days after the Huawei sanctions were issued, on May 20, the Chinese leader went on an inspection tour of the southeastern province of Jiangxi and made a point of visiting its leading manufacturer of rare earths—natural elements used for wind turbines, electric cars, and jet fighters. The visit was meant to remind the United States of its dependence on China for these minerals.

Xi also laid a wreath at a monument marking the starting point of the Long March, the long retreat to safety made by Communist revolutionaries that official media now portray as paving the way for ultimate victory over the Nationalists. The message to Washington couldn't have been clearer: China was prepared for another Long March, this time toward ultimate victory over America.

"This was a watershed moment in how China views the trade war," says a senior Beijing official. "It's crystal clear that the U.S.'s motive isn't just trade. It's both political and strategic. They want to keep China from becoming stronger."

Through a series of threats, counter threats, and miscalculations, the world's two biggest economies were edging toward a new Cold War. This one wouldn't be defined by missiles and nuclear weapons, but by a struggle over economic and technological supremacy. Rather than working together, two great economic powers were on a path of suspicion and separation, a fissure that would damage global commerce and upset the lives of workers, consumers, and businesses from Sichuan to Seattle. The global marketplace was in danger of shattering.

• • •

Donald Trump started the biggest trade war since the 1930s with only a superficial understanding of how China worked, and without a specific goal in mind or a plan to achieve success. Some of his advisers, especially Navarro and former chief strategist Stephen K. Bannon, claimed they had a plan: the administration would show it was serious on trade by quickly blocking imports of steel and aluminum, as Trump had pledged during the presidential campaign. Then the United States would promptly renegotiate the North American Free Trade Agreement so that American companies that left China could resettle in Mexico, on terms the Trump administration approved, if they didn't move back to the United States. Having accomplished all this, the United States would press China on economic, political, and military grounds.

Trouble was, Trump never signed on to the plan, and it was far-fetched.

Rather than dispose of the steel and aluminum tariffs, the United States embarked on a lengthy, bitter fight with some of its closest allies in Canada and Europe, which still wasn't settled by early 2020. Trump went out of his way to alienate allies the United States should have recruited to confront China. He pulled out of the Trans-Pacific Partnership, a twelve-nation pact of Pacific Rim countries that included heavyweights like Japan, Australia, and Vietnam, rather than try to renegotiate it to his liking. When French President Emmanuel Macron arrived in Washington for a state visit in April 2018, Trump rebuffed his offer to join forces on China. "I've got this one," he told the French leader.

Renegotiating NAFTA also took far longer than expected. In January 2020, the deal finally cleared Congress. While Lighthizer praised the results as presaging a new model of trade deals supported by labor Democrats and business Republicans, many trade associations backed the deal to try to end Trump's threats to pull out of NAFTA, not because of their enthusiasm for the agreement. Their support for future Trump trade deals was far from assured.

Companies still couldn't count on Mexico as a safe haven if they relocated from China. After NAFTA negotiations were completed, but before the pact passed Congress, Trump had threatened to impose tariffs on Mexico as a way to pressure the country to take a tougher immigration stance. To U.S. companies, that meant a Mexican location would always be subject to Trump's whims. One big U.S. consumer goods company was so confounded about where to locate facilities outside the United States that it started searching for low-wage nations that had a trade deficit with the United States. The company figured the president only targeted nations that ran big bilateral trade surpluses.

Trump's China offensive, as we will lay out, was marked by clashing ideologies and personalities, and hesitation about what actions to take. The president never made the case to the public that the United States might be in for a long and costly struggle with China—one that might require sacrifices, but was necessary to rebalance relations. He never put together a plan to keep the United States ahead of China technologically. Instead he proposed cutting research-and-development budgets year after year. He also claimed, against all economic evidence and common sense, that his tariffs didn't cost American consumers anything.

Trump was both a China hawk and a China dove. He truly wanted to get China to change objectionable policies, as the hawks did. But he feared upsetting global markets, as did the doves. Different aides played to different parts of his China schizophrenia, as U.S. policy to China lurched back and forth.

Beijing was also to blame for the escalating trade battle. Previous generations of Chinese leaders had used U.S. pressure to push through needed economic reforms at home, especially reducing the role of state-owned companies, which are subsidized, protected, and fed cheap loans by the government. Not Xi Jinping. He relied on state firms to move the country ahead technologically, reduce the widening income gap, and expand the country's power. They were the lynchpin of his "China Dream" of national revival. Complaints of unfair competition from U.S. firms and many privately owned Chinese ones were shunted aside.

From the 1990s until around 2012, when Xi Jinping took power, the role of state firms had steadily diminished. Xi was widely seen as a reformer who would continue that trend. Instead, state investment grew faster under Xi and state firms took on more debt even though they were significantly less profitable and contributed less than 30 percent to China's GDP. "This picture of private, market-driven growth has given way to resurgence of the role of the state in resource allocation and a shrinking role for the market and private firms," wrote Nicholas Lardy, an expert on the Chinese economy at the Peterson Institute for International Economics, who had earlier promoted the Xi-as-reformer thesis.

Xi and other Chinese leaders were also blind to the changing reality in the United States. Working-class Americans long ago had turned against Beijing, as Chinese imports, aided by an undervalued currency, decimated manufacturing towns in the Southeast and Midwest. In places like Hickory, North Carolina, the unemployment rate rose from less than 3 percent in 2000 to more than 15 percent by 2010, creating a new American underclass that would tie its hopes and resentments to Donald Trump.

Corporate America, long compliant to the demands of Chinese authorities, was also pressing the White House to take action. U.S. firms were angry that Chinese officials helped domestic firms steal their technology. The Americans also feared Chinese plans to spend hundreds of billions of dollars to overtake the United States in artificial intelligence, advanced semiconductors, aviation, and other technologies of the future.

Rather than reexamine the policies that caused such a reaction, Beijing turned to its old playbook: court and threaten U.S. multinational companies, which need the Chinese market to grow. Chinese leaders expected them to lobby Washington to back off, as they had in the past. Beijing also lavished attention on sympathetic officials in Washington, especially Treasury Secretary Mnuchin, thinking that would help raise their standing in bureaucratic face-offs with

China skeptics like Trade Representative Lighthizer. The strategy had worked in the past but no longer did.

Hawks on both sides of the Pacific say the result of the trade battle will be a "decoupling" of the two economies—a kind of complete estrangement. To us, that is fantasy, unless the two nations confront each other in a shooting war. The two nations are too intertwined. American multinationals spent a quarter century building global supply chains that stitched the economy of the two nations together. China is also one of America's largest lenders, holding more than $1 trillion of U.S. government debt.

America depends for growth on a burgeoning Chinese market. China is already the world's biggest market for luxury goods, automobiles, and online shopping, among other sectors. Its middle-class spending significantly tops the United States, according to Homi Kharas, a Brookings Institution economist. Cut off U.S. companies from that market, while European and Japanese companies remain entrenched, and the U.S. firms will become laggards, as will the American economy. Cut off consumers from the cheap goods they get from China, and Americans will balk at the higher prices at Walmart and Target.

Eurasia Group analyst Michael Hirson, who was a U.S. Treasury representative in Beijing, talks instead of a "derailment" of the two countries. The battle threatens to derail China's rise because it can no longer depend on the U.S. market or technological expertise. With broad segments of the U.S. population suspicious of China, the United States has become an unreliable partner, whether Trump is in the White House or not. China needs to turn elsewhere for technological expertise or further develop it on its own. "We're trying to give China a bloody nose," says Christopher Johnson, a former China analyst at the Central Intelligence Agency. "But if the assessment is that China will realize the error of its ways and embrace market economics, that's laughable. They will double down on industrial policy."

The fight also could derail the United States, which needs China's workers and markets to continue as the world's economic superpower. Now China's openness to the United States is in doubt. The United States is trying to woo other big markets, especially India, to replace what China offers. But the others lack China's singular combination of a huge population, diligent workforce, big-spending consumers, competent—though authoritarian—government, and aspirations to become a leader among nations. "We are telling the Chinese people that their growing rich is something we view as unfair and shouldn't be allowed," says Adam Posen, president of the Peterson Institute. "That is a very potent political message that could be quite destructive."

Between 1999 and 2018, the number of poor Chinese living on less than two dollars a day dropped by nearly 500 million, a miraculous achievement, supported in part by the U.S. decision to welcome China into the world trading system. Rather than see it as a great achievement for capitalism, many Americans now see it as a strategic blunder. And many Chinese, rather than appreciating U.S. support, now see America as an adversary.

One way to think about the lasting impact of this trade battle is to imagine the U.S.-China relationship if Trump were to lose the 2020 election. Whichever Democrat beats him would inherit a world where the United States has tariffs on hundreds of billions of dollars in imports from China and other nations. No president would simply roll back those tariffs. He or she would want a lot in return, meaning that the trade fight with Beijing would continue. A Democrat would also probably add other issues to the mix that Trump has, at best, paid lip service to: human rights in Hong Kong, Xinjiang, and Tibet; environmental issues; labor standards. Any of those issues is bound to make a deal much more difficult. They did during the Clinton presidency, as we will explore.

Trump has reinvigorated the use of tariffs, and they are now a part of the arsenal of any president. He can rightly point out that only tariffs got the Chinese to bargain seriously and Mexico to crack down on immigration. Only tariffs prompted the Europeans and Japanese to negotiate seriously over automobiles and agriculture, though tariffs haven't settled any of these problems. Should Trump be reelected, he's bound to use this weapon more and more. Should he lose, the weapon becomes a powerful one in the hands of Democrats looking to force nations to adopt environmental and labor standards acceptable to a Democratic White House.

The losers in all this are the consumers who have to pay the tariffs and the workers in the industries that are being harmed by the trade fight. More broadly, the battle damaged a global trading system that helped to lift more than 1 billion people out of poverty over the past forty years and delivered material prosperity to billions more. From the end of World War II until Trump's election, the United States championed an increasingly liberal trade order where tariffs were minimal and countries had started to agree on rules to cover the rest of the global economy, including services, intellectual property, and state-owned firms. Trade expanded globally and helped power the postwar boom. Both the left and the right in the United States criticized the system as too concerned with corporate interests, not the interests of everyday Americans, and there is truth to their criticism. But the system could be overhauled. Now it's on the verge of collapse, as the United States watches out for its own interests instead of also considering the global good. America First.

As we write this book in early 2020, the two sides agreed to a limited deal that paused the trade fight. The agreement contained detailed pledges by Beijing to protect U.S. intellectual property and end pressure on American firms to give up their technology—longtime U.S. goals—though it didn't compel China to change laws to carry out the pledges. In exchange for small cuts in U.S. tariffs, China promised huge purchases of American products, though many trade experts doubt exports will meet the targets. But the deal left untouched many of America's deepest concerns about Chinese mercantilism and technology policies. The so-called phase-one deal is supposed to lead to other phases that will tackle tougher issues.

It was as if the two sides were locked in a bad marriage and thought they wanted a divorce. Then when they saw the costs of the split, they decided to think it over again. But the rot in the marriage remains and the coronavirus pandemic, which was spreading globally as we finished work on this book, threatened to cause more rot.

The chances for a true rapprochement—for a deal that could change the way China does business—still seem remote, especially before the November election. With the global economy listing badly in the pandemic, that could change. The U.S.-China conflict remains an obstacle to global growth. Tariffs undermine corporate confidence in the future. That reduces business investment crucial for growth. With reduced investment comes reduced employment. Laid-off workers will find that the goods they buy are more expensive because of tariffs.

If pressed, the two sides could also pursue a follow-up deal before the election that is less ambitious than originally conceived by Trump's economic team. Treasury Secretary Mnuchin has hinted that is the administration's plan. That could give the president another talking point during the campaign.

Xi also may find it in his interest to strike another limited deal with Trump rather than risk the unknown. Should Trump win, his pressure on China is bound to continue, although Beijing will have had four years to figure out how to deal with him. Should he lose, a new president may make additional demands that are even tougher to meet. It's a quandary. The Chinese leadership finds it increasingly difficult to cut a deal with Washington, whoever is president, without being seen as caving to what it views as American hegemony.

Wei Jianguo, a former commerce vice minister, predicts that the U.S.-China economic and trade war will last thirty years or even fifty years. "The essence of the trade war is that the United States wants to destroy China," he says. "The U.S. is unwilling to accept China as a rising power."

To understand how we have come to this point—a trade war like no other since the Great Depression—it's important to look back in history to see how the relationship developed. It may seem fanciful now, but not long ago America was the shining city upon a hill to many Chinese, not just to impoverished peasants but to the Communist elites who would transform the nation. We trace the arc of the relationship from the 1990s when the United States was a model for China to emulate economically, if not politically, to the current day when the United States fears China is plotting a path to surpass it.

2

CHINA'S RISE, 1980s AND 1990s

Before getting anointed China's leader, in the fall of 2012, Xi Jin-ping disappeared from the public eye for two weeks. His meetings with foreign dignitaries including U.S. Secretary of State Hillary Clinton and Singapore Prime Minister Lee Hsien Loong were canceled, one after another. Xi's absence, never explained by the government, sparked speculation about his health, and trouble in the Communist Party's secretive leadership transition process. Some China watchers suspected a coup.

At a press briefing at China's Foreign Ministry, a Western journalist asked the ministry's spokesman whether Xi, who was then China's vice president, was still alive. "I hope you will raise more serious questions," the spokesman replied tersely.

Out of the public eye, Xi spent days brooding over his plans to restore China to its central position in global affairs. He felt he needed time to plot his next moves after the party leadership had purged his most powerful political rival and cleared the way for him to take over the reins of the country. Would he be able to continue China's historic economic rise while keeping the party in power? What should he do differently from his predecessors? Xi chose Zhejiang province as the place to mull over his choices. He had served as party chief from 2002 to 2007 in the coastal province, in eastern China known as "a land of fish and rice." Xi had scored early success there, presiding over an economy that grew 14 percent a year.

His record in Zhejiang put him in the running to one day lead China and taught him how to foster a vibrant private economy, while at the same time motivating entrepreneurs to become loyal party members. Huddling with a few close advisers in Zhuji, a Yangtze River city in Zhejiang, Xi mapped out the outline of what he would call his "China Dream," a slogan that conveyed his desire to make China a global superpower. To make the dream a reality, Xi concluded, he would need to make sure he became as effective as the man who started China's economic boom decades earlier, former paramount leader Deng Xiaoping.

Most Western economists see Deng only as a reformer. A short, stocky survivor of the lunacy of the Cultural Revolution, Deng heralded an era of "reform and opening up" in the late 1970s, after Mao Zedong's death and the end of decade-long political chaos. He unshackled the nation from the ideological constraints of the Mao era, embraced market-oriented policies, and opened China to the world. The Communist Party under Mao had triumphed in the bitter civil war and united China. But Mao also sapped the country of its entrepreneurial drive while millions of peasants, intellectuals, and party officials lost their lives in various campaigns he launched to boost production or weed out dissent.

Although Deng and his family were persecuted during those years, he remained loyal to the party. He saw the party as a powerful force he could harness to make the changes he sought. The government should play a central role in directing the economy, he believed, and in China, the government is ultimately run by the party. With firm party control, China was able to shut down inefficient companies that were holding back the country's rise without kicking up massive opposition from those thrown out of work. The party also focused China's scarce resources on promising industries

and organized vast projects to build highways, railroads, and air-
ports to link the country's interior to the coastal areas where factories were being built to serve Western markets.

At the same time, Deng opened the country up to foreign investment, markets, and ideas, a remarkable feat given the internal opposition to any policy that smacked of capitalism. "We mustn't fear
to adopt the advanced management methods applied in capitalist
countries," Deng once said. In doing so, Deng also began an era of
export-led growth for China, taking a page from Japan and the Asian
Tigers of Singapore, South Korea, Taiwan, and Hong Kong, which
embraced export markets to drive industrialization.

Xi Jinping thought he could further advance Deng's policy and
sought to emulate Deng's market openings as well as Mao's unrivaled control of the party apparatus. Many in the West saw those
two efforts as contradictory. How could China truly liberalize the
economy if it was under the thumb of the party? Xi didn't see a con-
tradiction. The party helped build China under Deng, Xi believed,
and would continue to do so under his direction.

Zhejiang taught Xi about both liberalization and control, and so
it made sense for him to choose it as a place to ponder his future.
The province was at the forefront of China's revitalization and became a thriving center of entrepreneurship. In the farming town of
Yiwu, a market started in 1982 with some 700 stalls selling socks and
other small consumer goods. It grew into the world's largest wholesale bazaar for bargain hunters from all over the world—46 million
square feet, or the size of nearly 800 American football fields. A port
in northeastern Zhejiang became the busiest in the world, measured
by cargo tonnage. The city of Wenzhou, located in a mountainous
region in southeastern Zhejiang, became famous for its small businesses and as a source of emigrants to the United States and Europe. Wenzhou people, as they are known, deepened the country's
ties to the outside world.

When Xi went to Zhejiang in the fall of 2002, the province's economy was already growing at a pace of more than 10 percent, faster than the national rate of about 8 percent. He largely took a hands-off approach to the private sector and focused on finding ways to encourage local shoe and clothing makers to expand into more sophisticated industries like machinery and chemicals. "He believed in limited government intervention at the time and spent a lot of time talking to companies," a Zhejiang official says.

But Xi wasn't a market cheerleader. Following Deng, he used the market when it suited his purpose—continued growth—and also pushed to strengthen the party's rule.

One of the first places he went to visit after arriving in Zhejiang was Fengqiao, a township of some eighty thousand residents. The little-known town gained national fame in the early 1960s when Mao praised the way Fengqiao officials mobilized the masses to energize the party rule. He named it "the Fengqiao experience." Back then, Mao celebrated Fengqiao's enthusiasm for identifying so-called enemies of the proletariat—capitalists, traditionalists, and the like—and punishing them, which led to some of the most brutal aspects of the Cultural Revolution. After that tumultuous period, "the Fengqiao experience" faded into history.

Xi sought to revive the concept but gave it a new meaning. He wanted to mobilize the masses to fix problems and complaints at the local level before they led to widespread social unrest. In a speech in November 2003, Xi urged Zhejiang officials to "cherish the Fengqiao experience, promote the Fengqiao experience, continuously improve the Fengqiao experience and effectively maintain social stability." Xi's effort to revive and evolve the Maoist concept was all the more remarkable given his personal experience. His father, Xi Zhongxun, a party revolutionary, was purged around the time that Mao called for class struggle and promotion of "the Fengqiao experience." The experience didn't sour the younger Xi on party power. He wanted to use it for different purposes.

Xi's government has tried to use modern technology to revive "the Fengqiao experience," especially the use of informants. An app launched in Zhejiang in 2016, "Safe Zhejiang," keeps users informed about laws and regulations and lets them notify authorities of issues ranging from domestic violence and corporate disputes to traffic violations. They also can use the app to lodge complaints against officials. In return, informants receive rewards such as shopping discounts. Today's "Fengqiao experience," as Zhejiang officials put it, has gone digital.

In the village of Fengyuan, which is part of the Fengqiao township, average disposable income is almost 40 percent higher than the national average and most every household owns a Honda, Toyota, or BMW. No resident in recent years has trekked to Beijing and filed petitions against local authorities, says Luo Gentu, head of the Fengyuan village. Instead, complaints are handled locally.

Beijing wants to replicate that experiment nationwide. Since the beginning of 2019, officials across the country have been encouraged to attend "study sessions" hosted by Luo and his colleagues to learn how to use the Internet and big data to mobilize the masses. In a late spring session in 2019, Luo told a group of visiting prosecutors from northern Shanxi province about the challenges of governing an increasingly wealthy population. "Back in the 1980s, all you had to do was to round up those who had lots of grievances and tried to stir up trouble," said Luo, who has served as a village official for three decades. "But now, as people have more money, they also know how to fight for their rights through legal means. So we have no choice but to adapt."

• • •

China's rise is one of the world's greatest economic success stories. It's a complicated tale.

Henry Kissinger, the U.S. diplomat who helped open the United States' diplomatic relationship with China, said that when he first visited China in 1971, "there were practically no automobiles, very limited consumer goods, and no high-rise buildings. The technology was fairly backward." A year later, when President Richard Nixon traveled to China, Kissinger added, "We had to bring a ground station with us in order to communicate effectively and for our media to communicate."

Over the following four decades, China increased per capita income 25-fold and lifted more than 800 million Chinese people out of poverty, according to the World Bank—more than 70 percent of the total poverty reduction in the world. China evolved from a nation filled with famine and deprivation into the world's second-largest economy, and America's greatest competitor for leadership in the twenty-first century. Skyscrapers and high-rise apartment buildings sprouted like glass-clad bamboo all across China. Rail lines and expressways zigzagged the country and began to knit together rural regions whose mountains had made them nearly separate countries. Made-in-China products came to dominate the store shelves of the developed world. Rising incomes made Chinese consumers the main pursuit of multinationals.

The country's economic rebirth was even more remarkable, given the chaos of the late 1960s and early 1970s, when the country was in the grips of the Cultural Revolution. Mao launched the mass movement in 1966 to root out so-called capitalist and traditional elements of Chinese society and reassert his authority. The result was ten years of turmoil, bloodshed, hunger, and near paralysis. Millions of families were ruined.

Nationwide, schools were shut and the youths were sent to the impoverished countryside for reeducation. Intellectuals and party officials deemed to have "impure" thoughts were murdered or driven to suicide by youthful Red Guards. Classical literature and paintings were torn apart. Temples were desecrated. Many people sought to rid any bourgeois connotation from their names. Among those who did was the mother of one of the authors of the book, Lingling. Her mother, the daughter of Mao's former aide, changed her Russian-sounding name, Lina, to Tao, which means waves, and only changed it back after the violence of Cultural Revolution ended.

Traditionally a nation of farmers, China under Mao had devastatingly low agricultural production because of government mismanagement. Under his centralized planning system, farmers were given a production quota but had little incentive to produce beyond that quota. By the late 1970s, there were widespread famines, including the disastrous Great Leap Forward of the 1950s. Tens of millions of peasants died then, as Mao's program to boost steel production wrecked farms while failing to modernize the countryside.

All that was to change soon. During the Cultural Revolution, Deng Xiaoping was purged twice, paraded through the streets of Beijing wearing a dunce cap, and sent to work at a tractor factory for punishment. His eldest son fell off the fourth floor of a building during interrogation and was paralyzed for life.

But Deng persevered, outmaneuvered his rivals, and came to power after Mao's death. He experimented with a splash of capitalism to increase food supplies. Deng changed the rigid quota system through policies that gave farmers formal control of their land, reduced their production quotas, and allowed them to sell whatever they produced above the quotas in free markets at unregulated prices. The new system increased China's agricultural production by 25 percent in the decade following the change and gave Chinese leaders confidence that market reforms could work in other areas as well.

In urban areas, China deregulated prices for industrial goods and commodities, allowing the Chinese to avoid the shortages of the Mao era. Private businesses were permitted to operate for the first time since the Communist takeover in 1949.

Xi Jinping's father, Xi Zhongxun, an ally of Deng at the time, played an important role in wooing foreign investors, who had been chased out of China by revolutionaries during the Chinese civil war. The elder Xi was assigned to run Guangdong province, which bordered the far wealthier city of Hong Kong, then a British colony. Daily wages in Guangdong were about 1/100th of those in Hong Kong. To try to prevent Guangdong residents from fleeing to Hong Kong, Xi proposed to Deng to carve out some areas in the province where the local government could experiment with economic liberalization and invite foreign capital.

Deng signed off on the proposal in 1979. "Let's call them 'special zones,'" Deng told the elder Xi, while adding: "The central government has no funds, but we can give you some favorable policies."

The special zones on China's southern and eastern coasts experimented with lower tax rates and reduced regulation. Guangdong and Fujian provinces—the latter two hundred miles off the coast of Taiwan—targeted foreign makers of clothing and electronics, often ethnic Chinese, to set up plants to make goods for overseas markets.

Deng later authorized more provinces and localities to take initiatives instead of waiting for directions from Beijing. Many townships and counties started companies and contracted them out to individuals to manage. They essentially operated like private businesses, giving local party bosses more experience with markets and market incentives. Many of those firms moved into textiles, chemicals, and other industrial sectors previously dominated by companies owned by the state and run by government officials.

Those de facto private firms "stimulated competition with state-owned enterprises (SOEs) and drove the process of marketization in the entire economy," wrote professor Hong-Yi Chen at Soka University of America in Aliso Viejo, California.

China's economy took off. Gross domestic product jumped thirty-fold from 1978 to 2001, vaulting China from the size of Mexico's economy to the size of France's. Foreign investments in factories and other projects, nonexistent before Deng's reform, surged to $46.9 billion two decades later, bringing to the country much-needed technological and management expertise and helping Chinese firms move into more lucrative industries. With its armies of cheap labor, China started to become the world's factory floor, with exports soaring 27-fold from 1978 to reach $266 billion in 2001, when China joined the World Trade Organization.

The process wasn't pretty. Deng's experimentation with liberalization didn't include political liberalization. When students filled Beijing's Tiananmen Square demanding democracy in June 1989, Deng unleashed the army, which killed hundreds, if not thousands, of the protestors.

The legacy of the party-led development model includes corruption, political repression, overspending, and inefficiency. Chinese economist Chong-en Bai of Tsinghua University says China has become a "special deal" economy, where local party leaders dole out aid, loans, and other help to favored firms. But he says the system has been saved from kleptocracy, so far, because local governments compete ferociously with one another for new development schemes. When one town comes up with a winning strategy—technology zones to lure computer chip companies—others copy and compete.

• • •

Xi Jinping sought to understand the elements of China's success during his five years running Zhejiang province as party secretary and add to the region's development. Like his predecessors, Xi wasn't entirely comfortable with capitalist dynamics. He saw an important role for the government and party in keeping control of development and guiding private businesses to ensure they stayed on the right track.

A government adviser described Xi as someone who believed private businesses should be allowed to prosper so long as they stayed in the good graces of the party. Among the private entrepreneurs in the province that received Xi's blessing was a village girl turned billionaire, Chen Ailian, who is now in her sixties and runs one of China's largest makers of auto parts. Her story is the story of China's rise, with its combination of guts, entrepreneurial drive, and party direction.

Chen is chairman of Wanfeng Auto Holding Group, based in a mountainous county in Zhejiang, though she sees herself as a party member first. She holds positions on government advisory bodies—an honor bestowed by the government to successful entrepreneurs—and devotes significant resources to party building. She works with the party to identify workers for party membership and also trains reserve forces for the People's Liberation Army. Those efforts benefit her personally and professionally. Cultivating party officials has helped her turn the small company she founded in a dilapidated factory in 1994 into one that sells quality auto wheels and rims to Ford, General Motors, BMW, and other foreign firms. Her company now is expanding into aviation.

"We only support one party, which is the Communist Party," Chen says. A photo of Chen and Xi, hung on the wall of Wanfeng's exhibition center, illustrates the dynamics in greater detail: "The party and the government have built a beneficial environment for companies to grow," the company wrote on the photo. "They encourage us when we make achievements, help us solve problems when we get into trouble, and show care and concern as we develop."

One of five daughters of a veteran of the Korean War—or "the War to Resist America and Aid Korea," as the Chinese call it—Chen grew up during the Cultural Revolution in a rural county in Zhejiang. With three big rivers and dense creeks winding through the county, Xinchang has a tradition of commerce. To enrich their land, local residents traded the green tea they grew for chicken feathers and other materials that could be used as fertilizer.

During the Cultural Revolution, all forms of trade stopped and, like the rest of the country, the area suffered from food shortages. Chen received little formal education during the decade of chaos. By the time she turned twenty, in 1978, when Deng started to give farmers more incentives to produce as part of his reform policy, Chen wanted nothing more than to become a tractor driver for the local commune—a prestigious job at the time when such vehicles were rare throughout the country.

She got her wish. Whenever she wasn't working in the rice fields, Chen would drive around the town in the tractor from the local commune, helping farmers ship goods and observing how Deng's policy turned the sleepy county of Xinchang into an increasingly vibrant one. "People became hopeful again about their lives, about the future," she recalls.

In the early 1980s, Chen got a job at a textile mill owned by the county government and met her future husband there, Wu Liangding. He was a catch. A state company promised a job for life and the "iron rice bowl" of comprehensive cradle-to-grave benefits. Companies clothed their workers, housed them, fed them, and educated their children. But the expenses made the companies enormously inefficient. As China changed, most of the firms foundered. They faced fierce competition from a growing army of more nimble and efficient private businesses, especially in Zhejiang, with its traditional entrepreneurial zeal and lack of heavy-handed government intervention.

That's when Chen and many others throughout the province and the rest of the country started to think about starting their own businesses. A Honda motorcycle her husband gave her as a gift for her thirty-fifth birthday in 1993 provided the entrepreneurial spark. The government was stepping up efforts then to build an auto industry, as the country started to transform from a kingdom of bicycles. But foreign imports remained scarce because of China's high tariffs. Chen's husband, then manager of the state textile firm they both worked at, had to use connections to sneak in a motorcycle from Hong Kong. "My Honda was the only imported vehicle in the entire county," Chen says.

As she drove around town, she noticed how much more stylish

and lightweight her Honda alloy wheels and rims were than the steel ones used in Chinese motorbikes. The aluminum alloy made for more agile performance and better acceleration. She investigated why Chinese motorcycles used inferior products and realized that state-owned firms used steel to make wheels and saw no reason to change. They sold all they made anyway.

Chen invited a few technicians from a local aluminum plant to tear apart her Honda. "I wanted to see if we could make such wheels," she recalls. "And the answer was yes."

Chen decided to set up her own alloy wheel business. She convinced a local bank to lend her 500,000 yuan ($58,000 at the time), a big loan when the average annual income was less than 5,000 yuan. She used it to purchase equipment and lease a facility from a teetering state-owned paper mill. In 1994, she founded Zhejiang Wanfeng Alloy Wheel Company and hired fifteen employees, who averaged thirty years old. Her employees included the technicians she invited over to dismantle her Honda. They worked out of a shabby single-story factory building located on a narrow street by a river.

In the early 2000s, Zhong Shan, then the province's top trade official, went to visit Chen and her company as part of a mission to encourage more exports. That was when many businesses in China, especially in the coastal province, started to find more opportunities overseas. But they still needed to apply for export quotas from the government to venture abroad.

"I said to him, 'I want to do more exports,'" Chen recalls.

"Yes, you can," replied Zhong, who was picked by Xi Jinping as China's commerce minister in 2017. Afterward, Wanfeng began an aggressive expansion overseas.

In recent years, the company has received government funding and other support to build a state-of-the-art factory that uses artificial intelligence and advanced robots to make wheels. A banner in the hallway of the factory celebrating Wanfeng's use of AI, with

Chen's signature, promises to implement China's "Made in China 2025" plan and promote AI manufacturing. The initiative aims to make the country a leader in technology of the future, but it has been assailed by the Trump administration as a protectionist policy that hurts U.S. firms, as we will see in later chapters.

Trump officials singled out one of Chen's foreign acquisitions as an example of how the Chinese government uses subsidies to get the technology it needs to advance. In 2016, Wanfeng acquired Paslin Company, a Warren, Michigan–based maker of advanced manufacturing robots, for $302 million. The deal was financed in part by a $45 million investment from the city of Shaoxing, which oversees Chen's county. The financing was designed to "activate a strategic industry," according to the city's finance department.

Around the same time, Chen's company started to build an aviation complex in accordance with the city's industrial plan. Within a year of buying Paslin, Wanfeng invested some $118 million—money raised from the government, other businesses, and the company itself—to improve its ability to use robots for manufacturing. A report by the Commerce Ministry credited Wanfeng for obtaining "key technology for the field of robotics" through the Paslin transaction. Such deals, Chen now says, help the country move from "'made in China' to 'created in China.'"

At five feet six, Chen likes to dress in bright red and pink and boast about her connections to party leaders. Separate pictures of Chen meeting with Xi, Premier Li Keqiang, and Vice Premier Han Zheng are prominently displayed at the company's exhibition center. On Wanfeng's website, she's listed first as the company's party secretary and then as its chairman. Her friends in the party help in many ways. In 2017, when an extravagant wedding she threw for her son drew negative headlines from China's social media, the government's propaganda department intervened to put a stop to the bad publicity.

Chen is also an admirer of the West, and all its excesses. She drives a Rolls-Royce and lives in a mansion in the scenic county. Her company's new headquarters are modeled on the twin towers of the World Trade Center. A sprawling aviation complex she is constructing features buildings that resemble the Arc de Triomphe, the White House, and the Great Hall of the People. Facing the complex is a famous local temple, where a giant wooden Buddha sculpture serves as a reminder of China's past and its onetime embrace of simplicity.

In 1998, she traveled with a team from her company to an auto show held in Las Vegas. She set a strict no-gambling rule for her teammates and required them to be in bed no later than midnight. But several of her crew couldn't pass up the city's attractions and wandered around the city until the morning. "They couldn't stop talking about the Las Vegas water fountains with the combination of music, water, and light," Chen recalls. "But I told them, 'Whatever the U.S. has now, China will have it someday.'"

• • •

Other companies in Zhejiang prospered too, although not on the scale of Chen's.

The number of private manufacturers in Zhejiang with annual revenue exceeding 20 million yuan—about $3 million—has more than tripled in the past two decades to nearly 28,000 now, making up 70 percent of all sizable industrial companies in the province. The vibrant private sector has helped Zhejiang achieve an annual growth rate of 12.4 percent on average from 1993 to 2001, when China joined the WTO and committed itself to adopting Western capitalist trade rules. After that, the province's economy soared further, powered by exports of socks, ties, chemicals, auto parts, and many other products.

When Xi was running Zhejiang from 2002 to 2007, he courted overseas capital, offering tax breaks and other incentives to those setting up plants in the province. Foreign direct investments tripled in that period, to $10.4 billion. Today more than forty U.S. multinationals, including Ford, Boeing, and Harley-Davidson, have investments in the province.

In 2007, when Hank Paulson, a former Goldman Sachs chief executive with long experience doing business in China, made his maiden trip to the country as Treasury secretary, he chose to meet with Xi first, as he recounts in his book, *Dealing with China*.

"'We need to foster a better climate for innovation,'" Paulson recalled Xi saying to him. The would-be Chinese leader told Paulson at the time: "'Small and middle-size companies in the private sector can lead the way.'" Years later, after Xi took over the party in late 2012, his turn to greater state control over the economy contrasted sharply with the pro-market reputation he established while running Zhejiang, although he never hid his commitment to party rule. The switch shows the difficulty even seasoned China watchers have in understanding Beijing. Market people like Paulson see the market side of Xi, but overlook his party allegiance.

As for Chen, in 2018 her family made *Forbes* magazine's list of China's richest people, with total net worth valued at $1.1 billion. Wanfeng now has 15,000 employees with about $1.5 billion in revenue annually. But business hasn't been easy, despite her party ties.

Time and again she's found herself having to battle. A growing Chinese economy provided companies like hers huge market opportunities, but also increased competition. When Chen formed Wanfeng in 1994, 3 million motorcycles were produced in China. That figure more than doubled to 8 million in 1997, and by 2000 it reached 20 million. More companies started competing to sell wheels to Chen's foreign customers.

Some of Chen's competitors are state-owned firms, which have to worry far less about profit margins than private firms because they have easy access to loans from state-owned banks and subsidies from provincial authorities. Rarely do state-owned firms go bankrupt, whatever harebrained schemes they might pursue. In the 2000s, Wanfeng's foray into the auto sector, dominated by state players, ended with a thud.

Foreign firms face these and other disadvantages when they compete with state-owned Chinese companies, including pressure to hand over their technology. Those complaints grew over time and helped ignite a trade war when Donald Trump entered the White House and faced off with Xi Jinping.

3

TAKING ON CHINA, 1993

The newly elected president was ready to make good on his campaign threats to take on China. Hadn't he told big crowds that Beijing exploited U.S. goodwill? Hadn't Chinese leaders played the prior occupant of the White House for a fool? While the new commander in chief lacked foreign policy experience and appointed aides who were as ready to fight with each other as with China, that shouldn't pose a problem, he figured.

If there was one thing that Bill Clinton had in abundance, it was self-confidence. To his critics, that came across as arrogance or even narcissism.

There is much to learn from President Clinton's experience battling with Beijing. While Clinton is now seen as the great globalizer—the man who paved the way for China's full membership in the global trading system—he didn't enter office that way. In 1992, he ran as a populist looking to revive U.S. manufacturing. He threatened to bash Japan with tariffs and to oppose the North American Free Trade Agreement unless it was rewritten, an early tryout for themes Donald Trump would use effectively twenty-four years later. President Clinton's turn to globalization reflected pressure from business interests and a search for ways to ensure U.S. economic growth and influence, along with heavy doses of idealism and naïveté.

Back then, China was too poor and too backward to worry many as an economic challenger, aside from the clothing, electronics, and luggage makers trying to compete with importers who jumped from one low-wage nation to another. Clinton's beef with China was about human rights. Three years after Chinese troops fired on student protestors in Tiananmen Square in June 1989, Bill Clinton said he would not "coddle tyrants from Baghdad to Beijing," unlike his election opponent, President George H. W. Bush, a onetime U.S. ambassador to China. Clinton's campaign went further, attacking "the butchers of Beijing," a phrase that became identified with Clinton, though there is little evidence that he used the term.

Clinton wanted to turn his focus on Chinese repression into American policy. But his party was split between business-friendly lawmakers who wanted U.S. firms to cash in on the Chinese market, and China critics appalled at Beijing's repressiveness. The split was illustrated vividly to him during the first weeks of his administration. California Representative Nancy Pelosi, a rising star who made China's human rights a top priority, pressed him on the issue during a White House meeting. The next day Louisiana Senator Bennett Johnston stopped by to make sure Clinton would help energy and chemical companies expand in China.

The president recruited a venerable China expert, Winston Lord, to oversee China affairs at the State Department and work out a human rights policy. As a young Nixon White House aide, Lord accompanied Henry Kissinger on his secret trip to China in 1971, and rose in Republican ranks to become President Ronald Reagan's ambassador to China. Feisty and patrician, Lord left China shortly before Chinese soldiers opened fire in Tiananmen Square, an event that turned him into a sharp critic of Chinese repression. Even more important for the Clinton White House, Lord had broken with his onetime allies in the Bush White House when they rushed to repair ties with Beijing. The new administration could count on his loyalty.

In December 1989, about six months after Tiananmen, newspapers reported that Bush's national security advisor, Brent Scowcroft, flew to Beijing to warn that Congress was planning new sanctions. TV and newspaper photos of Scowcroft clinking wineglasses with China's foreign minister at a state dinner were especially galling to Lord. The Bush White House had "forfeited moral reproof to seek improved bilateral ties," Lord wrote in the *Washington Post* a few days after news of the Scowcroft visit surfaced. He later found out that Scowcroft had visited China even earlier, in September. "This was sort of the last straw for my growing impatience with the Bush Administration's posture on China," Lord told a State Department historian in 1998.

A few months after Clinton took office in 1993, Lord cut a deal with Representative Pelosi and Senate Majority Leader George Mitchell of Maine, who represented the Democratic Party–controlled Congress. No longer would Washington give China the trade preferences it needed to export to the United States unless Beijing made sweeping changes in the way it treated dissidents. Under a May 1993 executive order, China was required to allow free emigration, bar exports made by prison labor, and show "overall, significant progress" in other areas, including releasing political prisoners, protecting Tibetan religious freedom, and ceasing the jamming of Voice of America. To Lord, the conditions would give the United States a cudgel to prod Beijing to make changes.

"I was a great hero for negotiating this," says Lord now. "There wasn't a lot of moaning."

That may have been true among China's critics, but that was hardly the case among U.S. businesses—or members of the Clinton economic team.

Since Tiananmen, Congress had voted every year whether to end trade preferences, known as Most Favored Nation (MFN) status, which guaranteed Chinese imports the lowest possible tariff rate. Without MFN, Chinese goods would have been priced out of the U.S. market and Beijing's economic growth stymied. During the Bush administration, MFN approval was routine. U.S. multinational businesses teamed with the White House to lobby Congress for MFN renewal.

Now that certainty evaporated. If Beijing didn't meet the tough human rights criteria by the summer of 1994, trade with China could halt.

These days, U.S. business relations with Beijing are fraught. China is seen as a crucial market for investment and exports, but feared for its ability to pressure companies into handing over technology, or stealing it. In the early 1990s, there was no ambivalence. Big U.S. firms were all-in for China, whose potential seemed limitless. "The Chinese government came to rely on us as an ally," says a former business executive who helped put together a coalition to boost China trade. "Early on, they had no idea how effective we could be."

Eleven days after Bill Clinton was elected president, the National Association of Manufacturers, the nation's largest manufacturing trade association, wrote the Clinton transition team to make the case that granting China MFN status was essential to the revival of U.S. competitiveness, which candidate Clinton had promised. Without the trade preferences, businesses "cannot afford to make the investments that would be necessary to take advantage of market opportunities in China," NAM's president wrote.

Later, as Lord was negotiating with Congress, NAM followed up, arguing against making human rights improvement a condition for trade with China. A new business group, the Business Coalition for U.S.-China Trade—an umbrella trade group made up of trade associations focused on China—sent the president a letter signed by 334 companies and trade associations that opposed additional requirements for MFN approval. "The persistent threat of MFN withdrawal does little more than create an unstable and excessively risky environment for U.S. companies considering trade and investment in China, and leaves China's booming economy to our competitors," the coalition charged. By the time the president made his decision on MFN in May 1994, the number of companies and trade groups signing a similar petition topped eight hundred.

At the center of the business lobbying was Boeing Company, the nation's largest exporter, which viewed the China market as a do-or-die proposition. Boeing had established a China office in 1980, as the country looked to modernize its air fleet, and helped Beijing improve its deplorable air safety record by training air traffic controllers and helping install modern safety systems. That paid off as Boeing became the leading aircraft supplier to the burgeoning economy.

Should Beijing freeze out Boeing because of unhappiness with the Clinton administration and shift its orders to Boeing's European competitor, Airbus SE, Boeing would lose the manufacturing scale necessary to compete globally. Boeing pressed its vast network of suppliers to lobby their local lawmakers and organized other big companies to do the same. Within the Clinton administration, Boeing reminded cabinet members, especially Commerce Secretary Ron Brown, that tens of thousands of jobs depended on keeping China happy and airplane orders flowing.

"The Boeing Company's access to foreign markets, including the rapidly growing China market, is essential to our efforts to remain globally competitive and to provide good, high-paying jobs for U.S. workers," Boeing declared in a set of talking points it used in lobbying sessions. "Today approximately $5 billion in Boeing aircraft sales are at risk if MFN status to China is conditioned" on improvement in human rights.

As the decision to extend MFN in 1994 drew close, Boeing paid for a television ad featuring Democratic party luminary Robert Strauss, who had been chairman of the Democratic National Committee and then U.S. trade representative. "The simple truth is that pursuing U.S. commercial interests with China is fully compatible with the achievement of long-term U.S. human rights objectives,"

Strauss said. Boeing also made sure to keep party leaders in Beijing up to date on its lobbying activities.

"Boeing worked to strengthen commercial relations, including pressing MFN extension, de-linkage of trade and human rights, and ultimately commercial normalization," says Lisa Barry, Boeing's former vice president of trade policy, who helped plot strategy for the business coalition.

Other companies in the top tier of lobbyists included automaker General Motors Company and insurer American International Group (AIG), which became leaders in the China market. Boeing's relationship with Chinese leaders was so close, says Barry, that Liu Huaqiu, a Chinese vice foreign minister who handled U.S. relations, would say of air transportation: "If it's not Boeing, I'm not going."

Business groups had plenty of allies within the Clinton administration, whose top priority was to lift the nation out of an economic funk. ("It's the economy, stupid," wasn't just a Clinton campaign catchphrase; it reflected the new administration's priority.) Although the recession that had doomed President Bush's reelection campaign officially ended in March 1991, the rebound was tepid and the unemployment rate hovered near 7 percent in 1993. Commerce Secretary Brown, senior White House economic aide Bowman Cutter, and others complained that Lord had cut them out of the discussions with Congress over the MFN conditions, a charge to which Lord now pleads guilty.

But Lord still resents what he calls the efforts of economic officials to "sabotage" the administration's pressure campaign through leaks to the press and complaints to the president. At a meeting in October 1993, for instance, Deputy U.S. Trade Representative Charlene Barshefsky and her counterparts at Commerce and Treasury stayed afterward to complain that Lord was putting too much emphasis on human rights at the expense of trade and economics. Cutter, the White House aide, took those complaints to National

Security Advisor Sandy Berger, who was sympathetic to arguments about the economy.

One White House official joked to a *Wall Street Journal* reporter that while many Americans go to China to buy shirts, U.S. Secretary of State Warren Christopher—Lord's boss—went there to lose his. Brown, meanwhile, was putting together a trip to China with two dozen chief executives, timed to arrive in the summer of 1994, shortly after the president had to decide on whether to extend MFN.

China scholar Michael Pillsbury writes in *The Hundred-Year Marathon*, a book that highlights the influence in China of anti–United States hard-liners, that Beijing put together a secret plan to bolster ties between Clinton economic officials and China's allies among U.S. businesses. They called it "the Clinton coup," Pillsbury says. If the Chinese did so, they wasted their time and money; the Clinton officials needed no convincing.

"President Clinton, to his detriment, didn't rein in those economic agencies," Lord told the State Department historian in a transcript that tops eight hundred pages. "He refused to knock heads as he should have done in ensuring that his own policies were carried out. Therefore, we had splits in our position, which the Chinese could see and which totally undercut our leverage."

"The Chinese could say to themselves, 'Well, the White House is not policing its own agencies,'" Lord continued. "'All of the economic types in the American administration are unhappy. The business community is lobbying the administration. They're unhappy.' So why should China make concessions?"

Mack McLarty, President Clinton's chief of staff at the time, dismisses Lord's claim of sabotage. "We worked hard to have really serious and engaged and candid conversations at the White House and cabinet levels," he says. "At some point, the president had to make a decision about where the proper balance should be struck."

• • •

In Beijing, party leaders showed no signs of caving to U.S. demands. When President Clinton met for the first time with Chinese President and Communist Party chief Jiang Zemin during an Asia-Pacific conference in Seattle in November 1993, the meeting went poorly. Jiang stuck to his briefing books, despite Clinton's best efforts to charm him. When the president asked Jiang about economic reform, figuring that was a good icebreaker, he "was then treated to about a 45-minute monologue in which Jiang Zemin cited statistics," says Lord in the oral history. The two leaders made no headway on human rights, either.

In late February 1994, John Shattuck, the State Department's top human rights official, flew to Beijing to check on progress, ahead of Secretary of State Christopher. As a warning shot, the State Department released its annual report on China's human rights record shortly before Shattuck arrived. Beijing "fell short of internationally accepted norms," the report found. In Beijing, Shattuck agreed to meet with one of China's most prominent dissidents, Wei Jingsheng, who had been in and out of jail for years for advocating democratic change.

Wei picked the lobby of Beijing's opulent China World Hotel, a meeting place that could hardly be missed by Chinese security agents. Afterward, Wei held a press briefing where he urged President Clinton to hang tough on human rights, once again tweaking his jailers. Some Chinese dissidents sought publicity, figuring that an international reputation gave them some protection at home from harassment. Wei was picked up by security agents after the session, but then released before Christopher was due to land in Beijing. To guard against a repeat performance, Wei was forced to leave Beijing while other dissidents were arrested, hardly a sign that China was taking Clinton's demands seriously.

Relations only worsened when Christopher was ushered into

the Great Hall of the People to discuss human rights and other issues. There he met with Chinese Premier Li Peng, a hard-liner who
had supported the Tiananmen Square crackdown and who was
known for his sarcasm and opposition to opening China to Western
business.

Li, a protégé of Zhou Enlai, a revered Chinese revolutionary who
advocated building diplomatic ties with America, represented the
conservative wing of the party. His political pedigree and years running a state-owned Beijing power company made him one of the
most effective defenders of party control during his time.

The Chinese premier turned his meeting with Christopher into
a harangue. How dare Washington interfere with China's internal
security issues in the name of human rights, he lectured the secretary of state. Why should he take Clinton's threats seriously? If
Washington were to revoke MFN, "the U.S. would lose its share of
the big China market," he told Christopher. U.S. executives had already let him know they were pressing the administration to change
its policies, including those from General Electric, AT&T, and "Gold
Sacks," an apparent reference to the Wall Street firm of Goldman
Sachs.

Li made it clear that "China will never accept the U.S.'s human
rights concept," says a former Chinese diplomat. Years later, Christopher recalled the Li talks as "one of the most difficult meetings I
ever had. He basically dared us, 'Go ahead and deny us MFN and
then we'll see who they say lost China.'"

Deflated, the State Department team jetted home and felt they
were slapped once more in the face, this time by Clinton. The president didn't publicly object to the way his team was manhandled in
Beijing or make a statement defending the administration's human
rights policy. "He let us hang there in the wind," says Lord now. Not
so, argues his former chief of staff, McLarty, who says the president
"was thinking how to engage the Chinese privately, compared to
publicly."

Back home, President Clinton convened a series of White House meetings where he asked national security and economic officials for ideas on how to deal with China. Pressure on human rights clearly wasn't working. Cutting off U.S. companies from the fastest-growing economy in the world was also a nonstarter. Aside from economics, the United States needed China's help on nuclear proliferation, the global environment, and other important issues. Turning China into an enemy made no sense. The former Soviet Union and its onetime Warsaw Pact allies seemed to be liberalizing; China could be the next Communist country to change.

A decision on MFN renewal was due in May, two months after the Christopher trip fiasco. The Commerce Department ran computer simulations of the impact of targeting exports only from Chinese military-owned industries. The economic results were insignificant. Another idea: slash imports from mainland China but spare those involving Hong Kong and Taiwan. That proved to be impractical, given the large role investors from those regions played in Chinese manufacturing. Trade sanctions would also damage U.S. firms that owned factories in China and prompt retaliation from Beijing.

"We are constantly reminded by our Chinese partners that the annual fear of MFN renewal withdrawal raises serious questions about the credibility of our commitment to China," AT&T's China chief told Christopher at a session with U.S. business officials in Beijing following his Li Peng meeting. To make sure that message was heard widely, the U.S. executives voted to open their meeting with Christopher to the press.

Finding no good alternative, Clinton canceled his policy. MFN approval would no longer be linked to Chinese progress on human rights. In an Oval Office meeting in May, he explained his rationale to senior officials, citing the examples of Cuba and Russia.

"The Chinese threw out the Soviets when the Soviets were their only friends in the world," he said, according to the recollection of several attendees. "That's interesting. And we've been trying to change human rights in Cuba, just ninety miles away, in a place with a similar culture to ours, and we have gotten nowhere. That's interesting, too. Now with China, with 1.2 billion people halfway around the world, we're going to dictate to them? We have no leverage."

President Clinton learned other hard lessons too that continue to apply to China. It's tough, if not impossible, to get China to make changes that it views as opposed to its national interests, especially ones that might weaken the Communist Party's hold on power. In Clinton's time, Beijing feared the democratic change sought by dissidents, seeing what had happened in the former Soviet Union. These days it worries that the Trump administration's demands that China remake its economy could weaken the party's economic control.

It's also hard to convince Beijing that the United States is fully committed to change when the president's top advisers are feuding over China policy and the U.S. business community is staunchly supporting Beijing. Those same issues will come into play later in the book as President Trump moves to confront China.

Late in the afternoon of May 26, 1994, President Clinton stepped to the podium of the White House briefing room to formally delink human rights from trade. In a tone that struck some reporters there as defensive and almost apologetic, he said that China had failed to achieve "overall significant progress" in human rights, as his policy required. But even so, he would recommend continuing China's trade preference. His goal wasn't to isolate China by cutting off trade, he said, but rather "to engage the Chinese with not only economic contacts but with cultural, educational, and other contacts, and with a continuing aggressive effort in human rights"—a position that business groups had been advocating for months, and which became U.S. policy for every succeeding administration until Donald Trump took office.

Clinton said he would push American companies to adopt a code of conduct for doing business in China, an effort that quickly fizzled. He invited CEOs to meet him in the White House Cabinet Room and lectured them that the administration wasn't giving up on human rights in China, a cause they should champion, too. "If you don't understand that, shame on you," he told them.

Businesses focused instead on their China expansion plans. Kentucky Fried Chicken, then a subsidiary of PepsiCo Inc., said it would spend $200 million to establish fast-food restaurants in forty-five Chinese cities by 1998. After the delinking decision, "the door to China is open wider," KFC's president told the *Wall Street Journal*.

PepsiCo spun off KFC in 1997. Today the chicken restaurants are part of Yum China Holdings Inc., China's largest restaurant company, which is incorporated in the United States but run out of Shanghai. Yum operates 5,900 KFC restaurants across 1,200 Chinese cities.

4

BOSS ZHU ARRIVES, APRIL 1999

When Chinese Premier Zhu Rongji landed in Washington, D.C., on April 7, 1999, expectations couldn't have been higher for an historic change in relations between the world's most populous country and its most powerful one.

For the past six years, Zhu had helped steer the Chinese economy, and he believed the country's future relied on market competition and foreign investment. That would mean a bigger role for U.S. companies and U.S.-style policies. Specifically, Zhu was traveling to Washington to finish work on a trade deal with President Clinton that would pave the way for China to become a member of the World Trade Organization. The Geneva-based organization oversaw global trade but required members to follow capitalist rules.

If all went well, China's WTO membership would banish any remaining fears that China would backslide to the inward-looking China of Mao Zedong, where private property was expropriated and businessmen persecuted. Many of China's American allies hoped that WTO membership would wrap Beijing so tightly in a cocoon with Western economies and ideology that a democratic China would eventually emerge.

"The bottom line is this," President Clinton said at a think tank gathering on the morning of Zhu's arrival: "If China is willing to play by the global rules of trade, it would be an inexplicable mistake for the United States to say, 'No.'" Bill Lane, Caterpillar Inc.'s chief trade lobbyist, was so excited by Zhu's arrival that he texted the construction equipment maker's Peoria, Illinois, headquarters: "The Eagle has landed."

But by the end of Zhu's three-day spring visit, Zhu was humiliated, U.S. businesses were livid, Clinton was scrambling to figure out what he had done wrong, and U.S.-China relations had sunk to their lowest point since the Tiananmen Square shootings.

Eventually, the two sides recovered. But the memory of the Clinton-Zhu negotiations over WTO membership, and the distrust they engendered, remains vivid today.

It's worth recounting in detail what happened. When Chinese leaders worry that President Trump might undermine them with a tweet or an offhand remark, they think back to the Clinton-Zhu encounter. When U.S. officials worry that Chinese leaders are trying to play them for fools, rather than negotiate in earnest, they hark back to the haggling over the WTO.

China had begun negotiations to join the WTO's predecessor organization, called the General Agreement on Tariffs and Trade, in 1986. It wasn't an easy decision for Beijing. At the time, China's economy was nearly fully controlled by the Communist Party and the government's state-owned firms. Private real estate barely existed. Export industries and foreign investors were confined to special export zones along the coast. It wasn't until 1992 that the Communist Party, at the 14th Communist Party Congress, adopted the goal of creating a "socialist market economy."

Even then, China's bureaucracy fought any easing of government control over banking, telecommunications, agriculture, and many other industries where Western companies hungered to get a foothold. High tariffs protected local firms from foreign competition; high subsidies kept many lumbering state firms from bankruptcy. Joining the WTO would mean scaling back government protection for millions of bureaucrats who ran the economy and hundreds of millions of laborers.

The WTO works by consensus. To join, China needed approval of all 142 members at the time, a process that involved laborious negotiations over tariffs, subsidies, government protection of industries, and other issues. No negotiation was more important than the one with the United States, the nation that had the most to offer—untrammeled access to the world's largest market—and drove the hardest bargain. Under WTO rules, any concession China made to the United States (or another nation) had to be offered to every other member. All for one and one for all.

After years of halting progress, China focused on gaining WTO entry by 2000. A big reason was the ascendancy of Zhu to the premiership in 1998. Although Zhu was the leading voice on economic issues as vice premier, a position he held for the previous five years, his enhanced status gave him a more powerful perch to push through changes. A financial crisis that swept across Asia in 1997 and 1998 had battered China's export industry, cut China's supercharged growth rate by half, and slowed foreign investment. Chinese leaders cast about for new ways to boost growth.

The strong-willed premier was dubbed "Boss Zhu" by admirers and detractors alike. Puffy-eyed and forceful, Zhu followed a path similar to many senior officials at the time. In 1970, during the chaos of Mao's Cultural Revolution, he was purged from the party and banished to the countryside as a manual laborer for being a "rightist," or one deemed as favoring capitalism.

When Deng Xiaoping prevailed in the power struggle following Mao's death, Zhu was allowed to rejoin the party. Deng tapped him for a senior post at the powerful state economic-planning agency. Then in late 1987, he became the mayor of Shanghai, the most Western-oriented of Chinese cities. "There aren't many people in our party who know about the economy," Deng said at the time. "Zhu is one who does."

Zhu's strategy of revamping the state sector, called *zhua da fang xiao*, or "grabbing the big ones and letting the small ones go," pushed many firms out of business and jolted the Chinese economy. Workers could no longer count on the "iron rice bowl" provided by state companies, which housed, clothed, fed, and educated them and their families. Many Chinese started small businesses or moved hundreds of miles to the coast to get jobs in new, privately owned factories because they could no longer find work in government-owned plants. Zhu's plans endeared him more to foreigners, who needed laborers for their factories, than to many of the workers whose lives were scrambled.

Zhu's agenda also faced fierce resistance from state-owned firms and Zhu's predecessor as premier, Li Peng—the same Li Peng who had badgered Secretary of State Warren Christopher over human rights. Although Li was no longer premier, he outranked Zhu in the party hierarchy. His new job as leader of China's legislature, the National People's Congress, had no real power, but it provided Li an important platform in political debates.

Li argued that China should move more slowly than Zhu wanted and ensure employment for those already laid off before moving ahead with changes that would push millions more out of work. Li also attacked Zhu's initiative to privatize some state firms as selling out to foreigners.

Zhu hoped to use foreign pressure to his advantage. It would no longer just be him and his allies who demanded change in China; the United States and other WTO members required such change as the price of WTO membership. "If China wants to join the WTO, wants to be integrated in international community, then China must play by the rules of the game," Zhu explained later. "China can't do that without making concessions. Of course, such concessions might bring about a very huge impact on such state-owned enterprises, and also on China's market."

For his plans to succeed, Zhu relied on the backing of Communist Party General Secretary Jiang Zemin, the nation's top leader, who focused more on foreign policy and national security. (Jiang also had the title of president, a largely symbolic position in China. His power stemmed from his party position.)

Elevated by Deng Xiaoping in 1989 after the Tiananmen Square crackdown, Jiang's top priority was continuing the "reform and opening up" policy begun by Deng. Jiang also displayed charisma and candor rare among senior Communist leaders, and a sense of humor.

Many in China recall how Jiang criticized a Hong Kong reporter who questioned one of his appointments. "You're too young," Jiang called out, speaking in English. "Too simple, sometimes naive!" Chinese netizens create Jiang Zemin memes today. Some show him combing his hair in front of a foreign dignitary; others have him playing the ukulele. They remind Chinese society of a leader with a colorful style, a big contrast to today's stepped-up state control over every aspect of the Chinese society.

With Jiang's backing, in February 1999, China's Politburo—the top twenty-five members of the Communist Party—approved the economic concessions Zhu felt necessary to get China into the WTO. China was ready to address nearly all the big issues that had divided Washington and Beijing for years. Dissenters held their tongues. "Opposition within China was not won over, but rather was run over," wrote University of Maryland professor Margaret Pearson.

• • •

The Clinton administration was a willing partner. Zhu had wowed Clinton Treasury Secretary Robert Rubin and his successor, Larry Summers, with his daring policies and his candid admissions that he needed foreign pressure to accomplish his goals. The Treasury also complimented China for ignoring pleas by domestic manu-facturers to devalue the yuan during the Asia financial crisis, even though a stronger currency harmed Chinese exporters. Runaway devaluations would have made recoveries by other Asian nations even more difficult.

Clinton had come to see his historic role as weaving China and the former Soviet Union into the U.S. orbit through trade and economic policies. After Clinton's first frosty meeting with Jiang in 1993, the two leaders developed a warm relationship. During a 1997 trip to the United States, President Jiang went out of his way to impress his American host.

Just before he was to meet the president, Jiang gathered staffers at the Chinese embassy in Washington, including cooks, drivers, and barbers, to practice his English. "Good evening, I am going to speak English tonight," he told the group. He recalled how he had practiced English in college by reciting Lincoln's Gettysburg Address, and then went off to the White House.

A trip by Clinton to China the following year also went well. He and Jiang did a live, televised press conference, where the president discussed human rights and urged Jiang to meet the Dalai Lama, the Tibetan religious leader despised by Chinese leaders. "The main point of the press conference was the debate itself" with Jiang, Clinton wrote in his autobiography. The president said Jiang impressed him as "intriguing, funny and fiercely proud."

The Clinton team was prodded by business lobbyists who had long been pressing the administration and Congress to help China with its WTO bid. In the mid-1990s, Boeing formed what it called "the Rump Group" of ten major U.S. exporters, including AT&T, AIG, Chrysler, and General Electric, to push a "normalization initiative" for improved economic relations between the United States and China. Boeing put up $2 million in seed money for a lobbying campaign that would spend far more in the years ahead. The group flooded U.S. negotiators with information about Chinese markets and the trade barriers they wanted dismantled as part of a "commercially meaningful" agreement for China's entry into the WTO.

A series of letters from Clinton to Jiang between November 1998 and February 1999 convinced Chinese leaders that a deal was within reach. In the February letter, President Clinton expressed the hope that a WTO deal could be wrapped up during Premier Zhu's already scheduled visit to the United States in April 1999. That visit was endangered by the start of the U.S.-led bombing campaign of Yugoslavia in March after that country's president, Slobodan Milosevic, rejected a peace deal drafted by the North Atlantic Treaty Organization (NATO). What more proof was needed, asked Zhu's opponents, that the United States sought global hegemony, not fair deals with less powerful countries? But Jiang batted away such concerns.

"President Jiang Zemin decided that I should come according to a schedule and he is number one in China, so I had to obey him," Zhu joked with reporters during his April visit to Washington.

But unknown to the Chinese, the president's top advisers had been holding a series of meetings in March, chaired by White House Chief of Staff John Podesta, to decide whether to try to wrap up a WTO agreement during Zhu's visit.

Charlene Barshefsky, now promoted to trade representative, Secretary of State Madeleine Albright, and members of the National Security Council and Central Intelligence Agency made the case for completing a deal. Although the United States still sought concessions from China in a number of important areas, Barshefsky said she was confident she could get Zhu's approval. The United States had an historic opportunity to transform China and the global economy. "If you don't empower him, and you humiliate him, you're making a terrible mistake," she argued.

Her confidence surprised some of the others, who had thought the two sides weren't close to a deal. "Trade negotiators can smell a deal," Podesta told colleagues after one meeting, holding his finger to the side of his nose and sniffing.

But Podesta, a savvy political operator trusted by the president, along with National Economic Council (NEC) Director Gene

Sperling and the White House legislative director, argued against accepting a deal. Democrats in Congress hadn't been notified that an agreement could be imminent, they said. They already suspected the Clinton White House was too wedded to free trade and didn't fight hard enough for Democrats' labor allies. A quick deal would fuel their suspicions.

The White House had just started discussions on China with Representative Sandy Levin, a Michigan lawmaker who was influential with House Democrats on trade issues. A premature announcement was bound to lose his vote and the votes of colleagues. "Rushing this so that you don't do the full consultation with key House Democrats that was promised wouldn't be in the long-term interest of getting this deal done," Sperling argued.

Perhaps the most important voice was that of Treasury Secretary Rubin. The influential former Goldman Sachs co-chairman was impressed with Zhu's sincerity and ambitions, and initially lined up with Barshefsky for finishing a trade deal. But he changed his mind during the White House discussions. "If we tried to do a deal with Zhu when he was there, it could have blown up in Congress," he says now. "The chance to get it done was better if he left without a deal." Others in the administration suspected that Rubin also wanted to impress upon Democratic lawmakers that he was with them in order to clear the way for Larry Summers, no favorite of the Democratic caucus, to succeed him as Treasury secretary. Rubin says that wasn't the case.

Hanging over the White House debates was the memory of congressional defeats in 1997 and 1998 when President Clinton sought authority for negotiating new trade deals in Latin America and at the WTO. The losses were the most significant setbacks for trade expansion since Franklin Delano Roosevelt started reducing tariffs in the wake of the Depression. Perhaps unfairly, Barshefsky took a lot of the blame for the defeat, as did business lobbyists, who didn't give her much support on Capitol Hill. The trade representative was nicknamed "Stonewall Barshefsky" by her White House colleagues for her negotiating ferocity, but politically she was viewed as a naïf.

In the 1998 congressional debacle, only 29 Democrats backed the administration in the House. Podesta figured he needed 60 to 70 to win approval of a China trade deal. "We had to take more time to get them," Podesta says now. "None of the groundwork had been laid." President Clinton agreed.

Worried that Zhu might feel sandbagged in Washington, Barshefsky flew to Beijing a week before the premier was scheduled to depart for the United States. Before the caravan of U.S. embassy vehicles arrived at the ornate gate at Zhongnanhai, the Chinese leadership compound, she stopped the cars, fearing they were bugged. "Step outside," she asked her chief China negotiator, Robert Cassidy.

"Bob, I'm doing everything I can to get a deal through this administration," she said.

"What do you mean?" he asked.

"I'm having trouble getting this through."

At Ziguang Hall, a two-story pavilion where Chinese leaders meet foreign dignitaries in front of elaborately carved Chinese panels, she delivered the same message to Zhu. She also used her visit to press for even deeper trade concessions.

"If we agree to this package, the president will sign?" Zhu asked.

She couldn't speak for the president, Barshefsky replied, but she was doing her best to put a deal together despite opposition. "We have to get the best package we can to get the best outcome in Washington," she told the Chinese premier.

• • •

Zhu arrived in Washington on April 7 after a short stay in Los Angeles. The Chinese premier settled into Blair House, the president's stately welcome center, and then made the short walk to the White House to meet Clinton at 9 p.m. in a second-floor parlor called the

Yellow Oval Room for its shape and décor. A handful of aides accompanied the two leaders, who sat facing each other under a crystal chandelier. A waiter stood by, ready to bring the two men drinks.

The president quickly got to the point. There wasn't going to be a deal, at least not now.

Clinton said that Barshefsky believed that if the two sides worked intensely the following day, they could put together a satisfactory WTO deal. "But that isn't my inclination," Clinton said.

The issues dividing the nations were still deep, and Congress would be suspicious of any outcome unless it was "bullet proof," the president said. The goal wasn't simply to get a deal, but to get one that Congress would approve.

Clinton looked to shift onto Zhu some of the responsibility for scrapping negotiations. The president told him that some of his aides thought Zhu could be hurt politically if he failed to bring home a deal. If Zhu wanted to try to wrap up an agreement, "we could work all night," Clinton said, according to his former aides and his recollections in his autobiography. But it was up to Zhu to ask for further negotiations.

To some of Clinton's political aides, the president was being as straightforward and candid with Zhu as he would be with a Western ally. Yes, a deal was possible. But why push for one now if Congress was so wary of the negotiations that it might reject the results? Better to continue to negotiate, make progress, and finish up sometime later.

Additional rounds of talks would help convince lawmakers that he wasn't settling too easily—"for a photo op," as one of Clinton's aides put it. Unmentioned by the president was that Republican distrust of Clinton on China dated back years to a scandal involving Chinese efforts to influence the Democratic Party through campaign contributions.

But others in the administration, who worked closely with the Chinese, felt that Clinton was putting Zhu in an impossible situation.

If Zhu took the president at his word and pressed him to finish negotiations during his Washington stay, he would lose any negotiating leverage and would be second-guessed back home. He would look like a beggar. "I can't imagine those words"—asking an American president for political help—"would come out of Zhu's mouth," says Barshefsky today.

Zhu kept his disappointment to himself for the time being. "If the timing was bad, we could wait," he told Clinton. The two sides would agree to keep talking and try to reach what Chinese advisers later described as "seeking common ground, while reserving differences," a reference to a strategy made popular by Zhou Enlai for dealing with nations that disagree with China. The idea is to acknowledge differences, but still treat each other with respect and maintain communications.

Early the next day, April 8, Barshefsky met with China's trade negotiators. They detailed the deep changes in trade and economic policies China was willing to make. Beijing would reduce or eliminate tariffs, quotas, price controls, and other barriers on thousands of agricultural and industrial goods. Foreign companies would get greater access to banking, telecommunications, insurance, and other politically sensitive industries. Intellectual property protections would be expanded and pressure to transfer sensitive technology curtailed. Barshefsky had the Chinese negotiators sign the documents outlining the offer.

One exception: the United States didn't push especially hard to get China to ease joint venture requirements and other restrictions on banks and securities firms, say U.S. negotiators. They lay the blame on Treasury, which was responsible for that part of the negotiations. Clinton Treasury officials don't dispute the criticism. They say they were pursuing other priorities and believed that U.S. financial firms were doing well in China despite limited access there.

At about 4 p.m., Clinton and Zhu met the press at the White House's presidential hall. Clinton put his best spin on his decision to spurn Zhu. "We have made significant progress toward bringing China into the World Trade Organization on fair commercial terms, although we are not quite there yet," the president told reporters.

But Zhu was no longer willing to play along with Clinton. He told reporters he saw their discussions quite differently. "If you want to hear some honest words, then I should say that now the problem does not lie with this big difference or big gap, but lies with the political atmosphere," the Chinese premier said.

Two hours later, Barshefsky and Sperling, the NEC director, held their own press conference. She had a surprise for the Chinese: the U.S. trade representative's office was publishing a seventeen-page document detailing the Chinese offers. The press release broke the rules usually governing trade negotiations. Any offers are considered tentative—and kept secret—until a final deal. In trade lingo, there is no agreement on anything until there is a final agreement on everything.

Many in Barshefsky's staff opposed her decision, saying it broke protocol and broke faith with the Chinese. The release was bound to weaken Zhu at home. Barshefsky shut down the argument with a curt, "That's enough." Her main concern was preventing China from backsliding on its commitments after Zhu went home.

"We have captured and memorialized—in agreement language—what has been achieved," Barshefsky told the afternoon press conference. "All of that is now locked in place."

Zhu's top trade adviser, Wu Yi, a female Chinese politician who matched Barshefsky in passion and intensity, felt betrayed. "The Iron Lady of China," as she was known, was "absolutely furious," recalls Cassidy, the U.S. negotiator. In a meeting with Barshefsky, "she had enough English to swear, but the translator had even more words."

That atmosphere was about to get a lot more poisonous. The *Wall Street Journal* reported the next day, April 9, that Clinton had never intended to cut a deal with Zhu during his visit. The story detailed the series of White House meetings that occurred before Zhu landed in Washington.

That night Zhu made his anger clear at how he was treated. At a dinner with U.S. business leaders, he complained that the U.S. side "made public many documents and said we had agreed to them, but we have not agreed. If you want too much too soon, in the end you may wind up with nothing."

U.S. business leaders were also outraged. After Zhu left Washington to start a tour of U.S. cities, about one hundred lobbyists were invited to meet with Sperling and Barshefsky in the elegant Indian Treaty Room of the Old Executive Office Building, across from the White House. Barshefsky, who they knew had pushed for a deal, was met with a standing ovation. Sperling was booed.

Looking to ease the tension, Sperling told the crowd that the president wanted a deal and "we're all in agreement" with that.

"No we're not," shouted Robert Kapp, the usually courteous president of the U.S.-China Business Council, which represents big businesses operating in China. He launched into a diatribe against the administration's handling of the negotiations. "I interrupted Sperling. I hogged the floor. I was beside myself," Kapp says now, embarrassed by his outburst.

The press portrayed Clinton's spurning of Zhu as a debacle. The *New York Times* called the talks "fruitless." *Washington Post* columnist David Ignatius was more withering. "Clinton's flip-flop on the WTO sullies one of the few areas—free trade—where he reasonably can claim to have acted consistently on principle," he wrote. *Newsday* called Clinton's decision to send Zhu home empty-handed "a missed opportunity that may never come again for Clinton."

The president struggled to understand what had gone wrong, his mood lurching between anger at his advisers and bewilderment at the Chinese reaction. Hadn't he offered Zhu Rongji the chance to negotiate further if that was what he wanted to do? When Sperling handed him a positive editorial, he batted it away. "Everyone knows

I made a mistake," he said. He asked his aides what they could do to get negotiations back on track or even convince Zhu to return to Washington.

With the skill of a veteran politician, Zhu barnstormed Denver, Chicago, and New York, portraying himself as the jilted partner and reminding business audiences of the opportunities they might miss in China. Clinton "didn't have enough courage" to sign an accord because he feared congressional opponents, he told a meeting of lawmakers before leaving town. In Denver, he told a luncheon hosted by the city's mayor that the Chinese "are not sure [Clinton's] judgment is the right one." In Chicago, he toured the Chicago Mercantile Exchange, met with Chicago-born Commerce Secretary William Daley, and warned the business community that "America is not the only country in the world. There are other countries and continents" happy to do business with China.

When Zhu reached New York on April 13, the White House had had enough. President Clinton called him at his suite at the Waldorf Astoria and the two men talked for about twenty minutes, during which Zhu regaled him with stories of all the Americans he met who favored China's WTO membership. The president said he would issue a new statement committing the United States to getting China into the WTO by the end of the year and to restarting negotiations as soon as U.S. negotiators could travel to Beijing. A satisfied Zhu told a dinner of business leaders afterward that "I think we are very, very close to achieving a final agreement on the WTO. Some observers say we are 95 percent of the way there. I myself think it is more like 99 percent."

About a month later, on May 7, 1999, that agreement was blown apart by B-2 stealth bombers flying from Whiteman Air Force Base in Missouri to the skies over Belgrade, Yugoslavia. There, the aircraft dropped five precision-guided bombs on the Chinese embassy, destroying the building, killing three Chinese staffers, and injuring twenty-seven others. Demonstrations erupted across China. Angry Chinese threw stones, bottles, and even some homemade bombs at the U.S. embassy in Beijing. For one of the authors of this book, Lingling, the bombing made her question whether to reject a full-scholarship offer to New York University's graduate journalism program. (After an editor at state-owned *China Daily* talked sense into her, she went ahead with her American Dream.)

"Don't worry, our three martyrs! The motherland and the people will remember you forever," said an announcer on the main evening newscast on China's state-owned broadcast. "Getting stronger is the only way we can avoid being humiliated." Plans were shelved for negotiations with Washington over the WTO. The talks could be portrayed in China as the United States taking advantage of China's weakness.

• • •

President Clinton was beside himself. How could the United States have screwed up so badly? How could he possibly convince President Jiang that the bombing had been a mistake, that someone had used an outdated map to load coordinates into the jet's computers? Chief of Staff Podesta tried a joke: "Some of your own staff weren't that sure it was a mistake, either," he said, unleashing a presidential tirade. Later, in his autobiography, Clinton said, "I had a hard time believing it, too."

At an emergency Politburo meeting in Beijing, not a single leader accepted the U.S. explanation. "This incident, more than anything else, reminds us that the United States is an enemy," Li Peng declared. "It is by no means a friend, as some say," he added, in a pointed reference to his adversary, Premier Zhu. But after three days of closed-door deliberations, the Chinese leadership concluded that China's relationship with the United States was too important to make it another casualty of the bombing. In a May 13, 1999, speech welcoming the return of Chinese embassy staff from Yugoslavia, Jiang said, "China will not deviate from the policy of developing the economy and carrying out reform and opening because of this incident."

The following day, Jiang told Clinton by telephone that he didn't believe he personally ordered the bombing, but figured that others in the Pentagon could have "rigged the maps intentionally to cause a rift" with China. He urged the U.S. leader to conduct a thorough investigation. Clinton offered his apology for the tragedy.

Still, the combination of Clinton's rejection of Zhu's WTO offer followed by the embassy bombing badly weakened the premier. As soon as Zhu returned home from his U.S. trip, committees under Li Peng's National People's Congress questioned whether Zhu had gone too far in offering concessions. Wu Jichuan, the head of the Ministry of Information Industry, threatened to resign over Zhu's offer to open the telecommunications industry to foreign competition. At a meeting of senior Communist Party officials, Zhu offered Mao-style self-criticism, or *jiantao*, for his U.S. trip. He said he was too anxious to get a deal done, said a senior government official at the time.

Many of China's Internet users, increasing at a rapid pace at the time—and far less controlled by censorship than they are now—labeled Zhu a *maiguozei*, or traitor, in their online postings. Some compared his WTO offer to the infamous "Twenty-one Demands" made by Japan in 1915 that would have greatly extended Japanese control of China during World War I.

The bombing deepened his problems further. Jiang sought to quell criticism by offering Zhu's critics some concessions. In the summer, the job of reforming the state sector, which had been Zhu's signature program, was handed to Vice Premier Wu Bangguo, Zhu's subordinate. Still, Zhu held on to the premiership, giving him the chance again to conclude a WTO deal.

Getting relations back on track took months of difficult discussions. U.S. officials were never really certain that their Chinese counterparts believed their explanations for the bombing. In an ice-breaking session in September, the two sides resumed formal talks, although the subject matter in Washington was limited to whether Zhu had agreed in April to allow foreigners to buy a majority stake in Chinese telecommunications firms.

On October 16, Clinton called Jiang, offering to clear up what the United States wanted from China to assure WTO admission. A week later, Larry Summers, then Treasury secretary, flew to Beijing to meet with Premier Zhu, signaling a further easing of tensions. Around that time, the United States formally dropped one of its toughest demands of China, which would have allowed Washington to impose high tariff walls to block all Chinese imports if Beijing flooded any U.S. market. U.S. negotiators called that the "nuclear option" and figured there was very little chance China would accept the provision anyway.

Final negotiations were to start on November 10 in Beijing, with the U.S. side uncertain whether Beijing really wanted a deal then or was looking to embarrass the United States by rejecting the negotiators, as Clinton had done to Zhu in April. For the Chinese, their suspicions of Clinton and his team continued unabated. Nevertheless, a day before the Americans arrived, the Politburo's seven-member Standing Committee, its most senior leadership group, including President Jiang and Premier Zhu, voted to support a deal. Only Li Peng dissented, as he had in the past.

Barshefsky, the U.S. negotiator, recruited NEC Director Sperling to accompany her on the trip, even though he had helped convince Clinton to reject Zhu. Having him in Beijing, she calculated, would signal to China that the U.S. side was united and represented the president. "They are going to be looking to you for help," Barshefsky advised Sperling. "They will want to talk to you during the breaks and try to peel you away. Be that friendly person they want you to be." If they trusted him, they would take his demands more seriously later on, she calculated.

Negotiations, expected to last a few days, started slowly. Sperling was mum as Barshefsky talked with her counterparts. On the second day, when the issue of auto tariffs came up, she advised Sperling to pounce, as a way to show the Chinese that slashing 80 percent tariffs on automobiles was a Clinton priority. When the Chinese balked, Sperling, usually friendly and ingratiating, pounded the table and said, "Let me be clear. President Clinton will never, never, never, never, never, never take that deal on autos," leaving the Chinese nonplussed.

Looking to move the negotiations along, Zhu came to the negotiating room on the fourth day of talks, November 12, and took over for his trade advisers. The premier apologized that he hadn't been able to get involved in the negotiations earlier, but said he had been reading the transcripts of the talks. As Zhu continued in Chinese, before his translators could explain his words in English, the Chinese officials cracked up at any mention of the word "Sperling." Why? the U.S. side wondered.

"I even know Mr. Sperling said, 'no,' six times," Zhu said. "We find that unusual because in China we tell our children not to repeat the same word even twice." Zhu encouraged negotiators on both sides to continue talking until a deal was struck.

But discussions remained stalled, again making the U.S. side wonder whether they were being set up to take the blame for a failure. During some of the many pauses in negotiations, Sperling went to see *Star Wars*, which was playing in local theaters, and called his father from the cavernous Great Hall of the People to get updates on the Michigan–Penn State football game. When the Chinese side said that they couldn't make a decision and needed to confer with more senior leaders, Barshefsky had had enough.

She and Sperling left to get dinner without telling their Chinese hosts where they were heading. "Trust me, they know how to find us if they want to," she told Sperling. Later, she telephoned President Clinton in a secure embassy room nicknamed "the refrigerator" and told him the team was flying home. The Chinese were jerking them around. "We had been there one week already," Barshefsky says now. "I only brought two outfits. I thought if we stayed longer, we'd look weak." Clinton agreed, saying he didn't want to be played.

But Sperling, who had backed Barshefsky's plan, had second thoughts. What if the Chinese really did need some additional time? Was Barshefsky acting too hastily? Without informing her, he placed a call to National Security Advisor Sandy Berger, who then telephoned Secretary of State Albright. She phoned Zhu in the middle of the night, Beijing time, to press him on the negotiations. With the U.S. delegation threatening to fly home the next day—and sending their luggage ahead to the airport to show they were serious—Zhu phoned his senior negotiator, Long Yongtu, to make another stab at discussions.

Around 4 a.m. on November 15, Long and U.S. negotiator Robert Cassidy met at China's Ministry of Commerce. "Do you really want to conclude an agreement?" Long asked Cassidy, who had donned what he calls his lucky shirt—a worn collarless garment with broad stripes. Of course, replied Cassidy, who said they should proofread the hundreds of pages of text they had negotiated over the years, which Long took as a sign of good faith. The Chinese negotiator telephoned Zhu with the news that "based on my many years of experience in dealing with the Americans, they want to sign," pointing to Cassidy's willingness to proofread the documents as evidence.

"Very well. I trust your judgment," Zhu said. "You must manage to talk to the Americans and don't let them leave." That wasn't only his order, he said, but the order of President Jiang and other top leaders.

By the time Barshefsky and Sperling drove up to the ministry, ostensibly to say good-bye before heading to the airport, the negotiators had a surprise for them. Premier Zhu would be coming to the ministry to handle negotiations. That was a crystal clear sign that he planned to finish a deal, because the premier rarely deigned to leave the leadership compound for the far less prestigious Commerce Ministry. Zhu, Long, Barshefsky, Sperling, and a small number of aides went to a back room of the ministry to cut the deal.

In some ways, the final talks were almost anticlimactic. The two sides didn't so much negotiate as listen while Zhu made clear what he needed politically and what he knew Clinton had to have. He agreed to U.S. demands that for twelve years China would accept provisions that made it simpler for U.S. firms to block Chinese imports. He also agreed that China would be classified at the WTO for fifteen years as a "nonmarket economy"—a designation that also made it easier for Americans to win lawsuits to stop Chinese imports. China would also reduce automobile tariffs from 80 percent to 25 percent.

Long, the Chinese negotiator, passed Zhu notes saying that he thought the premier might be exceeding his authority with these concessions, especially by accepting nonmarket economy status. An angry Zhu pounded the table and told his aide to stop bothering him.

But there were areas where Zhu wouldn't budge. He wouldn't agree to let foreign firms buy majority stakes in Chinese telecom firms, telling U.S. negotiators not to even bother arguing the point. Zhu said he understood the need for more competition, but this demand was politically impossible. "You're telling me what your president has to have," Zhu said. "I have political needs, too."

"He wasn't acting like the negotiator," says Sperling now. "He was saying each side had to respect and ultimately give on the other's top priorities." Boss Zhu.

After Barshefsky and Sperling telephoned President Clinton at a NATO meeting in Ankara for his approval—retreating to a bathroom in the ministry for privacy—the two sides signed the trade deal for China to join the WTO and broke out champagne. That marked the formal embrace of China into the world trading system, a designation that would clear away any doubts about China's economic direction and supercharge foreign investment and Chinese exports. The United States was to make little use of the concessions Zhu made on import restraints and, until the Trump administration, did very little to try to slow China's ascent.

5

NAILING JELL-O TO THE WALL, MARCH 2000

With Congress getting ready in 2000 to vote on the China trade deal that President Clinton and Premier Zhu battled over so fiercely, Clinton marshaled his best arguments for passage. "Economically, this agreement is the equivalent of a one-way street," the president said at the Johns Hopkins School of Advanced International Studies (SAIS), a Washington, D.C., training ground for China hands. That certainly seemed true. Beijing had agreed to slash tariffs, subsidies, and other trade barriers as the price of admission to the WTO. The United States didn't have to match any of China's concessions. None.

But that wasn't the heart of the president's argument. WTO membership required China to play by Western-style capitalist rules involving private property, the encouragement of innovation through free choices, and open communication. Those are hardly the hallmarks of a party dictatorship. "By joining the WTO, China is not simply agreeing to import more of our products; it is agreeing to import one of democracy's most cherished values: economic freedom," the president said on March 8, 2000. "The more China liberalizes its economy, the more fully it will liberate the potential of the people. . . . And when individuals have the power not just to dream, but to realize their dreams they will demand a greater say."

Although Clinton didn't outright promise a democratic China, he came close. What would guarantee change? The growth of the Internet and the ability of ordinary Chinese to criticize government officials and organize themselves. China had 9 million Internet users, he said, a number that was expected to grow to 20 million by 2005. "Now there's no question China has been trying to crack down on the Internet. Good luck!" he said to gales of laughter. "That's sort of like trying to nail Jell-O to the wall."

It wasn't just Clinton at his dreamiest who foresaw WTO membership remaking China; so did hardheaded foreign policy realists. Harry Rowen was about as gimlet-eyed as they come. He had been president of RAND Corporation, the Cold War national security research group, and then ran President Reagan's National Intelligence Council when the administration launched its Star Wars project to zap Soviet missiles midflight.

In a 1999 article, "Why China Will Become a Democracy," Rowen predicted the year for the momentous change: 2015. By then, China was projected to have a per capita income of about $7,000, and a middle class itching for change. "Although no one is likely to confuse China that year with, say, Sweden, it's likely that the Chinese will join the club of nations well along the road to democracy," he wrote. (China hit the $7,000 mark two years ahead of schedule without signs of freedom breaking out.)

Evidence for change abounded. South Korea, Taiwan, and a slew of nations in Latin America had shucked off dictatorships for democracy after mass protests by unions and the middle class. The inability of the Soviet Union to produce a decent middle-class life for its citizens helped lead to its demise, too.

U.S. labor unions weren't persuaded that China would change. They feared job loss through intensified competition from low-wage workers in a country where independent labor unions were prohibited. When China joined the WTO in 2001, Chinese factory workers earned on average roughly $1,800 annually, about 5 percent of U.S. manufacturing wages. (With liberal adjustments for the different costs in the two nations, Chinese workers made about 20 percent of what U.S. workers did. Still, quite a gap.) About a month after Clinton's SAIS speech, fifteen thousand AFL-CIO members, decked out in textile worker red-and-blue baseball caps and blue United Auto Workers jackets, rallied at the Capitol carrying signs: "No blank checks for China!"

The arguments used by the two sides of the congressional fight continue to frame the debate over China today. Engage or disengage? Faith in markets as agents of change or skepticism? The Clinton view that drawing China closer to the United States economically would help both countries prevailed then and guided the Republican and Democratic White Houses that immediately followed. A 2005 speech by George W. Bush's deputy secretary of state, Robert Zoellick, urging China to act like a "responsible stakeholder" in the global economic system, could have been written by a Clinton speechwriter. "While not yet democratic, [China] does not yet see itself in a twilight conflict against democracy around the globe," Zoellick said.

Donald Trump and his aides have seized on the arguments by labor that doing business with China results in massive job loss and instability at home. Like left-wing activists then, the Trump team argues that the threat of isolating China is a more effective way of handling China than embracing its leaders. For Trump, like the unions, high tariffs keep out the imports that cost U.S. jobs. But the Trump team only accepted part of labor's agenda. The administration hasn't pushed to strengthen U.S. unions or invest in regional development, retraining, and research and development. Those policies might have given communities competing with China a better chance to thrive.

• • •

The vote on China in 2000 recalled the early days of the Clinton administration. Once again, Congress was to vote on whether to give China trade preferences, called Most Favored Nation, which would award Beijing the tariffs, quotas, and other trade policies the United States gives its closest trading partners. In 1994, Clinton said he would no longer require China to make significant progress on human rights to qualify for MFN. Now he proposed another big step. He would eliminate the annual review of China altogether. That was the reward Beijing sought for the many trade concessions it was offering to join the WTO. China would no longer face the threat of losing access to the world's largest market, depending on congressional whim. China's leaders would be released from the probation they had been on since the 1989 Tiananmen Square repression.

In some ways, the MFN struggle on Capitol Hill wasn't a fair fight. Labor and its allies on the left were a tired force. On December 1, 1999, they had shut down a World Trade Organization meeting in Seattle, which was supposed to launch a new round of global trade talks to slash tariffs, regulations, quotas, and other forms of protection. The left portrayed those changes as a way for global elites to further undermine worker wages and attack environmental protections.

The Seattle protests quickly got out of hand. Anarchists costumed in black T-shirts, pants, and bandanas rampaged through the city, smashing store windows, spray-painting signs, and showering police with rocks and bottles. Overmatched and poorly trained police fired tear gas and rubber bullets at the protestors, but couldn't clear a way for the delegates to get from their hotels to the convention site to start negotiations. "The battle of Seattle" doomed the talks, perhaps fatally; the WTO hasn't finished a global trade round since then.

But the battle also tarred the left as a disruptive, antidemocratic force, even though labor unions and environmental groups generally weren't in league with the anarchists. In the fight over MFN, labor unions put together peaceful protests, produced reams of talking points for Capitol Hill lobbying, and shadowed pro-MFN Democrats back to their districts. Their goal was to keep the number of Democrats voting for the proposal well below the sixty to seventy that Clinton Chief of Staff Podesta thought necessary to pass the legislation.

In March 2000, about fifty Tibetan activists pulled up in a school bus at the LaCrosse Footwear Factory in Wisconsin to protest Democratic Representative Ron Kind's support for the China bill. Their labor allies held placards reading, "Hey Ron, Be Kind to Our Jobs" and "Vote Against Normal Trade Relations with Slave State Red China." Representative Kind wound up voting for the bill anyway.

The opponents faced long odds. The issue was arcane. What was MFN anyway? Polls at the time said the majority of people weren't paying much attention to the fight. Labor-backed research groups forecast that closer ties with China would cost nearly one million jobs over a decade but they were largely ignored. Didn't labor always make such predictions? In 2000, after years of Clinton free trade deals and dire union forecasts, the U.S. economy was humming.

Business lobbyists overwhelmed the opposition, as they sought the rich prize of broader access to the Chinese market at greatly reduced tariffs. So many business groups wanted to claim credit for the campaign—and be seen in Beijing as fighting for China's interests—that they established an unwieldy management committee of twenty-five companies. The groups hired a facilitator to teach them to work together during a session at Boeing's offices.

The business coalition spent more than $100 million on the lobbying campaign, says U.S. Chamber of Commerce Executive Vice President Myron Brilliant, who played a leading role in the MFN fight. That's more than business spent in all the trade lobbying battles afterward, through 2019, he estimates. The battle was sometimes heated. Brilliant says anti-China Republican lawmaker Representative Dana Rohrabacher of California kicked him out of his office, yelling, "You're selling us out," and threw a Nerf ball at him.

The Chamber targeted 66 districts of wavering lawmakers; the Business Roundtable, a group of big business CEOs, focused on 83 others. Trade groups paid for more than a dozen "fly-ins" of CEOs and local Chambers of Commerce to lobby their lawmakers.

Individual companies adopted the grassroots lobbying of their labor foes, particularly Boeing. Three years earlier, when China's president toured the United States and signed a $3 billion deal to buy aircraft, the company flew one hundred Boeing and supplier employees, from forty states, to a celebration in Washington, D.C. Boeing turned the lobby of the Commerce Department into a faux political convention in October 1997, with the attendees carrying placards from their states and lining up like delegates. "Celebrating Boeing Airplane Sales to China," said a big sign at the front of the lobby. A giant map of the United States was covered with airplanes representing different Boeing or supplier facilities.

In 2000, Boeing dialed up its efforts. It pressed 10,000 suppliers in 420 House districts to lobby their local lawmakers and helped the media find vignettes of small businesses that would benefit from future Boeing sales to China. The *Washington Post* profiled Daylight Donuts in Wellington, Kansas, which sold pastries to Boeing suppliers in the area.

Motorola copied Boeing's tactics in Illinois and Texas. Farmland Industries, the largest farm cooperative, with 17,000 employees in thirty states, printed messages about the value of exports to China on the stubs of employee paychecks. The Farm Bureau, a farm organization, with 4.9 million family farm members, met with each of the House's 435 members.

Business had a powerful argument. With China set to join the WTO, all the concessions it made to the United States would be available to every other WTO member. If the United States rejected MFN, it would cede the huge China market to competitors, and

Beijing would surely take out its wrath on U.S. firms. Better to get rid of the annual MFN renewal drama altogether. That would create the certainty in which business thrived.

The business groups had earlier successfully lobbied to change the name "Most Favored Nation"—a term that sounded as if the United States were doing China a favor—to the duller "Normal Trading Relations." By 2000, the fight was no longer over permanent approval of Most Favored Nation status for China but rather "Permanent Normal Trading Relations" (PNTR). The more boring the terminology, the less likely the public would care.

Business and the Clinton administration also recruited Chinese dissidents to make the case for China's WTO accession. The White House trumpeted the words of Martin Lee, Hong Kong's de facto opposition leader, who argued that WTO accession would make Beijing more likely to accept the rule of law. The Business Roundtable featured Chinese dissidents in advertising and news conferences.

To ensure Democratic votes, the administration made accommodations. Representative Sandy Levin of Michigan, an influential free trade skeptic who Clinton aides had targeted, wanted side deals with China on human rights and WTO compliance. He got the creation of the Congressional-Executive Commission on China, a joint administration-Congress panel, to review Chinese human rights progress. The administration got Levin's vote and those of his allies.

To secure other votes, the administration promised funding for a pipeline, environmental cleanups, and urban development zones, according to a study by the anti-free-trade group Public Citizen.

Clinton and his trade negotiator, Charlene Barshefsky, made speech after speech casting China's joining the WTO as a vote for a brighter future, and one anchored in the Democratic Party's past. Clinton chose Princeton University, where Woodrow Wilson had once been president, to make the point most clearly. Helping China join the WTO brought the United States "closer than ever to redeeming the vision of Woodrow Wilson, of reaching his dream of a world full of free markets, free elections, and free peoples working together," Clinton said. Barshefsky reached back to the legacy of FDR. "U.S. trade policy ever since the Second World War has been one element in a larger response, conceived under Franklin Roosevelt," of collective security, commitment to human rights, and the fostering of open markets, she told congressional panels.

In the end, the congressional vote wasn't close. PNTR passed in the House by a 237–197 margin. Seventy-three Democrats voted for the measure, somewhat more than Podesta, Clinton's chief of staff, had thought necessary. The Senate was a romp; the measure passed 83–15. "This is a great day for the United States and a hopeful day for the twenty-first-century world," Clinton said in October 2000 when he signed the bill into law.

At the time of the signing, the United States was at the height of its power, with its economy purring, markets rising, and its Internet technology remaking society. The American model was the envy of the world. But within months, all that would change. The economy fell into recession in March 2001. America was attacked by Al-Qaeda six months later. A housing bubble was building that would burst disastrously later in the decade. Economic stagnation was to follow, with China's rise taking a lot of the blame.

• • •

Two decades later, some of the most prominent opponents of China's WTO bid say it wouldn't have made much difference if they had won the 2000 showdown. China was too powerful a magnet for international business. If U.S. firms hadn't been able to cash in on China's WTO concessions, European and Asian traders would have taken their place. At some point—probably quickly—the United States would have scrapped its annual review of Chinese behavior.

"I don't know that it [rejecting PNTR] would have made a difference," says former Democratic whip David Bonior, a longtime critic of China's human rights and labor practices. "They were large enough that they could have gone their own way. They might have felt that they could have manipulated other economies to go along with them."

In a dash of humility, he added, "none of us are completely right or wrong on these things."

At least one China WTO critic, though, thinks that keeping China out of the WTO was not only the right thing to do, but possible. Back then, Robert Lighthizer was an obscure trade lawyer helping steel firms block Chinese imports. In a 1997 opinion piece in the *New York Times*, he warned, "if China is allowed to join the WTO on the lenient terms it has long been demanding, virtually no manufacturing job in this country will be safe."

Barshefsky negotiated tougher terms than Lighthizer expected, and economists say he vastly overstated China's impact on U.S. manufacturing. But later, as Donald Trump's U.S. trade representative, Lighthizer had a chance to undo the work of his predecessor, Barshefsky. Continuing the annual review of China's behavior would have made foreign businesses think twice before investing, Lighthizer says. "Uncertainty would have kept the trade deficit from growing and probably would have saved millions of manufacturing jobs in the U.S.," he now argues.

From the vantage point of 2020, the proponents of China's accession don't look prescient. President Clinton had counted on the growth of the Internet to make China more free through an engaged public and ideas imported from the West. He underestimated Beijing. At about the time when he compared controlling the Internet to nailing Jell-O to a wall, a Chinese computer scientist, Fang Binxing, was figuring out Jell-O nailing. By designing the technology behind the Great Firewall, Fang helped Beijing first block messages from abroad and then censor internal discussions.

Fang had plenty of critics at home. In 2010, his Internet account was filled with messages from people cursing him. When he spoke at Wuhan University the following year, a student pelted him with eggs. He remained defiant. "I regard the dirty abuse as a sacrifice for my country," he said, according to China scholar Elizabeth Economy. China now has more than 800 million Internet users, but the technology is closely monitored by the government.

Robert Rubin, Clinton's Treasury secretary, and many other Clinton economic officials say they made the right choice by guiding China into the WTO. "It would be overwhelmingly nonsensical to have the world's second largest economy—on its way to becoming the world's largest economy—outside the world trading system," Rubin says now.

China's markets would be less open to the United States and Beijing wouldn't have to follow WTO rules. "In any negotiation, no one gets everything they want," he says. "You can't coerce them into doing what they don't want to do."

China's growth has helped many nations that supply it or invest there. From 2001, when China joined the WTO, until 2008, when the world fell into a deep recession, China accounted for 23.9 percent of global economic growth, the International Monetary Fund estimates. Since 2010, China's share of world growth jumped to 31.9 percent.

Still, China is no closer today to democracy than it was in the 1990s, though individual Chinese do have more freedom to choose where to live, what to do for a living, and how to dress. New York University law professor Jerome Cohen, who has defended human rights cases in China since the 1970s, backed China's WTO membership because he thought it would improve the country's legal system. Now he says, "when it comes to civil rights—protection of the individual against arbitrary power—China has fallen backward. Human rights lawyers are being persecuted; their clients are being persecuted."

In a powerful foreshadowing of how opinion in the United States would change from hopefulness about China to anger and regret, consider Robert Cassidy, the U.S. chief China negotiator during the WTO episode. He left the government shortly before China joined the WTO in 2001. Unlike many former negotiators, he didn't cash in by working for law firms that greased the way for clients to invest in new opportunities in China. He worked for firms defending companies battling the onrush of Chinese imports.

In 2008, he published a kind of lamentation about his trade negotiating career. "The beneficiaries of the agreement with China fall into two groups: multinational companies that moved to China and the financial institutions that financed those investments, trade flows, and deficits," he wrote in an article published by the left-wing Institute for Policy Studies on the anniversary of the Tiananmen Square killings.

Cassidy says he hoped his life's work would help ordinary workers. But it didn't. "I have wrestled with this for many years," he says from his home in Fort Lauderdale, Florida. "When you retire, you like to think that you have accomplished a lot. I went over all the agreements I did. What kind of benefit did I produce from working around the clock? I was incredibly disappointed."

He believes the U.S. economy gains overall from trade with China because of greater efficiency and more consumer choice. "But politicians didn't make sure everyone was better off" by funneling relief to those laid off and retraining them, he complains. "Benefits went to business, not to labor," a conclusion that many shared over the coming years and which eventually helped elect Donald Trump as president.

At age seventy-five, Cassidy says he hardly ever tells friends that he was once a trade negotiator. "I tell them that I was a bureaucrat," he says. He raises orchids in his spare time.

6

CHINA TO THE RESCUE, 2008

After China joined the WTO, its economy boomed and many in Beijing started to rethink their views of America, especially as the 2008 global financial crisis brought the Western economic system to its knees. The country's leaders saw an opportunity in the crisis to expand their influence and promote a Chinese model of development that combined government direction and authoritarian rule with market incentives and massive spending on infrastructure and other projects. Beijing felt it had plenty to teach the rest of the world. World leaders reached out regularly to their Chinese counterparts for help.

A week after the Wall Street firm Lehman Brothers filed for bankruptcy in September 2008, exacerbating the financial crisis, President George W. Bush placed a call to Chinese President Hu Jintao. Hold on to China's $1 trillion–plus portfolio of U.S. government debt, Bush asked. Don't sell, especially now. If China were to sell large amounts of Treasuries, it risked driving up U.S. interest rates and squeezing American households and businesses that were already reeling. A big sale also threatened to drive down the value of the U.S. dollar, making Chinese exports to the United States more expensive. Hu did what President Bush asked.

A month later, on October 21, Bush dialed China's Zhongnanhai leadership compound again. This time he wanted to recruit President Hu to attend a summit of the leaders of the top twenty economies in the world, called the Group of 20, or G-20, to figure out how to deal with the deepening financial turmoil. Again Hu quickly agreed.

Earlier that month, the United States had proposed a $700 billion plan to bail out tottering banks and other financial institutions. Bush wanted China also to commit to emergency measures to buck up its economy and help stabilize global growth. Since joining the World Trade Organization in 2001, China had grown to become the third-largest economy in the world behind the United States and Japan. While China's GDP was still expanding in late 2008, the pace of acceleration was slowing—to a rate of 9 percent from a rate of 11.5 percent a year earlier—because foreign demand for Chinese goods was plummeting. A steep Chinese slowdown threatened to injure countries from Brazil to Australia, whose economies fed China's immense appetite for copper, iron ore, and other raw materials.

Three weeks after Bush's call, China announced a 4 trillion yuan plan, about $586 billion, to build housing, highways, airports, and other big infrastructure projects, all of which would consume billions of dollars in imported commodities. The stimulus plan had been in the works for much of the year. All levels of China's government would be involved, especially state-owned banks, steel mills, construction firms, and other entities. Years later, the activities of those companies would draw the ire of the Trump administration, but in 2008, they were celebrated.

China's leaders believed the plan showed the advantages of the country's state-led growth model and Beijing's ability to adapt quickly to changing circumstances. When top party officials had gathered earlier at a heavily guarded government hotel in Beijing in December 2007, there was little hint the world would tumble into recession. They were focused on the opposite problem—how to prevent the economy from overheating. Chinese GDP grew at a gaudy 14.2 percent in 2007, and economic planners believed that they needed to cut back aggressive lending.

But as 2008 wore on and the global financial crisis kicked in, those worries were set aside. Instead of tightening credit, some officials argued in early 2008, China should dramatically increase spending. With financial woes in the United States and other developed countries worsening, this was China's moment to move ahead, suggested officials, including Xu Shanda, the nation's former deputy taxation chief. China's stimulus spending could become the country's version of the Marshall Plan, the American initiative passed in 1948 to help rebuild Western Europe after World War II.

Rather than continue to invest in U.S. Treasuries, Xu and other proponents of the plan said, China should use its vast foreign-exchange reserves to make loans to developing nations rich in coal and other natural resources. The loans would finance mines, railways, and shipping docks to help the countries supply the Chinese market, and also create jobs for Chinese construction firms and other companies overseas. Advocates said their "Plan for a Harmonious World" would support and increase Chinese influence globally.

Around the summer of 2008, then–Vice Premier Li Keqiang called a meeting of senior officials from the government's main advisory body, known as the Chinese People's Political Consultative Conference. He wanted to discuss whether China should ditch the initial economic agenda focused on inflation prevention in favor of one aimed at ensuring growth—going beyond the "Plan for a Harmonious World" to create a stimulus plan to bolster domestic investment and shore up global growth.

The growth camp won. Inflation was then running around 5 percent. To drag it below 3 percent, as originally targeted, the central bank would have to dramatically tighten the money supply, which would cause the yuan to appreciate, exports to tumble, and growth to plummet. That was the wrong medicine when the global economy was starting to contract. Days later, the Politburo, the party's top 25 officials, decided to discard the original plan intended to fight inflation and put together a plan to prop up growth. On November 8, China released the 4 trillion yuan stimulus package to keep the economy humming. The announcement triggered a massive stock market rally worldwide.

Shortly afterward, Hu flew to Washington to attend the G-20 summit. On November 14 and 15, the leaders gathered first around a big conference table in a State Department dining room named after Benjamin Franklin. Hu made the most of his star turn, celebrating China's efforts and proposing that international financial institutions give emerging-market economies like China more say in governing. "Let us tide over the difficulties through concerted efforts and contribute our share to maintaining international financial stability and promoting economic growth," Hu told the attendees. China's state-owned media followed him throughout his stay, beaming back video of him from the conference's venues, including the White House, where Bush hosted a dinner for the G-20 leaders.

After decades of following in America's shadow, China was now stepping into the sunlight. Beijing was coming to the aid of the United States, and the rest of the world, a change that bolstered the confidence of China's leaders that they had chosen the correct path to development. Gone was the notion that the United States' economic system was superior. The Chinese model was to be emulated. Adding to Beijing's self-assurance was a chorus of praise from Western officials and scholars on how Beijing handled its economy. Even Hillary Clinton, who as first lady in 1995 had embarrassed Chinese leaders by stressing human rights during a trip to China, gave Beijing a pat on the back in 2009. As the secretary of state, she stressed the need to work with China to tackle the financial crisis and global warming, while downplaying its rights record.

Some of China's sense of triumph was surely misplaced. As

became apparent a few years later, the stimulus plan also saddled China's economy with debt and wasteful projects and turned its skies gray with smog. Still, the reception China's stimulus efforts received was a head-spinning moment for many in Zhongnanhai, who had spent the prior two decades following U.S. advice in re-making the Chinese economy.

In the late 1990s, when big Chinese banks teetered on the brink of bankruptcy following years of unscrupulous lending, Chinese regulators paid American investment bankers to help straighten out the mess. Premier Zhu Rongji backed Wall Street plans to sell to American firms stakes in the country's biggest four state-owned banks, whose total assets, Zhu said then, "couldn't even match those of one single U.S. bank, Citibank."

China sought to copy America by creating its version of Wall Street. It turned a big parcel of farmland along Shanghai's Huangpu River into a bustling financial district with skyscrapers, a stock ex-change, bank branches, and trading houses.

Later on, the Western-oriented central bank governor, Zhou Xiaochuan, instructed his underlings to study Wall Street's "finan-cial engineering," such as stuffing securities with mortgages that could be bought and sold similar to stocks and bonds. Those se-curities had led to rapid growth in home ownership in the United States, but also were to lead to shady lending that would help bring the nation's financial system to the verge of collapse.

Zhou's question to his staffers at the People's Bank of China (PBOC), prior to the financial crisis: Should China create its own version of this popular American financial instrument to help de-velop its housing market?

PBOC staffers also examined whether to restructure the cen-tral bank and close its thousands of branches across China. The PBOC wanted to look more like the Federal Reserve System, with its dozen regional Fed banks located across the nation. "Then the global financial crisis broke out," says a senior PBOC official. "That caused us to indefinitely shelve the plan." America was no longer the model to emulate.

After the crisis hit, Beijing started thinking about how to lessen its dependence on the dollar. In March 2009, Governor Zhou published a paper on the PBOC's website calling for replacing the U.S. dollar as the international reserve currency with a new global currency system controlled by the International Monetary Fund. While that proposal didn't gain much traction, it did start a successful effort by Beijing to include the yuan as an official part the IMF's reserves, a status it gained in 2016—another example of China coming into its own.

• • •

China's economy, which expanded rapidly during the 1980s and 1990s, rocketed after the country joined the WTO in December 2001. As the price of admission, China agreed to relax more than seven thousand tariffs, quotas, and other trade barriers and to open, albeit with limitations, nine broad sectors to foreign capital, including financial services, automobiles, and information technology. Many in China feared that foreign competition would destroy domestic industries and cause massive layoffs.

But those fears soon gave way to a sense of pride and accomplishment. Easing trade barriers made China a much more attractive place for foreign firms to invest, as did the elimination of America's annual review of whether China qualified for Most Favored Nation trading rights. Foreign investment in China soared from $49.7 billion in 2001 to $108.8 billion in 2010, as the country became an ever-larger export platform. A Mattel executive's reaction was typical. He told a congressional committee that his company wouldn't invest heavily in China if there was a chance the country could lose its favored trade status. While the risk was small, "the consequences would be catastrophic," the executive said, because Mattel's toy imports from China would have been hit with 70 percent tariffs.

The decade after China joined the WTO was one of the most prosperous in the country's long history. China's economy more than quadrupled from 2001 to 2011; total trade increased seven-fold; foreign investment in factories, shopping malls, and other hard assets more than doubled, helping to generate millions of jobs domestically. China cemented its status as the world's factory floor for everything from clothes and toys to televisions and tires. The government maintained a visible hand in redrawing the economic landscape, combining market opportunities presented by the country's engagement with the world with traditional state planning. China evolved from a Maoist planned economy to a hybrid state capitalism.

Bill Clinton's hopes that political freedom would go hand in hand with economic freedom were dashed. China's leaders pushed for market-oriented changes to create wealth and lift people's living standard. They figured that prosperity would strengthen support for the party's rule, not lead to political liberty. Those officials included Premier Zhu Rongji, the economic reformer admired by the West, who had sparred with President Clinton over the WTO.

In a speech to senior provincial officials in early 2002, soon after China joined the WTO, Zhu warned that "western hostile forces are continuing to promote their strategy of westernizing and breaking up our country." A year later, during China's annual legislative session, Zhu again stressed the government's effort to fend off such hostile forces. "We remained vigilant against and cracked down on all infiltration, subversion, and sabotage by hostile forces at home and abroad."

The eastern Chinese county of Guangrao, located in the fertile Yellow River Delta, illustrates the changes brought by China's WTO entry. The county is the hometown of Sun Tzu, the Chinese general who wrote the influential work of military strategy *The Art of War* 2,500 years ago. But the county had little commercial significance until China's entry into the global trading system. During the

2000s, Guangrao was designated by the government as a hub for tire manufacturing and exports. Now the county is one of the richest in the country.

Shortly after China's WTO entry, Guangrao officials and local businesses sensed an opportunity to create a tire industry. Rich in oil, natural gas, and other resources, the county already had factories that produced rubber tubes used in oil fields and wells. As the Chinese leadership began to develop an auto industry in the 1990s, a few of those plants shifted to producing tires for trucks and sedans. When China joined the WTO, it reduced export restrictions, which gave Guangrao rubber makers additional opportunities. Shipping tires to the huge U.S. market was more profitable than competing fiercely with their peers at home.

By 2003, the county's skyline was dominated by construction cranes hoisting up dozens of new plants. The local government herded them into an industrial park it financed, crisscrossed with roads, electricity grids, and sewage systems. Companies that set up manufacturing facilities there also received tax incentives and other forms of government support—the kinds of help that would soon kick up complaints from tire makers abroad. Peasant workers from the countryside poured in, helping to keep costs low. Before long, some one hundred tire factories were operating in the area and more were planned.

Tire sales soared, especially to the United States, and Guangrao factories ramped up production further. Town officials patted themselves on the back as local tax revenue soared. By 2005, Guangrao vaulted into the top one hundred counties in China based on tax revenue. Nationwide, China's tire exports increased almost tenfold between 2000 and 2011, with half of the sales coming from Guangrao, now dubbed "Rubber Valley."

The fortunes of Liu Zhanyi, a Guangrao tire boss, mirror that of Rubber Valley. In 1986, when most in Guangrao still worked on the land, Liu moved into manufacturing. With help from local officials, he leased a facility from the county government and bought a handful of extruding machines that produce long, hollow tubes of rubber, much as a meat grinder produces long strings of meat. His business was an instant hit.

A decade later, when the auto industry started to take off, he reconfigured his plant to produce tires and, after China joined the WTO, he expanded rapidly overseas. By the end of 2002, his company, Shandong Yongsheng Rubber Group, became one of China's largest tire exporters, employing thousands of workers.

Liu worked tirelessly and lived modestly. Townspeople frequently mistook him for a tire truck driver because of the black, slip-on, cloth shoes he wore and the compact Chinese sedan he drove. (He later upgraded to a Subaru.) "He likes to keep it simple and keep the cost down," says his son, Liu Zijun, who has taken over the company. "That's a main reason why we've managed to continue to expand our business."

But the successes of the Liu family and others in Guangrao came at the expense of American tire makers. Between 2004 and 2008, Chinese tire exports to America tripled in volume, while U.S. tire production dropped by one-fourth. Employment in the American tire industry shrank by 14 percent. Political pressure on the Obama administration from its labor allies increased so much that in 2009, the president approved duties of up to 35 percent on imports of Chinese-made tires. The action marked the first time—and the only time—that the United States used a special provision that U.S. WTO negotiators fought for, which made it easier for the United States to shut off import surges from China.

The tariffs stalled China's export growth in the United States for a while. But American tire wholesalers and retailers had become so dependent on Chinese goods that the sudden increase in prices when tariffs were imposed—and the sharp reduction in prices when the tariffs ended in 2012—bankrupted some businesses stuck with mispriced inventory. "We're just biding our time here," said Alex

Alpe, a manager at a nearly empty Del-Nat Tire Corporation ware-house, in 2015. The Memphis, Tennessee, tire distributor exited the business that year. "Either someone buys us or we're out of work," said Alpe. "It's wearing on all of us."

So much export money was pouring into China that its foreign reserves soared 15-fold to $3.18 trillion at the end of 2011, as China became a major buyer of the U.S. government bonds. That turned the onetime economic basket case into America's banker. How did that happen? As Chinese companies' sales overseas surged, Chinese exporters sold the dollars they received to the country's commer-cial banks in exchange for yuan to carry out their business opera-tions within China. The commercial banks then sold the dollars to the central bank, which pooled all the dollars in a giant fund called foreign-exchange reserves, nicknamed the "blood and sweat" of the Chinese people.

This series of operations also helped China keep down the value of its currency as the central bank continued to release more yuan into the financial system in exchange for the dollars from the com-mercial banks. China's U.S. critics long complained that Beijing simply replaced the mercantilist measures it agreed to give up to join the WTO with an undervalued yuan, which made Chinese products cheaper overseas. China's cheap labor gave it a competitive advantage in manufacturing; it's undervalued yuan supercharged its exports.

Across the world, China became the target of aggrieved indus-tries that complained, with justification, that China subsidized production in ways that violated global trade rules. Chinese banks doled out cheap loans, often to companies that were already pro-ducing goods far in excess of demand, including makers of steel and aluminum. Those companies then shipped their lower-priced goods to the outside world, depressing prices globally and bank-rupting producers in other countries. More and more, China was hit with trade complaints from around the world, alleging that Chinese companies "dumped" products at below-market prices.

Antidumping cases soared in industries marked by Chinese excess production, notes Mark Wu, a Harvard law professor who studies international trade. In 2007, before the financial crisis, twenty-three such cases were filed with the World Trade Organization, a number that more than doubled in 2011 and doubled again to reach a peak of 129 in 2016. Chinese companies, by far, were the most frequently targeted, amounting to more than one-third of the antidumping investigations during the period.

• • •

China's massive stimulus spurred the Chinese economy, helped pull the global economy out of recession, and won praise from the United States and international financial organizations. But it also led to a sense of hubris—and massive debt, oversupply, and economic inefficiency.

The country's stoked-up steel mills, aluminum smelters, cement plants, glass factories, and tire producers exported their excess production at below-market prices, deepening trade battles with the United States, Europe, and Japan. China's leaders now derisively call the 2008 plan "flood-irrigation stimulus," referring to the ancient, destructive farming practice of flooding land to grow crops. They vow not to repeat it.

But back in November 2008, Premier Wen Jiabao publicly pressed the banking industry to "increase its support to China's economic growth." Factories continued in overdrive. They counted on loans from state-owned lenders to keep them afloat even if they couldn't find buyers for their products or had to slash prices so steeply they lost money on each sale.

Some critics at the time warned that easy credit could eventually lead to disaster. Overproduction sapped profits, wasted money, worsened pollution, and started a spiraling debt problem. A 2011 report by British bank Standard Chartered estimated that more than $1 trillion of loans taken out by local governments and companies to build railways, plants, and other projects, much of it incurred between 2008 and 2010, would eventually have to be written off by banks.

But most state bankers put aside whatever doubts they may have had and continued to boost lending, as party leaders directed. Jiang Jianqing, the longtime chairman of the Industrial and Commercial Bank of China (ICBC), the country's most profitable state lender, didn't go along with the rest. He worried that hastily made loans would produce buckets of red ink. That decision cost him his career. In 2013, he was the only chief executive of a major state-owned bank to be passed over for promotion—another reminder to state bank officials to keep their mouths shut and follow government and party orders. "He should have done more," a regulatory official said in early 2013. In other words, the official said, Jiang should have followed what ICBC's largest shareholder, the Chinese government, wanted him to do.

By then, some others in the government were beginning to recognize that the stimulus plan had created serious problems. In 2013, the Ministry of Industry and Information Technology named nineteen sectors marked by overcapacity, ranging from steel, cement, and aluminum to tires and other auto products, up from only three a decade earlier. "There was an oversupply problem even before the global financial crisis," recalls a Chinese policy maker. "We just didn't pay too much attention then because our focus was on how to keep the growth going, especially after the financial crisis."

Reversing course was difficult politically. The central government ran into determined opposition from the thousands of government officials charged with carrying out its plans. Shutting down redundant factories meant that local officials would have fewer tax dollars and more problems. Unemployed workers would have to be

cared for or they would cause the kind of protests that drew un-
wanted attention from Beijing and could threaten their careers.
"We've always been judged on whether we hit growth targets," says
an official in Hebei province, an industrial powerhouse that produces most of the crude steel made in China.

Hebei officials did their best to keep local steel mills humming
despite Beijing's orders to do the opposite, even if the mills were
operating at a loss and the local officials had to use subterfuge.
In late 2013, Hebei staged an event called "Operation Sunday" in
which it dispatched demolition squads to blow up blast furnaces
owned by fifteen mills. Video of imploding furnaces was broadcast
on state television. The razing reduced the province's steel-making
capacity by 6.8 million tons, the Hebei government claimed, nearly
half the province's annual goal. But all of the furnaces targeted for
destruction turned out to be so outmoded that they long ago had
been mothballed and could never have been turned back on.

"Do any of the blasted furnaces affect capacity at all?" asked
Du Wenhua, an executive at Jinan Steel Group, a big steel company
in Jinan, east of Hebei, after he watched the TV broadcast of the
event. "No. They have been in limbo for a long time."

The legacy of the stimulus spending now haunts China. Lending to state enterprises and local governments led to overcapacity
and overbuilding. Empty shopping malls, half-built apartment complexes, unfinished resorts, and bridges to nowhere became common-
place. Many cities are ringed with apartment complexes that stand
empty. At night, the only lights from these unpopulated neighbor-
hoods are the air-traffic beacons on top of the buildings beeping red.

Total debt levels in China soared from 132 percent of its GDP
in 2008 to 205 percent in 2013, and ballooned further to 244 percent in 2018. The International Monetary Fund said in 2018 that in
the forty-three cases internationally where credit grew as rapidly
as China's over a five-year period, "only five ended without a major
growth slowdown or a financial crisis in the immediate aftermath."

Even so, Beijing's success in weathering the global financial crisis left future generations of leaders, including President Xi Jinping, more assured of the government's big role in the economy and the one-party system. Chinese leaders also felt more emboldened to speak out against their foreign critics and assert themselves more openly, a sharp contrast from the Deng Xiaoping era of the late 1970s and 1980s, when the paramount leader talked about keeping a low profile and hiding your capabilities.

In September 2012, Xi visited Mexico when he was vice president and heir-apparent to President Hu. He laid out China's contribution to the global economy during the financial crisis. Then he lashed out at critics of China's human rights record. "There are a few foreigners, with full bellies, who have nothing better to do than try to point fingers at our country," he said. "China does not export revolution, hunger, poverty, nor does China cause you any headaches. Just what else do you want?"

Two months later, he became general secretary of the Communist Party—his true source of power—and, in March 2013, president. He took pains to show he was committed to market reform, announcing in late 2013 that market forces would play a "decisive role" in the economy. But in reality that meant simply fine-tuning the country's government-led development model. China's economic system today is just as wedded to industrial policy, state-owned companies, and protection of homegrown industries as ever.

In a cavernous government exhibition hall in Guangrao's Rubber Valley is the area's Hall of Fame. Liu Zhanyi's Shandong Yongsheng Rubber Group is featured there. An electronic display shows the major markets for the county's tire makers: the United States remains the top destination, followed by Japan, the European Union, and countries in the Middle East, such as Saudi Arabia.

A bright red poster lists the kind of support that the Guangrao government offers the country's tire makers: "industrial policy support" that helps companies improve their manufacturing capabilities; "financial policy support" that features a government-sponsored fund and loan guarantees to aid local tire makers; "fiscal policy support" that involves subsidies to big tire producers; and "tax policy support" that promises tax reductions for companies making acquisitions or new investments.

The Hall of Fame could have been named China Inc.

7

AMERICAN BACKLASH, 2009

Until the 1990s, western North Carolina was the center of the U.S. furniture industry. Laid-off steelworkers from West Virginia, Tennessee, and beyond trucked over the Blue Ridge Mountains for jobs making tables, dressers, and beds for American homes. They knew they had arrived at Hickory, Lenoir, and other furniture-making towns by the smell of wood lacquer in the air.

The elegant headquarters of Broyhill Furniture was the area's unofficial capital. Locals called the white brick building, fronted by columns and set in a fifty-acre park, "the White House." A few years after China joined the World Trade Organization and its furniture exports wiped out thousands of local jobs, a Broyhill factory hand got fed up. He drove to work before his shift started and raised a Chinese flag over "the White House."

What was happening in North Carolina was repeated across the nation. Business owners, starstruck by China's unbeatable combination of shockingly cheap labor and a potentially enormous consumer market, jetted to Beijing, Shanghai, and Guangzhou to see what kind of business they could do there. The trade concessions that U.S. negotiators had wrung out of Beijing—lower tariffs, eased regulations, fewer subsidies for state-owned firms—made China a far more attractive place to invest and import made-in-China goods back home.

For many millions of Americans, U.S. business investment in China was a clear win. Clothing, toys, furniture, appliances, phones, computers, and hundreds of other goods stuffed the shelves at Walmart and Target at stunningly low prices. Between 2000 and 2017, average U.S. prices rose 47 percent. During the same period, there was little inflation in areas dominated by Chinese imports. Clothing prices didn't rise, while prices for furniture tumbled by 18 percent, appliances by 24 percent, and phones and other telecommunications equipment by 75 percent. The imports also produced jobs in trucking, retail, logistics, marketing, and the many other industries that fuel the U.S. consumer economy.

But for workers in targeted industries, China's rise was disastrous. During that same period, employment in furniture and appliance manufacturing fell by 42 percent, while clothing manufacturing employment plummeted 75 percent. Chinese imports focused on labor-intensive industries—sectors where workers rarely made it beyond high school, were poorly paid, and were unequipped for change. Many of the affected industries were clustered in the Appalachian region of the Southeast and smaller industrial cities in the Midwest.

Workers there were devastated. Some used government assistance to attend community college and try to figure out another field of work. But after years of factory work, wrenched backs, and bad knees, many other took a different route. They qualified for disability payments, a path that all too frequently led to opioids and other painkillers, and sometimes to drug overdoses.

Stuart Shoun, a mountain-sized Tennessee machinist who speaks with an Appalachian twang, says he took the Hillbilly Highway to North Carolina to work in wood. The saddest part of the layoffs, he says, was discovering that some of his colleagues were illiterate or could barely read and write. "There would be lots of tears," he says, and some coworkers would ask his help deciphering severance forms handed out by factory bosses. "How would they even go out and fill out applications" for new jobs, Shoun asks.

For years, such complaints were largely ignored by the top echelons in business, academia, and government. They looked at China trade as good for the overall economy and an important way for the United States to remain at the top of the heap in international competition. Decades later, Donald Trump figured out a way to channel the frustration of those who were battered by China's rise, while his many detractors wondered how things had gotten so out of hand.

• • •

China almost seemed too good to be true, says Alex Shuford III, the chief executive of Century Furniture, a Hickory, North Carolina, firm that makes higher-priced goods. Not yet forty years old, he moved back from California around 2000 to join the family business. To the Shufords, China looked a lot like the United States after World War II, when Alex's grandfather, a textile baron, opened a factory to sell furniture to millions of returning GIs and their families. The United States was a growth market; Depression-era parents rarely had furniture worth passing down to their children who were setting up house in the suburbs. Now the growth market was China. Hundreds of millions of Chinese laborers were moving away from peasant farming to city life, and they too would need furniture for their new apartments.

Before selling to the Chinese market, though, Century started to use Chinese workers to make less expensive furniture to sell to Americans, which it called "Destinations by Century." Chinese laborers earned roughly 5 percent of what the Shufords paid in Hickory. Century flew North Carolina workers to China to show managers there how to produce furniture that had the look and finish U.S. consumers wanted. Many of Century's competitors did the same. Importing Chinese-made furniture promised much fatter margins than producing domestically.

But the strategy proved risky. Import competition quickly drove down prices. The promise of fat margins evaporated, and brand images suffered. By training Chinese factories, U.S. furniture makers created competitors who started to sell directly to U.S. retailers.

"China came on faster than expected," says Shuford. "They sustained it longer than expected and they adapted faster than expected because we helped them. It was like Ford helping Toyota to understand American tastes."

By 2004, Century recognized the trap it had laid for itself. It started phasing out its import division and gave up competing with Chinese mass-produced goods. Instead, Century shifted to customized designs and offered hundreds of different finishes, which Chinese manufacturers, an ocean away, couldn't match. It remade its factories through automation so it could profitably produce tables and chairs in smaller production runs.

The change helped Century survive, unlike dozens of other furniture makers that went broke or stopped making wood furniture. In the late 1990s, there were fifty wood furniture factories within fifty miles of Hickory; now there are perhaps a half dozen. Some of the abandoned structures were sold and demolished after their hardwood floors and ceilings were removed and used to make reclaimed-wood furniture.

Still, Century's workforce paid a steep price. The company employed 1,323 people in 2003; now just 875. In Hickory's Catawba County, the falloff was more severe. In 2001, when China joined the WTO, 14,203 people worked in county furniture factories. By 2010, the number had fallen 40 percent, to 8,117. In all of North Carolina, furniture manufacturing jobs declined by 55 percent between 2001 and 2010. Since then, furniture factory employment has picked up by only 10 percent in the county and state, despite a long U.S. economic recovery before the coronavirus pandemic.

Different industries in different communities fared just as poorly. Makers of electronics in San Jose, California, sporting goods in Orange County, California, costume jewelry in Providence, Rhode Island, shoes in West Plains, Missouri, toys in Murray, Kentucky, and lounge chairs in Tupelo, Mississippi, among many other industries, were felled by Chinese imports.

In Hickory, Stuart Shoun was laid off three times because of Chinese competition. The most galling was in 2005, when a Broyhill manager asked him to figure out how to machine a mirror that the company's Chinese suppliers were having a tough time making. After he produced a sample, the company boxed up the forms, knives, and patterns and shipped them to China. "That got everyone mad at me—friends I had for fifteen years," Shoun says, even though layoff notices had already gone out. "They thought it was my fault they were losing their jobs."

Resentment grew against China and company executives. After Kroehler Furniture laid off sewing machine operators in nearby Conover, North Carolina, around 2001, a shipment of Chinese-made sofa covers arrived, which were mismeasured. Management asked the upholstery crew to return and repair the shipment. Half of them refused. "They said, 'Cram it, you sent it to China. Let them fix it,'" says Shoun, who worked at Kroehler at the time.

After his Broyhill layoff, Shoun started attending community college in 2006, with tuition paid by a government program to retrain workers hurt by import competition, called Trade Adjustment Assistance. He made good grades and wanted to work as a draftsman designing homes. By the time he got out of school, though, the housing crisis was in full swing, making hash of his plans. Eventually he returned to the furniture industry and was laid off once more in 2018, at age sixty-one, and retired.

Shoun's experience with the trade adjustment program, which paid for extended unemployment insurance payouts and two years of college tuition, wasn't unusual. A 2012 evaluation ordered by the U.S. Labor Department found that program participants, especially those older than fifty, generally made less money four years after starting the program than those who didn't sign up. The others went back to work more quickly.

Many who couldn't get a job wound up collecting Social Security Disability Insurance, which provided income and health care, but required them to stay home to keep their benefits. Too often, disability led to painkillers and opioid addiction. In Hickory's Catawba County, the percentage of workers collecting disability topped the state average after 2009. Opioid prescription rates ran about 40 percent to 50 percent higher than the average in North Carolina, as did the rate of deaths from drug overdose.

Academics debate whether layoffs and other economic shocks are responsible for the addiction scourge. Drug usage has been pervasive in furniture factories for years, say managers and workers. But layoffs meant more than a lost paycheck; they wreaked havoc on community life, especially in furniture factories where children followed parents into the plants. Gone were company picnics, softball teams, and bowling leagues. When a factory closes, "it's like losing part of your family," says Jackie Starnes, a former upholstery manager in the Hickory area. "You lose your golfing buddies and your fishing buddies."

His older son, now in his mid-forties, was one of many to get laid off at furniture factories. Starnes doesn't blame that for his son's lifelong battle with drug addiction. He's been in rehab eight times, he says, and is now clean. But with the layoffs, Starnes says, "you lose direction."

• • •

Why were the changes in blue-collar America so frequently overlooked?

Business executives had profit opportunities in China on their mind, not the concerns of workers at home. Having lobbied ferociously to get China into the World Trade Organization in 2001, they were ready to cash in. U.S. investment in China quadrupled to $20.9 billion in 2008 from 2000, according to Rhodium Group, a market research firm.

Some leaders of the lobbying campaign prospered. Boeing saw its China revenue jump from 2 percent of sales in 2000 to 13 percent in 2015. Although General Electric doesn't break out China revenue, its Asia revenue increased from 10 percent of sales in 2000 to 16 percent in 2015. General Motors also doesn't identify China revenue. But in 2009, as it battled bankruptcy, China was one of its few bright spots. Vehicle sales there nearly equaled sales in the United States. Earlier, U.S. car sales far outpaced China's.

Apple Computer didn't have enough sales in China or Asia to note them in financial filings in 2000. In 2015, China accounted for 24 percent of its revenue. Intel saw similar growth. Qualcomm technology became the global standard in cellular telephone technology after China adopted its system.

Others didn't fare nearly as well. Of the ten members of the Rump Group—Boeing, GE, GM, and seven other companies that started lobbying in the mid-1990s for China to join the WTO—one died (Digital Equipment Corporation); another nearly brought down the global economy in 2008 and had to be rescued by the government (American International Group); and a third became a shell of itself (Eastman Kodak Company).

Motorola, another Rump Group member, had an especially tough time. In a 2010 lawsuit, the company accused Huawei Technologies of stealing its wireless network technology, but eventually dropped the suit, under pressure, when China's Commerce Ministry investigated it for antitrust violations. In 2011, Motorola split into two companies. One, Motorola Mobility, was eventually sold to China's Lenovo Group. The other, Motorola Solutions, sued a different Chinese company, Hytera Communications, for ripping off its technology. That dispute hadn't been resolved by March 2020.

The corporate cheerleading for China died down in the wake of the global financial crisis of 2008, as China's massive stimulus spending wound up leading to overproduction of commodities like steel, aluminum, and glass. The excess swamped foreign markets and clobbered domestic firms. Concern also escalated about Chinese firms pressuring foreign partners to hand over technology. American companies took note of how the Chinese began to dominate the market for high-speed trains. Around 2004, Kawasaki Heavy Industries and other Japanese and European bullet-train makers transferred know-how to China's Railways Ministry and Chinese companies. Afterward, China train makers used the technology to become powerful competitors.

The dampened enthusiasm was reflected in surveys of American businesses. In 2008, 64 percent of the members of the U.S. Chamber of Commerce in China said they were optimistic about their two-year prospects in China. By 2014, that percentage had fallen by half. Still, corporate criticism of Beijing was rare. GE chief executive Jeffrey Immelt got widespread attention in 2010 when he complained to Italian executives at a dinner in Rome that China was becoming increasingly protectionist. "I am not sure that in the end they want any of us to win, or any of us to be successful," he said, according to the *Financial Times*. But Immelt hardly stuck to his guns. GE quickly said his words were spoken in private and taken out of context.

There were plenty of examples of American companies kowtowing to Beijing. In 2018, Gap Inc. apologized for selling a T-shirt showing a map of China that didn't include Taiwan. U.S. and other foreign airlines made sure their websites referred to Taiwan as a part of China after Chinese authorities objected. In 2019, a Houston Rockets executive quickly took down a tweet backing pro-democracy protests in Hong Kong, as the National Basketball Association tried to limit any damage to its brand on the mainland.

The corporate unwillingness to take on Beijing differed sharply from the 1980s and 1990s, when Japan was the target of U.S. economic concern, as we will see in the next chapter. Then some of America's most famous business leaders—Lee Iacocca of Chrysler, Ross Perot of Electronic Data Systems, and Robert Galvin of Motorola—challenged Japan's trade restrictions and domestic subsidies.

Back then, the United States complained that Japan closed its doors to American companies. That isn't the case in China, where localities compete for foreign investment. U.S. executives in China complain privately that their companies face discrimination and threats. But they speak softly in public to make sure they don't anger Chinese leaders, who have plenty of ways to make their lives miserable.

In 2015, companies started to push back more publicly after China published an industrial development plan called "Made in China 2025." The report laid out strategies to master technologies in ten important sectors, including information technology, aerospace, robotics, and electric vehicles. In some ways, the report was similar to other long-range reports in a country that has produced a dozen or so Mao-style five-year plans. Many of them didn't work out.

China has long looked to substitute domestically made products for imports, even if that means discriminating against foreign firms. In 2006, the government under President Hu Jintao mapped out a comprehensive blueprint to promote what it called "indigenous innovation," to reduce China's reliance on foreign technology and turn the country into a global leader of advanced manufacturing. "The National Medium- and Long-Term Plan for the Development of Science and Technology" heralded an era of increased policy bias for homegrown products but didn't do much to advance China.

The Made in China report was different. It had specifics that ticked off foreigners. China aimed to have 40 percent market share in its chosen markets by 2020 and 70 percent by 2025. The only way to accomplish that, foreign executives figured, was through massive subsidies and technology theft. The European Union Chamber of Commerce in China was among the first to issue a call to arms. "The numbers attached to this initiative are staggering," the group's

March 2017 report said. "It seems that the Chinese Government is determined to maintain a prominent role in guiding the economy."

Joerg Wuttke, the EU Chamber head who launched the report, was blunter. "It's one thing to plan a road or a power plant in China," he says. "It's another thing to tell companies around the world that their market share will be reduced" because of Chinese inroads. The U.S. Chamber of Commerce published a similar report two days after the EU Chamber, as a one-two punch to get Beijing's attention. Think tanks in Europe and the United States also joined in.

Although many Chinese leaders downplayed "Made in China 2025" and said they hadn't bothered to read it, the report acted as a signal to provinces and cities to invest in the highlighted technologies. The U.S. Chamber later detailed how twenty-four provinces and municipalities used the report to set priorities and provide subsidies. In high-tech Guangdong province, the report said, local officials encouraged companies to become "backbone" robotics enterprises, create "secure and reliable" next-generation information technology systems, and establish the region as a "Made in China 2025" demonstration zone. The rust-belt province of Liaoning, where mining and machinery industries have struggled for years, provided subsidies for advanced manufacturing and scientific investment.

The Trump administration would later use the report as its main evidence that Beijing intended to replace the United States as the global economic leader and had to be stopped.

· · ·

Academics also underplayed the challenge to the United States from China's rise, as did many journalists who rely on their work, including one of the authors of this book (Bob). Journalists and economists have a symbiotic relationship. Reporters act like frontline troops, ferreting out information and uncovering problems by traveling around the country and interviewing people caught in economic struggles. Academics use that work as raw material, but mainly base their research on economic data that can be years old. They produce studies journalists use to show that the anecdotes they collect are part of a significant trend.

From the vantage point of many journalists and academics, free trade with China, Mexico, and other developing nations was generally positive for the United States because consumers benefited through lower prices and product innovation. While many workers blamed trade for holding down wages or taking their jobs, newspaper and television stories, bolstered by academic research, frequently pointed out that the larger threat was automation. Robots and other new machinery reduce the need for factory hands, whether or not the United States trades with low-wage nations. "All the evidence points to the role of technology" as the workers' problem, said Robert Z. Lawrence, a Harvard University professor, in a 1993 *Wall Street Journal* article by Bob. (This is not to pick on Lawrence; those views are typical of the economics profession and rightly point out the powerful role of technology in factory job loss.)

Some labor-backed economists predicted that 1 million jobs would be lost in the decade after China joined the WTO. Even if that was correct, it didn't seem to be all that significant. That would amount to a loss of a 100,000 jobs a year in a labor force of more than 150 million people, where 3 million to 4 million workers quit their jobs every year. Worker hardship had to be weighed against consumer gain.

But that wasn't the best way to think about the impact of China trade. It took three economists, in 2012, to make a powerful case that Chinese imports were doing far more harm than commonly understood. In "The China Syndrome: Local Labor Market Effects of Import Competition in the United States," David H. Autor of the Massachusetts Institute of Technology, David Dorn of Centro de Estudios Monetarios y Financieros in Spain, and Gordon H. Hanson of the University of California, San Diego, demonstrated that the impact of China trade wasn't spread evenly around the country. Instead it hit very specific industries very hard—furniture, clothing, costume jewelry, electronics, and others—and those industries tended to cluster in specific parts of the country. The disruptive power of Chinese imports devastated those communities, while many other parts of the country went largely untouched or benefited.

The three economists attributed a loss of 1.5 million manufacturing jobs to Chinese competition between 1990 and 2007, concentrated in industries that employ workers who rarely made it to college. In those regions, laid-off workers were far more likely to end up on disability than to try their hand at community college. In a later paper, they updated their estimates to 2.4 million jobs lost in manufacturing and services between 1999 and 2011—again concentrated in regions where industries were competing with Chinese goods.

Chinese imports to the United States had been climbing since the 1990s, so why did it take so long to arrive at this finding? Hanson has several explanations. On a technical level, it required a combination of different academic skills. Autor is a labor economist who looks at the United States as a series of very different local labor markets. Hanson is a trade economist who tracked the impact of Chinese imports on specific industries. Dorn is a stats whiz who figured out how to use U.S. Agriculture Department data that divides the country into about seven hundred commuting zones—groups of counties that share a labor market—to track the industry impact to specific regions. According to their data, the commuting zones surrounding Hickory and many other furniture-making parts of the country were in the top 5 percent of regions most affected by Chinese imports.

Hanson met Autor around 1999, when he was looking to hire the freshly minted PhD who wears Mr. Rogers–style cardigan sweaters. Autor chose a position elsewhere, but the two men, then in their mid-thirties, remained friends. The younger Dorn bonded later with Autor during a 2007 stint at MIT. A few years afterward, the three joined forces. "I could bring in the trade perspective and they could bring their hard-core, empirical labor data," says Hanson, who now teaches at Harvard's Kennedy School of Government "The stars aligned."

Cultural issues also slowed the work. Academic superstars might have been faster to focus on the communities harmed by China if they lived there. Few did. "Places that were getting hit weren't places that had universities," says Hanson.

Most economists also defended free trade with the ardor of missionaries. "We developed the ethos that protectionism was the greatest evil, and we had to fight against it," Hanson says. "We got lulled into complacency." The trio took extra time to check their work, certain that their findings would be used to attack trade deals they still defend. All three think the world is better off with China in the WTO and that policy makers should have provided the spending necessary to help regions hurt by trade.

Their work rocketed to academic fame. "The China Syndrome" has been cited more than 2,500 times in other academic studies. Of the nearly 2,500 articles published between 2011 and 2015, only 15 were referenced more frequently. The three economists have become so prominent in their field, they are known simply as ADH.

• • •

The pain caused by Chinese competition also wasn't a priority for leaders of either political party. After President Clinton ushered China into the WTO, the two administrations that succeeded his— one Republican, one Democrat—continued his policy of engagement. Their goal was to further bend China to Western norms.

The WTO deal with China gave Washington a way to shut off Chinese imports when they overwhelmed industries. In conventional trade cases, industries must prove that imports cause economic "injury" before tariffs are slapped on imports. That's a pretty tough standard to meet during economic expansions when an industry's sales may grow despite Chinese competition. The WTO agreement gave U.S. industries an alternative, which lasted twelve years. Under the import-surge provision, industries simply had to prove that Chinese imports were disrupting markets and threatening industries, as they surely were, not that they were actually harming companies.

Charles Freeman, then an assistant U.S. trade representative for China, spread the word about the new provision, looking for import-surge cases, but he found little interest. When industries complained about Chinese imports, he asked whether they were interested in using the new provision. "Uniformly, they weren't," says Freeman.

Some officials speculated that trade lawyers didn't want to file the cases because they weren't as complicated as traditional anti-dumping suits, so there would be fewer billable hours. Trade lawyers certainly were busy. From 2001 to 2017, the United States imposed tariffs in 158 antidumping and subsidy cases. Others thought that industry didn't believe President Bush would approve import-surge cases, the last step in the procedure.

Whatever the reason, the Bush administration considered only six cases. The industries involved were minuscule. One company complained that China was flooding the market with pedal actuators—a part in a brake pedal. That involved just seven jobs, Freeman recalls. Another complaint about Chinese imports of wire hangers affected about 150 workers.

The U.S. International Trade Commission, which had to make the preliminary ruling, turned down two of the cases; President Bush turned down the rest. Following Bush, President Obama approved one case involving tires, described in chapter 6.

Freeman says he was able to use the threat of bringing import-surge cases to get China to settle some disputes. But the disuse outrages former U.S. Trade Representative Barshefsky, who fought for import-surge provisions in negotiations with Chinese Premier Zhu

Rongji. She and other WTO negotiators believe that if the United States had used the tool liberally, China would have gotten the message to go slowly in ramping up exports, giving communities more time to adjust. "As with any trade agreement, you've got to enforce," she says. "You can't pussyfoot around."

Top officials in the Bush and Obama administrations saw it differently, particularly Bush's first U.S. trade representative, Robert Zoellick, and Obama's chief economic adviser, Larry Summers. They worried about encouraging protectionism and figured U.S. industries had plenty of weapons to sue Beijing for unfair trade practices. Their bosses also wanted China's help on many different issues. "The [Bush] administration decided that the national interest was not served by raising protectionist barriers," says a senior Bush trade official.

President Bush sought China's help in its antiterrorist campaigns after the 9/11 attacks and later pressed Beijing to boost spending to fight the global recession of 2008 and 2009. If China stimulated its economy, it would need more imports from hard-pressed nations, giving them a lift. China's banks would also lend to companies facing hard times. President Obama continued to rely on China as an ally in the downturn. Later, he recruited Beijing to help craft the Paris global climate pact. China trade was secondary in both White Houses.

Both the Bush and Obama administrations wanted to restore a sense of trust and confidence in U.S. financial systems. That meant convincing China not to start selling its $1 trillion cache of U.S. Treasury bills and other government debt, which could panic others into selling, too. Bush Treasury Secretary Hank Paulson briefed Chinese leaders regularly about U.S. policy changes. "We're watching this very carefully," Chinese Vice Premier Wang Qishan warned Paulson. "We want to make sure you are going to protect our financial interests."

Paulson and Wang had been close since the 1990s, when Paulson was a rising star at Goldman Sachs and responsible for Asia.

The two put together initial public offerings for Chinese banks and telecom companies and boasted of their friendship. But the financial crisis strained relations. "You were my teacher," Wang told Paulson during a visit to the Treasury in 2008. "But now I am in my teacher's domain, and look at your system, Hank. We aren't sure we should be learning from you anymore."

Paulson set up annual meetings between U.S. and Chinese officials to hash out economic differences, which he called the Strategic Economic Dialogue (SED). Although China is an authoritarian state led by the general secretary of the Communist Party, Paulson understood that Beijing's leaders often operate by consensus. A retinue of Chinese officials would meet their U.S. counterparts during SED sessions. Paulson knew he needed buy-in from a range of Chinese officials on the economic issues discussed.

In his book, *Dealing with China*, Paulson claims successes from the SED, including contracts for U.S. firms, pressure on China to let its currency rise somewhat, and launching negotiations for an investment treaty (never completed). In an interview, he says that the close coordination he arranged with Chinese leaders during SED meetings helped the United States convince Beijing not to sell U.S. securities and deepen the global downturn. "Our ability to communicate and coordinate with the top Chinese leaders 24/7 during the height of the panic was important in helping us avoid another Great Depression because China was a huge holder of corporate, banking, and Fannie Mae and Freddie Mac securities," he says.

When Russians approached Chinese officials to suggest they both sell Fannie and Freddie securities, which would have worsened the crisis for the two U.S.-backed mortgage firms, Paulson says the Chinese informed him and said no to Moscow. "The Chinese refused, and we quickly found a creative way to nationalize the mortgage giants," he adds.

Others involved came to view the meetings as gabfests that produced long lists of pledges by both nations to change policies, but with no way to enforce anything.

Under President Obama, the talks were renamed the Strategic and Economic Dialogue and added security issues to economic ones. On the U.S. side, Treasury Secretary Timothy Geithner shared top billing with Secretary of State Hillary Clinton, but he found the proceedings so dull that he delegated most of the responsibility for the meetings to a deputy. For her part, Secretary Clinton wondered how best to handle China. "How do you deal toughly with your banker?" she asked Australian Prime Minister Kevin Rudd, who had long experience in China, in 2009, according to a State Department cable disclosed by WikiLeaks.

By the end of the Obama administration, White House attitudes toward China hardened somewhat. Worried that Beijing was trying to leap ahead of the United States in advanced computing, the administration in 2015 started blocking Chinese purchases of U.S. computer chip firms. That work was carried out by a secretive interagency group, called the Committee on Foreign Investment in the United States, which reviews foreign purchases to make sure they don't endanger national security.

President Obama also played hardball after numerous reports that Beijing was hacking U.S. companies and handing their secrets to Chinese competitors. With Chinese President Xi Jinping due for a Washington visit in September 2015, the White House made clear that it would impose sanctions on Chinese companies, a move that might cause Xi to cancel his trip. Instead, Beijing dispatched a high-level delegation to Washington to discuss cyber spying.

On a cloudy fall day in Washington, the two presidents stood at adjoining podiums in the White House Rose Garden to announce they had reached a deal. Neither nation would use cyber technology to steal business information and give companies a competitive advantage. Obama aides say commercial spying subsided for a time, although their successors in the Trump administration say any improvement was short-lived.

Some of Obama's top national security advisors say the administration should have pressed China harder on issues ranging from trade to China's transforming some specks of land in the South China Sea into military outposts. "We had much more space to push on China," says Ely Ratner, a China specialist in the Obama State Department. "In every instance where the Obama administration threatened negative consequences if China didn't change its behavior, China changed its behavior. There was too much risk aversion." He is now executive vice president of the Center for a New American Security, a Washington, D.C., think tank.

On the trade front, the Obama administration's energies were focused on negotiating a twelve-nation pact with Pacific Rim countries, including Japan and Vietnam, called the Trans-Pacific Partnership. TPP members planned to cut tariffs and write rules governing Internet communications, intellectual property, and the behavior of state-owned enterprises—all areas of contention with China.

Over time, TPP could grow to include more countries in Asia and perhaps Europe. At some point, China would find it irresistible to join, which would require Beijing to make big changes in economic policy, as it did to join the WTO, Obama aides figured. If China chose not to join, it would be isolated. During a 2012 stop in Australia, an enthused Hillary Clinton said TPP "sets the gold standard in trade agreements to open free, transparent, and fair trade."

But by the time she ran for president in 2016, TPP was seen by American blue-collar voters as just another trade agreement that would help their bosses ship their jobs overseas. During the campaign, she said she opposed the deal. "My message to every worker in Michigan and across America is this: 'I will stop any trade deal that kills jobs and holds down wages, including the Trans-Pacific Partnership,'" she said during a stop at Futuramic Tool & Engineering in Warren, Michigan. "I oppose it now. I'll oppose it after the election. And I'll oppose it as president."

Some of her aides believe that if she had won, she would have tried to renegotiate the trade deal, not scrap it, as Donald Trump did on his first workday in the Oval office.

· · ·

Back in Hickory and other factory towns, the pain from China didn't let up by the time of the 2016 election. Manufacturing was slow to recover. The opioid crisis was worsening. Blue-collar voters were split between blaming China and other low-wage nations for their lost jobs or management for selling them out. They found an ally in Donald Trump, who they believed understood the forces threatening them.

"We can't continue to allow China to rape our country, and that's what they're doing," Trump told a rally in Fort Wayne, Indiana, in May 2016. "It's the greatest theft in the history of the world." He promised to bash China with 45 percent tariffs. (That is far more than even he put into effect once in office.) It worked. In Republican presidential primaries and the general election, he won 89 of the 100 counties most affected by competition from China. In the November voting, he carried those counties by seven percentage points more than the Republican presidential candidate did in 2012.

Alex Shuford III, Century Furniture's CEO, who says he is no fan of Trump, says he couldn't miss Trump's popularity among his workers. Around the time of the November election, he was touring Century factories, telling workers that he thought the company was having a tough year because consumers were keeping their wallets closed until after the election. When he gave the talk a few days before the election, there was no reaction, even among the many in the crowd wearing Trump T-shirts. When he gave the same talk a few days after the election, the workplaces broke into raucous cheers: "Trump! Trump! Trump!"

"Parts of America wanted a bully," says Shuford. "People felt, 'We keep getting picked on and pushed around. I want the guy who punches back. I want the guy who punches first.'"

In a tight election decided by some tens of thousands of votes in a handful of states, there are any number of explanations for Trump's victory. Russian bots. FBI director James Comey's harping on Clinton emails. Clinton's neglect of midwestern voters.

Economists Autor, Dorn, and Hanson have a different explanation.

For every one percentage point increase in Chinese imports in local markets between 2002 and 2014, they calculate, Trump's countywide vote increased by 2 percentage points, compared with the share of the vote won by George W. Bush in 2000. In places where Chinese imports didn't play much of a role, including big swathes of the Great Plains, the political impact from China was negligible. But in areas where Chinese imports walloped local industries, as in the swing states of North Carolina, Pennsylvania, New Hampshire, Wisconsin, and Michigan, the China impact was substantial.

Trump carried North Carolina by 3.8 percent and other swing states by narrower margins. If Chinese import growth had been 50 percent slower than it was—a rate that still would have made China's import surge one of the fastest in U.S. history—the economists figure Clinton would have nearly carried North Carolina and would have won Pennsylvania, Wisconsin, and Michigan. That would have been enough to defeat Donald Trump.

8

THE LEADERS: TRUMP'S CHINA; XI'S AMERICA

Donald Trump was toying with a presidential run in 2011 and wanted to make sure a Las Vegas crowd understood precisely how he would deal with a China that he believed had ripped off the United States for years.

"People say, 'What can you do? What can you do?' It's so easy," Trump said, in the exaggerated speaking style he uses to make clear that only idiots would disagree. "I'd drop a 25 percent tariff on China." The crowd applauded.

"And, you know, I said to somebody, 'It's really the messenger. The messenger is important.'

"I could have one man say, 'We're gonna tax you 25 percent,'" he said, switching to a whiney, high-pitched voice.

"And I could say [to] another, 'Listen you motherfuckers, we're going to tax you 25 percent,'" he said, reverting to New York tough guy. "Now you said the same exact thing. You've said the same exact thing. But it's a different messenger." The crowd erupted in laughter and cheers.

Trump cleaned up his language about trade and China after that, but his Las Vegas remarks are probably the clearest distillation of his approach to trade battles. For Trump, trade is more about atti-tude, swagger, and grievance than it is about policy. Trump's world-view, shaped by cutthroat New York real estate competition, divides people into winners and losers, champs and chumps—and Donald Trump was going to make sure he was never a chump. Global trade gave him a way to project his hypercompetitiveness onto a global stage. Nations can rise and fall on the wiles of their leaders. Trump used trade to argue that if he were in charge, America would be a winner, whatever tactics he had to use and whatever damage to the existing international order.

"He sees trade as a chance to make a stand and define himself as a strong, aggressive masculine leader who will stand up for the U.S. in a way no one else can," says Jennifer Miller, a Dartmouth historian who has studied the origins of Trump's trade views. "He latched on to trade as a way he can make this claim about himself."

Some of Trump's closest economic aides say trade is the issue he is most comfortable discussing and most confident in his judg-ment about. Trump on trade and tariffs is like Reagan on tax cut-ting, they say. President Reagan was sure that cutting taxes was the right move every time to boost the economy. President Trump looks at tariffs in the same way—a surefire winner. In his 2020 State of the Union address, he said that "unfair trade" was probably the "single biggest reason" he ran for president. That's surely an exaggeration. But it isn't an exaggeration to say that his focus on trade helped put him in the White House.

Trump's confidence on trade doesn't come from long study or experience. He made his mark in what economists call nontradable sectors—real estate development, marketing, and television. He didn't have to compete with imports in any of those fields.

On policy, even now, after decades of talking about trade, he con-fuses simple concepts. In an interview with the book's coauthor, Bob, for the *Wall Street Journal*, he kept calling tariffs "interest rates" and couldn't think of the term "developing country" until Bob helped him out. Trump claims tariffs are paid by other countries, when they are actually paid by importers and often passed along to U.S. consumers as higher prices. He regularly argues that reducing the trade deficit with China would boost jobs and U.S. growth when there is scant economic evidence to back that up. Often when the trade deficit declines, it is a sign of falling demand overall, as when the United States tumbles into recession.

Trump's initial foray into international trade was a marketing ploy. He wanted the public to see him as more than a gossip-column Manhattanite, famous for squiring models and plastering his name on New York landmarks and Atlantic City casinos. In 1987, shortly before he was to publish his autobiography, *The Art of the Deal*, he paid for a full-page ad in the *New York Times, Washington Post,* and *Boston Globe*. At the time, he was also contemplating a presidential run.

Designed as an "open letter" written in his office, Trump complained that Japan and others were getting rich because they closed their markets to imports and the U.S. military protected them. "For decades, Japan and other nations have been taking advantage of the United States," he complained. "The world is laughing at America's politicians," he wrote, using a line he would repeat for thirty years.

The ad was coupled with an appearance the same day, September 2, 1987, on *Larry King Live* where he complained of countries that "laugh at us behind our backs because of our own stupidity." Not long after, he used *The Oprah Winfrey Show* to say, "I do get tired of seeing this country get ripped off." In 1989, he told Diane Sawyer that he would impose a 15 percent to 20 percent tariff on Japanese imports, declaring "I'm not afraid of [a] trade war."

The trade offensive was "part of a strategy to float his name as a presidential candidate," Roger Stone, an early Trump adviser who helped place the newspaper ads, told the *Wall Street Journal*'s Jacob M. Schlesinger. He wanted "to get an enormous amount of coverage; to show a different side of him," Stone explained.

It was a masterstroke. "For this entrepreneur out of New York real estate and casino gambling to say, 'Free trade is ripping you off!' That would get people's attention," says Trump biographer Gwenda Blair. "It's not what you'd expect."

Japan was the obvious target. The country's startling success in the 1980s and early 1990s rattled many Americans. Fuel-efficient Japanese imports were grabbing market share from Detroit gas-guzzlers. Japanese televisions, video recorders, and cameras were erasing American mainstay brands. President Trump's former campaign chief, Steve Bannon, calls Trump "the last of the Mad Men generation"—an era when U.S. multinationals bestrode the world and Japanese imports were dismissed as "Jap crap." How could Japan possibly be winning at trade, other than through cheating and U.S. political incompetence?

Theodore H. White, the Pulitzer Prize–winning journalist who had watched Japan's leaders surrender on the deck of the USS *Missouri*, wrote in 1985 how flabbergasted he was by Japan's rise. "Today, forty years after the end of World War II, the Japanese are on the move again in one of history's most brilliant commercial offensives, as they go about dismantling American industry," he said.

Trump had plenty of company in corporate America when he complained that Japan's markets were closed. The auto industry pressed Washington to limit Japanese car exports; the semiconductor industry lobbied for tariffs on Japanese chips. Among the most outspoken were Ross Perot, who founded Electronic Data Systems, and Robert Galvin, whose father had formed telecommunications maker Motorola Inc.

In 1987—the same year as Trump's "open letter"—Galvin testified in Congress that Japan's market was so shuttered that it acted as a "sanctuary to home industry while we have no and ask no sanctuary here." Intel's CEO Andrew Grove went him one better. In 1990, he predicted that the United States would become a "techno-colony of Japan" unless it imposed heavy tariffs on Japanese semiconductors.

Lee Iacocca, the voluble, plainspoken Chrysler Corporation chairman, whose 1984 autobiography was a bestseller, had an especially large megaphone and became a model for Trump. "I for one am fed up hearing from the Japanese, and I might say some Americans too, that our problems in this industry, all our problems are our own damn fault," he thundered. He attacked "insidious Japanese economic and political power within the U.S."

Iacocca palled around with Trump for a time. In May 1986, Iacocca bought a condominium for his daughter in Trump Plaza. That summer, the two men put together a $40 million purchase of a West Palm Beach, Florida, condominium complex that would be called "Trump Plaza." Later in the year, Trump received an "Ellis Island Medal of Honor" from a foundation Iacocca chaired. Trump wrote *The Art of the Deal* after seeing how well Iacocca's book sold.

Robert Lutz, Iacocca's executive vice president, figures his boss's trade views had to rub off on Trump, who was twenty-two years his junior. "Trade was uppermost on Iacocca's mind; he never stopped talking about it," says Lutz. "I'm sure the mature Lee Iacocca spent a lot of time indoctrinating the impressionable, much-younger Donald Trump."

The two publicity hounds later may have had a falling-out. In a 1991 *Playboy* interview, Iacocca said, "I know Trump fairly well. Now that's an ego that's gone screwloose, gone haywire." They also began to differ on trade. Trump attacked the North American Free Trade Agreement during a 1993 conference held under a huge tent in Bakersfield, California, while Iacocca mocked those who were "scared to compete" with Mexico. Auto companies used NAFTA to move a lot of production south of the border.

Trump's interest in trade issues only went so far, though. He never participated in the burgeoning anti–free trade movement, which fought pacts with Mexico, the Caribbean, and China, and united opponents from the left and right who agreed on nothing aside from the insidiousness of global trade deals. Participants compared the secretive Capitol Hill dinners of what they called the "No Name Coalition" to the intergalactic bar scene in *Star Wars*. International Ladies' Garment Workers Union lobbyist Evelyn Dubrow, a firebrand who fought to unionize southern factories, would greet one of her chief nemeses, courtly textile magnate Roger Milliken of South Carolina, with a kiss on the cheek, as they plotted their next moves. Naderites and environmentalists sought advice from the sister of right-wing anti-globalist Pat Buchanan.

Trump never sought to join the coalition, unlike another billionaire, Sir James Goldsmith. Milliken's chief lobbyist, Jock Nash, who was responsible for recruiting CEOs, didn't try to tap him. "The accent he had and the way he sashayed around was off-putting to me," says Nash, who now says he wishes he had reached out to Trump.

During the fight over admitting China to the World Trade Organization, Trump was invisible. In 2000, when Congress was debating whether to end its annual Most Favored Nation review of China's behavior, Trump was again considering a run for president. In his campaign book, *The America We Deserve*, he identified China as a long-term threat but didn't mention the WTO fight. His main policy recommendation was to make himself chief trade negotiator as well as president. "I'd lower our trade deficits and I'd save the salary of our U.S. trade representative because I wouldn't accept it," he wrote. Then, in perhaps the most un-Trumpian comment he has ever made, he said: "I've learned in the business world that bluster gets you exactly nowhere" and he criticized the Clinton administration for making "threat after threat after threat."

Still, his regular flirtation with presidential runs kept Trump thinking about trade and the next big challenger on the horizon, China. By the early 2000s, however, corporate America had changed. "Big Red" Milliken—as a young man his hair was red—stepped down as chief executive of textile maker Milliken & Company in 2006. His successors dropped the firm's anti–free trade lobbying and expanded in Asia. Unlike Japan, China welcomed foreign investment, and CEOs feared offending their hosts. Facebook's Mark Zucker-berg was typical of the new corporate generation. He made news in 2016 when he jogged around Tiananmen Square despite hazardous air pollution. "It's great to be back in Beijing!" Zuckerberg posted on Facebook, which has long been blocked in China.

The change in CEO behavior made Trump stand out more. In 2011, he told CNN host Piers Morgan that he saw firsthand that China was cheating when he bought glass for his buildings. Chinese glass was much less expensive than American-made glass because Beijing kept its currency undervalued, he said. "I don't want to buy glass from China," he said. "But our companies can't compete." A year later, he backed the GOP's eventual presidential nominee, Mitt Romney, who sharply criticized Chinese trade practices. Romney returned the favor, praising Trump as "one of the few people who stood up and said, 'You know what? China has been cheating.'"

Iacocca was replaced as Trump's trade guru by TV news anchor Lou Dobbs, who around 2001 transformed his show from what the *New Yorker* called "a sort of video clubhouse for corporate Amer-ica" into a populist "full-throated champion of the little guy." China, illegal immigration, and treasonous CEOs were regular subjects. In the early 2000s, Dobbs started a series he called "Exporting Amer-ica" and named U.S. companies that were shipping jobs overseas. A companion book, written by Dobbs, was titled *Exporting America— Why Corporate Greed Is Shipping Jobs Overseas.*

Trump, who refers to Dobbs as "the Great Lou Dobbs," was a rapt viewer, say his aides. Bannon and Sean Spicer, Trump's first presidential spokesman, go so far as to call their former boss's trade views "Dobbesian."

Trump's 2016 campaign combined the themes Trump had de-veloped concerning Japan with the updated journalism of Dobbs. Japan was "interchangeable with China, interchangeable with other countries," Trump told the *Wall Street Journal*. "It's all the same thing."

China became the Trump campaign's symbol for lost manufacturing jobs and the bosses and politicians who sold out blue-collar America. Huge bilateral deficits were the proof that China was cheating. Tariffs were the solution—as high as 45 percent on all Chinese goods, Trump pledged.

Trump focused on the deficit, says his former campaign spokesman Jason Miller, because he thought it proved his point that China was treating America unfairly, and fairness was the crux of Trump's campaign. Immigrants flooding into the United States were unfair to American workers. Endless wars were unfair to the working-class families whose sons and daughters signed up to fight. A nuanced message about the challenge China posed to America's future wouldn't work, says Miller. "That's a loser," he says. "It's hard to understand. 'Industries of the future' don't fit on a bumper sticker."

Trump took the argument a step further. Don't blame Beijing for taking advantage of America, Trump said; blame the feckless American politicians who sold out their country. Bannon says that message jibed with campaign polling showing that working-class voters "would follow a leader that would return America to its former greatness."

An April 2016 Trump rally in Watertown, New York, an old mill town in New York's perpetually depressed upstate region, was typical of Trump's pitch. "I don't blame China. I don't blame Mexico. I don't blame Japan," he told the cheering crowd. "I blame our leaders for being stupid people, okay?"

The clarity of his message, repeated over and over for thirty years, resonated. "He's been incredibly consistent" on trade issues, which gives him "the mantle of authenticity," says Miller, the Dartmouth historian. "He developed clear and direct language. There was no hedging. He didn't talk with nuance. It's what he believes."

His trade views were attacked by economists on the right and left, who put together models of how much damage tariffs would inflict on the U.S. economy. He also attracted ultranationalists like

Bannon, who had run Breitbart News, a populist, hard-right news site that regularly attacked Beijing. Bannon had admired Trump's anti-China rantings for years, and Bannon appealed to Trump's anti-establishment side. Overweight, unshaven, with a shock of gray hair and surfer-dude patois—"Dude, Emperor Xi is going to fall"—Bannon played the role of outré political outlaw.

Another stalwart was University of California, Irvine economist Peter Navarro, who had morphed from a scholar studying electricity regulation into a pamphleteer about China. In *Death by China*, Navarro warned that China is "rapidly turning into the planet's most efficient assassin" because of the dangerous Chinese food, drugs, and other products shipped to the United States and jobs stolen away. Trump wrote a promotional endorsement for the video version of the book, which starts with the image of a dagger, labeled "Made in China," stabbing the heart of America, as blood spurts out. Navarro became the campaign's top economic policy aide.

Navarro says he had read a 2011 blog post in the *Los Angeles Times* that said Trump had listed one of Navarro's books, *The Coming China Wars*, among his twenty favorite China books. The *Times* item referred to a Xinhua News Agency story about Trump. But as Loren Collins pointed out in a 2017 *Medium* article, the Xinhua article was probably phony. It doesn't exist on Factiva or other newspaper databases (and Trump advisers roll their eyes when asked if Trump has read any China book).

Navarro had little firsthand experience with China. He says he had visited the country just once before joining the campaign, though he advertised himself as a China expert. "You don't need to go to China to understand their seven deadly protectionist sins against American workers any more than an astronomer has to go to Mars to understand the solar system," he says in written comments for this book.

In 2015, Trump's campaign manager, Corey Lewandowski, said he heard a radio interview with Navarro on China while he was riding in a taxicab in New York City. Intrigued, he conferred with Trump's son-in-law, Jared Kushner, and then invited Navarro to Trump Tower to meet first with staffers and then Trump. "We should hire this guy," Trump told Lewandowski.

For a campaign shunned by established academics, Navarro, a Harvard-educated PhD in economics, was a "difficult find and a big get," says Lewandowski. The protectionist economic plan Navarro produced with Wilbur Ross, a longtime Trump business associate who became Trump's Commerce secretary, called China "the biggest trade cheater in the world." Navarro's credentials didn't help. It was panned by prominent economists on the left and right.

Harvard's Greg Mankiw, who was George W. Bush's chief economist, said the work was "truly disappointing" and had mistakes that "even a freshman at the end of EC 10" would recognize. The errors included failing to recognize how the economy responds to changes in trade. Given how well the economy performed under President Trump—at least until the pandemic—Navarro believes he has the last laugh. "I point to one of the best performances of a president in modern economic history," he says.

Bannon and Navarro see themselves in Churchillian terms. To them, China is the gravest threat to America since the fascism of the 1930s. They oppose free trade for aiding China's ascent. (Bannon is self-aware enough to realize that his liberal critics consider him one of the biggest fascist threats to America. He dismisses the criticism. "Fascism worships the state," he says. "We're trying to deconstruct this kind of state capitalism.")

But Trump isn't truly an ultranationalist. To him, China isn't much different from Germany, Mexico, Japan, or any country that runs big trade surpluses with the United States. In the Trump worldview, they all take advantage of the United States.

He also learned from his business career that personal relations matter enormously, and he figured he could talk anyone into anything. Hadn't he convinced hard-assed bankers in 1990 to keep him as head of his casinos when his Atlantic City empire was crumbling into bankruptcy? The bankers figured his star power would convince more gamblers to take the bus from New York for a night out.

With China, Trump would always flatter Xi Jinping as a friend with whom he could work out any problem. His notoriously undisciplined administration kept to that line as well. The tactic gave Trump a chance to build his relationship despite the trade battle. In the administration's eye, this also gave Xi a way out if he wanted to cave to the United States. Since he wasn't personally at fault, Xi could also blame underlings for leading him astray.

Trump has benefited greatly from one form of globalization, the massive flow of capital across borders, and takes advice as much from rich business friends as from anti–free trade followers. In the 1980s and 1990s, he hunted in Tokyo for investors in Trump Tower and other properties. (This is the flip side of trade deficits—they are funded by foreign capital, some of which found its way into Trump's pockets.) After *The Art of the Deal* became a bestseller in Japan, real estate agents put together packages of photos of Trump and his Mar-a-Lago estate in Japanese mass mailings, although some would-be investors were put off by his anti-Japan rhetoric.

Asked by *Time* magazine in 1989 about his net worth, he said, "Who the eff knows? I mean, really, who knows how much the Japs will pay for Manhattan property these days?" The following year, he told *Playboy*, "Japanese investors literally gave their subordinates instructions to buy apartments only in Trump buildings." One "just paid me $20 million bucks for seven apartments he's turning into one."

The bursting of Japan's financial bubble in the early 1990s came at an especially difficult time for Trump, whose business empire was teetering on bankruptcy. Tentative deals he had reached with Japanese buyers fell apart, including plans to buy his 281-foot

Trump Princess yacht and a stake in the Plaza hotel. Japanese banks were also among the final holdouts in a deal to restructure the debt for his Taj Mahal casino.

When China became a world-class market, the Trump Organization tried and failed to do at least four property deals. His lawyers sought copyrights for Trump-branded goods, including clothing and beauty products. "It was a living, breathing demonstration for him it's a tough place to do business, a tough place to protect intellectual property," says Ross.

Trump's business dealings also brought home to him that Japan first and then China weren't simply enemies. They were also rich markets, from which the United States couldn't easily disengage, as Bannon, Navarro, and other Trump backers hoped would occur. Trump's wealthy friends pressed him to stay involved with China and explained how the rise and fall of the Dow Jones Industrial Average—an index that Trump consults as avidly as he does political polls—depended in large measure on how well U.S. companies exploited opportunities in Asia.

"Trump is a successful businessman," says Bannon. "I'm not. He looks at the world in a pragmatic sense," while Bannon calls himself "an unreasonable man." That meant that Trump was bound to disappoint his nationalist followers, at times, when it came to China, by being more willing to compromise than they would be. It also meant it was especially hard for Chinese leaders to understand what Trump really wanted—to fight with them unless they remade their economic system or to cut a sales deal. Trump was caught between Lou Dobbs and the Dow.

• • •

Donald Trump campaigned for president by promising to "Make America Great Again." Xi Jinping had the same idea for China. He called his version "the China Dream."

Upon taking over the Communist Party's reins in November 2012, four years before Trump won the election, Xi made it clear he wanted to restore China to the position of global primacy the Middle Kingdom had held for centuries before being eclipsed by the West. He chose to announce his plans at a massive exhibit in China's lavishly renovated National Museum, called "The Road of Rejuvenation."

The display told the story of China's rise from subjugation to triumph, thanks to the Chinese Communist Party's leadership. Featured were cannons used during the Opium Wars between Britain and China in the 1800s, which forced China to open up trade with other countries; the first Chinese translation of *The Communist Manifesto*, as a reminder of the party's ideology; and the five-star Chinese flag that was hoisted above Tiananmen Square when Mao Zedong declared the founding of the People's Republic in 1949.

At a section highlighting the country's achievements under former paramount leader Deng Xiaoping, Xi stopped and gave a ten-minute speech that was broadcast nationwide. He was flanked by the six other members of the Politburo Standing Committee, the party's ruling body, most dressed like Xi in dark navy windbreakers. The Chinese leader talked about everyone's right to dream and then laid out his vision. "The greatest dream of the Chinese nation in modern times is the great rejuvenation of the Chinese nation," Xi said. That was the task he set for himself. "We're more confident and capable of achieving this goal than at any time in history," he said.

To fulfill his ambition, Xi believed, he would first have to revitalize the party and purge it of the corruption that had turned many ordinary citizens into cynics. He would also have to rid himself of rivals and secure his position as unchallenged leader, as Deng—and Mao before him—had done decades earlier.

Xi's "China Dream" also meant putting the nation on a collision course with the United States, as China strove to be a rival econom-ically, militarily, and politically. Under Xi, Beijing moved aggres-sively to enforce what it called "indisputable" sovereignty claims to almost all of the South China Sea, one of the world's busiest shipping routes. China's military developed and equipped islands, rocks, and reefs across the South China Sea with military hardware, including electronic jamming equipment meant to cloak activities from U.S. surveillance.

To drive home the point that China aspired to become a global power, five Chinese naval vessels sailed into international waters in the Bering Sea just off Alaska when President Obama visited the state in September 2015. That was the first time the Pentagon had seen Chinese naval vessels there.

Beijing also competed for influence with Washington in trade and economics. In 2015, China launched a new development bank, called the Asian Infrastructure Investment Bank, as a rival to the U.S.-dominated World Bank, and won support from Washington's allies, despite the Obama administration's lobbying against the AIIB. Xi also put together a trillion-dollar infrastructure plan called the Belt and Road Initiative, which sought to pull Asian, European, and African nations into Beijing's orbit.

Under the plan, China offered financing and other aid to cash-poor nations that agreed to use Chinese construction companies and buy Chinese-made goods. Washington warned that the Chinese initiative would leave borrowers indebted to China financially and politically, but had little success blunting China's efforts. In 2019, Italy joined the project, giving China a major inroad into Europe.

Donald Trump's victory caught Beijing's leaders by surprise, as it did many in the United States and abroad (and even Trump himself). Although his victory owed much to working-class angst over Chinese competition, the results of the election did little to shake Xi Jinping of his faith in the superiority of China's system. The Chinese leader frequently compares American democracy to "a sheet of loose sand"—his way of describing the partisan division that dominates Washington politics these days. By comparison, Xi says in leadership meetings, the one-party system in China allows things to get done as long as the party itself is united in thoughts and actions.

• • •

Xi Jinping learned about the privileges of being part of the Chinese political elite and the cutthroat nature of Chinese politics at an early age. His later experiences confirmed his faith in the party, but also instilled a respect for the role of markets. That complicated mixture of experiences and beliefs makes it hard for Americans to predict how Xi will react and frequently leads the White House to miscalculate. Chinese officials have the same difficulty understanding Donald Trump.

Born in 1953, four years after Communists took over China, Xi led a privileged childhood because of his father, Xi Zhongxun, who had fought alongside Mao during the revolution. The Xi family lived in a large courtyard house in Beijing reserved for party leaders. Guards, nurses, and a cook catered to the family, which was chauffeured around town in Soviet-made cars. Xi Jinping attended elite schools and had access to foreign books and films. But those privileges came to an abrupt end in the early 1960s, when Mao launched his Cultural Revolution.

Xi's father was purged for supporting a book deemed critical of Mao, and his son was also punished. At age sixteen, Xi Jinping was dispatched to the Liangjiahe village in northern Shaanxi province. He remained there for seven years and spent most of the time in a cave digging ditches with villagers to extract methane from pig waste. He persevered by burying himself in the books he had brought from Beijing. One of his favorites was a trilogy of short stories by a Ming Dynasty writer in the 1600s: *Stories to Instruct the World*, *Stories to Caution the World*, and *Stories to Awaken the World*.

Xi got a break in the mid-1970s when village officials helped him gain party membership and a place at Beijing's prestigious Tsinghua University. There he studied chemical engineering as a "worker-peasant-soldier student"—meaning a student who was accepted because of his class background and recommendations, not his academic qualifications. His family's persecution did little to erode his faith in the party. If anything, it hardened his belief that the sacrifices made by his father and his generation to establish the party's rule should never go to waste.

Years later, as China's top leader, he would set straight anyone who doubted the one-party system. "Although our party has made some large mistakes in its history, including in the thirty years since the founding of the People's Republic, even mistakes as large as the Cultural Revolution, in the end it was our party that made the revolution successful," Xi told two hundred or so senior party officials in 2013.

In the late 1990s though the mid-2000s, Xi rose through the political ranks in China's coastal provinces, first as deputy mayor of the port city of Xiamen, later as governor of the surrounding Fujian province, and then as party secretary of neighboring Zhejiang. In all these assignments, he experimented with market incentives.

Fujian is located across the strait from Taiwan, the island viewed by China's leaders as a rebel province. The province had long been an economic backwater as the government turned it into a military stronghold to repel a possible invasion from the island, presumably backed by America. In the late 1990s, Xi focused on economic development instead, taking a page from his father, who helped spur Guangdong province's growth by enticing foreign businesses to locate there. In 1999, Xi endorsed a free trade pact between China and Taiwan, and offered lower tariffs and other incentives to Taiwanese companies, whose executives often had family roots in Fujian.

Xi also tried to lure foreign capital to Zhejiang, a Chinese hub of entrepreneurship. A U.S. diplomatic cable released by WikiLeaks suggests that Xi helped FedEx, Motorola, and Citibank establish operations in Zhejiang. Those companies all expanded in the province.

In 2007, Xi went on to run Shanghai, the most sophisticated of Chinese cities. Shanghai is usually celebrated as a showcase for the power of the market and foreign investment to remake China, but Xi took away a different lesson. After seeing the successful transformation of some of the big state companies owned by the city government, Xi became convinced of the value of state-owned enterprises. Private-sector development wouldn't be sufficient to transform China, Xi believed.

One of the Shanghai-owned firms, SAIC Motor Corporation, is now China's largest automaker. "It struck him that state companies like SAIC can be just as successful as privately run businesses," says a Shanghai official. SAIC Motor went public in 2012, the year Xi rose to the top of China's political apex, and has been one of the most profitable companies owned by the city government. It has joint ventures with many foreign carmakers, including General Motors and Volkswagen.

"He is a master politician who understands power," former U.S. Treasury Secretary Hank Paulson says of Xi. "It is not easy to reconcile his absolute faith in big government and the Communist Party with private markets. First and foremost, he sees the party as the future of China and his own power."

• • •

When Xi rose to power in late 2012, he had a relatively weak political base. His two most recent predecessors, Jiang Zemin and Hu Jintao, were handpicked as Communist Party general secretary and president by former paramount leader Deng Xiaoping, which gave them immediate legitimacy. Xi was a compromise candidate, chosen through the intense backroom politicking by current and former leaders that is common in China.

But Xi managed to turn that weakness into strength. He silenced party elders, who traditionally retain enormous power, by launching an anticorruption crusade that swept away those who opposed him or were deemed as potential threats. Heading the campaign was Wang Qishan, a friend dating back to the years of the Cultural Revolution, when both were banished to the countryside for reeducation. Together they used a scandal involving Bo Xilai, who was Xi's chief rival for leadership and was ultimately jailed for abusing power, as justification to target others.

The campaign brought down President Hu's chief of staff, Ling Jihua, and a former national security chief loyal to President Jiang, Zhou Yongkang. In 2013 alone, some 182,000 party members were investigated, compared with roughly 10,000 to 20,000 graft investigations a year before Xi took power. The drive curbed the influence of networks centered around Presidents Jiang and Hu and prevented overt challenges to Xi's authority.

President Hu had already sworn he wouldn't interfere with Xi when he retired in late 2012. Shortly before Xi was about to introduce his new seven-member leadership team, Hu told a gathering of the party's most senior leaders, past and present, that he wouldn't meddle in politics as other retired senior officials had. He also announced his decision to relinquish all his positions—president, Communist Party chief, top military official—rather than cling to the military title as his predecessor, Jiang Zemin, had done.

Xi was "qualified" to be the party and military leader, Hu told the gathering. "After I retire, I absolutely won't interfere with the next generation of leadership," he added, emphatically. The surprise action by Hu, often viewed as a bland figurehead, helped pave the way for the newly minted leader to assert control.

Xi overturned the way China had been ruled since Deng Xiaoping came to power in 1978. Fearful of Mao-style one-man rule, China's top leader had to negotiate decisions with other members of the Politburo Standing Committee until the group reached a consensus, making the party chief a kind of first among equals. Xi turned himself into the Chairman of Everything. He now takes personal charge of the economy, the armed forces, foreign affairs, and other power centers, though he still must take into account the political views of top party officials to make sure they don't line up against him.

As part of his power grab, he downgraded the role of the premier, Li Keqiang, whom President Hu had backed as his successor, rather than Xi. For nearly two decades, China's premier was responsible for managing the economy. Xi hinted at his plans to assume that responsibility in early 2013 soon after his rise to power, in a fashion that was unsubtle by Chinese standards. In a conversation with Vice Premier Ma Kai, Xi asked whether he thought the party (meaning people like himself) or the government (meaning the premier) had been more effective in running the economy.

In responding, Ma referred to the different areas of Zhongnanhai, the compound in Beijing that houses the offices of the party and the government's top decision-making body, called the State Council.

"The northern courtyard," Ma answered, referring to the section of the compound that houses the State Council.

"I don't necessarily think so," Xi replied.

Since then, Xi's economic adviser, Liu He, has mapped out the country's economic policy, essentially preempting the premier. Liu, a childhood friend of Xi's, focused on stabilizing the economy while Xi strengthened his grip on the party. Liu also sought to carry out Xi's view of economic development: push forward with some market-oriented changes, but make sure the party keeps firm control of any changes. In early 2018, when trade tensions with the United States started to escalate, Xi made Liu his chief trade negotiator. Xi's imperative of retaining party control was bound to collide with the Trump White House's bid to force China to operate more as a Western-style economy.

• • •

Xi had his reasons to try to consolidate power and strengthen the party. He believed Hu Jintao's consensus-style approach had resulted in policy drift, internal infighting, and rampant corruption. China's economic growth, driven by exports and debt-fueled investment, was reaching its limits. Labor costs and social unrest were rising. Debts were piling up at various levels of government and in state-owned companies. Environmental woes were worsening.

The problems were starting to undermine the party's main claim to legitimacy—that it would continue to deliver prosperity for the Chinese people. Hu's tenure as president and party chairman, from 2002 to 2012, was regarded by some senior party members as a "lost decade" because of the lack of economic and political change. All that convinced Xi that he needed to consolidate power in his own hands to save the party.

But recentralizing power didn't translate into bold economic reforms. Initially Xi dabbled with enhancing the market's roles in the economy. For Xi, that was a natural continuation of Deng's reform policies. He even considered a proposal to scrap a hulking ministry that owns and supervises state firms in favor of the "Temasek model," named for Singapore's sovereign wealth fund.

Under that plan, investment firms funded with the central government's money would take over the ownership of state companies from the ministry, called the State-Owned Assets Supervision and Administration Commission (SASAC). The investment funds would allow professional managers to run the companies rather than party overlords.

Fighting for their survival at the time, senior officials at SASAC argued that the ministry was necessary to carry out Xi's plan to strengthen the Community Party. That was best done, they argued, by increasing, not reducing, the role of state companies in the economy and the ministry's oversight. SASAC prevailed.

In the years since, the state ministry has spearheaded a wave of mergers in powerful sectors including energy, heavy machinery, and steel. The consolidation hasn't led to improved efficiency or profitability. Rather big state companies absorb loss-making smaller ones and keep them going.

Xi became more wary of market forces during the summer of 2015. An epic stock rally that year, dubbed by many Chinese investors "the Uncle Xi bull market" because the government encouraged stock investing, turned into an epic bust. The tumble pounded markets around the world and embarrassed Xi. At a closed-door meeting with senior economic officials in July 2015, he made clear his unhappiness with how the government had handled the market. A few days earlier, the *Economist* magazine had put him on its cover, portraying him with arms raised, trying in vain to hold up a plunging Chinese stock index.

"I didn't want to be on that cover," Xi told his underlings. "But thanks to you, I made the cover." Xiao Gang, at the time China's top securities regulator, went pale upon hearing Xi's remarks. He had spent months talking up the market as a way to reform China's economy. In early 2016, he was removed from his post.

Then in August 2015, global investors seized on a brief Chinese experiment with a freer currency to pummel the yuan. In response, Xi approved a plan that relied heavily on the state. A team of state companies stepped in to buy stocks and boost the market. The government cracked down on investors who had bet on stocks to fall. The central bank set aside all other priorities to prop up the yuan, whose weakness was driving huge amounts of capital out of the country. In Xi's view, the market had failed, while the state had come to the rescue.

Today, private investment is growing much more slowly than state investment in China. Authorities have limited the expansion plans of privately owned Chinese conglomerates, which had made inroads in Hollywood and bought trophy hotels in the West.

Instead, capital is flowing to government-approved infrastructure projects overseas.

The party is also taking a more visible and expansive role. Publicly traded Chinese companies now must set up party committees for their employees. "Party discussions are prerequisites for major business decisions," according to a directive issued in early 2020 by the Central Organization Department, a Communist Party office that oversees major personnel appointments. At Baowu Steel Group, China's largest steel producer, the party cell held 55 meetings in the past two years and reviewed 137 business and other proposals, according to Plenum, a research group in China. The party cell turned down two of the proposals and amended 16 before sending them to the company's board of directors. Some foreign firms also are pushed to give party representatives a bigger say in business decisions.

"The direction of policy under Xi has been clear: the power that the Party had over business decisions and personnel in state firms, once wielded behind the scenes, would not only be strengthened," wrote Richard McGregor in his book *Xi Jinping: The Backlash*. "The Party's power would also increasingly be exercised explicitly, with a demand that it be recognized and acknowledged."

• • •

Despite being a fervent believer in the party, Xi Jinping still retains affection for the United States. His coining of the phrase "the China Dream" was a nod to the global appeal of the American Dream, where ordinary individuals can get ahead through hard work and gumption. Xi has also told foreign leaders and his lieutenants that "we have a thousand reasons to get the China-U.S. relationship right, and not one reason to spoil it."

He visited the United States first in 1985 when he stayed with a family in the small city of Muscatine, Iowa, and was warmly received. He sent his only child, a daughter, to Harvard. In a written interview with the *Wall Street Journal* ahead of his first official state visit to the United States in 2015, the Chinese leader talked about his admiration for the Americans he met. "During my last visit to the United States, my old friends in Muscatine, Iowa, talked to me about their dream," Xi said. "I have the impression that the Americans and people in all other countries share the same dream about the future: world peace, social security and stability, and a decent life."

But there are limits to what he thinks China can learn from the United States. While he wants to emulate America's economic prosperity and military prowess, he views Western-style democracy as a serious threat to the party's hold on power. To fend off that risk, Xi stresses the need to unify the party under the banner of Marxism. His goal: to remake the party into a disciplined organization, loyal to him personally and able to reshape society and the economy.

He often talks about the fall of the Soviet Union as a lesson for China. "Why did the Soviet Union disintegrate? Why did the Communist Party of the Soviet Union fall to pieces?" Xi said in a closed-door speech to senior party officials in January 2013, shortly after he took the reins of the party. "An important reason is that in the ideological domain, competition is fierce."

Robert Zoellick, the former World Bank president, recalled a documentary film about the end of the Soviet Union that Xi had commissioned after he assumed office. Instead of portraying Mikhail Gorbachev, the last Soviet leader, as a hero who helped end the Cold War, Zoellick said, the Chinese version showed that "Gorbachev was the fool who abandoned the Communist Party."

"The not-so-subtle message was, 'It won't happen here,'" said Zoellick, at a Washington party hosted by the U.S.-China Business Council in December 2019.

Today Xi's leadership is undisputed. In 2018, he eliminated the two-term limit on the presidency, allowing him to rule China for as long as he chooses. (His role as general secretary of the party never was subject to term limits.)

Yet he still faces constraints. He has a limited number of people he can truly trust. His emphasis on obedience and austerity has prompted many officials to leave government while others simply pass along orders and avoid taking initiatives. He also has antagonized many party leaders with his anti-graft crusade, and they might try to bring him down if he is perceived as deviating from the party's core interests.

Xi turns to economic liberalization if it helps him further cement the party's rule. "No matter how we reform and open up, we should always adhere to the socialist road with Chinese characteristics," he told senior party leaders in the January 2013 speech. "Socialism with Chinese characteristics is socialism, not any other 'ism.'" That speech, which wasn't publicly disclosed by state media until six years later, leaves no room for misinterpretation: Xi is not the kind of reformer America has hoped for.

9

FLOOD THE ZONE, DECEMBER 2016

Not long after Donald Trump surprised the world by winning the presidency, a familiar Washington rite began—the courting of power. Within days of the election, a parade of big names auditioning for a job or influence with the new administration arrived at Trump Tower in Manhattan to meet with the president-elect or his senior aides. Camera crews in the marble lobby recorded their comings and goings, which had to be an ego boost to the president-elect. When it came to China policy, says Steve Bannon, the campaign chief who viewed China as a mortal enemy, "everyone who ever ate chop suey" came calling.

None had better credentials than Henry Kissinger, whose secret diplomacy in 1971 paved the way for China to reestablish relations with the United States, rejoin the global trading system, and emerge as American's greatest rival. At ninety-three years old, Kissinger still had unrivaled access to Chinese leaders and a thriving corporate consulting business that benefited from those contacts. On November 17, 2016, he was ushered into Trump's office. The president-elect had a message he wanted conveyed to Beijing: "Everything is on the table."

From one perspective, the message was surprisingly positive coming from a president-elect who had threatened to hit Chinese imports with 45 percent tariffs and who had accused China of rape. But the message had a touch of menace, too. If everything was on the table, that could include China's claims of sovereignty over islands in the South China Sea, or even Taiwan or Tibet.

Trump told Kissinger that he wanted to establish a personal relationship with Chinese leader Xi Jinping that would help the two nations solve conflicts. Kissinger said he was scheduled to meet soon with Xi and would deliver the message. On December 2, he did just that. The two men met at the Great Hall of the People, where Xi told Kissinger that he also wanted a fresh relationship. He sought a one-on-one meeting with Trump and was ready to travel to meet him.

Later that day, though, before Kissinger could fly back to New York and deliver the positive response, Trump had a different interchange, which would stun Beijing and call into question whether any Chinese leader could do business with him. Trump took a phone call from Taiwan's president, the first time a U.S. president or president-elect had spoken to a Taiwanese leader since at least 1979, when the United States broke off diplomatic ties with Taiwan as part of its agreement to recognize China.

The substance of the twelve-minute phone call didn't seem like much. Taiwan's president congratulated Trump on his election victory, and the two leaders cited "close economic, political, and security ties," according to a Trump office statement.

But the symbolism was breathtaking. China views Taiwan as a breakaway province and has never ceded sovereignty. As part of a Kissinger-negotiated deal in 1972 to resume relations between the United States and China, Washington said it accepted there is "one China and that Taiwan is a part of China," although the United States and China disagreed on what the One China policy entailed.

The Trump call suggested that the new president might be willing to accept Taiwan as an independent entity, perhaps even a sovereign nation. A front-page commentary in the *People's Daily*, the Communist Party's mouthpiece, warned that "Trump and his transition team ought to recognize that creating trouble for China-U.S. relations is just creating trouble for the U.S. itself."

For the independence-minded new president of Taiwan, Tsai Ing-wen, the call was a big win. Bob Dole, the former Republican senator and presidential nominee, stepped forward to say that his law firm did work for the Taipei Economic and Cultural Representative Office—Taiwan's U.S. quasi-embassy—and that "we may have had some influence" in arranging the phone call.

The full story was both more mundane and troubling because it showed how unprepared the new Trump team was to govern. The president-elect hadn't decided to jettison the One China policy; he hadn't approved any China policy at all, other than signaling he was open to a new relationship. A lower-level Trump staffer sympathetic to Taiwan placed the call on an Excel spreadsheet of upcoming telephone calls for the president-elect, fully expecting someone more senior to knock it off the list. No one did.

Bannon, who saw the schedule, liked the idea of shaking up the China relationship, given his distaste for Beijing and his to-the-barricades temperament. Jared Kushner, the president's son-in-law, also reviewed requests from foreign leaders to talk to Trump. Bannon didn't brief him on the significance of the call or the potential blowback.

A senior White House official said Kushner learned of the call just a few minutes before it was made, and Trump had already decided to go ahead. But another staffer said that Bannon had "cuckolded" Kushner, whom he viewed as a rival. Well, Bannon says, chuckling, "maybe I didn't fully explain."

In any event, Trump wanted to talk to the Taiwan leader. Who was China to tell him who he could talk to? "I don't give a shit" about Beijing's reaction, he said, according to staffers.

Trump's election had stunned Beijing, which had focused during the 2016 campaign on Hillary Clinton's China aides, including former Obama Assistant Secretary of State Kurt Campbell. China's ambassador, Cui Tiankai, invited Campbell to his residence in January 2016 for what Campbell described in a memo released by WikiLeaks as a request for "an informal, private, off-the-record get-together with a few of us to discuss the next year and the current state of U.S.-China affairs."

Clinton had known three generations of Chinese leaders, including Xi Jinping. As secretary of state in 2012, she had hosted Xi, who was then vice president, for lunch at the State Department. Xi discussed the difficulty of building a "new type of cooperative partnership" between two countries with such different political systems. "There's no precedent for us to follow, and no ready experiment for us to refer to," Xi said.

Whatever difficulties Beijing expected with Clinton were magnified with Trump, whose campaign was an enigma to Chinese leaders. At internal meetings, Xi marveled at Trump's ability to anticipate shifting voters' sentiment in the United States and his ability to sway public opinion. Trump's attacks on China didn't have much impact on their sentiment; even ordinary Chinese were used to U.S. presidential candidates lambasting China.

Trump actually had plenty of admirers on the mainland. His reality TV show, *The Apprentice*, was a hit and had spawned local copycats. His perceived directness and decisiveness appealed to Chinese viewers, who dubbed themselves *chuan fen*, or Trump's fans.

Chinese leaders, who rarely comment on U.S. elections in public, couldn't hide their amusement at Trump the candidate. Premier Li Keqiang, at his annual press conference in March 2016, noted that the U.S. election was "lively" and had "caught the eyes of many." A few, though, were wary. "Trump is an irrational type," Lou Jiwei, then China's finance minister, told the *Wall Street Journal* a month later. "If the U.S. were to do what he proposed, then the U.S. would

not be entitled to its position as the world's major power," added the
blunt-talking Lou.

• • •

The fury of Beijing's response to Trump's Taiwan phone call and the
criticism of Trump domestically for roiling China relations caught
the Trump team by surprise. Beijing was also uncertain how to proceed. "We're somewhat ill-prepared for the Trump administration,"
an official in the Zhongnanhai leadership compound lamented at
the time. "How can we get him back on track?"

Chinese officials were accustomed to following long-standing
procedures and protocols, not to handling someone as combative
and freewheeling as Trump. China had long been the unpredictable
partner in the bilateral relationship, and U.S. diplomats sought to
understand the intentions of China's secretive Communist leadership. Now Beijing was in the uncomfortable position of trying to
make sense of a mystifying change in U.S. politics.

Beijing dispatched its most senior foreign affairs official, Yang
Jiechi, to meet with the Trump team. Yang started out as a factory
worker during the Cultural Revolution and later earned a master's
degree in economics from the London School of Economics. His
career blossomed, in part, because of his excellent English. In the
1970s, he worked as an interpreter for George H. W. Bush when the
future American president was setting up the U.S. government's
liaison office in Beijing before the two nations established diplomatic relations.

Bush called him "Tiger Yang" because his name contains the
Chinese character for tiger, a nickname that other foreign dignitaries used too, including Kissinger. He continued to rise through the
ranks in China's foreign policy establishment after he served as an
interpreter to Deng Xiaoping in the 1990s.

On December 9, Yang, Ambassador Cui, Bannon, Kushner, Peter
Navarro, and Trump national security aide K. T. McFarland huddled

in the 666 Fifth Avenue headquarters of Kushner's family real estate firm. The Trump team wanted to avoid the camera crews posted at Trump Tower.

"The territorial integrity and sovereignty of the People's Republic of China is not to be questioned," Yang began, in what amounted to a two-day lecture. "It was perfect English," says Bannon. "He never looked at a note, never missed a beat. [It was] actually magnificent." Then after a short coffee break, Yang repeated his talk nearly word for word, this time reading from papers, which Bannon interpreted as Yang's need to tell his Beijing superiors that he had delivered the formal message. "That's how mad they were," Bannon said.

Ultimately, Bannon found Yang's message "incredibly condescending," though the Trump aides heard Yang out respectfully. "The Trump people at the time, they listened to us very carefully," recalls Cui, the Chinese ambassador. "They wanted to learn more about the Chinese position and the sensitivities on issues like the Taiwan issue."

The meetings ended on a Saturday, the Jewish Sabbath, so Kushner, an observant Jew, didn't attend. In his place was retired Lieutenant General Michael Flynn, the campaign's top national security aide, who was to have a very short-lived career as the Trump White House national security advisor. Relations seemed to be back on an even keel.

The next day, December 11, though, Trump again created an uproar, this time telling *Fox News Sunday* interviewer Chris Wallace, "I don't know why we have to be bound by a One China policy unless we make a deal with China having to do with other things, including trade." Trump listed concessions he might require to keep the policy intact: help on North Korea, a revaluation of the yuan so Chinese exports would be less competitive, and a halt to military construction in the South China Sea.

The message was aimed at Beijing: "I don't want China dictating to me," he told Wallace. But it reverberated in Taiwan. Did the president-elect consider Taiwan a bargaining chip to be tossed to Beijing as part of some deal? Would he trade Taiwan for more U.S. exports to China?

In less than two weeks, Trump had sent contradictory messages about Taiwan—yes, I'll take your president's call because I have some sympathy for Taiwanese sovereignty, but no, don't count on me defending Taiwan if Beijing offers a great deal. Those contradictory impulses still define Trump, say his national security aides. On some days, he is rankled by China's insistence that Taiwan is off-limits; on other days, he is rankled that Taiwan is an obstacle to an agreement with China.

A few days later, Trump's flip-flopping earned him a rebuke from President Obama, who still had a month to go as commander in chief and whose team considered their successors to be amateurs. "If you're going to upend this [One China] understanding, you have to have thought through what the consequences are because the Chinese won't treat that like they treat some issues," Obama told the White House press corps.

• • •

The Trump China team was full of hard-liners with plenty of ideas, but no overall strategy. They listened to the counsel of business leaders with deep China experience, who made pilgrimages to Trump Tower, though they were deeply skeptical of what they heard. Trump aides blamed the China hands for being naïve in their assessment of Beijing; now they would have to deal with China's unchecked rise. Insurance executive Maurice "Hank" Greenberg was one of the most successful American businessmen in China, although his standing in Washington had plummeted after his American International Group teetered on bankruptcy in 2008 and had to be rescued by the federal government. He was also a multimillion-dollar contributor to Trump's opponents during the Republican primary, another strike against him.

When Greenberg, then ninety-one years old, met with about a dozen Trump aides, he tried to impress them with the importance of the U.S.-China relationship. Russia and China were America's two greatest adversaries, he said, and the United States couldn't afford to take them both on. Continuing to work closely with China made the most sense because it benefited the United States and the global economy, he said. Don't treat China as an enemy.

Navarro, hot-tempered even when unprovoked, grew red in the face and lashed out at Greenberg. Others in the room got him to back off. Michael Pillsbury, the Hudson Institute China scholar working on the transition, says he told Navarro that Greenberg deserved respect. "You may disagree with him, but Hank landed at Normandy," he said of the World War II veteran. Says Greenberg of the session: "Navarro was very hostile about China."

A meeting with former Treasury Secretary Hank Paulson at the General Motors building in midtown Manhattan was friendlier. He laid out for the group his reasons to continue the annual meetings he started, called the Strategic Economic Dialogue. Though Paulson considered the sessions, which brought together a slew of senior Chinese and American officials, crucial to ironing out problems with China, the Obama team found the sessions less useful.

Many Trump advisers considered them an enormous waste of time. In their view, the meetings locked senior officials into legalistic negotiations that did little to change how China operated. Worse, there was no mechanism for enforcing Chinese pledges. Although there was some interest in continuing the efforts among Trump's more moderate economic advisers, Kushner later told Paulson they weren't going to go ahead with them.

Before Bannon had turned into a nationalist provocateur, he had a short career at Goldman Sachs, when Paulson was a senior executive. Bannon addressed him as a onetime colleague. How should the Trump team approach governing, he asked Paulson. "Do you think we should do things strategically, one after the other? Or should we just flood the zone and come out with everything all at once?" The surprised Paulson chose the former. "Hank, you're such an aggressive guy," Bannon said. "I thought you'd say flood the zone."

Flood the zone was precisely what the Trump transition team had been thinking.

For Trump's first workdays in the Oval Office, Navarro was planning an economic and trade offensive. If he had his way, the new president would accuse China of manipulating its currency, a process that could lead to tariffs on Chinese goods; impose tariffs on steel imports, to help the struggling U.S. industry cope with excess production from Chinese mills; and threaten to pull out of the North American Free Trade Agreement unless Mexico and Canada negotiated a replacement within ninety days.

The Trump team wanted to make Mexico a place where U.S. companies could relocate their China operations, but they first wanted a more advantageous trade deal with Mexico. Bannon was planning an additional provocation: have a U.S. aircraft carrier battle group sail through the Taiwan Strait separating the island from the mainland.

The transition team also put together a China strategy group, including Pillsbury, the Hudson Institute scholar whose book, *The Hundred-Year Marathon*, controversially argues that the United States is blind to China's secret plan to overtake it as the global superpower. Bannon carried a dog-eared copy of the Pillsbury book in his backpack and tried—he figured unsuccessfully—to get Trump to read it.

The new team also included Matt Pottinger, who had served in the Marines under General Flynn as an intelligence officer. The boyish-looking Pottinger, in his mid-forties, had an unusual background. From 1998 to 2005, he was a journalist based in China for Reuters and then the *Wall Street Journal*.

As a reporter, the Mandarin-speaking Pottinger had covered the Chinese energy industry, politics, and Beijing's cover-up of the

SARS epidemic. He was enormously skeptical about Chinese intentions. After leaving the Marines in 2010, he moved to New York City and founded a business investigating Chinese companies for American exporters and investors, where he turned up cases of fraud. That further reinforced his wariness of China's government and party.

Explaining his decision to leave journalism for the military, he wrote in the *Wall Street Journal* in 2005 that "living in China also shows you what a nondemocratic country can do to its citizens.

"I've seen protesters tackled and beaten by plainclothes police in Tiananmen Square, and I've been videotaped by government agents while I was talking to a source," he continued. "I've been arrested and forced to flush my notes down a toilet to keep the police from getting them, and I've been punched in the face in a Beijing Starbucks by a government goon who was trying to keep me from investigating a Chinese company's sale of nuclear fuel to other countries."

The China strategy group churned out about a dozen papers on meeting the Chinese challenge, whether in Antarctica (seabed minerals) or deep space (satellite warfare). They focused especially on what some team members called national security "seams"—areas where rules of engagement weren't clear and China could try to exploit the uncertainty. Wary about possible Chinese surveillance of Trump Tower, the team resolved not to send their work via Wi-Fi, other than to print out papers.

Toward the end of the transition, Pottinger put together a ten-page paper on overall strategy and briefed the president-elect that he shouldn't expect engagement alone to bring about economic and political liberalization. The new administration needed to increase pressure on Beijing economically and diplomatically.

"The key is actually getting leverage on China," Bannon emailed Pillsbury on December 20.

By the time Trump took office on January 20, 2017, none of the work was ready to execute. Only one proposal went into effect.

On workday number one, Trump scrapped U.S. participation in the Trans-Pacific Partnership, a proposed trade pact of a dozen Pacific Rim nations, including Japan. That agreement spelled out rules that the United States someday hoped would hem in China economically. They included requirements that state-owned enterprises operate like commercial ones, antitrust policy not be used arbitrarily to punish companies, and data be allowed to flow freely across borders and not be blocked by something like the Great Firewall of China.

Trump had argued during his campaign that TPP was yet another trade deal that encouraged U.S. companies to move factories offshore. The Trump trade team feared that China's auto industry would get a huge boost by shipping auto parts to Japan and other TPP nations, where they would be assembled into automobiles and shipped to the United States, tariff-free.

But Trump's national security advisors saw the scrapping of TPP as a lost opportunity. The trade pact would have strengthened ties with Japan, which they considered a frontline state in any clash with China.

• • •

One idea broached during the transition did immediately carry over to the new administration: a one-on-one meeting between Trump and Xi Jinping.

Trump had marketed himself to the American public as a deal maker since at least his 1987 bestseller, *The Art of the Deal*. He saw himself as a businessman who could pull off agreements that eluded others. During the campaign, he was careful not to attack Xi personally; all blame went to his predecessors, who had let China get away with murder. He needed to meet Xi to gauge what kind of guy he was and how best to deal with him.

Xi suggested he was open to such a meeting, Kissinger told Trump when they conferred again on December 6. Around that time, John Thornton, a former Goldman Sachs senior executive, also met with Trump and encouraged him to move ahead with a meeting.

Thornton had been responsible for Goldman's China business and developed deep ties among Beijing's Communist Party elite. They included Wang Qishan, whom Xi Jinping had entrusted to run his anticorruption campaign and then appointed vice president. Thornton was also one of the few Goldman Sachs alumni whom Bannon still admired, and he helped Thornton get an audience with Trump. Though Thornton was a Democrat, he was excited that Trump was promising to put China at the center of his new administration's agenda.

"You must have a relationship of trust with Xi Jinping," Thornton advised the president-elect. "Invite him and his wife to Mar-a-Lago and make it entirely personal. Get to know each other and what your visions are for your countries." Xi's personal history, he told Trump, was like a metaphor for modern Chinese history. Trump liked the idea. "Let's do it," he ordered Bannon.

But Trump's disparagement of the One China policy had complicated a possible meeting. Beijing sought out an ally among the Trump team and turned to Kushner as a go-between, a role he readily embraced. Both Trump and Xi rely on a small circle of trusted advisers. China's tightly controlled media built up Kushner, calling him America's "first son-in-law," and in reference to his slim build, "a fresh breeze in the world of potbellied CEOs."

Kushner was aware he was being courted and tried not to put the Chinese too much at ease. Kissinger had advised him earlier that foreign nations would be nervous about Trump because of his America First campaign and because they knew so little about him. "Don't make them not nervous because that could be a real strategic advantage for President Trump," Kissinger advised.

Beijing demanded that Trump make clear his support for the policy before Xi would meet with him. Beijing was pushing Trump to back off, and he did, despite his tough talk about China.

In December, after consulting again with Kissinger, the Trump team turned down a proposed meeting with the Dalai Lama, the Tibetan religious leader whom China views as an enemy. The following month, Pillsbury, the Trump China team member, published an article in the *National Interest* called "Trump Can Stand Up to China Without Sparking War." Trump didn't plan to change the One China policy, he argued, and hinted that the president-elect opposed selling Taiwan F-35 stealth fighters.

Kushner's wife, Ivanka Trump, helped out, too. On February 1, 2017, shortly after the inauguration, she attended a Chinese New Year celebration at Beijing's embassy in Washington. The next day, she posted a video of her daughter, Arabella, singing a New Year's song in Mandarin, which went viral in China.

On February 9, Trump made his first phone call to President Xi after taking office. In a highly scripted exchange, negotiated by Kushner and Ambassador Cui, Xi said to Trump: "I would like you to uphold the One China policy."

"At your request, I will do that," the U.S. president replied.

Trump then invited him to Mar-a-Lago, as prearranged, and Xi accepted. The decks were cleared for the summit.

Before they met, though, Japanese Prime Minister Shinzo Abe, who was wary of any U.S.-China détente, got his own Mar-a-Lago meeting. To make sure nothing went wrong, Abe consulted with psychologists for advice on dealing with Trump. "He strongly dislikes being told what he does not know," one of the psychologists said, according to a *Nikkei* report.

The mid-February meeting went well. The two men played golf at Trump's Florida resort and plotted a response to a North Korea missile test while sitting in a Mar-a-Lago dining room. Club members gawked and took mobile phone videos.

With the Abe session out of the way, Ambassador Cui sent Kushner drafts of a joint statement that China and the United States could issue after President Xi and President Trump met in Florida.

Elsewhere, the two nations' top officials were growing closer, too. In March, Secretary of State Rex Tillerson made his first trip to Beijing since taking office. Before meeting with China's Foreign Minister Wang Yi at the Diaoyutai State Guesthouse, Tillerson described the basis for U.S.-China ties as "nonconflict, nonconfrontation, mutual respect, and win-win cooperation." That was the exact language used by Xi in 2013 to define a "new model of great power relations" between the two nations. The choice of words stunned many in Washington while pleasing Tillerson's Chinese hosts.

Kushner played a role in Tillerson's choice of words. Says a White House official: "Diplomats love to get hung up on the wording when the actions are a lot more important and relevant."

Xi and his stylish wife, Peng Liyuan, a prominent folk singer in China, arrived at Mar-a-Lago on April 6. Beijing did all it could to make sure the meeting would be a success. In the past, Chinese leaders announced purchases of Boeing aircraft at such occasions—sometimes taking credit for purchases they had announced earlier. This time, on the day Xi touched down in Florida, Beijing approved three of thirty-six product trademarks that Ivanka Trump had applied for in 2016, beginning a pattern of approving Ivanka trademarks before important trade events. (A Chinese government spokesman said the decision simply reflected "the principle of giving equal protection to foreign trademark holders.")

After a series of internal fights at the White House about whether to turn the meeting into a formal summit, the Thornton idea of a friendly encounter carried the day. Eighteen honor guards lined up to salute the leaders. Chinese and American flags flapped in the breeze.

The two leaders spent hours together at teas, working lunches, walks around the compound, and chats on elegant sofas. The first ladies visited Bak Middle School of the Arts in West Palm Beach to watch student performances. The Kushner children, five-year-old Arabella and her three-year-old brother Joseph, were wheeled out to sing a Chinese folk song, "Jasmine Flower," for Xi and his wife.

"Mr. Trump was at his convivial best," reported the *Straits Times* of Singapore.

The agenda for the meeting was clear from the planning sessions. Trump wanted to convince his Chinese counterpart to narrow the United States' vast trade deficit with China, and to police Chinese companies that trade with North Korea in order to hobble Pyongyang's nuclear and missile programs. Xi wanted to stabilize the bilateral relationship so he could focus on assuring his dominance in a Communist Party leadership reshuffle scheduled for late 2017.

The two leaders bonded over military action. As they ate dessert, the president confided to Xi that he was about to launch fifty-nine missiles at targets in Syria in retaliation for a gas attack by the Assad regime on Syrian rebels. "We had the most beautiful piece of chocolate cake that you have ever seen," Trump later said. "And President Xi was enjoying it." During their conversations, Xi explained the long, tangled history of China and Korea. Before that, Trump later said he thought Beijing could easily take care of any North Korean threat. "But after listening for ten minutes, I realized it's not so easy," he said later.

The leaders even did some business. They agreed to create the United States–China Comprehensive Economic Dialogue, which was Trump's version of Hank Paulson's Strategic Economic Dialogue. Officials from both sides would work on "an ambitious agenda and meeting scheduled to show progress and demonstrate meaningful results." The negotiations were to cover national security, law enforcement, cybersecurity, and social and cultural issues. But the heart of the new talks was the Comprehensive Economic Dialogue, bureaucratic-speak for trade negotiations. The only difference with past efforts was a short deadline—just one hundred days to show "meaningful results."

President Trump appointed his longtime business ally Wilbur Ross to oversee the trade portion. Trump called Ross, whom he had made Commerce secretary, one of his "killers"—the awesome negotiators who would, like Trump's campaign motto, make America great again. Ross seemed cut out for the job. As a private equity investor, he had made money when Washington turned to protectionism and he had made money when it turned to free trade.

In 2002, when President George W. Bush imposed steel tariffs, Ross bought bankrupt steelmaker LTV Corporation and merged it with Bethlehem Steel, Weirton Steel, and Acme Steel to form International Steel Group. He took the company public in 2003 and sold it later for $4.5 billion. Ross started scooping up steel companies before Bush decided to go ahead with tariffs and says he lobbied the administration to adopt protection.

When Congress passed the Central America Free Trade Agreement (CAFTA), which eliminated tariffs with Central American nations and the Dominican Republic, his textile firm, International Textile Group, shipped factory jobs to Nicaragua. CAFTA passed the House by two votes in 2005; opponents blamed Ross's lobbying for making the difference. It was the kind of trade deal that Donald Trump had spent the presidential campaign attacking as a job destroyer.

"I think I helped" get the trade deal approved, says Ross in an interview. "I testified quite a bit for it." He defends CAFTA because the United States generally runs a trade surplus with the six CAFTA nations.

Despite the bonhomie of the Mar-a-Lago meeting, Beijing started to prepare for the worst. China's Commerce Ministry assigned a senior economist at a government think tank to lead a study on the impact of a U.S.-China trade war. Pei Changhong, director-general of the Institute of Economics of the Chinese Academy of Social Sciences, often gets tapped by government agencies for advice on trade and investment issues.

"The entire cabinet picked by Trump seem to be China hawks," said a Chinese policy maker at the time. "We need to be prepared for the high likelihood of increased trade frictions with the U.S."

10

THINGS FALL APART,
SUMMER–FALL 2017

It didn't take long for the new Trump White House to dissolve into acrimony over trade policy. China wasn't the cause, at least not at first. Steve Bannon, Peter Navarro, and other campaign veterans tried Bannon's idea of flooding the zone and prepared to pile one trade offensive on top of another. They would protect steel workers with tariffs (although that would piss off European, Japanese, and Canadian allies that export steel) while preparing to pull out of the North American Free Trade Agreement (again pissing off Canada and adding Mexico to the aggrieved) and gearing up to battle China (for which the United States would need as many allies as possible). Navarro prepared charts with a timeline showing all this was possible by the end of the first year.

Except it really wasn't possible, not if much of the economic team hired by the new president had its way. National Economic Council Director Gary Cohn, a combative, plain-talking former Goldman Sachs president, warned the president that tariffs would tank the stock market. Treasury Secretary Steven Mnuchin, another Goldman Sachs alum who also had been the campaign's finance chief, cautioned about the impact on the global economy. Both reminded the president of his other priorities, especially passing a huge corporate tax cut, for which the White House needed the votes of Senate Republicans who, unlike the president, were generally free traders. The battle lines were drawn.

Trump had campaigned like a Bannon-style nationalist but had his feet firmly in the camps of both the nationalists and the financiers, whom Bannon and company dubbed the globalists. Yes, Trump wanted action on trade. But no, he didn't want to risk a stock market plunge or a defeat of his tax bill, which his economists told him would lift growth and let him show up his many critics. A Blue-Collar Trump was at odds with a Wall Street Trump, as would be the case throughout his presidency. His aides jockeyed for power by playing to one side of the president's personality or the other, never knowing whether a Trump decision would stick.

Navarro, especially, seemed outmatched by his Wall Street foes. Before the inauguration, the *Economist* magazine predicted the one-time academic would become "one of the world's most powerful economists" because of his prominent campaign role. The president-elect named him the head of a new, grandly titled National Trade Council.

But after Trump was sworn in, Cohn and company made sure the council was stillborn; no members were ever appointed. Navarro was assigned a staff of one, given a small office across an alley from the White House, and had no scheduled time to see the president. Bannon had to intercede to make sure Navarro wasn't consigned to a job in the basement of the Commerce Department.

Stewing, Navarro told colleagues in March 2017 that it had been fifty days since he had time with the president. "It's like fucking 'Game of Thrones' around here," he complained. He was saved from a Red Wedding–like demise when Trump finally noticed his absence. "Where's my Peter?" the president asked his aides in March, and Navarro was once again included in meetings. Afterward, on

March 27, Navarro prepared a memo for the president: "Subject: Future Direction of Trade Policy."

"It is impossible to get a trade action to your desk for consideration in a timely manner," Navarro complained. "If this situation is allowed to persist, this Administration is likely to fail on trade and suffer catastrophic consequences." To make sure the president didn't miss the point, he underlined the part about failing on trade and catastrophic consequences.

Who was to blame? Two White House trade staffers, Kenneth Juster (he later became ambassador to India) and Andrew Quinn (he was quickly sent back to his home agency of the trade representative's office), and Navarro's two biggest rivals: Cohn and Mnuchin. The "Wall Street Wing" has "effectively blocked or delayed every proposed action on trade since the President signed the order withdrawing the U.S. from TPP [Trans-Pacific Partnership]," he wrote, underlining the accusation.

How could the president rectify the situation? Navarro urged Trump to have Cabinet Staff Secretary Rob Porter, a Navarro foe, "fast track" trade initiatives and make clear to White House staff that none of Navarro's many opponents "have the ability to delay, or veto any trade action OR make changes to any proposed trade action" unless the changes are approved by him, his ally Wilbur Ross, and an unnamed "senior policy adviser." That probably referred to either Steve Bannon or another trade hard-liner, Stephen Miller, who focused far more on immigration than trade.

In the memo, Navarro admitted that his National Trade Council so far was "a weak legal fiction rather than a strong administrative fact." Why? "I was not provided the rank, authority, staff, or access to fulfill my assigned mission," he wrote, again underlining the sentence for emphasis. Journalist Bob Woodward reported that Porter didn't forward the memo to Trump—yet another example of the globalists frustrating Navarro.

With fresh White House access, the wiry, resourceful Navarro would try to slip into the Oval Office without others noticing. He saw himself as the protector of the president's trade agenda doing battle with those who would turn Trump into a conventional free trade Republican. The president had promised during the campaign to withdraw from NAFTA; now Navarro told the president that Cohn and others were keeping him from fulfilling that pledge. By April 2017, Trump's patience had run out. He told his aides he wanted to get out of NAFTA, a process that required giving Mexico and Canada written notice sixty days before exiting.

In the intimate world of Washington policy makers and influence peddlers, word of the president's threat rocketed from administration aides opposed to NAFTA withdrawal to lobbying firms, embassies, and trade associations supportive of the trade pact. They, in turn, had their most influential members deluge White House and cabinet contacts with warnings of disaster should Trump carry out his threat.

Mexico's president and Canada's prime minister phoned Trump asking him to reconsider. "Let me think about it," the president replied. Business groups urged their CEOs to call the highest-ranking Trump officials they could reach. Since the 1994 enactment of the trade deal, Mexico, Canada, and the United States had operated as an economic zone, with auto components, farm produce, and electronics shuttling across the border duty-free. Unraveling that arrangement could injure companies and workers in all three nations.

A political presentation by Agriculture Secretary Sonny Perdue ended the threat. He showed Trump a map of the United States with the states and counties that would be hit hardest by NAFTA's dissolution, especially agricultural areas that had voted heavily for Trump. "It's your base in states that are important presidential swing states," Perdue said. "You just can't do this."

Trump relented, but Mexico and Canada had been put on notice of his impatience, which was perhaps the theatrical president's purpose. The White House put out a statement saying the president agreed "not to terminate NAFTA at this time," but said he expected renegotiations to begin shortly.

By contrast, in the spring of 2017, confronting China wasn't even the president's top priority in Asia. North Korea was. Starting in February 2017, the Kim Jong Un regime fired a series of ever-more-powerful missiles, including some that flew over Japan, one that could reach U.S. troops in Guam, and, in July, one that could hit the U.S. mainland. In September, North Korea detonated underground what it claimed was a hydrogen bomb. Trump matched the military show with escalating rhetoric, threatening in August "fire, fury and frankly power, the likes of which the world has never seen before" if North Korea continued along this path.

A frustrated Trump turned to China for help. During his April summit with Xi Jinping in Mar-a-Lago, the two leaders had spent much of their substantive discussions on North Korea. Trump's national security aides, led by National Security Advisor H. R. Mc-Master, briefed the president on how best to convince Xi to help. Pressing North Korea to give up nuclear weapons was in China's interest, McMaster advised the president to argue. North Korea was bound to sell missiles to other nations, which could threaten China. A nuclear North Korea would unleash an arms race, with South Korea, Japan, and maybe even Taiwan building their own city-busting weapons.

There was no need, McMaster and others argued, to offer China a better deal on trade if it cooperates. Mixing China trade and North Korea nuclear issues would give Beijing an edge in upcoming trade talks, where Beijing could dangle help on North Korea in exchange for Trump dropping his trade threats.

In some of the conversations, Trump hewed to the advice, translating it into his own vernacular. "You know," he said to the Chinese leader, "you could solve this if you wanted to." But to Trump, trade was at the center of everything he did, both to reduce the U.S.

trade deficit, which he saw as the cause of America's slow growth, and as leverage for other issues.

"I explained to the President of China that a trade deal with the U.S. will be far better for them if they solve the North Korean problem!" he tweeted on April 11, two days after Xi jetted from Mar-a-Lago to Beijing. "Had a very good call last night with the President of China concerning the menace of North Korea," Trump tweeted the following morning. Security aides shrugged; the president's tweets caught them by surprise nearly as often as they did everyone else.

With North Korea on his mind, Trump quickly made peace with Beijing on another economic front. In mid-April, he decided not to fight China over its currency policy, despite his campaign promise to do so.

Twice a year, the Treasury Department puts out a report on currency manipulation, as a warning that it is watching to see whether trading partners are cheapening their currency to give their exporters an edge. During the 1990s and early 2000s, many economists accused China of keeping the yuan undervalued by as much as 30 percent to help it gobble up U.S. markets. Steel makers, machine tool companies, furniture makers, and labor unions added China's currency practices to their list of complaints. Trump took up their cause during the campaign.

A designation as currency manipulator has little immediate consequence. Treasury is only required to "take action to initiate negotiations" with the offending country—and the United States and China are continually negotiating anyway. But the designation has political importance. The United States would be accusing China of cheating, which would offend Beijing and raise pressure on the White House to impose sanctions. A succession of Treasury secretaries warned Beijing that they would be forced to label China a currency manipulator—or that Congress would force them to do so—to cajole their Chinese counterparts to push up the value of the yuan. But they didn't carry out their threats.

By the time Trump was sworn in, American pressure had largely succeeded. China's central bank by then had spent more than $1 trillion in reserves to prop up the value of the Chinese currency, not drive it down. With China's growth slowing, the People's Bank of China feared Chinese investors would trade their yuan for dollars as a way to preserve their savings, triggering a run on the currency that would further weaken the yuan. China also depended greatly on foreign oil, iron ore, soybeans, semiconductors, and many other goods and services priced in dollars, all of which would become more expensive to purchase with a devalued yuan.

Still, breaking a major campaign pledge related to China was a big move. North Korea was the justification. "Why would I call China a currency manipulator when they are working with us on the North Korean problem?" Trump tweeted on April 16. Later, the president explained in an interview with the book's coauthor, Bob, "For the first year, I was focused—I was doing North Korea and I didn't want to let the negotiations [with China] come in the way."

Around the same time, Commerce Secretary Wilbur Ross was trying to work out a quick trade deal with China as part of the Comprehensive Economic Dialogue announced at Mar-a-Lago, which had a hundred-day deadline. In May, Ross reported a breakthrough that he breathlessly characterized as a "herculean accomplishment."

After only one month of negotiations, the two nations released a joint statement on May 11 touting a consensus in ten broad categories, including agricultural trade, financial services, investment, and energy. Ross even endorsed Xi Jinping's pet trillion-dollar project, the Belt and Road Initiative, aimed at building infrastructure in nations around that world, although Trump's national security team viewed the initiative as a threat that could expand China's power in Asia. Privately, Ross also offered to start free trade negotiations with China, say members of his negotiating team, a position that was the opposite of the hard-line approach Trump promised during the 2016 campaign.

"China just agreed that the U.S. will be allowed to sell beef, and other major products, into China once again. This is REAL news!" an enthusiastic Trump tweeted the following day.

But the real news was that the Chinese were repackaging stale offers and Ross, who was new at his job and inexperienced in trade negotiations, didn't realize it. China had discussed reopening its beef market as early as 2006 after banning U.S. beef imports three years earlier amid concerns over mad cow disease. In 2013, then–Vice President Joe Biden made another pitch for beef sales during a visit to China. "You can make me a hero" if you reopened the market, he told Xi Jinping. The Chinese thought about helping Biden but eventually did nothing.

For Beijing, beef sales were a concession it could offer whenever the political heat from Washington reached a boil, as was now occurring. Before sales could proceed, though, China insisted on tough regulations. Cattle producers had to track the birthplace of the cattle, slaughter them before they were thirty months old, and make sure they hadn't been injected with certain growth hormones—all this from a government that was unable to keep domestic suppliers from selling rotten food.

At least that pledge led to some sales. China also promised to open its electronic payment and processing market to Visa, Master-Card, and other U.S. firms. This was a replay of the pledge China made when it joined the World Trade Organization sixteen years earlier and which it hadn't carried out. Rather than allow foreign competition, China created its own card-processing firm, state-owned UnionPay. The Ross deal committed China to "begin the licensing process," which "should lead to full and prompt market access."

More than a year later, Visa was still waiting for the regulatory okay to set up a wholly owned business in China. American Express won approval to set up card-clearing services, but as a joint venture with a Chinese firm, not as a wholly owned company. MasterCard was even more frustrated. In early 2019, the company restarted its efforts to crack the Chinese market by joining with a Chinese company close to the country's central bank, which is in charge of approving credit card businesses. The joint venture finally won regulatory approval in March 2020.

Over the two months following the joint statement, Ross focused on curbing China's steel production to relieve import pressure on U.S. steelmakers, say members of his negotiating team. That was a cause Trump championed and an issue that Ross, a former steel executive, presumably knew well. "No steel, no deal" was the Ross group's motto. In his autobiography, Blackstone Group CEO Stephen Schwarzman says Ross asked him to help out. He pressed the Chinese to cut their steel capacity by 15 to 20 percent. When Beijing accepted, Schwarzman wrote, "Wilbur was delighted." But the Chinese offer amounted to simply speeding up by a year its schedule of closing outmoded steel mills.

Beijing's lead negotiator was Vice Premier Wang Yang, a savvy politician who had burnished his role as an economic reformer when he ran the southern province of Guangdong, which borders Hong Kong, and is known for entrepreneurship and technology development. He had been a political star since he was named mayor of a Yangtze River port city when he was thirty-three, where the locals dubbed him "baby mayor."

Despite Trump's tough campaign rhetoric, Wang was certain U.S.-China bonds were strong. In 2013, he had compared the bilateral relationship to a married couple. "We fight often, but in the end we have to live together," he said during a meeting with Obama's Treasury secretary. The two countries can't divorce like Wendi and Rupert Murdoch had just done, he continued, referring to the high-profile split between the media mogul, who owns the company publishing this book, and his younger, Chinese-born wife. "It's just too expensive."

In his negotiations with Ross, Wang believed he didn't have to give much to satisfy the Americans. Chinese money would deliver the kind of results Trump wanted, he figured.

Encouraged by the progress made by Ross and Wang, China's giant sovereign wealth fund, China Investment Corporation, sought out the book's coauthor, Lingling, to make sure U.S. investors and government officials knew that it would "significantly increase" its investment in the United States, especially in highways, rail lines, and high-tech manufacturing plants. At the time, CIC had more than $200 billion in foreign assets and frequently complained about the difficulty of investing in the United States. "There is a potential for Chinese companies to make more investments in the U.S. and vice versa," said the firm's president, Tu Guangshao.

Chinese officials considered sweetening the deal they offered Ross by opening China's market further to foreign banks, insurance companies, and brokerages. But they decided that wasn't necessary for an agreement, at least at that time. Besides, Wang had his eye on a Communist Party meeting in the fall where a new slate of leaders would be appointed and he was in line for a promotion. Better to play it safe than be criticized as yielding to the Americans.

Ross didn't push back hard enough, say members of his team. With a tight deadline, he ignored the tough issues that were to become the heart of the U.S.-China trade battles of the following two years. The United States was certain that Chinese firms pressured their American counterparts to transfer technology, and Chinese government agencies threw up barriers to foreigners selling electric cars, computing networking, and other equipment in China, while forcing U.S. firms to store sensitive data locally. None of these issues were addressed.

"Wilbur Ross was crucified on a cross of steel," says James Green, then the senior trade negotiator in the U.S. embassy in Beijing.

In July, the two sides planned to finish talks and declare victory. They would issue a joint statement, hold a White House press conference, and then celebrate over drinks at a Washington party hosted by Ross. But on the morning of July 19, those plans were scrapped. Details of the proposed deal circulated among senior officials, including the new U.S. trade representative, Robert Lighthizer, a trade policy veteran who hadn't been in office when the talks began. Ross had been naïve, Lighthizer told the president. It was a terrible deal. National Economic Council Director Gary Cohn and others echoed the criticism. Infuriated, Trump berated Ross as incompetent. "Shut the fucking thing down," he said. You're not running China trade any longer, he told Ross.

No longer able to produce a joint statement, the two sides made separate comments in the afternoon. Both noted that reducing the trade deficit was a shared objective. They disagreed on everything else. China said that the two sides would follow up with year-long negotiations. The Americans denied that. They had no interest in the endless negotiations pursued by previous administrations, they told reporters.

Ross, then seventy-nine years old, says he didn't screw up. "The president changed his mind [on what he wanted] and was upset," he says in an interview. Some of the deals he negotiated played a role in later talks, Ross says.

"It's the first time in decades that I've had a boss," he adds. "There are inherent frustrations with having a boss. A boss doesn't always accept your opinions." Still, Ross says, the Commerce job is "the most invigorating thing I've done in twenty years."

Many in the administration, though, say he performed woefully and blame that on his inexperience in government and his advanced age. Susan Thornton, a longtime State Department China expert who served for a year in the Trump administration, said Ross misunderstood what was needed. He was trying to deliver what he thought Trump wanted—some progress on steel and increased exports—and didn't realize that was insufficient.

"The Chinese were happy to deal with Ross," she says. "They knew he was a businessman, that he does deals. They thought, 'We're Chinese. We know how to do deals. We'll sit down and haggle.'" But lost in the back-and-forth were more nuanced issues that aren't the stuff of business deal making—how to negotiate the opening of markets, which takes a combination of legal, regulatory, and political decision making, and enormous patience. "That's what Lighthizer does," she says.

· · ·

For Wang Yang, the talks ended happily. In October, he was promoted to the Communist Party's top ruling body, the seven-member Politburo Standing Committee. He is now in charge of the nation's top political advisory body, called the Chinese People's Political Consultative Conference. For Robert Lighthizer, the talks marked his ascension to the upper ranks of Trump advisers, with a major say on China issues.

Trump didn't bond quickly with the tall, gravelly voiced Lighthizer, a steel industry lawyer who was about to turn seventy years old in the fall of 2017. When Trump was toying with the idea of running for president in 2011 and was pilloried as a protectionist, Lighthizer wrote an opinion piece for the *Washington Times* defending him. Many Republicans supported tariffs, Lighthizer argued, including Abraham Lincoln. "Skepticism toward pure free-trade dogma can be seen as well in more recent Republican leaders," Lighthizer wrote, citing Ronald Reagan's battles with Japan. But the op-ed was aimed more at bolstering Lighthizer's trade philosophy than it was at establishing a relationship with Trump, whom he didn't meet until the 2016 campaign.

Trump's anti-China advisers recommended Lighthizer for the trade job. "Lighthizer is my trade lawyer," Ross told the president, which wasn't the case, though the two were allies in fighting steel imports. (Ross kept repeating the claim after Lighthizer joined the administration, as a way to try to become top dog on trade policy.)

"What is his name? Lighthamer? Lighthimer? Lighthower?" Trump would say to his aides, running through a half-dozen mispronunciations of Lighthizer's name. Lighthizer seemed stiff and wooden to Trump, who responded to big personalities.

Still, Lighthizer was the obvious candidate to help a president who wanted to make trade deals a focus of his administration but who lacked expertise. As deputy U.S. trade representative under Reagan, Lighthizer had battled Japan on steel issues in the mid-1980s, once getting so frustrated he took a Japanese proposal, turned it into a paper airplane, and floated it back to the Japanese negotiators, in what he considered a joke. "Missile man," Tokyo dubbed him.

As a prominent attorney for U.S. Steel, he sued to halt Chinese imports, though his team of lawyers rarely visited China to investigate. He also wrote opinion pieces opposing China's entry into the World Trade Organization. His practice had done well enough that he was worth between $20 million and $76 million, according to government filings. In 2010, he laid out for a congressional panel how to contain a rising China, using trade law to challenge Chinese currency practices, protect domestic industries, and strip China of the benefits of WTO membership. "We must stop being so passive," he told the panel's members. "We should not assume that aggressive action on our part would automatically make the situation worse."

Lighthizer's friends said he never expected to have a chance to put his ideas into action. Neither political party was looking for an avowed protectionist to lead trade policy. He considered his testimony a kind of valedictory as he contemplated retirement in a few years. When Trump named him U.S. trade representative, battling

China became his mission. "This is what he had been preparing for his whole life," says his brother Jim.

He also wasn't the uptight Washingtonian that Trump assumed he was. Although he was a doctor's son, he saw himself as a blue-collar product of his struggling hometown, Ashtabula, Ohio. On his iPhone, he has two versions of the Bob Dylan song with the line, "I'll look for you in old Honolul-a, San Francisco, Ashtabula." One is by Dylan, the other by Madeleine Peyroux.

For years he raced a red Porsche 911 Targa at a track in West Virginia. When he turned forty years old, he installed a big oil painting of himself in the parlor of his suburban Maryland home. "I think everyone should have one," he joked with friends. "I don't mean a painting of yourself; I mean a painting of me." (He still has the painting, though he displays it less ostentatiously in his new home not far from the president's Mar-a-Lago estate.)

Lighthizer caught rides to his Florida home on Air Force One and used it to develop a rapport with Trump, who shares a similar chip-on-his-shoulder sense of humor and appreciates Lighthizer's off-color jokes. The two began to banter about who was tougher when it came to tariffs. The trade representative also struck up a friendship with Kushner and made him a part of negotiations with Mexico, which brought him closer to the first family.

Kushner helped Lighthizer understand how Trump thought and what he wanted from different deals, and to understand when a Trump "yes" was actually a "yes," and not just a lukewarm okay. That helped Lighthizer avoid the pitfalls that ensnared other Trump officials.

Lighthizer had once been a senior staffer to Senator Bob Dole and learned how to succeed at working for a politician who doesn't want to share the limelight. "Bob recognizes there's one king and he ain't it," says his brother. Or as Lighthizer puts it: "I stay in the trade lane and out of the press."

As the new administration sought to rebound from the Comprehensive Economic Dialogue debacle, Lighthizer convinced officials that they should dust off a part of trade law that hadn't been used much for decades: Section 301 of the Trade Act of 1974.

To justify tariffs or other sanctions under that provision, administration lawyers had to show China engaged in a policy or practice that is "unjustifiable and burdens or restricts United States commerce." How hard could that be? Didn't that define China's trade practices? Grounding their China strategy in long-standing U.S. law would also reduce the chances that a district court judge somewhere would halt their plans if sued, as had happened many times with Trump's hard-line immigration policies.

Since China joined the World Trade Organization in 2001, successive U.S. administrations had largely given up on unilateral trade actions and sued China through the WTO instead, a frustrating process that would take years to get a decision, and where the United States could lose the case. Lighthizer had criticized that change in trade policy during his 2010 congressional testimony. He called Section 301 "a powerful tool with which to influence our trading partners." The United States would act as trade prosecutor, judge, and jury.

Years earlier, Section 301 had been criticized for precisely that reason. In April 1989, forty economists, including four Nobel laureates and four former chairmen of the White House Council of Economic Advisers, signed a statement criticizing the measure because it allowed the United States to bully less powerful nations. Two years later, University of Minnesota law professor Robert Hudec, a major figure in international trade law, attacked the law's "towering self-righteousness." Now Lighthizer would revive it.

In early August, Lighthizer made his case to senior White House advisers and cabinet officials gathered in the White House's Roosevelt Room. "China is tap, tap, tapping us along," he said, using one of President Trump's favorite phrases, which he brought to Washington from the New York real estate world. The New Yorkers used the term to describe being jerked around; for Lighthizer it meant that Beijing regularly promised policy changes but didn't deliver them. He punctuated his talk with bar charts showing how the U.S. trade deficit with China ballooned despite one U.S.-China negotiation after another. Beijing continued to unfairly subsidize its companies and rip off American technology, he argued.

U.S. Ambassador to China Terry Branstad, linked by telephone, asked for a delay. He wanted time to start another round of trade talks based on the rapport he was developing with Chinese leaders, but found little support. The group backed Lighthizer's proposal to start a formal investigation of China for unfair trade practices using Section 301. "Lighthizer's historical narrative hit home," says a senior Trump official.

The president wasn't part of that meeting, but he eventually agreed, though he wasn't sure why they needed to go through such legal contortions. "Bring me tariffs," he regularly told his advisers.

Bluster aside, Trump was wary about making a public announcement of his decision. Once again, the reason was North Korea. In early August 2017, the United Nations Security Council was debating sanctions on Pyongyang for its missile tests. UN Ambassador Nikki Haley argued that the effort was useless without Chinese support. Why risk angering Beijing now? The White House was putting together a Section 301 announcement for around August 3, when the president, surrounded by supportive business leaders, would launch his China trade offensive. That was called off until after the Security Council voted on August 5. When the resolution passed unanimously, Haley personally thanked China for its help.

The Section 301 announcement was rescheduled for August 14, when the White House was once again in turmoil. White supremacists had marched through downtown Charlottesville, Virginia, several days earlier carrying tiki torches and shouting, "Jews will not replace us." A young protestor was killed in the melee. President Trump's response was tepid, at best, blaming the violence "on many sides" and then staying silent for forty-eight hours before condemning the hate groups. (He would soon further inflame the controversy by saying there were "very fine people on both sides"— equating the protestors and the white hate groups.)

While White House officials debated what to do next on Charlottesville, they also had to convince the president to follow through with his Section 301 announcement. That would signal a looming trade war against the world's second-largest economy, which had just given the United States critical support on North Korea. "I don't want to target China," the president told his senior aides. "Let's leave China out of it." He was fine with the United States investigating intellectual property theft but he no longer wanted to single out China.

Nonplussed, his aides reminded him that the point of the Section 301 investigation was to single out China. "They're the ones stealing the intellectual property. They're the ones forcing technology transfers," senior aides said. "There's no way we can do this without targeting China."

Fine, Trump said, "but let's take the word 'China' out of the speech I'm going to give." At that point, China was mentioned more than a dozen times in a draft of his prepared remarks.

In the afternoon, the president signed the document during a short ceremony in the White House's Diplomatic Reception Room, as Lighthizer, Treasury Secretary Mnuchin, and a handful of business officials watched. In his two-minute talk, he mentioned China just once and then tried to distract the attention from Beijing by broadening his attack. "We will stand up to any country that unlawfully forces American companies to transfer their valuable technology as a condition of market access," he said.

A reporter shouted the question that was on most journalists' minds: "Mr. President, can you explain why you did not condemn the hate groups by name over the weekend?" To which Trump replied: "They've been condemned. They have been condemned." Then he added with a flourish: "You're fake news."

• • •

In October, Chinese Vice Finance Minister Zhu Guangyao flew to Washington to attend the fall meeting of the International Monetary Fund and to deliver a message to his counterparts at the U.S. Treasury. With President Trump due to head to Beijing the following month for a state visit, China's leadership wanted to offer a gift. It was considering granting foreign firms broader access to China's fast-growing banking, securities, and insurance sectors.

This was the same offer Wang Yang had decided against giving Wilbur Ross during the ill-fated Comprehensive Economic Dialogue, and one that previous administrations had sought for years. Beijing had learned its lesson. It wanted to make sure the Trump visit was a success and the two sides could tout the financial sector opening as a breakthrough.

Not interested, Zhu was told. Too little, too late. Beijing needed to do much more than dangle partial openings of individual markets, U.S. officials informed him. The United States was looking for broad-based changes.

"No, we're not going to take your gifts because you're just trying to sucker us," a U.S. official told the book's coauthor, Lingling, explaining Washington's decision. Starting negotiations then "will just make us beholden to them and reluctant to slam them on other stuff." Besides, the United States had just begun its Section 301 investigation where it was going to lay out precisely how China was screwing U.S. companies and workers.

Wilbur Ross, looking to stage a comeback in the president's esteem, lined up deals to be announced during the Beijing trip. The president had been thrilled by a similar outcome during a May visit to Saudi Arabia. There Trump announced an arms deal worth

$110 billion, with the prospect of another $350 billion in sales over the coming decade, though much of those contracts still needed to be negotiated. A delegation of top-shelf executives accompanied Trump and his entourage to Beijing, including Goldman Sachs CEO Lloyd Blankfein, General Electric vice chairman John Rice, and DowDuPont executive chairman Andrew Liveris.

On November 9, the second day of the Trump visit, the Commerce Department announced $250 billion of deals that "will bring thousands of new jobs to Americans." But hours later, the *Wall Street Journal* dissected the deals under the headline: "Something Old, Something New: $250 Billion in U.S.-China Deals Don't Add Up."

The announcement, the *Journal* explained, didn't involve actual contracts. In many cases, they were nonbinding offers. Commerce highlighted a $43 billion investment in a natural gas project in Alaska. But the U.S. and Chinese participants, including China Petroleum & Chemical Corporation, known as Sinopec, were still negotiating big parts of the deal. The $43 billion figure also reflected the estimated cost of building the natural gas project, not revenue from selling gas to Chinese buyers. "The deal is politically expedient, yet its nonbinding nature gives Sinopec the flexibility to quietly back away from the deal down the line," according to an Asia analyst quoted by the *Journal*.

Other publications also criticized the supposed deals. "Trump doles out deals in China, but will they stick?" headlined *USA Today*. "AP FACT CHECK: U.S.-China trade package mostly about symbolism," wrote the Associated Press.

With the press mocking the China deal, Wilbur Ross was once again in Trump's doghouse. During meetings between Trump and China's senior leaders, Ross generally sat outside in the waiting area.

Still, much of the trip went well, as Beijing rolled out what it called a "state-visit plus." This was the first state visit to Beijing by a foreign leader since the October Communist Party meeting where Wang Yang was promoted and Xi Jinping unveiled a top leadership lineup that didn't include an obvious successor. The session confirmed Xi's status as China's preeminent leader.

Hundreds of elementary school students and a motorcade of twenty-one motorcycles welcomed the president at the airport. On his first day in Beijing, the Chinese leader and his wife escorted the president and Melania Trump on a private tour of the Forbidden City, for centuries the home of China's emperors. The couples had afternoon tea and dinner there, making Trump the first president shown such treatment.

Trump returned the compliment by presenting the Chinese leader with a video of his granddaughter, Arabella Kushner, singing in Mandarin and reciting Chinese poetry. (Once again, five-year-old Arabella was cast in a diplomat's role.) Later Trump tweeted his thanks to the Chinese leader for "an unforgettable afternoon and evening," even though Twitter is blocked in China.

The most significant part of the trip occurred behind closed doors on the second day. Trump had meetings with Xi Jinping and Premier Li Keqiang, who oversees the State Council, the Chinese government's top decision-making body. In both sessions, the president asked Lighthizer to explain U.S. complaints about Chinese trade practices. Lighthizer did so, with lawyerly detail. He lectured the Chinese leaders how the new administration considered past negotiations to have been fruitless. U.S. firms had their technology poached in China. The trade relationship was unbalanced, as reflected in the ever-widening bilateral trade deficit.

Lighthizer's bluntness shocked the Chinese hosts, who complained later to Americans that they had been offended and mystified by his remarks. They had no idea that Lighthizer had replaced Ross as their interlocutor, though they should have noted something important had changed when they saw Ross sitting outside the meeting hall.

Afterward, President Trump was more conciliatory during a joint press conference. Trump called Xi "a very special man" and blamed the problems with China on past inhabitants of the White House, as he had done during his presidential campaign. Xi smiled broadly at that remark, but responded more formally. "I told President Trump that the Pacific Ocean is big enough for both China and the U.S."

The difference between Lighthizer's hard-line and Trump's soft touch confused their Chinese hosts. Was Lighthizer really talking for Trump? If he wasn't, who was? That's a question Chinese officials would ask themselves for the following two years.

In the state banquet that followed, the Chinese lavishly decorated a room in the Great Hall of the People and invited basketball great Yao Ming, who had starred for the Houston Rockets, to attend. The video of Arabella was played again, this time on a larger screen. Trump and his entourage were served grouper fillets in chili oil, coconut-flavored chicken soup, and wines from the Great Wall winery in Hebei province, next to Beijing.

Chinese state media touted "a new chapter of history" in the U.S.-China relationship. *The Australian* reported, "In Beijing, Trump was subject to world-class flattery."

Lighthizer and his staff found themselves suddenly the object of much attention. The Chinese seated two of the seven members of the ruling Politburo Standing Committee on either side of Lighthizer. His young chief of staff, Jamieson Greer, was seated between Vice Finance Minister Zhu and Vice Commerce Minister Yu Jianhua, both excellent English speakers. Their goal: figure out who Lighthizer was and how much influence he had on China policy.

After Air Force One left Beijing, China announced the market-opening plans that Vice Minister Zhu had offered a month earlier. Beijing pledged to allow foreign firms to take a 51 percent stake in Chinese securities firms, up from 49 percent previously. The two-percentage-point difference promised to give foreigners the chance to control Chinese ventures. The announcement didn't rate even a thank-you from Washington.

11

LIU HE GETS A LECTURE, MARCH 2018

As 2018 dawned, the world's two largest economies were starting to engage in a trade battle that would shake the global economy, upend markets around the world, upset corporate plans in the United States, Europe, and Asia, and affect the lives and jobs of more than 1 billion citizens. The power struggle between the United States and China is the most important geopolitical contest of the early twenty-first century.

For all that, the fight resembled a schoolyard brawl. The two antagonists relentlessly circled each other determined to settle old scores. To Donald Trump, China had been cheating the United States for decades. It was time for someone to smack down the cheaters. To Xi Jinping, America was a bully and jealous of China's ascent. America was trying to clobber China before it grew too powerful to challenge. It was time for someone to show the bully he wouldn't back down.

Over the following two years, the two sides landed punches and counterpunches, took breathers, called in allies, and tried to psych each other out. As night dawned on the schoolyard fight, the brawlers decided to take a break, but the fight was hardly over. Examining the struggle in detail reveals the strengths and weaknesses of the two combatants, their strategies and their mistakes. Each side thought it was more resilient than it really was; each side exaggerated the weakness of the other. With the two nations heading to a new Cold War, it's important to understand the calculations and miscalculations that produced the conflict. The following chapters lay that out.

Initially, Xi looked for a quick end to the fighting. At the beginning of 2018, China's usually reliable engines of growth—exports, real estate, and industrial output—were all showing signs of sputtering. The last thing the Chinese leader needed was another problem. In January, Beijing got a sense of the trouble that could lay ahead when the Trump administration slapped steep tariffs on solar panels, an industry dominated by China. The Chinese embassy in Washington also warned Beijing that the administration was preparing its Section 301 report, which could lead to heavy new tariffs.

Xi wanted to clear away problems before the annual meeting of the legislature on March 5, which would rubber-stamp changes he wanted to make to China's constitution. By then, there was little doubt that Xi wasn't the kind of reformer the United States had hoped for. Rather, he was all about party control and, like Trump, he wasn't shy about breaking with convention. Xi's policies and philosophy, known as Xi Jinping Thought, would be added to the constitution's preamble. Presidential term limits, introduced after Mao Zedong's death in 1976, would be eliminated. The Chinese leader wanted the moment to commemorate his hold on power—a grip rivaling that of Deng Xiaoping, if not Mao himself. He didn't want the event overshadowed by a battle with Washington, which could diminish him politically.

Xi directed his old colleague Wang Qishan, whom he planned to install as vice president, to figure out what the Americans wanted. Wang had worked closely with Americans since the 1990s, when they jointly cleaned up Chinese telecommunications companies and banks and arranged for China's first public stock offerings. He knew generations of U.S. business and political leaders and would invite them to what he called "old friend" sessions, where he would shed his suit and tie for Mandarin-collar jackets and soft-sole shoes. The sessions were meant to be casual discussions of changes in America and China.

In late 2017, he invited David Rubenstein, cofounder of the Carlyle Group, a U.S. private equity firm whose investments in China spanned financial services, health care, and technology. "Is Trump a rare phenomenon, or a trend?" Wang asked Rubenstein, as officials from China's Foreign Ministry took notes. (The informality of "old friend" sessions only went so far.)

"Trump is an indicator of the changing attitudes in the U.S.," Rubenstein responded.

Wang agreed. He said the "New York financial people" who came to see him were too optimistic about how the average American sees China and the average Chinese sees America.

In early January 2018, a group of visiting American CEOs, including former Clinton administration Defense Secretary William Cohen, who now ran his own consulting firm, weren't nearly as candid. Wang challenged them to tell him about problems they encountered in China, which he figured the Trump administration would echo. But the participants mainly used the time to pitch him on what their companies had to offer China. Annoyed, Wang admonished the group. He wanted intel, not hype.

A few months later, Wang met with the new U.S. ambassador to China, former Iowa governor Terry Branstad, who had hosted Xi Jinping in 1985 when Xi was a low-ranking official touring America. Wang flattered Branstad by telling him how much Beijing valued dialogue with Washington and how foreign pressure helped Beijing push through reforms. The ambassador was more forthcoming; he warned that the administration's patience with Chinese policies was running low.

In early February, Xi dispatched Yang Jiechi, China's top diplomat, to Washington to try to ease tensions. That was a big change in mission for Yang, whose visit to Washington in late 2016 to lecture Trump campaign staff that the president-elect shouldn't challenge China on Taiwan still rankled some Trump officials. Now Yang brought what Beijing considered a soothing message: China didn't want to fight. "We hear you," he told U.S. officials. China was ready to work on the trade issues near to Trump's heart over the next three to five years.

But all the Americans heard was Yang's time frame. More delay, U.S. officials fumed. They wanted change and they wanted it quickly. No more "bread crumbs," a U.S. official said at the time.

By the time Xi's trade envoy, Liu He, arrived in Washington at the end of February for the first round of substantive trade talks, Trump's bitterly divided trade team was, for once, united. Liu was to meet jointly with U.S. Trade Representative Lighthizer, a trade hawk, and the two senior administration officials most opposed to tariffs, National Economic Council Director Gary Cohn and Treasury Secretary Steven Mnuchin. The trio prepared to deliver a united message during meetings at the Treasury.

Liu, then sixty-six years old, was the kind of Chinese envoy who usually does well in Washington—friendly, English-speaking, well-connected at home, with a reputation as a reformer. A boyhood friend of Xi, he had the Chinese president's full support. The Liu and Xi families lived in the same Beijing neighborhood in the 1960s and both had been victimized by the cruelty of the Cultural Revolution. Liu's father, Liu Zhiyan, a Communist Party veteran who drafted many party documents during the early years of the People's Republic, was purged and committed suicide in 1967 when he was forty-nine years old. Liu He, fifteen years old at the time, was dispatched to the countryside to learn from farmers and workers.

Over the years, Liu rose through the ranks of the powerful National Development and Reform Commission, the old state-planning agency, which still approved large investments throughout China.

He helped put together China's five-year plans that set economic goals. But he had little power to make major policy decisions before Xi assumed power in late 2012.

Liu's career then blossomed. Xi named him to head a party agency, clunkily named the Office of the Central Leading Group for Financial and Economic Affairs, which works something like the White House's National Economic Council. Liu's agency frames economic policy options for senior leaders. When tensions arose between the central bank and the Finance Ministry over who should do more to spur growth, Liu would act as referee. Underlings called him He Shu—Uncle He—for his mild, soft-spoken demeanor. (The "He" in Liu's name is pronounced "heh.")

When Xi wanted a trade envoy he could trust, he jumped Liu ahead of another senior party official who was in line for the job, Hu Chunhua. Hu had spent much of his time governing Tibet and tamping down the region's political independence movement. Although he was considered a rising political star, he didn't have the experience dealing with Americans that Liu did.

U.S. economists and China experts vouched for Liu as a reformer, who honed his English skills and learned market economics when he studied at Harvard's Kennedy School of Government, the same incubator as many in Washington's foreign policy establishment. His top aide during the trade negotiations, Liao Min, also had ample experience dealing with Westerners. In the 1990s, he got his start trading securities at China's central bank and acquainted himself with the ins and outs of capital markets—at the time still a novelty in China.

Liao's 1998 book, *The Rising Euro*, is the first book published in China on the birth of the single currency and its effects. Then Liao moved on to regulate banks in Beijing and Shanghai, and spent years pushing to make China's financial industry more open to foreign investors. A fluent English speaker, he has an MBA from the

University of Cambridge and sometimes wore a Cambridge hoodie when he wasn't darting in and out of negotiation rooms.

LIAO ALSO MADE A name for himself in a way that's not typical of Communist technocrats. He wrote folk songs, among them, "Fleeting Youth" and "Waiting for Someone Is Like Drinking," and released albums while studying at Peking University from 1986 to 1993. When he joined Liu He's team, China's online community dubbed him "The folk music singer."

Before Liu became a Xi adviser, he often met with visiting American politicians and business leaders at the private Chang An Club, above a Beijing Porsche dealership. He shunned big entourages and was always prepared with binders filled with statistics and charts on the Chinese and U.S. economies, and plans for reforming the Chinese economy. He was a Chinese official who could convince Americans that Beijing and Washington shared common goals and a common destiny.

Liu later drafted Xi's first economic blueprint in 2013, which promised to give market forces a bigger role in the economy. In 2016 he was the "authoritative person" who took to *People's Daily* to criticize the old way of stimulating China's economy through debt.

But Liu was also a Communist Party functionary who believed in a powerful role for the state and party. He was also relatively low in the Zhongnanhai pecking order. Even if Liu wanted to push through market-oriented reforms, he lacked the sway of Washington's favorite reformer, former premier Zhu Rongji, who had enormous political power and bureaucratic cunning. When China needed to change to join the World Trade Organization, Zhu was able to win President Jiang Zemin's support and push through reforms that eliminated thousands of state-owned firms, even though that produced massive layoffs.

Liu had much less room to maneuver because of Xi Jinping's

stepped-up emphasis on state control of the economy. "Ultimately, Liu He is dependent on his ability to keep Xi Jinping on board with his policy proposal," says Barry Naughton, an expert on China's economy at the University of California, San Diego. "This is his greatest strength but also his biggest limitation."

When Xi prepared to deliver his vision for China's development at an October 2017 party congress, Liu sought to convince the president to inject more market discipline into state-owned companies, which the top leader had described as the foundation of the party's rule. In a 30,000-word report, Liu focused heavily on one section. Rather than saying "state companies" should become "stronger, better and bigger," as Xi wanted, Liu was able to convince him to substitute the term "state capital." In the Chinese system, the one-word change was enough to signal to state firms that they must improve their returns and act more like commercial firms. But there is little evidence that the change in terminology led to any meaningful changes in the way state-owned firms operated, reflecting Liu's limited ability to push through fundamental reforms.

During a meeting in Beijing in January 2018, Liu met with a bipartisan delegation of former senior U.S. officials led by Myron Brilliant, the U.S. Chamber of Commerce executive vice president. The delegates included Bill Clinton's top trade negotiator, Charlene Barshefsky, and Carlos Gutierrez, George W. Bush's Commerce secretary. They pressed Liu on why China hadn't made more progress reforming markets and revamping the state sector. Liu indicated some sympathy for their position and said state firms must be held more accountable. But given how hamstrung he was by Chinese politics, he didn't give them much hope that a major overhaul was in the works.

"He's not an apologist for China's economic policy," says Brilliant. "He implied that, 'We're on the path to more market reforms, even if it's not at a pace Americans would like to see.'" An article Liu wrote for the *People's Daily* in November 2019 affirmed that approach. China will "promote structural adjustments of the state-owned economy, invest more in important industries and key areas related to national security, and serve the nation's strategic goals," he wrote. In other words, expect some state-sector reforms but China is sticking to its state-driven system.

When Liu conferred with Lighthizer, Cohn, and Mnuchin in Washington on March 1, 2018, he unveiled a five-point plan. Such initiative is unusual for Chinese officials, who routinely wait for their foreign counterparts to make an opening bid and then try to scale back the foreigners' demands. Beijing offered to reduce tariffs on U.S.-made autos and other products; move ahead with the $250 billion in commercial deals promised during President Trump's visit to Beijing; send trade missions to the United States to boost imports; open China's financial sector further to foreigners; and launch negotiations for a free trade agreement that would reduce trade barriers and boost investment opportunities in China.

The offer barely registered with the Americans. The pledge on financial liberalization was a rehash of previous offers, they believed. Free trade negotiations would tie up the two sides in years of negotiations and would ignite opposition in Congress, where even free trade deals with allies are controversial. More significant, Liu didn't make any offer on what the United States considered China's greatest economic sins: stealing U.S. intellectual property, and subsidizing state-owned firms to buy up American competitors or roll over them.

The Americans told Liu that the United States wanted Beijing to cut its $375 billion trade surplus with the United States by $100 billion—and quickly. As for the rest, the three Americans said repeatedly: China knows what it needs to do. Come up with solutions to the problems that have vexed American workers and companies for years, they told Liu. Let us know when you are ready to truly negotiate. The Americans didn't hand Liu a list of demands for a deal, another change from past practice.

"The message to China was 'We're serious,'" said a U.S. negotiator. "We're not going to be tapped along, like prior administrations. If you want to put real issues on the table, we're happy to talk twenty-four hours a day."

To the Chinese, the meetings in Washington were a series of humiliations. The American bullies were lording it over their Chinese guests. They approved only a handful of visas, not the forty Beijing sought. The meeting with U.S. officials turned into a harangue. President Trump left town to go golfing at Mar-a-Lago rather than meet with Liu, as the Chinese embassy thought the U.S. side promised. After that snub, Liu canceled a meeting with Blackstone Group chief executive Stephen Schwarzman, whom China counted on to set up the Trump meeting.

President Trump declared himself satisfied with the outcome. "Trade wars are good, and easy to win," he famously tweeted on March 2, the day after Liu He met with his American counterparts. "Example, when we are down $100 billion with a certain country and they get cute, don't trade anymore," he added. "We win big." Don't get cute with me, Trump was warning. The billionaire Manhattanite, who was chauffeured around town in limousines, spoke naturally in the language of New York City schoolyards.

Back in Beijing, officials were outraged. Liu's offer was "an excellent package," which Washington failed to appreciate, Fang Xinghai, a vice chairman of the China Securities Regulatory Commission, told American business representatives on March 20. Fang is a prominent economic reformer whom Americans consult to figure out the thinking of more senior leaders. As negotiations ground on over the following two years, Liu would tell foreign visitors that the February trip was "the best time to reach a deal."

• • •

Washington's apparent unity on trade policy was a façade. Internal divisions would undermine and hamper the U.S. efforts for the following two years. The splits reflected Trump's conflicting views on China and trade. Was he Blue-Collar Trump, looking to make good on his campaign promises to stop the pillage of America by Chinese imports, as he had promised during the campaign? Or was he Wall Street Trump, worried about the market reaction to a deepening trade dispute? The problem for people trying to figure him out—Americans and Chinese—was that he was both. It was hard to tell which side of him was ascendant at any particular time. In early 2018, Blue-Collar Trump was riding high and so were the advisers who played to that part of his personality.

While Liu was still in town, Trump finally made up his mind how to handle steel and aluminum tariffs, an issue that had tied up the administration for a year. Steel took precedence over aluminum in the administration's deliberations. Trump had promised to restore the industry to its glory days, and Lighthizer and Commerce Secretary Ross had long experience battling steel imports. Industry analysts also agreed that China's massive, subsidized steel production undermined prices globally and made producing steel in the United States frequently unprofitable.

Dealing with the problem wasn't simple. U.S. steel industry lawyers, including Lighthizer, had effectively shut out Chinese imports through trade lawsuits. Chinese producers managed end runs, though. Sometimes they shipped steel to buyers in other nations, who processed it somewhat and then shipped it to the United States, so the steel wouldn't count as Chinese exports. Chinese mills also expanded overseas and exported directly to the United States from other nations. Just the threat of additional Chinese steel exports was enough to depress the market. Ross's Commerce Department studied the issue and, dusting off another rarely used part of U.S. trade law, argued that steel tariffs were necessary to protect national security.

In heated White House debates, even the Pentagon objected that the rationale was bogus. The United States produced plenty of steel and could rely on Canada and other allies for more in pinch. Cohn and others objected that tariffs would backfire by raising prices on U.S. consumers of steel, a much larger industry than steel producers. "If you put tariffs on steel, you'll kill the RV industry," Cohn argued, because the cost of the big campers would jump. "Ask the vice president what he thinks of that," he said, knowing that the industry was based in Mike Pence's home state of Indiana. (Cohn turned out to be prescient about RVs.)

Former steel industry lawyer Lighthizer also raised concerns about tariffs, though rarely in front of Trump, letting others take the heat. The tariffs would have to be applied globally to work, which meant targeting allies the United States would need in a China trade battle. The timing was wrong, Lighthizer argued. Why anger Europe, Japan, Canada, and others when you want to present a solid front against China? An assault on steel could come later.

NEC staffers Clete Willems and Everett Eissenstat hatched a plan using a different approach, which they dubbed "Save Our Steel." Under the proposal, the United States would start a second Section 301 trade investigation, this one focused on China's steel excess capacity. The new investigation would substitute for Commerce's plan and eliminate the need to argue that steel imports harmed national security. Under Section 301, the United States could assess tariffs on Chinese imports and negotiate with other countries that imported Chinese steel, only to re-export it to the United States. Either stop the transshipments or the United States would hit them with tariffs.

Cohn and White House Staff Secretary Rob Porter, who played an important role in trade policy, embraced the plan and argued to Trump that the United States could line up allies to fight Chinese steel rather than fight with them. At a July 2017 summit of the G-20 nations in Hamburg, Germany, the United States had already won a pledge that the leaders, which included China's Xi Jinping, would "rapidly develop concrete policy solutions that reduce steel excess capacity." Save Our Steel would build on that.

Navarro, Ross, and others, though, thought the steel proposal would be ineffective and yet another effort by globalists to delay action. The plan wouldn't help U.S. industry steelmakers if other countries ramped up exports to the United States instead of China, says Ross now. Trump listened to the arguments and was noncommittal. But he wanted action quickly, and Save Our Steel was bound to be a complicated multiyear effort.

When the tax cut was signed into law in late 2017, the anti-tariff forces lost their best argument to persuade Trump to hold off. No longer could they say that the tariffs could cost Senate votes on the tax measure. The North Korea argument didn't work anymore, either. In 2018, China seemed to be cozying up to Kim Jong Un, White House officials believed. One said Xi had begun to act like Kim's lawyer. Confronting China on trade wouldn't make the situation with North Korea worse, Trump came to believe.

On the evening of February 28, 2018, Ross and Navarro walked into the Oval Office and were able to convince Trump to approve the steel tariffs. To make sure the president wouldn't backslide, they invited U.S. steel executives to meet in the White House the next day for a big announcement, without informing the chief of staff or their administration opponents. Cohn tried to get the meeting canceled, but failed. Ross and Navarro's White House opponents dubbed their ploy "the Midnight Massacre."

In the White House's Cabinet Room on March 1—around the same time Liu He was meeting with steel tariff opponents Lighthizer, Cohn, and Mnuchin—the president announced he would go ahead with 25 percent tariffs on steel and 10 percent tariffs on aluminum. "We're going to build our steel industry back, and we're going to build our aluminum industry back," the president promised. He then asked the leaders of U.S. Steel Corporation, Nucor Corporation, and United Aluminum Corporation to talk about how the decision would help their companies.

The Dow Jones Industrial Average fell 420 points after the announcement, not as far as Cohn had predicted or enough to make Trump recant. Europe and Canada also retaliated despite Navarro's assurances that they wouldn't dare do so. This was enough to remind Trump and others in the White House that the market was watching trade policy carefully. That would factor into the president's decision-making later on.

Within days, Cohn resigned. That followed the exit of Porter, who had been accused of abusing two ex-wives, an allegation he denied. Secretary of State Rex Tillerson, another globalist, was soon out the door. A fourth globalist, presidential son-in-law Jared Kushner, was also sidelined. He steered clear of China issues for some time after the *New York Times* published articles alleging that he met with China's Anbang Insurance Group about investing in his family company's property on 666 Fifth Avenue. (Anbang's founder, Wu Xiaohui, once one of China's most prominent tycoons, had sought the investment as a way to build himself up with Chinese authorities. Wu was convicted of fraud and embezzlement in 2018.)

The personnel moves tilted the playing field further toward the White House's nationalist wing, with its hard-line views on China. The nationalists had lost their ringleader, Steve Bannon, who flamed out spectacularly in August 2017 when he did an interview saying the Trump strategy on North Korea was bound to fail. By then, though, Bannon was a spent force in the White House.

With the steel issue decided, for better or worse, attention focused again on the Section 301 report, which was to lay the foundation for the economic battles ahead with China. With lawyerly attention to detail, the trade representative's office held hearings on the proposed report, while White House economic officials debated what actions to take. The results were easy to predict.

The October 2017 hearings led off with a statement by Richard Ellings, who had directed a 2013 private sector Commission on the Theft of American Intellectual Property. He repeated the report's findings that China was responsible for 80 percent of the theft, which cost the United States hundreds of billions of dollars a year and millions of jobs. He was followed by executives of an American solar panel company and a wind energy company, who blamed Chinese theft, espionage, and underhanded tactics for their firms' woes.

The National Security Council pushed to declassify documents involving Chinese cyber espionage and other issues. That work was included in a February 2018 report by the White House Council of Economic Advisers, which calculated that "malicious cyber activity" cost the U.S. economy between $57 billion and $109 billion in 2016 alone. The report examined 290 cyberattacks and detailed some of the largest ones involving China.

At the same time, seventy-four petitioners filed comments with the trade representative's office on Chinese trade practices—mainly trade associations because individual companies feared retaliation from Beijing. Government officials claimed that some business executives were afraid to walk into the trade representative's building on Seventeenth Street because they believed the Chinese tracked who entered.

Even longtime China allies urged the trade representative to take strong action. The U.S.-China Business Council, an organization of big exporters that had lobbied furiously for China to join the WTO, submitted an eighteen-page paper detailing the many ways Beijing pressured its members to hand over valuable technology. "The requirement to transfer technology as a condition to gain market access in China is an acute concern of American companies in key sectors, who often must make difficult choices about managing the tradeoff of technology sharing and access to the world's second-largest economy," the trade group wrote.

There was some dissent. Mark Cohen, then the U.S. Patent and Trademark Office's senior counsel for China, who had long experience in the country, criticized the interagency effort for relying too much on anecdotes and not insisting on data to show whether

China was an outlier in protecting intellectual property. Although Chinese data is suspect, he says now, it could be used to see whether certain technologies get heavy subsidies or how China stacked up against other countries in granting patents. The report was "a data-free zone," says Cohen, who says he resigned in disgust in April 2018.

The White House ran interagency sessions to examine different ways to discipline China, including cutting off Beijing's access to advanced U.S. technology. But with the president regularly pressing his staff to "bring me tariffs," it was clear to most everyone what the outcome would be. Council of Economic Advisers chairman Kevin Hassett analyzed the economic loss to U.S. companies from forced technology transfer—the heart of the Section 301 complaint—and arrived at a $30 billion figure and presented the research to the president. "We gotta make the number bigger," Trump told him. He wanted to double what Hassett found. But that wasn't so simple. Administration lawyers worried they could lose a lawsuit if the tariff penalty seemed arbitrary.

Hassett went back to his spreadsheets, updated the information, and came up with a figure of $48 billion, which the trade representative's office rounded off to $50 billion. Trump never seemed to notice—or care—that the number was still smaller than what he wanted. When he announced the Section 301 report on March 22, in the White House Diplomatic Reception Room, he said that tariffs on China "could be about $60 billion." To boost the numbers higher, he repeated the demand Lighthizer had given Liu He earlier in the month. "I've asked them to reduce the trade deficit immediately by $100 billion," Trump said. "It's a lot."

The threat of tariffs captured the headlines. But the heart of the Section 301 report was ultimately more important. The United States was filing a brief accusing China of being the world's biggest trade criminal and providing evidence of Beijing's crimes. Under U.S. law, the United States didn't have to prove the case; it could judge China and punish it. The 215-page document alleged that

China sought technological dominance and either stole U.S. technology through cyber espionage or old-fashioned theft, or pressured U.S. companies to give up their technology through joint ventures, regulatory reviews, antitrust investigations, licensing requirements, and other means.

The report cited Beijing's "Made in China 2025" report 114 times, treating it as a kind of Chinese confession of guilt. "In comparison to previous plans, 'Made in China 2025' expands its focus to capturing global market share, not just dominance in the China market," the report said. It also listed ten instances where Beijing pledged to halt coercion of U.S. companies over technology between 2010 and 2016, but failed to do so. Despite the gravity of the charges, the report was consciously written in unemotional language with no obvious sound bites. About as close as the report comes to quotable material are sections like this: "Ultimately, China's acts, policies, and practices that require or pressure technology transfer undermine U.S. companies' valuable IP [intellectual property], weaken their global competitiveness, and stunt investment in innovation." Hardly a call to arms.

The report was meant to convince by an accumulation of facts, testimony, and anecdotes. Its audience was U.S. industry, which wanted action on China, but which opposed the administration's resort to tariffs; U.S. political and opinion leaders; and other trading nations, which the White House hoped would back American actions. Convincing the public that China was up to no good was the responsibility of the president and other policy makers, who could use the Section 301 report as a resource.

On the morning the report was released, Lighthizer tried his best to explain the administration's rationale for acting. "I think at the end of the day, no matter what I do and what you do during your career, China is still going to be a market-driven Communist country. It's never going to be like us," he told Senator Ron Wyden, an Oregon Democrat, at a Senate Finance Committee hearing. "There

are some areas that you just have to protect yourself from them."
Tariffs would help provide that protection, Lighthizer believed.

In Beijing, the report and the threat of tariffs drew swift con-
demnation and started a war of words. Within twenty-four hours,
China said it would retaliate with levies on $50 billion of U.S. im-
ports. Trump upped the ante, threatening tariffs on another $100 bil-
lion of Chinese goods—$150 billion in all. Not to be outdone, China's
Commerce Ministry said, "China is fully prepared to hit back force-
fully." The trade war was on, or at least the threat of a trade war. The
United States needed time to prepare the list of Chinese goods subject to tariffs, giving the two sides several months to try to negotiate
a settlement. The adversaries were getting ready to land blows, but
as happens in many a schoolyard battle, they also were looking for
a way out.

Beijing studied the U.S. trade fight against Japan in the 1980s
and 1990s for lessons in dealing with Washington. Like Japan, China
could try to deescalate the fight by giving in to the United States
somewhat and lowering tariffs and opening its markets further, the
leadership concluded. But Beijing rejected some Japanese tactics.
Tokyo, which depended on Washington militarily, never retaliated against U.S. sanctions. That passivity wasn't for China, which
viewed itself as a rising power that would eventually challenge the
United States. China's days of kowtowing were over.

In a closed-door economic forum, China's former Finance Minister Lou Jiwei said America had treated Japan like its mistress
back then and ordered it to do whatever it wanted. China was more
like a wife, he said, who should be treated with more respect and
who is entitled to fight back against a bullying spouse. His message
would be repeated over and over again when Chinese officials met
with their American counterparts: China is an equal to the United
States and it won't yield to pressure tactics. Back off, buddy.

12

AMERICAN DISARRAY, MAY 2018

With the two sides moving closer to a trade war, some officials looked for a way out. In Washington that job fell mainly to Treasury Secretary Mnuchin, who had been overshadowed on trade issues first by Commerce Secretary Ross and then by Trade Representative Lighthizer. In the past, the Treasury secretary took the lead on China. Mnuchin's mentor, former Treasury Secretary Hank Paulson, urged him to reassert Treasury's primacy. Treasury was the cabinet agency responsible for overseeing the health of the U.S. economy and, especially, the U.S. financial sector, which had complained for years that it was largely shut out of the enormous Chinese market.

During the George W. Bush administration, Paulson had what he called in his book on China a "'super-Cabinet' position to lead and coordinate other Cabinet members" because he ran the annual Strategic Economic Dialogue talks involving dozens of U.S. and Chinese officials. Although the Trump team had rejected Paulson's advice to restart the dialogue, Paulson still pressed his protégé to show more bureaucratic backbone. Earlier in their careers at Goldman Sachs, the two men had worked closely together. As CEO, Paulson promoted Mnuchin to the firm's management committee, had him work on corporate strategy, and put him in charge of the firm's information technology. According to Mnuchin's public calendar, he spoke more frequently to Paulson than to any business leader.

On March 23, the day after Trump unveiled the Section 301 report and threatened tariffs, Mnuchin called Liu He at 8 p.m., at Paulson's suggestion, and spoke to him for thirty minutes. The two went over the contents of a letter Mnuchin and Lighthizer had sent Liu pressing China again for a $100 billion reduction in the trade deficit and an end to forced technology transfer, among other items. Mnuchin also congratulated Liu on his recent promotion to vice premier. Liu responded that he hoped both sides would remain "rational" and keep trade relations stable. The two were to play leading roles as peacekeepers. In schoolyard terms, they were trying to keep the combatants from taking the first swing and making a battle inevitable.

Two weeks later, Xi Jinping made his own attempt to mend relations. In an April 10 speech at the Boao Forum, an annual gathering of world political and business leaders on the resort island of Hainan, he promised a host of changes that could appeal to Americans. They included increased imports, financial sector opening, lower tariffs, and other parts of Liu He's five-point plan. While Xi didn't mention Trump or the trade fight with the United States during his forty-minute speech, Washington was the clear target.

Although Xi wanted negotiations, he would bend only so far. "While we're crossing the river by feeling the stones"—a reference to Deng Xiaoping's metaphor for China pragmatically opening its economy—"we're also strengthening top-level planning," Xi said at Boao. In other words, don't expect Beijing to ease the party's control over the economy, as Washington sought.

Sensing an opening, Mnuchin lobbied the president to send him to Beijing to start negotiations. "The Treasury secretary's job is to look across the economy—all the things that impact the economy," says Mnuchin in an interview. "And trade is obviously one of them."

But he faced opposition from Lighthizer, who thought the United

States would have a better chance of forcing China to change if negotiations were delayed until tariffs were ready to be imposed, which was still months away. White House adviser Peter Navarro was also deeply opposed. He doubted China would live up to any deal it signed. As he wrote in *Death by China*, "based on China's abysmal track record to date, with Beijing we must appropriately 'mistrust and constantly reverify.'"

The struggle between Mnuchin and Navarro over China policy continued for the next two years and came to define the differences between the nationalist and globalist wings of the administration. Not only was the Trump administration tangling with China; it was tangling internally.

The two men couldn't be more different personally. Mnuchin, who turned fifty-seven years old in 2019, seemed perpetually ill at ease; his dark glasses gave him the look of a high school debate coach. He was born to wealth and privilege. His father, Robert, was a star Goldman Sachs trader whom the U.S. government turned to for help in preventing panic after the market crashed in October 1987. Mnuchin had been publisher of the *Yale Daily News* and a member of the college's Skull and Bones secret society. He made partner at Goldman Sachs in his thirties. He later ran a hedge fund backed by mega-investor George Soros, invested in Hollywood hits, and married a glamorous actress. *Fortune* magazine estimated his net worth at as much as $500 million.

Navarro, thirteen years older than Mnuchin, was lean and aggressive and looked constantly angry. He was raised by a single mother who often worked in low-paying retail jobs, went to Tufts University on a scholarship, served in the Peace Corps in Thailand, and then earned a PhD from Harvard. At the University of California, Irvine, he initially focused on electric utility regulation. Despite writing a series of investment books with titles like *If It's Raining in Brazil, Buy Starbucks*, his net worth was less than $600,000, according to government filings.

Mnuchin never showed much interest in public policy, according to those who worked closely with him. As the Trump campaign's finance chairman, he figured he had a good shot at a top government job if Trump pulled off an upset win. "It's like a cheap option" to become Treasury secretary, he told his market colleagues. As he explained to *Bloomberg Businessweek*: "Nobody's going to be like, 'Well why did he do this?' if I end up in the administration."

Navarro was a policy wonk—though his policy beliefs changed so often that his opponents labeled him a political chameleon. He initially made his reputation as an environmentalist who started the group Prevent Los Angelization Now!, or PLAN, which tried to slow development in San Diego. In losing bids for local office in San Diego, he ran as a Democrat, a nonpartisan, a Republican, and then again as a Democrat.

He was also a free trader. In his 1984 book, *The Policy Game*, he attacked tariffs and protectionism for raising consumer prices, destroying jobs and investment, and harming national security. Those were the same arguments that leading economists used against him after he enlisted in the Trump campaign.

"The economics of protectionism clearly indicate that the best trade policy is one that resumes the process begun after World War II—but aborted in recent years—of steadily lowering trade barriers through international cooperative efforts," Navarro wrote. He told *Axios* in 2018 that "the turning point in my trade thinking" came when he saw the impact of China on the U.S. economy in the early 2000s.

In emailed comments for this book, Navarro says he was "one of the first academic economists to conduct significant analytic work that revealed China for the mercantilist and protectionist it is." He says he considers himself a pioneer or visionary, rather than a chameleon.

In 2019, Navarro admitted to unusual conduct of a different kind. In some of his books—supposedly nonfiction—he created a fictional character, Ron Vara, and quoted him to make dramatic points. In *Death by China*, he also prominently quoted a Leslie LeBon, which was his wife's name. He told the *Chronicle of Higher Education*, which broke the story, that he considered Ron Vara, which is an anagram of the name Navarro, to be a "whimsical device and pen name." Vara is identified as fictional in one of his books, though not the ones on China.

Mnuchin and Navarro were similar in one regard—they used flattery to stay in Trump's good graces. Mnuchin praised Trump's "perfect genes" and claimed the administration's tax cut would pay for itself by spurring economic growth that would boost tax revenue. (It didn't.) He endorsed Trump's attacks on National Football League players who kneeled during the national anthem. He defended Trump from accusations that he encouraged anti-Semitism after Trump said neo-Nazis were some of the "very fine people" who marched through Charlottesville during riots there. Former Treasury Secretary Larry Summers tweeted that Mnuchin "may be the greatest sycophant in Cabinet history."

Navarro proved his allegiance to the president by attacking his critics in scathing language. "There is a special place in hell" for Canadian Prime Minister Justin Trudeau, Navarro said, after Trudeau clashed with Trump at a Group of Seven (G-7) leaders' summit in Canada in June 2018. (Navarro apologized a few days later.) Later in the year, he called Wall Street executives pushing for negotiations with China, some of whom were Trump's friends, "unpaid foreign agents." (He didn't apologize for that one.) Only "Donald J. Trump," as he invariably called the president, had the guts to take on China, he argued on television.

Navarro blamed Mnuchin for trying to get him cast out of the White House for a job in the Commerce Department's basement and attacked him ferociously. He called Mnuchin "Neville Chamberlain" behind his back for appeasing China and convincing Trump to ditch his campaign promise to label China a currency manipulator. Word of that got back to Mnuchin, who is Jewish and who found the label particularly insulting. "I take great offense to that," Mnuchin says in the interview.

By the end of April, the president approved Mnuchin's plan to negotiate with the Chinese, but with important caveats. Trump wanted Lighthizer and Navarro to go, too. Looking for allies, Mnuchin convinced the president to add Commerce Secretary Ross to the negotiating team. Mnuchin's plan of mano-a-mano negotiations with Liu He had come apart. Not trusting either his nationalist or globalist advisers to cut a deal, Trump sent them all, though that was bound to deepen Trump White House infighting. The president thought the Mnuchin wing (Wall Street Trump) was too soft and the Lighthizer-Navarro wing (Blue-Collar Trump) too harsh.

The divisions also flummoxed the Chinese, who weren't sure who was in charge and whether any concessions they might offer would be enough for the president. Trump wasn't sure, either. He would judge the results of the trip and decide.

Inside the Chinese bureaucracy, there were also divisions over how to deal with the Trump team. Some officials argued that offers of market openings should be tied to China getting something in return. Others thought that wasn't necessary because the changes would benefit China anyway. Still, the Chinese were much better at presenting a united front than their American counterparts.

On May 3, the U.S. team arrived in Beijing bearing an eight-part list of demands for deep changes in China's economic system. They included reducing the U.S. trade deficit by $200 billion in two years—twice what Trump had only recently demanded—and immediately ceasing subsidies in industries targeted by Beijing's "Made in China 2025" plan. Beijing was also to end pressure on U.S. firms to transfer technology, strengthen intellectual property, stop cyber spying of U.S. companies, broadly open up its market to U.S. companies, and slash tariffs and other impediments to U.S. exports. In addition, China must agree not to retaliate or to fight U.S. restrictions on Chinese investment in U.S. technology.

Beijing thought the demands were so onerous that it promptly leaked the document, although it held back the annexes where the United States laid out specifics. The proposal amounted to "surrender or die," said Erin Ennis, who was then senior vice president of the U.S.-China Business Council. Even Michael Pillsbury, the hawkish Trump adviser, thought the United States was expecting too much. "It would be like the Chinese flying into Washington and telling us to change our Constitution," he says.

Chinese officials had a similar reaction. "It reads like the twenty-one demands," says a Chinese official involved in the talks, referring to the demands made by Japan in 1915 that would have extended Tokyo's control of China during World War I.

In response, Liu He's team also presented a tough framework. The Chinese wanted the White House to drop its Section 301 investigation into Chinese trade practices and cease its tariff threats. Beijing also wanted better treatment for Chinese technology companies, especially ZTE Corporation, a big telecommunications firm that the Commerce Department had banned from purchasing American computer chips and components, a penalty that threatened the firm's survival.

As a sweetener, Beijing offered pledges similar to those made by Xi Jinping in Boao, including cutting levies on imported autos and increasing the quota of Hollywood films that could be shown in China.

Although the goal of the talks was to head off a fight, the meeting was making things worse. The tough U.S. demands provoked a similar Chinese response, and the divided U.S. team made it impossible for Beijing to know who—if anyone—it could turn to for help in Washington.

The negotiating sessions went badly, too. Most were led by

Mnuchin, who headed the U.S. delegation. Lighthizer attended many of the meetings but refused to say anything when prompted by Chinese officials. U.S. officials later said Lighthizer saw no advantage in tipping his hand in a negotiation that he didn't lead.

The fight with Beijing took a backseat to fights within the U.S. delegation. After the first day of talks, the jet-lagged team met in an embassy secure room. Mnuchin and Ross discussed what kind of purchases they could count on from the Chinese and whether that would be enough for a deal. For Navarro, acting as the group's China expert, this was just his second trip ever to Beijing. He mocked Ross for counting on the Chinese to carry out promises. The following morning, he confronted Mnuchin in a building at the Diaoyutai State Guesthouse. Mnuchin was planning one-on-one meetings with Liu. What gave him the right to do that?

The two continued their fight later on the complex's manicured lawns. Navarro assumed that they were far enough from any building that the Chinese bugged and let loose. What the fuck, he said to Mnuchin, in a tirade laced with profanity. Why are you cutting him and others out of some meetings? Ease off, the Treasury Secretary shouted back. They could make more progress in one-on-one sessions, rather than meetings with a roomful of officials where much of the time was taken up by translation. He was the leader of the delegation and got to make these calls.

From a distance, Chinese negotiators watched the two Americans go at each other, wondering what to make of the argument. They had put their hope in Mnuchin, who was close to Paulson, who had many friends among Chinese officials. (The officials teased Paulson that if he helped Mnuchin like he had helped Gary Cohn, Mnuchin would soon be out of a job.) They despised Navarro for his anti-Chinese writing. "We definitely didn't want to talk to someone like him," says a Chinese Commerce Ministry official.

After two days like this, the U.S. delegation left. Xi Jinping answered Trump's snub of Liu He during his negotiating session in

Washington by not meeting with the Americans. The two sides couldn't agree on a joint statement. The Americans had trouble agreeing among themselves what to say. Hours after the U.S. team flew off, the White House issued a statement citing "frank discussions"— diplomatic speak for disagreements. The statement claimed that the size of the delegation reflected the importance that the administration put on China trade and investment, rather than the disagreements among the Americans about how to deal with Beijing, and each other.

• • •

ZTE represented an opening.

In March 2017, the Commerce Department slapped the firm with an $892 million fine after ZTE pled guilty to violating U.S. sanctions law and obstructing a federal investigation. That capped a five-year probe, in which the Commerce Department threatened to bar U.S. companies from supplying ZTE with computer chips and other components. The penalty that could kill the company, which relied on U.S. parts to make mobile phones and other telecom gear. ZTE began cooperating, and Commerce suspended the blacklist during settlement talks.

As part of its evidence, the U.S. government released ZTE documents labeled "Top Secret Highly Confidential," which described how ZTE set up shell companies to avoid U.S. sanctions requirements. One document included flowcharts of the operations. ZTE tried not to mention the countries by name, but slipped up. Next to "YL" on one flowchart was the name "Iran." (YL might have been derived from the transliteration of the Mandarin name for Iran, "Yilang.")

A second document said, "Currently our company has on-going projects in all five major embargoed countries—Iran, Sudan, North Korea, Syria and Cuba. All of those projects depend on U.S. procured items to some extent, so export control obstacles have arisen."

That document also discussed how another company, called "F7," skirted U.S. sanctions law. "F7 found a big IT company serving as its agent to sign contracts for projects in embargoed countries," the document said. "This cut-off company's capital[,] credit and capability are relatively strong compared to our company; it can cut off risks more effectively." F7 turned out to be Huawei Technologies Company, which would later become a big factor in the U.S.-China battle.

In April 2018, about a year after the guilty plea, ZTE admitted additional problems to Commerce. ZTE had lied about complying with the settlement. It hadn't fired employees involved in the sanctions busting, as required; it had even given some bonuses. In response, Commerce banned U.S. companies from selling to ZTE— slipping the noose around ZTE's neck once again.

The action effectively turned what started as a trade battle between the United States and China into a technology and national security fight, too. That was fine with Navarro, the National Security Council, and intelligence agencies, as well as hard-liners in Congress, including Senator Tom Cotton, an Arkansas Republican, and Senate Democratic leader Chuck Schumer of New York. To them China represented an existential threat to the United States—a rising, hostile power that had to be confronted economically and militarily.

The administration's National Security Strategy, after all, labeled China a "revisionist power" and a "strategic competitor" and defined economic strength as an important part of national security. ZTE's thumbing its nose at U.S. law was an example of what the hawks feared.

But Trump wasn't looking to lash out at China over national security issues. Economics and trade were front and center with him. China was an economic competitor, bigger but not fundamentally different from other countries that run large trade surpluses with the United States, he believed. When Trump said, as he did often, that Europe "treats us worse than China," he meant it because Germany has a big bilateral trade surplus.

He also meant it when he said that closing the borders with Mexico would be a "profit-making operation" because then Mexico wouldn't any longer have a bilateral trade surplus. "He sees China similar to the way he'd see a crafty real estate developer," says an exasperated senior U.S. security official. "It's not like they are out for blood. It's like they got away with a lot in past negotiations and now they have to be reined in."

ZTE quickly became a bargaining chip in his trade battle with China. When Xi Jinping telephoned him to complain about U.S. treatment of the company on May 8—a rare move for Chinese leaders, who usually wait for Americans to initiate calls—Trump was ready to deal. The White House read-out of the call mentioned only that the two leaders discussed North Korea and made an oblique reference to Trump affirming his commitment to a balanced trade and investment relationship.

But others briefed on the call say ZTE featured prominently in the hour-long discussion. Xi looked to save the company and rattled off statistics to make his case. For the Chinese leader, U.S. help on ZTE was a precondition for continuing trade negotiations.

"President Xi of China, and I, are working together to give massive Chinese phone company, ZTE, a way to get back into business, fast," the president tweeted May 13. "Too many jobs in China lost. Commerce Department has been instructed to get it done!"

The concession was criticized inside the administration by intelligence agencies and the Navarro wing in the White House, and outside by lawmakers. Nodding to security concerns, Representative Adam Schiff of California, the top Democrat on the House Intelligence Committee, tweeted, "Our intelligence agencies have warned that ZTE technology and phones pose a major cybersecurity threat." He criticized Trump: "You should care more about our national security than Chinese jobs."

But for Trump, solving ZTE's problems was a way to keep up his personal relations with Xi and preserve jobs at ZTE's U.S. suppliers. Hadn't he been elected president to create jobs? ZTE is a big player in the telecom world, Trump later told reporters, and buys a lot of components from American firms. "They buy those parts in the United States," he said. "That's a lot of business."

On May 15, a big delegation of Chinese officials landed in Washington for the next round of negotiations. The Chinese, looking for a positive outcome, went to their go-to move. They approved about a dozen of Ivanka Trump's trademark applications around this time, covering baby blankets, perfume, and even coffins. The White House put out a statement naming Mnuchin as the leader of the U.S. side to try to head off backstabbing among American officials that had undermined previous talks.

This time, the United States wasn't chintzy and issued numerous visas for the Chinese, led again by Liu He. During the talks, which lasted until May 19, Liu negotiated in good faith, U.S. officials said. Liu also got his meeting with Trump in the Oval Office. Originally scheduled for fifteen minutes, the session stretched on for forty-five.

The Chinese trade envoy was surprised to see all the key members of Trump's economic team with the president during the meeting. To the Chinese, this showed how important the U.S.-China relationship was to Trump. But to Washington veterans, it signaled once again that the U.S. trade team was so divided that they all angled to get into the room to make sure one of them didn't get more time with the president.

There were few concrete results. National Economic Council Director Larry Kudlow predicted the Chinese would buy billions more in farm products, energy, and financial services. But after eighteen hours of negotiating on the text, Liu didn't commit to meet the trade deficit reduction target. Instead, the two sides agreed quietly that Beijing would come up with a detailed purchasing plan within a month or so.

Still, the talks didn't bomb, as they had the previous two times. There were plenty of positive vibes. The Chinese leadership issued instructions to state-owned media outlets to play down China's interest in buying advanced technology and carrying out the "Made in China 2025" plan that so worried Washington. Instead they were told to run more stories about Chinese consumers' growing appetite for quality American products. On the U.S. side, Mnuchin went on *Fox News Sunday* on May 20 to announce the United States was "putting the trade war on hold" and wouldn't assess tariffs on Beijing while the two sides talked.

The Treasury secretary, looking to play peacemaker, went too far. Over the prior two weeks, the United States had agreed to give ZTE a pass, feted Chinese negotiators, and got nothing specific in return. Now Mnuchin was announcing unilateral trade disarmament. This was too much for Lighthizer. Within hours of Mnuchin's announcement, Lighthizer's office released a statement saying tariffs, investment restrictions, and export regulations remained important tools to "protect our technology." He didn't cite Mnuchin by name, but he didn't have to. The statement was a smackdown of Mnuchin's peace-in-our-times statement, say administration officials.

Even worse for Mnuchin, Bannon had become an outside critic and was telling his allies in conservative media that the Treasury secretary was soft on China and letting down the president. On May 21, Lou Dobbs—Trump's guru on trade—attacked the negotiations. "The globalist wing of the White House economic team have their way in the China trade talks and so did China," said Dobbs. "Quite a performance for the Secretary Mnuchin–led trade delegations." To drive home his point, Dobbs also complained in a phone call with the president.

The following day the *Washington Post* editorial board chimed in. "President Trump's trade war with China is over, at least temporarily," the *Post* wrote. "And here's the after-action report: Advantage China."

Trump went ballistic. He had encouraged his Treasury secretary to make a deal and appointed him China chief for the talks. Mnuchin had encouraged him on ZTE, too. Now look at the results. Lou Dobbs, lawmakers in both parties, and even the *Washington Post*—the despised *Washington Post*!—accused his administration of weakness. If there was one thing Donald Trump couldn't stand, it was being called weak.

After digesting the *Post* editorial, Trump assembled his senior trade team at the White House on May 22 and dressed them down, singling out Mnuchin for criticism. He wanted a tougher approach, including tariffs, to force Beijing to bend. "Get moving," the president told them.

Trump kept his word to Xi on ZTE. The two sides informally agreed on a deal to save the company while Liu was in Washington. A few weeks later, the Commerce Department announced a settlement: a penalty of $1 billion plus U.S. enforcement officers posted inside ZTE to monitor its actions. In return, ZTE could resume buying parts from U.S. companies. Its life had been spared.

Trump held firm on the deal even after the Republican-controlled Senate voted to kill the agreement and reinstate the blacklist. The measure didn't advance further.

But elsewhere, Trump prepared to crack down hard on China. Over Memorial Day weekend, Lighthizer attended a dinner with the president while a drafting team readied a statement on sanctions that Trump personally edited. Not only would 25 percent tariffs on the $50 billion in Chinese goods be ready on June 15, the White House announced on May 29, but the United States would also start proceedings to restrict Chinese investment and toughen export controls on Chinese purchases of "industrially significant technology." The trade war was deepening. Blue-Collar Trump was in command and ready to strike the first blow. Lighthizer was his chief lieutenant (at least for the moment).

And Mnuchin? His nemesis, Navarro, went on Fox News the following day to say that the Treasury secretary's statement that the trade war was on hold should be dismissed as "an unfortunate sound bite."

13

A BUYING MISSION, JUNE 2018

Peter Navarro's triumphal comment was hardly the last word. Within days, Treasury Secretary Mnuchin was pushing ahead with a different plan to end the trade conflict. This time he teamed with Commerce Secretary Ross to press China to buy huge quantities of U.S. merchandise. Reducing the vast bilateral trade deficit remained the president's main goal. Maybe a big sales package would convince Trump to settle and drop his plans for tariffs. Maybe Beijing could buy its way out of a trade war. On a conference call in mid-May with the president and members of the trade team, Mnuchin appealed to the Wall Street side of Trump. The markets were now booming because of Trump's success in passing a tax cut and pushing deregulation. A prolonged China battle could derail those gains. A skeptical Trump gave his okay. "Go ahead and try but I don't think you'll get it done," he said.

What explains Mnuchin's persistence? He attributes it to stick-to-it-iveness and his closeness to the president, with whom he speaks nearly daily. "I tend not to give up on things," says Mnuchin in an interview. "I'm very focused on the president's economic plan being successful."

His allies say that he viewed himself as the administration's chief financial officer—the cabinet official responsible for the economy's overall financial health. The trade fight threatened that well-being and needed to be settled. As CFO, he didn't need the approval of the CEO—Donald Trump—to launch initiatives, and he didn't have to worry about the feelings of other officials.

When Robert Lighthizer was confirmed as trade representative in the spring of 2017, he received a letter, signed by the president, putting him in charge of trade policy. In interagency battles, the letter was worthless. Mnuchin had deeper ties to the president, stretching back to the presidential campaign, and Trump didn't block Mnuchin's way. "There is no more important relationship at 1500 Pennsylvania Ave."—the Treasury's address—"than the one at 1600 Pennsylvania Ave.," says a former senior Trump Treasury official.

Mnuchin and Chinese negotiator Liu He also needed one another. To fend off pressure from powerful party officials at China's state-owned companies and ministries who wanted Beijing to stand firm against American pressure, Liu had to show progress. Mnuchin was a sympathetic interlocutor, unlike the standoffish Lighthizer and the hostile Navarro. Liu frequently told visiting foreign business leaders how constructive Mnuchin was in trying to ease the trade conflict. Fellow peacemakers, as Liu saw it.

For Mnuchin, his ties to Liu made him the man to see in Washington when it came to Beijing. Chinese Ambassador Cui Tiankai met or telephoned Mnuchin more than forty times in 2018, according to the Treasury secretary's daily calendar. Cui contacted Lighthizer twice.

Ross arrived in Beijing on June 2, 2018, when the air was turning increasingly smoggy in the gathering summer heat. He led an interagency team comprising the Treasury, Commerce, Agriculture, and Energy departments. The Americans recorded possible deals on a color-coded Excel spreadsheet, organized by categories—energy, agriculture, manufactured goods, and the like. Beijing did its best to make the purchasing team feel welcome. The leadership worked to head off popular resentment against U.S. tariff threats, and censors banned the use of the term "trade war" in Chinese media. But Xi Jinping had strict instructions for Liu He: the price of Chinese purchases was a pledge by the Trump administration to abandon the threatened tariffs.

Liu presented Ross with a plan to buy more U.S. soybeans, corn, coal, natural gas, and manufactured goods, which the Chinese side valued at $100 billion in the first year. The Chinese thought coal purchases would be a big winner, given the Republican Party's concerns about upcoming congressional elections. The purchases would help Pennsylvania and West Virginia coal fields and reinforce Trump's boast that he had revived the industry. Throughout the negotiations, Liu made clear to Ross that the offer would be void if Washington proceeded with its plan to impose tariffs on $50 billion of China-made products. The message from Xi to Trump was clear: I can help you if you back off.

But Beijing's proposal was derided in Washington as yet another example of Ross not realizing he was being played by the Chinese. The Ross team estimated the Chinese offer at $70 billion, but even that figure was wildly optimistic. The plan didn't include signed deals. Energy purchases would largely come from sales U.S. firms would have made to other nations. U.S. farms weren't able to ramp up production as quickly as the plan assumed. The Commerce Department was double-counting some purchases, say industry officials consulted by the administration. China also wouldn't commit to multiyear purchases.

To really boost imports of U.S. goods, Chinese negotiators said, sell us more high-technology equipment, especially semiconductors. Beijing had tried for years to get the United States to sell it more advanced technology and was invariably turned down. This time the administration was intrigued; some officials asked some high-tech executives what products could be freed from export controls. Lawmakers, led by Senator John Cornyn, a Texas Republican, got wind of the plan and tried to kill it before the team reached Beijing. "We implore you to reject any proposal to soften restrictions on the transfer to China of U.S.-made military technologies and advanced dual-use technologies, including semiconductors," twenty-seven senators from both parties wrote to the administration on May 22.

Lighthizer was especially withering in his criticism of Ross's deal. "I don't see $70 billion. Have you seen $70 billion?" he would say, mockingly. Another skeptical official said the Chinese proposed purchases amounted to $20 billion, at most.

No one knew for sure. The Chinese proposal wasn't reviewed by officials from different U.S. agencies to see whether the package would boost exports or represented new sales. "No matter how you looked at it, the numbers literally didn't add up," says James Green, a U.S. trade negotiator at the time who was involved in the effort.

Ross defends his work and says, once again, that Trump changed his mind about what he wanted from a deal. Initially the president focused on purchases but then "he decided he wanted a more all-encompassing thing," Ross says in an interview.

"All we get to do is to try to negotiate as best we can to achieve the policies, and then bring [proposals] back to him," he says. "He will either accept them or not accept them."

Beijing was disappointed by the plan's failure. The combination of Mnuchin and Ross hadn't been able to win acceptance for a proposal Beijing thought was solid.

At a closed-door meeting with American CEOs in September, China's Foreign Minister Wang Yi vented. "Vice Premier Liu He and Secretary Mnuchin had very detailed discussions down to which products and how much of each," Wang told some ten senior executives from Cheniere Energy, Xcel Energy, and other companies. "There was no problem with importing $100 billion or more in additional U.S. goods," he said. "Unfortunately, after they brought this agreement back to the United States, it was tossed. It disappeared."

Mnuchin did manage to keep the relationship from unraveling

further. His Treasury Department never produced the restrictions on Chinese investment that Trump threatened on May 29.

As the June 30 deadline approached, administration officials met privately in the White House Situation Room to consider alternatives. Mnuchin and other Treasury officials argued that the restrictions faced legal land mines. How would the government know which investments are Chinese, unless you consider them all? What authority did the administration have to examine every investment? Even if the government could find such authority, lengthy reviews could gum up the financial system.

"There's not a way to design a system without a series of loopholes that are easy to exploit, or where well-intentioned investment that intends to seek out profits isn't allowed in the United States," said an official involved in the decision.

The administration had been considering using the extraordinary powers granted to the president under the International Emergency Economic Powers Act (IEEPA). If Trump declared a national emergency, he could block transactions and freeze assets. But IEEPA is used mainly to block assets of terrorist groups, and lumping Beijing in with ISIS would have been a slap in the face for China. Treasury was in charge of administering such sanctions and Mnuchin broadly opposed using the power for reasons outside of national security. Trump backed him on this.

Others, including Navarro, thought the Treasury was inventing excuses to block an initiative it opposed. This time the president rebuffed the hard-liners. Despite his constant resort to threats and tariffs, he wanted foreigners to invest in the United States. As a businessman, he had relied on overseas buyers for his real estate deals.

Rather than block Chinese investments, he directed the administration to endorse a bill making its way through Congress that toughened national security reviews of foreign investment in the United States. The bill had narrower restrictions than the White House had initially envisioned for China. "The president's view has never been that we should cut off investment from China," says Mnuchin in an interview.

• • •

With the failure of the purchasing initiative, the White House's National Economic Council started a quixotic effort to get the president to focus less on the trade deficit and more on the structural issues at the heart of the Section 301 report. It was a long shot. From the start, senior economic officials like Trump's first NEC director, Gary Cohn, had tried to convince Trump that a trade surplus or deficit—especially with one country—wasn't a measure of economic success. Neither economic growth nor job production depended on whether exports outpaced imports. The trade deficit fell by about half during the 2009 recession, for instance, because American consumers had less money to spend on imports.

The White House arguments got heated, with Cohn and Navarro trading insults. The U.S. economy would be far better off if the goods the United States imported were made in America instead, Navarro argued. When others made complicated arguments that linked budget deficits and trade deficits, Navarro dismissed them as "the same old globalist bullshit."

In early 2018, conservative economist Stephen Moore, who had advised Trump during the campaign, and Arthur Laffer, one of President Reagan's favorite economists, prepared a series of charts showing that "economic prosperity in America has been strongly and positively correlated with trade deficits, not trade surpluses," says Moore. The data stretched back to colonial times and showed how the trade deficit declined during the Great Depression. Their longtime friend, NEC Director Larry Kudlow, got them a session with the president to present the evidence. Trump listened, "but I don't think we persuaded him," says Moore. The septuagenarian president was hardly ready to rethink arguments he had made for decades.

In the summer, Kudlow held a series of lunches. This time he tried to recast the issue. Focusing on the trade deficit was less effective than concentrating on the Section 301 complaints. The deficit focus was bound to upset allies the United States could use in its battle with Beijing, Kudlow argued. They would worry that China would increase U.S. imports by reducing their sales. Concentrating on structural issues like subsidies and forced technology transfer could unite allies, who had similar complaints against China. Convincing China to reduce tariffs and other barriers was also a winner because it would encourage China to boost imports long-term, not just as a short-term fix to get the United States off its back. He urged CEOs who met with the president to make similar points.

The effort worked for a while. During the summer of 2018, there was a noticeable drop in how often Trump used the trade deficit to justify his trade war. Trump tweeted fifteen times between March 2 and June 10, 2018, about the importance of the trade deficit. He tweeted about it just three times the rest of the year, though he never dropped the concept entirely.

Other administration officials made a similar shift, including Mnuchin, who was ever-sensitive to changes in Trump world. Although Mnuchin had pressed Beijing to buy more farm produce to shrink the trade deficit, he had a different message in an August 28 appearance on CNBC. "As the president said, it's not just about buying more soybeans," Mnuchin said. "This is about structural changes that create fair market access."

But Trump never fully accepted his advisers' arguments. Clete Willems, the White House trade adviser, says he began to understand why the president focused so much on deficits when he accompanied him on a trip to London. There the president complained to British Prime Minister Theresa May about Germany backing the Nord Stream 2 natural gas pipeline between Russia and Germany because it transferred wealth to Moscow. "It's like the trade deficit with China," Trump told May. "We give them money, which makes them stronger."

For Trump, a trade deficit with China meant Americans were transferring their money to China, making China wealthier and more powerful at U.S. expense. Just another example of the United States making China a winner and the United States a loser. By that same logic, of course, Chinese purchases of trillions of dollars of U.S. bonds would be making the United States more powerful at Chinese expense because of the money flooding into the Treasury's coffers. But Trump never bought the latter argument; the administration looked at Chinese purchases of U.S. Treasuries as a weakness because Beijing could threaten to dump the securities and drive up U.S. interest rates.

• • •

On June 15, the administration announced the details of the 25 percent tariffs it would impose on $50 billion of Chinese goods. The United States divided the tariffs into two parts, with levies on the first $34 billion going into effect on July 6, and the rest later in the summer after additional hearings to get public comment. The tariffs hit 818 different product categories, though clothing, furniture, mobile phones, and other consumer goods weren't hit. Many of the proscribed goods were industrial components that only factory hands could identify. The Council of Economic Advisers had created a computer algorithm to go through every line of products the United States imported from China and picked those where tariffs hurt China more than the United States.

The administration claimed that putting levies on these goods would make it harder for China to move ahead with its "Made in China 2025" plan to dominate advanced technology, although the levies had big downsides. Raising the price of imported diodes, electric motors, plastics, and other widgets was bound to raise the costs of manufacturing in the United States and make American manufacturing less competitive.

Should China retaliate, as it quickly warned that it would, Trump threatened on June 18 that the United States would hit another $200 billion in Chinese imports with tariffs. Retaliate again and the United States would target another $200 billion in Chinese imports. That would mean tariffs on nearly all the $505 billion in goods that China sold to the United States in 2017. Trump, as schoolyard bully, was threatening to batter his opponent into submission.

With the deadline approaching, Beijing moved to line up allies and present itself as a victim of U.S. economic aggression. At meetings inside Beijing's gated Zhongnanhai leadership compound, officials worked out policies that would help U.S. trading partners get broader access to China's market, but deny the benefits to U.S. firms. Trump needed to understand what the United States would lose in a trade war.

By the early summer, the State Council, China's top government body, was ready to lower tariffs on imported washing machines, cosmetics, and other consumer goods. It was also drafting what it called a "negative list"—limiting the areas that were off-limits to foreign investors.

If the United States imposed tariffs on Chinese imports, Beijing would retaliate with tariffs on U.S. imports. Effectively, that meant U.S. exporters wouldn't benefit from China's planned liberalization, while exporters from Europe, Japan, and elsewhere would. Beijing figured that U.S. companies would press the Trump administration harder if they feared being left out of the growing Chinese market.

Beijing also sought multilateral trade deals as a way to help its exporters if they were blocked from the U.S. market. That included an investment agreement with the European Union, which would help EU companies expand in China ahead of American ones. Beijing also tried to speed up negotiations over the Regional Comprehensive Economic Partnership (RCEP), a trade deal involving fifteen countries in the Asia-Pacific region, which excluded the United States. By early 2020, China, Japan, South Korea, Australia, and other countries agreed on the outlines of a trade partnership but India pulled out for fear that its economy could be flooded with Chinese manufactured goods and Australian and New Zealand farm imports. Chinese leaders pledged to address those concerns.

But Beijing still found it difficult to tempt longtime U.S. allies to join forces. Japan, which saw China as a military threat, convinced Washington to explore multilateral pressure on China. Negotiators from the United States, EU, and Japan met periodically to plot joint policies on subsidies and forced technology transfer. Tokyo hoped to use these talks as a launchpad for negotiations at the World Trade Organization that would bring global pressure on China to change.

To improve their chances at winning allies, Chinese leaders worked on their image overseas. In March, China Film Group, a state-owned monopoly, started to distribute a ninety-minute documentary called *Bravo, My Country*. The film heralded the country's high-speed rail lines, a massive bridge-and-tunnel system linking the cities of Hong Kong, Zhuhai, and Macau, a supersized radio telescope that could be used to detect signs of extraterrestrial life, and the development of superfast wireless technology called 5G. A month later, however, the film was removed from video sites.

"It was just too boastful," said a senior editor at a state-owned newspaper in Beijing, especially when foreign competitors suspected Beijing was trying to overtake the West.

Looking for other ways to get its message out, Liu He instructed the Chinese Economists 50 Forum, an influential think tank he cofounded, to hold an event at Tsinghua University in Beijing, called "A Conversation of Thoughts between China and the World," and to invite Western opinion leaders.

Among the attendees were journalist Carl Bernstein, well known in China for his Watergate reporting; *New York Times* columnist Thomas Friedman, whose scathing pieces on the Trump administration often circulated among Chinese officials; historian Niall Ferguson, who coined the term "Chimerica" with a colleague to describe the symbiotic relationship between China and the United States; and *Financial Times* economics columnist Martin Wolf, who has a big following in China.

It's rare for Chinese officials to court foreign journalists, and officials wanted to control how they would be covered. Those invited could report on the gist of their messages, but the officials insisted that they not be identified by name. Under those conditions the officials sought to improve Beijing's image, or at least clarify the leadership's intentions.

Yang Weimin, at the time a top deputy to Liu He, explained that Xi Jinping's pledge five years earlier to give the market a "decisive role" in the economy didn't mean the government wouldn't play a role. The market was responsible for pricing assets and resources, while the government set macroeconomic policies and regulations, Yang said, according to a transcript of the forum. All in all, not much different from the market reform policy ushered in by Deng Xiaoping, which the West had applauded.

But he warned that China was suspicious of U.S. motives and believed that Washington wanted to keep China from advancing. "You can't let China only make T-shirts while the U.S. does high-tech," Yang said. "That is unreasonable."

Some speakers denied Washington's allegations that China subsidizes state companies. "There are no subsidies, that's for sure," said Ning Gaoning, chairman of the state-owned China National Chemical Corporation, known as ChemChina. But he did admit that the government had handouts for favored industries, such as wind power and fuel ethanol, though he said that was open to private firms, too. "That is industrial policy, not policy just for state-owned enterprises," Ning said.

Others at the forum were more forthright. Major General Zhu Chenghu, dean of the Defense College at China's National Defense University, said the Chinese military had learned a lot from the United States. By 2049, the hundredth anniversary of the People's

Republic, he said, China's armed forces would become a world-class military, as promised by Xi Jinping. That means "we can be benchmarked against the U.S. military," Zhu said.

As the date for the tariffs drew closer, Xi Jinping's hope for a quick deal all but vanished. He resorted to more of a bare-knuckle approach, looking to bully Trump's corporate friends. Washington couldn't miss the signal.

On June 21, a group of twenty mostly American and European multinational CEOs gathered at the Diaoyutai State Guesthouse for their annual meeting. The group, called the Global CEO Council, had in the past met with Premier Li Keqiang rather than the president. By taking the meeting himself, Xi sought to press business leaders to help him get American politicians to ease off on China and to warn them they could be wounded in a trade war if they failed.

"In the West you have the notion that if somebody hits you on the left cheek, you turn the other cheek," the Chinese leader said. "In our culture, we punch back."

Preferential treatment awaited those companies whose home countries weren't fighting with China. "If one door closes, another will open," Xi said, using the indirect language of the Chinese leadership to deliver a very direct threat. The group included executives from Goldman Sachs Group, Prologis Inc., Hyatt Hotels Corporation, and other U.S. firms. European firms included Volkswagen Group, AstraZeneca PLC, and Schneider Electric SE.

At the end of the gathering, Xi's frustration with the United States boiled over. "We respect your democratic system," the Chinese leader said. "Why can't you respect ours?"

• • •

July 6, 2018 was a typical summer day in Washington, D.C. The temperature neared 90 degrees at noon, and thunder showers passed through town at dinnertime. There was little to mark the day as the start of a trade war with China that would rock global markets and threaten to dump both nations into recession, as the United States put in place its first round of tariffs aimed solely at Beijing. Steve Bannon, President Trump's onetime chief strategist, was gleeful. "China has been in a trade war with us for twenty years," he said. "Now someone is standing up and fighting for American workers." But the White House was silent, not even putting out a press release to mark the moment. "The president didn't want to make a big deal of it," said a senior White House official. "He values his relationship with Xi."

The battle quickly deepened. Although White House trade adviser Peter Navarro had predicted that China would be too cowed to retaliate, Beijing did just that. In striking back, China chose 545 types of goods that would face the same 25 percent tariffs that the United States had picked to shut out Chinese imports. The initial targets included soybeans, pork, chicken, seafood, sport utility vehicles, and electric vehicles. Later in the summer, industrial components were added to the list. If Trump wanted a trade war, Beijing would make sure farmers and rural areas, Trump's core supporters, would suffer.

Both sides started with levies on $34 billion of goods, with tariffs on an additional $16 billion to roll out in early August. But before the second round of tariffs was put in place, Trump vastly upped the stakes. Angered at the temerity of China to match U.S. tariffs dollar-for-dollar, on July 10 the administration started legal proceedings to tag another $200 billion in Chinese goods with 10 percent tariffs, which Trump later said might be raised to 25 percent. Because U.S. imports of $505 billion in goods from China far surpassed China's U.S. imports of $130 billion, Trump figured the United States had the upper hand in a trade battle. The United States had far more room to assess tariffs than China did. "They'll run out of bullets first," he told aides.

The impact of the tariffs began to sweep through both nations during the summer. In the early part of 2018, exports had been one of China's strengths, rising 4.9 percent in the first half of the year. China's shipments to the United States also continued to grow, up 5.4 percent during the period. Both figures continued to increase in the following months despite the U.S. tariffs, as Chinese manufacturers raced to fill holiday orders from their American customers and ship goods before the trade conflict got worse.

But the trade fight cast a pall over business and investor confidence in China's economy, which was already slowing due to government efforts to control borrowing and rampant investments. China's markets swooned. Businesses delayed or canceled expansion plans, and consumers started to tighten their purse strings.

In the southern boomtown of Shenzhen, a few miles from Hong Kong, factory owners Du Yaliang and his wife, Shao Danping, were among the manufacturers who saw orders dry up as customers sought other sources of supply. The couple's Shenzhen Wonder Office Appliances Company made machines that print numbers, expiration dates, and other information on plastic cards. Shenzhen Wonder's customers were mainly American. Although the company's products weren't on Trump's initial hit list, sales dropped anyway because American customers were wary the firm would eventually be targeted.

By early fall of 2018, production machinery in the three-story factory was largely sitting idle. Half the factory's first floor was leased out to another company. "We didn't feel anything even during the 2008 global financial crisis," said Shao, an engineer-turned-entrepreneur in her late fifties. "The trade war is really killing our business."

In the United States, the initial tariffs jacked up the price of machinery components, which started a hunt for alternatives to China. In Elkhart, Indiana, where most of the nation's recreational vehicles are made, China tariffs piled on top of steel tariffs to increase prices of RVs and drive down sales. The decline came after eight years of stunning growth and unemployment so low that a Kentucky Fried Chicken restaurant in the area offered $150 signing bonuses for workers.

Robert Martin, chief executive of Thor Industries Inc., the nation's largest RV maker, says he was in the waiting room of Jim Cramer's *Mad Money* TV show in March 2018 when he heard that Trump decided to impose steel tariffs. He figured that the threat of tariffs was enough to get buyers to delay buying expensive RVs. Facing falling sales, RV makers "de-contented" some of the products, Martin says, meaning they started using less expensive flooring, cabinets, and sofas to try to keep prices from rising too much because of the tariff hit.

Still, Elkhart was a place where tariffs sometimes worked as the administration hoped they would to drive production out of China. When Chinese electric motors were hit with U.S. tariffs, LCI Industries Inc., an RV component maker, switched to suppliers in India, Vietnam, and Malaysia. LCI CEO Jason Lippert says he started manufacturing jacks and other hydraulic parts in Indiana rather than China after he reassessed his production costs because of tariffs.

FOR SAVANNAH LUGGAGE WORKS in Vidalia, Georgia, one of the few remaining American luggage makers, the impact of the tariffs was devastating. Savannah produces luggage for brand-name companies that want Made-in-America products. The wheels, hand assemblies, and plastic parts Savannah used came from China, where nearly all American luggage makers had moved their factories. After these components were hit by tariffs—or simply threatened with tariffs—Savannah's biggest luggage customer dropped the firm in the summer of 2018.

"They needed a certain margin," says Allen Rice, the company's president. "Once the tariffs came in, they couldn't get the margin."

Savannah leased out one of its three factory buildings that it no longer needed.

China's retaliatory tariffs also hit hard, especially in farm states.
Soybean prices dropped 20 percent as sales to China fell by more
than 90 percent after the tariff decision. Pork sales also fell sharply.
In Minnesota, soybean and corn farmer Keith Schrader said in July
that depressed prices had soured his outlook at his 5,000-acre operation. "When the trade stuff hit—boom—we went back to unprof-
itability," Schrader said.

Trump looked to cushion the blow for his farm state supporters
with a $12 billion program of farm payments, which the Agriculture
Department calculated would equal the impact of the Chinese tariffs. However, the United States had no answer for other forms of
Chinese retaliation.

China's antitrust regulator delayed for so long its approval of
Qualcomm Inc.'s planned $44 billion purchase of Dutch company
NXP Semiconductors NV—a deal widely seen as critical for the U.S.
chip maker—that the acquisition fell apart. In late May, when trade
talks between the United States and China looked promising, the
Chinese regulator hinted it was ready to wrap up the review and
clear the transaction. But after the United States imposed tariffs,
President Xi expressed reservations about approving the deal for
fear the combined company would be too tough a competitor for
Chinese firms. Xi didn't return Trump's favor when the president
took political heat for sparing China's ZTE Corporation from a
death sentence.

"No U.S.-related deal could be cleared without approval from
the higher-up," a Chinese official says.

By the summer of 2018, some lessons should have been clear to
Beijing, though China's leaders still didn't seem to get the message.
The road to a deal with Trump led through Lighthizer, not Mnuchin,
whom Trump and his trade guru Lou Dobbs saw as soft on China.
Trump saw little reason to back away from his tariff strategy, which

was hurting the Chinese economy, but hadn't so far frightened U.S. markets. The Dow Jones Industrial Average rose 1,500 points in the two months following the July 6 imposition of tariffs.

And China could no longer count on its U.S. business allies to be effective lobbyists in the White House on trade issues. Trade groups formed coalitions to halt the tariffs and failed. The most they received was a pledge by the trade representative to hold hearings on the impact of tariffs, which gave businesses the chance to state their case. Lighthizer, a careful lawyer who fretted about the trade offensive being overturned in U.S. courts, surely would have held the hearings anyway.

While the White House worked closely with business groups on tax cuts and deregulation, and the president nominated former lobbyists to cabinet posts, business had little sway when it came to trade. Years of lobbying for China—from pressing President Clinton to overturn his human rights policy to spending heavily to get China into the World Trade Organization—had caught up with Corporate America.

When Lighthizer spoke before the Business Roundtable, a big business trade group, back in September 2017, he made his views clear to an assembly of one hundred CEOs. "I understand where you're coming from and you have to maximize profits, and that means doing everything, including exporting jobs," he said. "My job is different. My job is to represent American workers." To the Trump White House, business groups were a stand-in for Beijing.

14

THE COMPLAINT: CHINESE ARM-TWISTING

Business Roundtable CEOs were furious at Lighthizer's comments. What arrogance. A White House trade lawyer claiming he cared more about their employees than they did, the people who signed the workers' checks. But Lighthizer and the rest of Trump's top advisers felt they were working for U.S. business, too. They had the guts to take on China over the issues that CEOs complained about privately but were too frightened to speak about publicly. Beijing was after their most valuable technology and would steal it either through spying or through arm-twisting. That had to stop, the Trump administration believed, or the United States would lose its edge economically and militarily. Beijing denied it was engaged in such outrageous practices. The clash was at the heart of the U.S.-China trade war. It was the reason the two antagonists had stopped circling each other and started to brawl.

Beijing has many ways to purloin U.S. technology. The most mundane is hiring away employees who have worked on advanced technology for U.S. companies and paying them to bring the secrets with them. More sophisticated is using cyber espionage to infiltrate company computer networks. But outright theft is less important to

China's technology drive than subtler means. Beijing coerces companies to hand over their technology to get access to the Chinese market. Sometimes the pressure is applied through joint venture arrangements. Sometimes through regulators who feed technology secrets to Chinese companies. Sometimes through raids by antitrust investigators. Sometimes through local courts ready to help hometown companies by invalidating American firms' patents and licensing arrangements.

Chris Padilla, an IBM vice president, has wide experience dealing with Beijing as a Washington lobbyist and a former U.S. trade official. During a January 2019 lunch at the U.S. Chamber of Commerce in Washington, he tried to explain to the visiting U.S. ambassador to China, Terry Branstad, how Beijing applies pressure. "It's like someone getting knifed in a dark alley," Padilla said. "You don't know who did it until the next morning. But there has been a murder."

DuPont de Nemours Inc. has yet to escape its knife fight. It suspected its onetime partner in China was getting hold of a prized chemical technology and spent more than a year fighting in arbitration to make the former partner stop.

Then twenty antitrust investigators showed up in December 2017. They fanned out through DuPont's Shanghai offices, demanding passwords to the company's worldwide research network. Investigators printed documents, seized computers, and intimidated employees, even accompanying some when they went to the bathroom.

The antitrust investigators left a message: DuPont should drop its arbitration case against its onetime partner, which DuPont felt had made off with valuable technology for producing textile fibers from corn, a $400 million business for the company in 2017.

In 2006, DuPont shared manufacturing processes with Zhangjiagang Glory Chemical Industry Company when it licensed the Chinese firm to produce and distribute Sorona, the textile polymer made from corn. DuPont executives labeled the Glory deal a "tolling" partnership—meaning that DuPont paid a kind of toll to get into the Chinese market. Over three years, DuPont trained Glory employees to set up a factory to produce Sorona polymer and to spin it into fibers.

"We believe our partnership with Glory will help us expand our business on a global level," said Peter Hemken, a DuPont vice president, in 2006. He praised Zhangjiagang Glory and its leadership for their "impressive operating experience [and] attention to quality."

Praise gave way to acrimony. Around 2013, DuPont didn't renew Glory's license because it suspected the Chinese firm was ripping off its intellectual property and selling products similar to Sorona. DuPont filed two arbitration cases in China, alleging patent infringement. Hearings stretched through 2017. DuPont especially worried that it would face Zhangjiagang Glory competition in other overseas markets.

Around that time, officials with the antitrust division of the powerful National Development and Reform Commission (NDRC) got involved and started holding meetings with DuPont. Chinese investigators focused on the DuPont-Glory standoff, not DuPont's upcoming mega-merger with Dow Chemical Company. With three days of meetings scheduled before Christmas 2017, DuPont worried that the NDRC would raid its offices. DuPont planned an employee training session on how to deal with one, but the antitrust cops showed up before the training session.

After the raid, DuPont had at least five meetings in 2018 with NDRC officials, who told them they were looking at antitrust behavior, specifically their unwillingness to license technology to Chinese firms and their pursuit of the Glory case. Expect a heavy fine, the investigators said. But after the late November 2018 session, NDRC went silent. With the U.S.-China trade war deepening, DuPont officials feared that even dropping the case wouldn't satisfy Beijing, which might want a hostage in the trade fight with

Washington. DuPont and Zhangjiagang Glory declined to make officials available for comment.

Other firms also say antitrust cops have bullied them. In 2013, InterDigital Inc., a mobile technology firm, refused to meet with the NDRC, which was investigating the firm for the licensing fees it charged Huawei Technologies. The company feared its employees would be arrested. "We are simply unable to comply with any investigation that is accompanied by a threat to the safety of our executives," said InterDigital's chief executive, William Merritt. The company eventually settled with the NDRC by reaffirming its licensing practices, including offering arbitration.

"Chinese enterprises should bravely employ antimonopoly lawsuits to break technology barriers and win space for development," said the Chinese chief judge in the InterDigital case, encouraging Beijing to use antitrust suits to pry away American technology.

In a 2018 survey by the U.S. Chamber of Commerce in China, one in two technology and industrial companies said they limited their investment in China because they feared their technology could be stolen. In August 2019, 91 percent of companies in a U.S.-China Business Council survey said they were concerned about China's enforcement of intellectual property rights. In 2013, about one-third of U.S.-China Business Council respondents said they had been asked to transfer technology to China recently. While that response shrank to just 5 percent in 2019, the change likely reflected China's reduced use of joint ventures to pry away technology. Beijing uses many more tools to acquire company secrets.

The U.S. companies felt bullied by Beijing and feared retribution if they complained publicly. They pressed the U.S. government quietly for action. U.S. semiconductor firms lobbied against Chinese efforts to buy U.S. semiconductor companies, which convinced the Obama administration to block such purchases. Then the chip makers complained that Beijing was using massive subsidies to create semiconductor rivals and pressured them to hand over technology.

That became a Trump administration priority. But the firms rarely make a fuss in public. China is the chip makers' largest market.

High-tech companies, however, were ready to criticize the administration for the massive tariffs it used to pressure Beijing, a position that struck many in the administration as ungrateful and two-faced. Tariffs raise their costs and make them less able to compete, the companies argued—the opposite of what the administration said it wanted to accomplish. To many high-tech firms, the trade offensive had an almost Vietnam War quality: "It became necessary to destroy the town to save it," a U.S. officer said at the time. Two networking companies, Cisco Systems and Juniper Networks, used less colorful language to make a similar point when they filed comments objecting to tariff hikes: "By raising the costs of networking products, the proposed duties would impede the development of cloud-based services and infrastructure and, perversely, would incentivize" customers to pick foreign competitors.

The administration also remained divided over how hard to push China. Aside from the nationalist-globalist divide in the White House trade team, there were other fractures. National security officials in the Pentagon, National Security Council, and Justice Department pressed for harsh measures and had to battle with the trade officials who sought a deal. Trump let the two sides fight it out.

In December 2018, the Justice Department unsealed criminal charges against two Chinese citizens who allegedly were part of a state-sponsored campaign to steal secrets from U.S. businesses and government agencies. The pair was accused of working for a company called Huaying Haitai in Tianjin, which worked with China's Ministry of State Security. The indictment said their efforts were part of a "continuous and unrelenting effort," called Operation Cloud Hopper, by a Chinese hacking group known as APT 10, for Advanced Persistent Threat, to steal advanced technology.

According to the charging papers, APT 10 used a technique known as "spearphishing" to convince targets to open emails laced with malware that would reveal their passwords to hackers. They targeted companies in at least a dozen countries, including IBM and Hewlett-Packard Enterprise Company. IBM said it was aware of the attacks and had taken measures to protect itself. HPE said the hacking affected customers of a business it had spun off in 2017. HPE products and services weren't affected, the company said.

U.S. allies applauded the detective work, including the four other members of the Anglophone intelligence alliance, known as Five Eyes, which includes Canada, New Zealand, Australia, and Britain. The Trump administration also cited the case to accuse China of violating the 2015 Rose Garden Agreement with President Obama, discussed in chapter 7, not to target businesses for cyber espionage to gain a competitive edge. "More than 90 percent of the [Justice] Department's cases alleging economic espionage over the past seven years involve China," said then Deputy Attorney General Rod Rosenstein. China's Ministry of Foreign Affairs denied the allegations and called the prosecution "a serious violation of the norms of international relations."

The episode was a public relations black eye for Beijing, but it had little practical effect. Beijing wasn't going to turn over the accused to the Americans. To strike back, national security officials wanted to sanction Chinese companies and individuals—which would cut them off from the global financial system. This would illustrate what they called a "whole of government" approach to China, and would have been a coda to what some were privately calling "Fuck China Week." A coordinated response would have been the toughest blow yet struck by the U.S. side in its schoolyard-style battle with China.

UNTIL ABOUT A WEEK before the announcement of the indictment, John Bolton, the national security advisor, thought he had the president's approval to package sanctions with the indictments. But Treasury

Secretary Steven Mnuchin, whose agency oversees sanctions, objected and prevailed. Sanctions have been reserved for countries branded as enemies, such as North Korea or Iran, or to hobble terrorist groups, he argued. He didn't want to extend them to cases of intellectual property protection. Besides, sanctions would screw up chances for a trade deal at a time when markets were already tumbling. President Trump, in his Wall Street mode, decided to ease off a bit on China.

• • •

To Beijing, the U.S. complaint about technology transfer was mystifying and insulting. Americans exported the concept of joint ventures to China four decades ago. During a trip to China in 1978, General Motors Chairman Thomas Murphy proposed the idea of joint ventures to Chinese officials looking for ways to boost China's antiquated auto industry. "Why do you only talk to us about introducing technology, not joint ventures?" Murphy asked his Chinese hosts. "A joint venture is like a marriage and building a family together."

Under the Communist Party, China had never done a joint venture and had no idea that a JV could help China get much-needed technology. As soon as the Americans' proposal was sent to Chinese leader Deng Xiaoping, he approved. "Joint ventures can be done," he said.

To Deng, JVs were a way to obtain Western technology but limit Western influence at a time when most senior officials were deeply suspicious of foreign interest in China. A year later, Deng laid out his reasoning. "To set up a joint venture, the counterpart has to make sure it's economically viable, and has to bring advanced technology with it. Even though it preserves the rights to some technologies, no matter what, we'll get to learn some." In 1984, he pronounced, China "needs to give up portions of the domestic market in exchange for advanced technologies we need."

Since then, generations of Chinese leaders have sought to interest American and other foreign companies to invest in China. A March 2018 paper by economists at universities in Colorado, Illinois, Hong Kong, and Nottingham, England, found that foreign technology "diffuses beyond the confines of the joint venture" and boosts competitors' technology.

When the Trump administration made forced technology transfer, through joint ventures or other means, the heart of its trade offensive, Beijing viewed the accusation as grossly unfair. U.S. companies willingly entered into contracts with Chinese partners, Chinese officials said. Nobody forced the Americans to come—or stay—if they were so upset about their treatment.

During a meeting with a group of U.S. corporate executives in March 2018, just before the United States released its Section 301 report accusing China of twisting arms to obtain U.S. technology, a senior Beijing official sought to explain China's offer to the world. It was "simple," said Fang Xinghai, a top financial regulator and a point person to the U.S. business community. "Foreign companies would be allowed access to China's huge market but would need to contribute something in return—their technology," he told executives from firms including Bank of America Merrill Lynch and buyout firm KKR & Company.

For example, Fang said, China didn't have the technology to make its own aircraft engines, so when the government started buying engines, it sought a company that would share technology so the Chinese firm could learn from its foreign partner. Two of the world's largest jet engine manufacturers, Britain's Rolls-Royce Holdings PLC and America's Pratt & Whitney, looked at the opportunity, he said, but decided not to accept the Chinese terms and walked away. But General Electric "saw the competitive opportunity" and agreed to enter a joint venture and share its technology with a Chinese partner, Fang said. "No one forced GE to share its technology," he added.

Chinese Vice President Wang Qishan also shared the dismay. If the U.S. companies were so concerned about their technology transfer deals, he asked former Obama Treasury Secretary Tim Geithner when he was visiting China, why hadn't the Americans made it a top priority earlier?

China was hardly the first country to try to advance economically by making off with foreign technology. After Britain invented the modern textile factory in the 1770s, it tried to block foreign competition by prohibiting artisans from emigrating until 1825 and forbidding most machinery exports until 1842. People and technology left anyway. France set up its first cotton mill in 1778; America followed in 1791.

As trade tensions escalated, Beijing ratcheted up its rebuttal. In a white paper issued in late September 2018, after Washington hiked tariffs on $200 billion of Chinese products, China called the United States' forced tech-transfer accusations "distorted and filthy." Any transfer of technology between a U.S. company and its Chinese partner was a result of negotiations between the companies, the paper said. It also detailed China's enormous investment in technology. Since 2000, according to the white paper, China's total research and development spending had grown at an average rate of nearly 20 percent a year. In 2017, it spent 1.76 trillion yuan, roughly $266 billion, on R&D, second only to the United States.

Chinese officials point to GE's experience in China as an example of their fair dealing. Aircraft manufacturing is a top Chinese priority. GE saw a huge market for its jet engines and other aircraft parts. China's needs became GE's opportunity.

When China set out to build its first large commercial passenger jet, the C919, in 2008, state-owned Commercial Aircraft Corporation of China, or Comac, made it clear it would buy components only from foreign suppliers willing to set up joint ventures in China and share technology. GE willingly agreed.

A year earlier, GE had spent $4.8 billion to buy Smiths Aerospace, a British-based aircraft component supplier. The Smiths business supplied avionics systems, which work like the operating systems on computers, to the Boeing 787 Dreamliner. But the business didn't work out well, and GE was at risk of having to write off a big portion of the Smiths investment, according to former employees. When the Chinese government put out bids for its C919 program in 2009, GE jumped at the opportunity to set up a joint venture, even though that meant sharing technology.

In 2009, Jeff Immelt, then GE's chairman and CEO, and Lin Zuoming, chairman of state-owned Aviation Industry Corporation, or Avic, did a handshake deal to set up a jointly owned manufacturer of avionics system. But it took the 50/50 joint venture, called Aviage Systems, three years to get up and running as the two companies squabbled over intellectual property protection, leadership and staff structures, computer safeguards, and other issues.

Avic at first wouldn't provide its own engineers for the venture. It wanted GE to supply all the key personnel so that the Chinese side could learn GE know-how. Eventually the two companies compromised: GE provided some engineers, and the venture, based in Shanghai, also hired locally.

Another issue: The Chinese partner wanted GE to set up the venture's computer servers, where all data are stored, in China. Western companies fear that arrangement makes it easier for Chinese hackers to steal information. As a compromise, GE insisted that IBM help manage the servers. In March 2012, the JV was officially formed. A year later, it got the contract from Comac, the state-owned aerospace manufacturer, to be a major supplier of avionics systems for the C919. Avionics systems are the second most-important component in aircraft after engines.

GE says it has protected its technology and is pleased with the arrangement. It also denies there had been a risk of a write-down to its avionics business. In recent years, China has become the second-largest market for the company after the United States, and the company has focused on China's power and health care sectors, along with avionics. No complaints from GE; only praise.

"GE believes that the only way to achieve growth in China is to grow together with our Chinese customers," Rachel Duan, president and CEO of GE China, told the country's official Xinhua News Agency in late 2017.

By 2015, China had selected sixteen foreign firms, including Honeywell and Rockwell Collins, to set up aerospace ventures in the country. These JVs, said Comac in a press release, had "improved the overall level of China's aerospace R&D and manufacturing through technology transfer, diffusion, and spillover."

For Beijing, the GE venture is Exhibit A in its defense against the Trump administration's allegations of coerced technology transfer. But Congress and the White House drew the opposite conclusion: the partnership illustrated how China uses JVs to pressure U.S. partners to relinquish technology.

Although GE got clearances from the Defense and Commerce departments to go ahead with the deal, the JV caught the attention of Senator John Cornyn of Texas, who feared JVs helped China move ahead militarily and who was pushing legislation to stiffen national security reviews of U.S. companies in China. "GE was a concern," says Senator Cornyn. "China is notorious for its theft of intellectual property, and very skillful at insisting on joint ventures, which give them access to technology and also know-how to make systems in China."

His staff noted that the Pentagon had listed avionics as a Chinese weakness in 2009 when the GE-Avic deal was announced. By 2011, the Pentagon no longer did, as Avic and GE were in final negotiations for the joint venture, which was established in 2012.

"'Voluntary' technology transfer takes place, but one that is only voluntary in the sense that the business transactions engaged in by the fictional gangster of the *Godfather* series, Vito Corleone, were voluntary," said the Trump administration's Section 301 report, quoting Carnegie Mellon economist Lee Branstetter. "China is effectively making an offer multinationals cannot refuse."

. . .

Complaints about Chinese pressure on foreign companies go well beyond joint venture arrangements. A big concern involves regulatory panels that scrutinize new projects by foreign companies, including those in the chemical and auto industries, to make sure they meet environmental, production, and other standards set by authorities. These panels can become a way for local officials to pass foreigners' trade secrets to Chinese competitors. In China, the government frequently staffs the so-called expert panels with members from Chinese universities, research shops, and state-owned firms. U.S. companies say they routinely demand more information than is formally required for approval and pass the data to Chinese firms.

"Companies have been required to disclose an amount of proprietary information sufficient for product duplication," the American Chemistry Council, a trade association of chemical companies, told the trade representative's office in 2018. That includes chemical identities, manufacturing information, and product formulations. Chinese companies steal microbial strains engineered to produce proteins, the ACC earlier said, and then rebrand them and sell copycat versions to the textile and grain ethanol industries.

Huntsman Corporation has singled out expert panels as a conduit for siphoning off trade secrets. The panels have drilled down on specialized knowledge, including how Huntsman makes plastics with high transparency and elasticity—the kind of materials used to make athletic shoes. Soon after the expert panels finished their work, Huntsman's Chinese competitors used the same kind of technology in their own products.

The Woodlands, Texas, chemical maker entered the Chinese market in 1992, when it opened a technical service center. Since then it has set up joint ventures with state-owned China Petroleum

& Chemical Corporation, or Sinopec, among others. China now is Huntsman's second-largest market after the United States, accounting for nearly 14 percent of its 2018 revenue.

But the company has grown increasingly worried about losing its competitive edge to Chinese firms that it suspects steal its technology. "Our competition isn't going to be standing on the sidelines cheering," CEO Peter Huntsman told analysts in June 2018, speaking of China. They could be "trying to either steal the technology or develop the technology themselves." Huntsman declined to be interviewed.

Huntsman laid out the risks it encounters in China in its 2019 annual report. "Certain of our competitors in various countries in which we do business, including China, may be owned by or affiliated with members of local governments and political entities," it says. "These competitors may get special treatment with respect to regulatory compliance and product registration, while certain of our products, including those based on new technologies, may be delayed or even prevented from entering into the local market."

For more than a decade, Huntsman has been battling in China over a crown jewel of its business, a black dye used in textiles that is less polluting to make. In 2007, it filed a lawsuit in Shanghai against a Chinese company for infringing a patent on the dye. Huntsman then found a court-appointed review panel stacked against it, it said in a 2011 complaint filed with the U.S. Commerce Department.

The three-member panel included an engineer from the company Huntsman was suing, another from a local dye research group, and a third who once worked at a local dye firm, according to the complaint and people with knowledge of the matter. The experts' work "effectively turned them into allies and 'spokespersons'" for the Chinese competitor, the complaint said.

Litigation of the patent infringement case has dragged on. In addition, Huntsman in 2017 filed another patent infringement suit involving the black dye against two Chinese companies. The Beijing intellectual property court in October 2018 dismissed Huntsman's case on the grounds that the samples in question were too out of date. Huntsman believes that the court ignored significant pieces of evidence submitted by the company and omitted much of this evidence in its final judgment. It has appealed the ruling.

In February 2019, Representative Kevin Brady of Texas, the top Republican on the House Ways and Means Committee, whose district includes Huntsman facilities, discussed the firm's problem in a congressional hearing with Lighthizer. "The Huntsman example is unfortunately one of many, many thousands," Lighthizer said.

• • •

Chinese firms can also use hometown courts to their advantage. Should a U.S. firm win a patent infringement case in a U.S. court against a Chinese competitor, the Chinese firm can push for a contrary ruling back home. That blocks the U.S. firm from selling products in China—a tactic that makes a company think twice about continuing to fight.

Veeco Instruments Inc., a maker of semiconductor manufacturing machinery in Plainview, New York, faced that dilemma. Veeco produces machinery, known as reactors, to make LED chips, a technology that's a priority to China. Heavy subsidies by the Chinese government in 2012 led to a boom in the LED chip industry, with 100 manufacturers producing the chips, including 60 in China, according to a report by Benchmark Company, a market research firm.

Those manufacturers needed reactors to make the chips and Veeco was one of the most advanced producers of such equipment. Veeco's sales from China jumped to $242 million in 2015 from $149 million in 2013.

Veeco's main Chinese competitor, Advanced Micro-Fabrication Equipment Inc., in Shanghai, known as AMEC, is run by a veteran of Applied Materials Inc., a Silicon Valley semiconductor equipment maker. Veeco suspected that AMEC reverse engineered its products to make a competitive product that infringed on Veeco patents. Veeco also suspects AMEC hired some of its employees in China who knew the technology well. AMEC sharply undercut Veeco's prices on the reactors, which go for about $2 million each, and started to gain big market share.

Worried about preserving its market, Veeco turned to the U.S. courts to sue one of AMEC's major U.S. component manufacturers for also infringing its patent, hoping to hobble AMEC's ability to produce LED-manufacturing machinery. In a seventy-six-page opinion filled with engineering drawings and a detailed examination of Veeco's highly technical claims, Veeco won a decision in U.S. district court in Brooklyn on November 2, 2017, that blocked AMEC from getting critical components. Veeco figured it scored a knockout because it would probably take AMEC a year to find another qualified supplier.

Instead, AMEC turned to a Chinese court in Fujian province, a big LED chip production center where AMEC has facilities, and sued Veeco for patent infringement. In Securities and Exchange Commission filings, Veeco said that the Fujian court didn't notify the company of the hearing or hear its position on the alleged patent infringement. Fujian courts are "very hospitable [to Chinese firms] because of Fujian's semiconductor industrial policy," said Mark Cohen, a former China expert at the U.S. Patent and Trademark Office. "It's the heart of darkness."

On December 6, 2017—one month after the U.S. court ruled in Veeco's favor—Fujian Higher People's Court forbid Veeco from selling its LED reactors in China. The four-page decision didn't include any discussion of the technical issues involved.

With Veeco blocked from China, in February 2018 it cut a deal with AMEC but couldn't obtain a long-term licensing agreement. Essentially, the Chinese firm was free to use Veeco-developed technology in its products. With AMEC's price advantage, Veeco's Chinese sales plummeted to $108 million in 2017. Although sales in

China rebounded in 2018, the company's losses widened substantially and Veeco executives say they don't expect China to be a big revenue generator in the future.

Veeco won't comment on the case; its SEC filings say it and AMEC "mutually agreed to settle." AMEC didn't respond to requests for comment.

Mark Miller, an analyst at Benchmark, says, "Veeco put up resistance. But in the end, the odds weren't in their favor. With a government like China's, you have very little recourse."

• • •

As the U.S.-China trade fight rolled on, China sought to address U.S. complaints about forced technology transfer, although it never admitted that it sanctioned the practice. During its annual legislative session in March 2019, the National People's Congress made last-minute changes to a proposed foreign investment law to tighten channels used to leak intellectual property.

Foreign businesses, which wanted to compete on equal terms as domestic firms, avidly sought the new law. Legislative and government bodies had worked on drafts for years, but then abandoned the efforts about four years ago, without explanation. Vice Premier Liu He, who has been leading the negotiations with the United States, helped push the law through. He saw it as a way to address U.S. complaints about intellectual property, investment restrictions, and other issues. The legislature then fast-tracked it for passage.

Earlier drafts of the law pledged broadly to protect foreign technology and said abuse of power by officials could be prosecuted criminally, but lacked specifics. The language in the final version of the law, which went into effect at the beginning of 2020, more directly addressed U.S. concerns over transgressions by Chinese officials. "Administrative agencies and their employees shall keep confidential the commercial secrets of foreign investors," the law says. They "should not divulge or illegally provide [them] to other people." The new language took aim at the regulatory reviews, known as "conformity assessments," that foreign companies must pass before manufacturing new cars and other products or setting up plants.

The new law reflected the proposed text of the trade agreement the two sides were negotiating at the time. Under that text, China would agree to "eliminate conflicts of interest" in such regulatory reviews to prevent the officials involved from passing foreign companies' proprietary information to Chinese competitors.

But when those negotiations broke down in early May 2019, as described in chapter 1, Beijing toughened its stance again. A white paper released a month later again called the U.S. accusation of China's technology theft "absurd."

* * *

With trade talks producing few results, U.S. companies hit on a different strategy—seeking financial sanctions on Chinese competitors to shut them down.

Micron Technology Inc., a large U.S. memory chip maker, got caught up in dueling lawsuits with a Chinese competitor, similar to the situation faced by Veeco. Micron helped Taiwanese prosecutors build a case that its technology was being stolen by former Micron employees who had gone to work for a Taiwanese chip maker, United Microelectronics Corporation. Taiwanese authorities say the evidence included stolen documents with detailed production secrets for producing Micron's chips. The data was ultimately intended to help a Chinese semiconductor company, Fujian Jinhua Integrated Circuit Company, which planned to manufacture its version of Micron chips.

In December 2017, Micron alleged in a California lawsuit that Jinhua masterminded the plan to learn the complicated processes involved in semiconductor manufacturing. Three months later, Jinhua sued Micron in Fuzhou Intermediate People's Court in Fujian province for patent infringement—essentially accusing Micron of stealing its technology instead of the other way around, and making the accusations in its home court. Jinhua is located in Fujian province; the Fujian government partly controls Jinhua.

In July 2018, Jinhua won a preliminary injunction prohibiting Micron from selling certain electronics in China. The injunction cost Micron about $300 million in sales, roughly 1 percent of Micron's total revenue. Company officials considered the Chinese action to be a warning shot. In a statement, Jinhua said Micron "recklessly" infringed on its patents. Micron says it intended "to vigorously protect our intellectual property."

Like Veeco, Micron had a choice: settle or fight. At risk, potentially, was Micron's China sales of $17.4 billion—more than half the company's $30.4 billion revenue in 2018. But the company figured it had leverage; Beijing needed its memory chips to supply the Chinese electronics industry. Shutting down Micron in China could damage Beijing's ability to produce advanced electronics. The company doubled down by lobbying the U.S. government to make its case a priority.

During August 2018 trade talks, U.S. negotiators brought up Micron's complaints that it was being ripped off by Jinhua and treated unfairly in China's courts. Commerce Vice Minister Wang Shouwen dismissed the concerns. Micron and Jinhua "are like brothers," Wang told negotiators. "And brothers fight."

Micron tried a second approach—convincing Washington to levy sanctions on Jinhua for violating Micron's patents. In July 2018, Micron's CEO, Sanjay Mehrotra, and other top executives met with Treasury Secretary Mnuchin. Again, Mnuchin was skeptical about using Treasury's ability to shut off companies from the global financial system to punish patent violators. Doing so could inadvertently block Western countries from buying Chinese equipment with dollars and ignite confrontations with allies. Micron officials suggested Mnuchin invoke emergency powers under the International Emergency Economic Powers Act—a course of action he had rejected a month earlier when he convinced the administration not to single out Beijing for investment restrictions, as recounted in chapter 13.

"I'm not using IEEPA for that," Mnuchin said, growing red in the face. He closed a book he was looking at and ended the meeting.

Micron had better luck with the Commerce Department in September. Although its powers aren't as sweeping as Treasury's, Commerce can block U.S. companies from doing business with foreign companies by putting it on its entity list—the same provision the administration used against ZTE and Huawei Technologies. Only companies that get a Commerce license can sell to a listed company, and Commerce rarely approves such licenses.

Commerce officials required Micron to demonstrate that its problems in China represented a national security threat. Should Jinhua be able to use its technology and produce chips at subsidized prices, Micron argued, that would threaten its survival and ability to supply the military. That was a concern of the Pentagon, too. "Micron has been vocal about the importance of protecting our IP investments," said a Micron spokeswoman, who added that the actions taken by the Commerce and Defense departments "have been based on their own independent review and analysis."

Commerce Secretary Ross was convinced. "The entity list is based on national security," he says in an interview. "IP is very much in the national security." In October 2018, Commerce placed Jinhua on its blacklist. Without access to U.S. technology and components, Jinhua was crippled.

Since the Micron decision, Commerce has used its entity list power in other intellectual property cases. In 2016, Advanced Micro Devices Inc., a Silicon Valley chip company, entered joint ventures with Chinese private and state-owned entities, including the government's Chinese Academy of Sciences and a state-backed supercomputer maker, Sugon Information Industry Company, to make chips licensing AMD's x86 processor technology.

For AMD, the licensing deal was a winner. It was set to receive $293 million, plus licensing fees. The revenue was enough to help boost AMD into the black for 2017, for the first time since 2011. "We created a joint venture that was very much a win-win," said the company CEO, Lisa Su, shortly after the deal was signed in 2016.

But the JV raised concerns in national security agencies that the venture would help China develop supercomputers used to design missiles and nuclear weapons. Intel Corporation also worried that its x86 technology would wind up in Chinese hands. AMD and Intel are the only two companies that make the semi-conductors. AMD initially sold chips that Intel designed but later made its own chips based on the x86.

"It's the Chinese state figuring out ways to get technology," said Mark Newman, a Sanford C. Bernstein & Company technology analyst in Hong Kong.

In June 2019, Commerce added Sugon to the entity list, effectively barring it from getting American technology. AMD says it won't get $93 million of the fee it anticipated, though it believes it can make up the lost revenue through other sales. All in all it was a raw deal from the U.S. government, the company argues. "AMD received no objections whatsoever from any agency to the formation of the joint ventures or to the transfer of technology," said Harry Wolin, AMD's general counsel, in a statement. The technology involved "was of lower performance than other commercially available processors."

Now producers of more mundane products are lobbying to see if they can get their Chinese competitors on the entity list. Brian Harker, president of Better Tools Company, a Granger, Indiana, maker of hand tools, went to the White House in August 2019 to plead his case. He says a big Chinese competitor is ripping off its patented technology, including different ways to make wrenches. Sometimes, he says, U.S. retailers ship his company's product samples to Chinese manufacturers that produce copycat versions at prices he can't match.

"We got tired of suing companies," he says, so he approached the Commerce Department and the Federal Bureau of Investigation for help.

Still, it's uncertain whether U.S. firms will come out ahead through entity listings. Beijing has so many ways to strike back. It is developing its own "unreliable entity" list, which could be used to bar American firms from selling in China.

Micron hasn't declared victory. In August 2019, a Chinese government official in Beijing relayed a message to the company through visitors. The Jinhua entity listing cost the Chinese government the $1 billion it had invested in the company. If Micron's fight with China isn't settled, the official warned, Micron could face damages well in excess of that.

15

OLD FRIENDS NO MORE, SEPTEMBER 2018

With the Trump administration bearing down on Beijing, China's leaders turned to their closest American friends, the Fortune 500 firms that had lobbied for decades on their behalf. In the early 1990s, as we have seen, China's corporate allies pressured President Clinton to drop plans to punish China for oppressing dissidents and other human rights violations. Later in the decade, they spent more than $100 million lobbying Congress to clear the way for China to join the World Trade Organization. The corporate campaigns were so successful that no administration since then, including Trump's, has tried to link China trade with human rights.

During the Hong Kong prodemocracy protests, Congress in November 2019 passed legislation by a near-unanimous vote mandating an annual review of Beijing's treatment of Hong Kong's autonomy, which certainly included respecting human rights there. Punishment would include ending the city's special status, which exempted Hong Kong from the U.S. tariffs and sanctions applied to other Chinese cities and helped make it an international trade center. While the measure reestablished a trade–human rights linkage, Trump only approved the bill reluctantly; a veto could have been easily overridden. He picked the night before Thanksgiving to sign the bill into law and his aides briefed the Chinese government on his plans. The symbolism was impossible to miss: Trump, like presidents before him, had little stomach to pick a fight with Beijing over human rights. A battle could hurt corporate America, which often chose Hong Kong as a gateway city to Asia.

In the schoolyard version of the U.S.-China trade imbroglio, Beijing was turning to its bodyguards for help. American CEOs had convinced prior presidents to back off. Trump, a businessman, would surely cave, too.

But this time when Beijing asked its old friends for help, it often got a cold shoulder. U.S. businesses were angered by a slew of Chinese practices, including technology theft, steep subsidies to their state-owned firms, rigged courts, and phony investigations. Quietly they fed Trump administration officials the information they needed to launch an offensive against Chinese economic policies.

And when the Trump team used tactics that both corporate America and China opposed—especially tariffs on hundreds of billions of dollars of Chinese imports—corporate America was powerless to stop the administration from moving ahead. The president, who relied on big business to fight for his tax cut, lobby Congress over deregulation, and bankroll his reelection campaign, rebuffed his business pals when it came to China.

"The Chinese figure that the bankers and big business own the American government. That's why they go to them," says James McGregor, who has worked for decades in China as a business consultant and a leader of the U.S. Chamber of Commerce in China. "The Chinese are discombobulated now."

In the 1990s, the three leading U.S. corporate trade groups— the Business Roundtable, U.S. Chamber of Commerce, and National Association of Manufacturers—competed for credit with Beijing for lobbying to get China into the WTO. Their members wanted to be first in line when China opened its markets. In the Trump trade war, the three groups took a much different stance. Each publicly proposed agendas for the administration to pressure China to drop objectionable practices. The government's Section 301 report on Chinese forced technology transfer, which served as a kind of declaration of war in the trade battle, cited submissions by the U.S. Chamber fifty-four times. Executives at the three groups presented a united front to press China for change.

"The U.S. business community in China, so long an advocate of good bilateral relations, can no longer be relied upon to be a positive anchor," declared the U.S. Chamber of Commerce in China in April 2019 when it released its annual report on the country's business climate. "The mood has shifted." The lobbying group's survey two months earlier showed a majority of its members favored Washington keeping at least some tariffs on Chinese merchandise as a way to make sure Beijing kept its word. The survey's results certainly didn't win the group any brownie points with the Chinese government.

The change in attitude toward China didn't have a single cause. American businesses faced a steady accretion of practices they found offensive, which accelerated after the global financial crisis in 2008 and 2009. Beijing's "Made in China 2025" report, which laid out goals in 2015 for China to become number one in advanced technology, crystallized concern, as we have seen. Western firms figured the only way Beijing could reach those goals was by stealing their technology and subsidizing their competitors.

Xi Jinping's increasing reliance on state-owned firms and government power also spooked American firms, as did a cybersecurity law that required foreign firms in China to store sensitive data in the country and favor Chinese network equipment over foreign products. Another concern: China had started to put in place an expansive system for monitoring company behavior, called the corporate social credit system, which could be used to blacklist firms that didn't yield to government demands.

A 2019 study by researchers at the University of Pennsylvania, the University of California, Berkeley, and Microsoft Corporation, called "Can a Tiger Change Its Stripes?" documented how Beijing increasingly subsidized state-connected firms. In 1998, before China joined the WTO, 15 percent of state-owned firms had subsidies. In 2013, 45 percent did, though the number of such firms was greatly reduced. Even firms that the state sold off could count on government aid. In 1998, fewer than 15 percent of the privatized firms were subsidized; in 2013, 25 percent to 35 percent received handouts. Formerly state-owned companies "enjoy lower interest rates, larger loan facilities, and more subsidies while suffering poorer performance" than private firms that had no state connections, wrote the researchers.

Market incentives that Beijing once saw as tools to invigorate the economy now were feared as beyond government control, and as potential agents of chaos. "Risks are everywhere in the society, and now more than ever, the government should play a bigger role" in guiding the economy, says Liu Shangxi, a senior adviser to the leadership and head of the Chinese Academy of Fiscal Sciences, a government think tank.

• • •

Corporate executives were able to influence Trump's China policy mainly at the margins, especially when they could argue that his sudden policy shifts threatened to backfire politically. That occurred when Trump suddenly proposed new tariffs on Mexico.

The president wanted U.S. firms to leave China and move to the United States, but his advisers realized a large-scale exodus to the U.S. was unrealistic given America's higher wages and shortage of skilled blue-collar labor. The administration renegotiated the North American Free Trade Agreement, in part, to give Trump's blessing to Mexico as a low-wage haven for China corporate refugees. In Mexico, they could get tariff-free access to the U.S. market, an increasingly powerful incentive as Trump piled on Beijing. The president announced the completion of the trade deal, renamed the

U.S.-Mexico-Canada Agreement, on October 1, 2018, in the Rose Garden. Trump's former chief strategist, Steve Bannon, called it "a great day to be alive."

But seven months later, Trump sought to use trade to squeeze Mexico on immigration. On May 30, 2019, he threatened Mexico with tariffs of 5 percent, which he said he would increase to 25 percent, despite the renegotiated NAFTA, unless Mexico did a better job of stopping migrants trying to cross the U.S. border. The threats made a hash of any plans U.S. companies had of moving from China to Mexico. Out went the promise that goods produced in Mexico would have tariff-free entry into the United States. Companies had to factor into their decision-making Trump's readiness to impose tariffs on any country on a whim.

Treasury Secretary Mnuchin convinced the president to hold off for a week. That would give Mexico time to react and also reduce the market impact. It also gave him time to organize CEOs to lobby the president. Executives from car companies, banks, and technology firms, among others, called into the White House and argued that the president's tariff threat was holding the U.S. border states ransom to his policy shifts. This would harm the U.S. economy and hurt Trump politically. The U.S. Chamber released a state-by-state analysis of the economic damage.

Others in the Trump cabinet objected, too. Trade Representative Robert Lighthizer warned that the move could endanger congressional approval of the new NAFTA. Secretary of State Mike Pompeo cautioned about the impact on U.S. relations with Mexico and other nations.

A week later, Trump dropped the threat, as Mexico pledged to toughen border enforcement, though businesses continued to worry that he could, at any time, threaten border trade again.

Mexico was the exception where business was able to convince Trump to reverse himself on a trade measure. There China policy was a secondary consideration to the tumult at the border and Trump's focus on illegal immigration. The president's closest corporate friends and advisers had little ability to influence the way he ran his trade battle with Beijing. For the most part, they acted as intermediaries, trying to get a new round of talks going after either side shut down communications. They provided intelligence about what the Chinese were thinking, and did the same for their Chinese friends who needed intel on the Trump team. Corporate executives also warned the president that layering tariff after tariff on China would tank the stock market, push the economy toward recession, and endanger his chances at reelection. Those warnings sometimes gave Trump pause, but they didn't stop his relentless use of tariffs to try to bludgeon China.

His cast of corporate advisers on China included casino owners whose businesses depended on a thriving Chinese economy. In 2017, former Las Vegas casino magnate Steve Wynn, whose Macau casinos relied on licenses from Beijing, hand-delivered a letter to the president from the Chinese government about Guo Wengui, a wealthy fugitive who criticized the Chinese leadership for corruption, the *Wall Street Journal* reported. Beijing wanted him sent back to China. The United States didn't return Guo, who some later accused of acting as a double agent for Beijing by helping to identify dissidents. Guo's attorney, Daniel Podhaskie, released a statement saying that the spy charge "utterly lacks credibility" and that Guo is Beijing's "most wanted dissident worldwide." A Wynn spokesman has denied he had tried to help Beijing.

In August 2019, the U.S. Chamber's executive vice president, Myron Brilliant, recruited casino billionaire Sheldon Adelson, among other big Republican contributors, to make the case to the president that he should patch up relations with China. Adelson depended enormously on China. His casino company, Las Vegas Sands Corporation, has had operations in Macau since 2002, and in 2018 the company derived nearly two-thirds of its income from the Chinese gambling hub. Most of Adelson's earlier lobbying involved Israel and his pet project of getting the United States to move its embassy to Jerusalem.

Now Adelson and other executives were worried that Trump would go through with a threat he tweeted in August to "order" U.S. companies to leave China. In discussions with Trump, Adelson warned that additional tariffs would makes businesses hesitant to invest and would damage Trump politically by ratcheting up prices for consumers. The calls came before the president delayed some tariffs and restarted talks. Adelson's lobbying came at an opportune time to get results. Both Beijing and Washington feared a market collapse if they didn't keep talking.

Adelson is especially close to the president. He wrote a $5 million check for Trump's inauguration and, along with his wife, gave $20 million to his presidential campaign. If Trump ignored Adelson's wishes, the casino magnate might be less generous for his 2020 run. The president certainly courted the Adelson family. He awarded Adelson's wife, a doctor, the Presidential Medal of Freedom, the nation's highest civilian honor, and flew to Las Vegas in April 2019 to address the Republican Jewish Coalition at Adelson's Venetian hotel.

Mnuchin praised Adelson on Lou Dobbs's cable show in September 2019. "When other people weren't stepping up, Sheldon was stepping up" to help the campaign in 2016, the Treasury secretary said. "He does have interests [in Macau]. But he has pretty good perception from having done business in China. And that's really his counsel."

Both Trump and the Chinese leadership also regularly turned for assistance to Stephen Schwarzman, the billionaire cofounder of the private equity firm the Blackstone Group. He worked hard to build relationships on both sides of the Pacific, and once remarked that most Americans "know next to nothing about China." In 2013, he sought to change that by donating $117 million to fund a scholarship program, named after himself, and over the years raising another $450 million to bring two hundred mainly American students to China every year for study at Beijing's prestigious Tsinghua University. Xi Jinping is a Tsinghua alumnus, as are many of the country's top political and business leaders. Schwarzman's largesse improved his access to them.

For a time, China's sovereign wealth fund, China Investment Corporation, owned 9.9 percent of Blackstone—just short of the percentage that could have triggered a U.S. national security review. The CIC investment, Schwarzman said in his autobiography, *What It Takes: Lessons in the Pursuit of Excellence*, made him a "minor celebrity" in China.

In April 2018, when Xi Jinping appeared at the Boao Forum, an international conference on the resort island of Hainan, Chinese trade negotiator Liu He tapped Schwarzman on the back during a dinner for Xi. Liu asked him to explain Trump's trade and political strategy to the group, which included Alibaba Group founder Jack Ma and former United Nations General Secretary Ban Ki-Moon. Trump isn't a conventional politician, Schwarzman told Xi. He wants a good relationship with China, but he'll use pressure tactics to get you to the table and make a deal. "He's not making empty threats," said the Blackstone CEO.

The Blackstone Group is one of America's largest real estate developers, a credential that goes a long way with Trump. Schwarzman and Trump have known each other for years and Trump regularly sought Schwarzman's approval—and cash for his political campaign. He is also friends with Mnuchin; the two have apartments in the same building in Manhattan and sometimes vacation together. Schwarzman backed other Republicans in the 2016 presidential race but did come through with $250,000 for Trump's inauguration and $344,000 through early 2020 for his reelection campaign.

Once in office, Trump appointed Schwarzman to run a business advisory group. In the wake of Trump's comments seeming to embrace neo-Nazis during the violent protests in Charlottesville in August 2017, Schwarzman polled his members to see what they wanted to do. They decided to disband but before they could act, Trump shut down the panel, although he didn't hold Schwarzman responsible for the embarrassment. The two men talked once every week or two, and the subject often turned to the economy and China. Schwarzman says in his book that he made eight trips to China on Trump's behalf in 2018, "trying to assure China's most senior officials that the president was not looking for a trade war" and reporting Chinese views to Trump or his advisers.

Other U.S. business leaders also had strong ties to the Chinese leadership and consulted with the administration on China policy. They include former Treasury Secretary Hank Paulson and his onetime Goldman Sachs colleague John Thornton, who played an important role as intermediary during December 2019 negotiations for a limited deal. But they didn't have close ties to Trump either, especially Paulson, who was a never-Trumper and backed Hillary Clinton in 2016. As we have seen, Paulson remains close to Treasury Secretary Mnuchin, who considered Paulson to be his mentor when both worked at Goldman Sachs.

At the same time that Adelson got involved in trying to patch up trade talks in mid-2019, Mnuchin reached out to Schwarzman, Paulson, and others for intelligence about what the Chinese were thinking and planning. Chinese leaders were no longer talking to the Americans. "We're flying blind," the Treasury secretary said. Schwarzman tried to make clear to the Chinese that they wouldn't intimidate Trump by not talking. To Trump, Schwarzman emphasized the economic costs of the continuing trade fight and the risks to market confidence.

The facilitator role played by Trump's business friends outraged the president's most hawkish aides, especially White House trade adviser Peter Navarro, as described in chapter 12. In a November 2018 speech at the Center for Strategic and International Studies, a Washington think tank, he let loose. "Globalist billionaires

are putting a full-court press on the White House" ahead of an upcoming meeting with Xi, Navarro said, his anger rising. "If there
is a deal, it will be on President Donald J. Trump's terms, not Wall
Street terms. If Wall Street is involved and continues to insinuate
itself in these negotiations, there will be a stench around any deal
that's consummated."

Navarro didn't name any particular business executives, though
he did cite Goldman Sachs. But it was clear from his private railings
that he was including Schwarzman in his list of unnamed backstab-
bers. To Navarro's enemies in the White House, this was a golden
moment to take him down. Navarro was attacking people the president admired and considered friends.

"He was not speaking for the president," White House economic
adviser Larry Kudlow told CNBC a few days later. "I actually think
he did the president a great disservice." Privately, Kudlow tried
to get Navarro banned from television, if not fired. White House
aides said the CSIS speech was Navarro's "Scaramucci moment"—
referring to the woebegone former White House communications
director, Anthony Scaramucci, who was dismissed after ten days on
the job for savaging White House officials during a magazine interview.

The anti-Navarro effort failed. Navarro was barred from TV for
a while. But as in the past, the president saved him. Trump appreciated Navarro's loyalty and toughness. "I have to keep him around,"
Trump would tell his staff, half-jokingly. "He's the only one who
agrees with me."

• • •

China's leaders took far too long to fully appreciate that their old
corporate pals were no longer able to bail them out. That made
Beijing unprepared to deal with Trump and his demands, and even
more unwilling to make the changes necessary to reach a deal.

Their obtuseness means the blame for the prolonged trade war lies as much with Beijing as it does with Washington.

Initially, Chinese leaders dismissed U.S. complaints as whining. American businesses still invested in China and made lots of money, they believed. Americans should have faith that China would liberalize, although at its own pace. They needed to learn how to compete in a rapidly developing China. "There is more competition on the Chinese market," says China's ambassador to the United States, Cui Tiankai. "Maybe the days of so-called easy money in China are gone. Maybe they are gone forever."

Early in the Trump administration, big corporations hardly presented a united front when they met with their Chinese counterparts. It would take time for the CEOs to refine their arguments and screw up the courage to talk candidly with their Chinese contacts.

At the Davos, Switzerland, meeting of the World Economic Forum—the epicenter of global capitalism—in January 2017, President Xi received a standing ovation from the business crowd when he attacked protectionism. No foreign power should attempt to dictate to other countries what economic path to follow, Xi said—a not-so-veiled criticism of the newly elected American president. Development should be "of the people, by the people, and for the people," the Chinese president continued, borrowing a phrase from Abraham Lincoln's Gettysburg Address.

As the trade battle progressed, Chinese leaders leaned on their old corporate allies. In May 2018, Xi's vice president, Wang Qishan, who had long worked with Americans on business, met with U.S. executives in Beijing. Wang was an old hand at mixing threats and blandishments, and considered himself an expert on American politics and culture, which sometimes made him sound smug. He loved Mark Twain and Jack London novels and had exhausted the supply of Western literature, both American and European, that existed in China during the Cultural Revolution. Following China's opening in the late 1970s, he watched American movies and television shows and was a big fan of Netflix's Washington melodrama *House of Cards*.

He lectured his visitors about Chinese military strategist Sun Tzu. "If you know the enemy and yourself, you need not fear the result of a hundred battles," he told them. China understood the United States better than the other way around and would endure far more pain rather than concede. The message: get your government to back off.

He repeated that message in a meeting with executives later in the year. He lifted his feet and showed them his Skechers sneakers to make it clear senior Chinese officials like him wanted to buy U.S. merchandise despite the trade war. (Some of the executives realized the sneakers were made in China and Vietnam.) He quizzed Walmart Inc. CEO Doug McMillon on whether the tariffs would hurt American consumers. Yes, they would feel the price increase, McMillon responded. Wang agreed.

He then turned to General Motors CEO Mary Barra for her opinion. GM's joint venture with state-owned SAIC Motor Corporation sold 4 million vehicles in China in 2017. She used the opportunity to lobby him to lower China's trade barriers. Chinese consumers would benefit if GM could import advanced foreign-made batteries for the electric cars the JV made in China, she said.

At the time, carmakers in China were required to buy from a "white list" of recommended domestic battery suppliers, which gave local firms a boost. But Chinese government-owned Volvo Car Group was exempted. Volvo was allowed to use batteries in its locally built cars based on more advanced technology licensed from South Korea's LG Chem Ltd. The unequal treatment rankled U.S. carmakers, who felt it was yet another example of how China favored domestic firms over foreign ones, even when they were part of a joint venture. (China scrapped the list in June 2019.)

During the meeting, Wang said that trade was just one component of a broader fight between the United States and China that also included national security, geopolitical, and cultural issues. China wouldn't be pressured or bullied. "History may show the problems of today will look like backpedaling" before both nations improved their relationship, said Wang, who was a history major in college. He emphasized that the Chinese leadership was unified and consistent, both strategically and tactically, on bilateral issues. In trying to solve the trade conflict, Wang said his boss, Xi Jinping, "is calm, clear-minded, disciplined, and responsible."

By September 2018, the message from American business to China—that things had to change—couldn't be mistaken. As global political leaders landed in New York for a meeting of the UN General Assembly, China's Foreign Minister Wang Yi met with U.S. business leaders in a midtown Manhattan conference room. The lineup was a who's who of corporate America: Evan Greenberg, CEO of insurer Chubb Ltd.; Schwarzman of the Blackstone Group; Ajay Banga, CEO of MasterCard Inc.; Alfred Kelly, CEO of Visa Inc.; and Thomas Donilon, chairman of BlackRock Investment Institute and a former national security advisor in the Obama administration.

Wang started the meeting by reminding his audience that it had been forty years since the two nations established formal diplomatic ties. "When a man turns forty, he has no doubts," he said, quoting the ancient Chinese philosopher Confucius. Meaning? Washington and Beijing should work together and not be distracted by "the rising negative factors" in the United States, as Wang put it. Those included intelligence agency suspicions that "Chinese spies are everywhere, that even Chinese students are spies," Wang said, and allegations that the Chinese are stealing American intellectual property. Beijing's top diplomat was putting the blame for souring relations solely on the Trump administration.

Not so, said one CEO after another. China shares the blame. Evan Greenberg, who was also chairman of the U.S.-China Business Council, spoke first. Chinese leaders had long viewed his father, Hank Greenberg, the former CEO of insurance giant AIG, as an "old friend of China." Evan was known in Beijing as "Greenberg Junior."

He was direct. "The lack of meaningful implementation of reforms for the last many years is a source of deep frustration" for the U.S. business community, Greenberg said. "The latest five-year plan has further thrown into doubt the trajectory of reforms," he added, referring to the planning document that turned Beijing's "Made in China 2025" technology development blueprint into a government priority.

The U.S. business community was very much on board with the Trump administration's effort to take China to task for unfair trade practices, Greenberg stressed. "There is a major trust gap right now in our relationship," he said, and urged Beijing to take immediate steps to liberalize its economy. "This would put a floor under the current situation and we could begin to build trust," Greenberg added.

Other CEOs backed him up. Those from MasterCard and Visa complained of the difficulty in cracking open China's market despite repeated government promises. "We left Beijing in March with the sense that movement seemed imminent," said Visa's Kelly, referring to a fresh Chinese pledge to open its electronic payment market to foreign competitors, a promise Beijing had made when it entered the World Trade Organization in 2001. "Absolutely nothing has happened," Kelly said. "It makes a difference when cabinet officials ask us what is happening and all we can say is that we have no idea. We have applications in. Just start reviewing them. Give us feedback. Tell us what we need to do to meet the needs of the Chinese government. Help us give the U.S. administration a sense that China's markets appear to be opening."

Blackstone's Schwarzman recounted how he had regularly explained to China's leadership the need to make structural changes in China's economy to make it operate more fairly. "Too many people in the U.S. simply haven't done well since the financial crisis and are frustrated. This kind of domestic frustration is inevitably projected onto the most successful non-American country," Schwarzman said, referring to China. "This is not about one president or one administration. There is now a shift. Without more openness in your market, things are just unbalanced."

Donilon, the former national security advisor now at BlackRock, wondered if Beijing understood how deeply U.S. attitudes toward China were changing. "There is a rethink under way in the U.S. about the bilateral relations. It is bipartisan, and it cuts across defense, foreign policy, and the economic arena," Donilon said. "I fear even a decoupling in the economic and investment sphere."

After listening to complaint after complaint, Wang responded defensively. China had been reforming, he said, ticking off a list of measures aimed at broadening foreign access to China's markets for banking, securities, auto, and other sectors. He also pointed out that China had slashed tariffs since its WTO admission. "The pace of China's reform and opening up is very rapid and faster than that of any developing country," Wang said. "I understand how you feel. I understand the sentiment, but facts are facts. We just started running a marathon and are twenty kilometers behind you."

China will continue to reform, Wang said, referring to Xi's promises to widen market access for foreign investors. "Our highest leader speaking for our entire central government and party said this," Wang said. "You know it is characteristic of China that if we say we're going to do something, we are going to do it." Watch what we do in the next three to five years, he said.

American business executives were tired of waiting. Two months later, former Treasury Secretary Paulson addressed a meeting of global corporate executives organized by Bloomberg in Singapore to discuss China issues. "How can it be that those who know China best, work there, do business there, make money there, and have advocated for productive relations in the past, are among those now arguing for more confrontation?" he asked. "The answer lies in the story of stalled competition policy, and the slow pace of opening over nearly two decades. This has discouraged and fragmented the American business community."

"An economic Iron Curtain" may be descending, Paulson warned, "one that throws up new walls on each side and unmakes the global economy as we have known it."

• • •

Beijing and U.S. companies did align on one issue—opposing tariffs. U.S. companies felt the pain of higher prices and lost sales as much as Chinese firms did. Beijing worried that the trade war would batter its economy. U.S. firms worried that they would be maimed, too.

American trade associations opposed tariffs with the enthusiasm they usually reserve for free trade deals. This time, though, the big three corporate trade groups played secondary roles. The Business Roundtable, National Association of Manufacturers, and U.S. Chamber of Commerce opposed tariffs, but they didn't join a coalition of more than 150 trade groups organized to fight them. Instead, they sought good relations with the Trump White House and continued to lobby for a pressure campaign to get China to make economic changes.

The anti-tariff effort involved two different groups. One was led by farm organizations, including the American Farm Bureau Federation, the American Soybean Association, U.S. Apple Association, and the Corn Refiners Association. They worried that Chinese retaliatory tariffs slashed farm exports and forced Beijing to buy agricultural products elsewhere. The United States could lose China altogether as a market. They took the name Farmers for Free Trade.

The second lobbying push was headed by retailers, technology groups, and manufacturers concerned that U.S. tariffs on Chinese goods would drive up their prices and drive away buyers. They included the National Retail Federation, the Toy Association, the American Petroleum Institute, and the Consumer Technology Association. Their group was called Americans for Free Trade. The two worked together under the name Tariffs Hurt the Heartland.

The lobbyists figured that the White House would listen most to farmers, given Trump's political dependence on rural America. They spent $2 million on three thirty-second television ads in 2018 that ran on Fox News, *Fox & Friends*, *Lou Dobbs Tonight*, and other cable shows in Washington, D.C. There was nothing subtle about the campaign. It sought to influence President Trump by advertising on the shows he watched.

The ads featured a Montana wheat farmer, an Indiana soybean farmer, and a Pennsylvania apple grower. In the soybean ad, Brent Bible from Lafayette, Indiana, climbs into a big green John Deere tractor and fingers a handful of soybeans. China is his top soybean customer. "Our farms and many others like it will be one of the first casualties of a trade war," he says, looking into the camera. "President Trump, support free trade and keep the ag economy strong."

Afterward, the coalition spent another $1.5 million through the fall of 2019 organizing town hall meetings in states that are crucial to Trump's reelection, including Ohio, Pennsylvania, Wisconsin, and Iowa. Farmers and businesses talked about how the trade war was hurting them. Local newspapers and television stations covered the events and produced sympathetic accounts.

Some free trade campaigns have had budgets ten times as large as the anti-tariff effort. But the trade groups weren't ready to spend that kind of money to run television ads around the country. Organizers said that could make the anti-tariff campaign an important part of the 2020 election. If successful, the groups could anger the Trump White House and get Democrats elected, an outcome their members weren't sure they wanted. If unsuccessful, the advertising spree would reinforce how unpopular China had become as a political issue.

By the end of 2019, the campaign hadn't managed to get the White House to hold off on tariffs. When the two sides signed a limited deal in 2020, a small set of tariffs were reduced. But that had little to do with the lobbying effort. By that point, the United States was threatening to hit mainstay consumer goods like mobile phones, laptop computers, and toys. The president's advisers realized that would be self-defeating. The vast bulk of tariffs remained in place.

"Wall Street, CEOs, and trade associations have been expecting Trump to flinch at points along this path [of tariff increases] because that is what traditional politicians do," says David French, a senior vice president of the National Retail Federation who is one of the coalition's field generals. "Instead of flinching, he veers closer to the cliff."

From Lighthizer's point of view, the groups never proposed an effective alternative to tariffs. Some wanted the United States and its allies to sue China at the WTO. Lighthizer argued that the United States brought cases against China when that made sense, but he didn't want to give allies a veto over what the United States did. Others, including the U.S. Chamber, urged that disputes be handled by international arbitration panels. Lighthizer distrusted such reviews, which gave power to outsiders. He was also pressuring the WTO to limit the power of its appeals panels by threatening not to approve new judges.

"The only fucking arbitrator I trust is me," he told U.S. business executives.

16

COUPLES THERAPY, FALL 2018

By the early fall of 2018, Xi Jinping was trapped in a dilemma. His tit-for-tat strategy hadn't stopped Donald Trump from ratcheting up tariffs on Chinese imports. But the Chinese leader couldn't back down. Xi's popularity depended on turning China into a global power and standing firm against foreign forces, especially the American hegemon.

The spiraling trade fight with the United States was starting to take a bigger bite out of China's growth. Business and consumer confidence was plunging, and foreign companies grew increasingly jittery about their operations in the country. The leadership urgently felt the need to resume negotiations with Washington. "The instruction at the time was to try to stabilize the bilateral relationship as soon as possible," a Chinese official says. To that end, Beijing sought out intermediaries. If Beijing's old friends in business couldn't get the Trump team to stop punching at China, perhaps they could at least get the White House to listen.

In early September 2018, Beijing tapped Blackstone's Stephen Schwarzman, who tried again to play couples therapist to the United States and China.

The estrangement between the two nations was growing deeper.

President Trump had already put in place 25 percent tariffs on $50 billion of Chinese goods. When Beijing responded with its own $50 billion hit list, an angry Trump threatened even more tariffs— 25 percent on $200 billion of Chinese imports.

If Trump gave the final okay, about half of what China shipped to the United States annually would suddenly cost 25 percent more, delivering a potentially crippling blow to Chinese exporters and a powerful message to U.S. importers to ditch China. Bound for a campaign rally in Fargo, North Dakota, the president told reporters on Air Force One, he would put levies on all Chinese imports if China didn't budge soon. No president since the 1930s had used the tariff cudgel the way Trump was swinging it.

On September 6, Schwarzman met first with Chinese Vice President Wang Qishan in the ornate Ziguang Hall, the building in Beijing's leadership compound used to greet foreigners. Later in the day, he conferred with China's top trade negotiator, Liu He. In his autobiography, Schwarzman doesn't provide much detail about the discussions, other than to say they focused on "finding a way to restart formal talks." Convinced the Chinese were trying to patch up their relationship with the United States, he says he passed along a positive message to President Trump, who asked him to set up a meeting in Washington for Liu and U.S. negotiators. Why play hard to get?

Treasury Secretary Mnuchin also wanted to restart negotiations. In a September Oval Office meeting, Trump told him of a Schwarzman call. In Trump's retelling, the Blackstone CEO had said the Chinese economy was in the toilet and Beijing wanted to settle. "Invite them right now, and here's the letter you should send," the president told Mnuchin, who scribbled down notes and sent an invitation to Vice Premier Liu He.

Talks were set for the end of September, and confident Treasury officials told Schwarzman and other business executives that the $200 billion tariff hit was on hold. (According to Mnuchin's calendar, he and Schwarzman spoke by phone on September 10, though the calendar doesn't disclose the subject.) If the talks were fruitful, maybe the tariffs would be shelved. Between September 10 and September 14, Mnuchin and Chinese Ambassador Cui Tiankai conferred daily by phone.

But Treasury, once again, had overestimated its influence with the president on China. During mid-September meetings in the Oval Office, Mnuchin and Trade Representative Lighthizer squared off. This wasn't the time to back off on tariffs, Lighthizer argued. To get China to move, the United States needed the leverage that only tariffs would provide. Mnuchin countered that hitting China with tariffs was a mistake. Beijing would probably cancel Liu's visit, and the negotiator would lose face back home. All the preparation would have been for nothing.

Trump had different qualms. How far had negotiations progressed since U.S. negotiators flew to Beijing in May and delivered their surrender-or-die demands, he wanted to know. Not very far, was the answer. The Chinese had turned U.S. demands into some 142 items to be negotiated, including more purchases of American goods, better U.S. access to Chinese markets, and elimination of all Chinese subsidies. They divided the items into three baskets: up to 40 percent could be done immediately; another 40 percent could be negotiated over time; and the remaining 20 percent were off-limits because they involved national security. But here was the kicker: the Chinese wouldn't say what items were in what category, other than to note they considered 122 of the 142 to be negotiable.

Clearly unimpressed, Trump told the group, "They're tapping you along." All you have to show for five months of talks is a list, Trump lectured the group, and the Chinese won't tell you what's on it?

Beijing wasn't ready to negotiate, the president felt. His national security advisors were convinced that the Chinese were waiting until the midterm congressional elections in November 2018 before tabling a serious offer. If the Republicans took a drubbing in the election, Beijing figured, Trump would be ready to make concessions for a deal he could claim as a victory. "They do not want me, or us, to win because I am the first president ever to challenge China on trade," Trump later told the United Nations Security Council, reflecting the conclusion of his senior national security officials.

As for the chance of upsetting the Liu He visit, Trump told cabinet officials in the Oval Office, "I don't really care if he comes."

Trump did approve one Mnuchin proposal. Tariffs would begin at just 10 percent through the Christmas season, a level that wouldn't hurt most importers. Only on January 1, 2019, would they jump to 25 percent. That gave the two sides several more months to negotiate before the tariffs bit hard.

The president later explained his thinking. "They were not ready to make a deal," he said of the Chinese. "Steve [Mnuchin] is doing an excellent job," he added, "but I disagreed with him on this."

• • •

In Beijing, the tariff decision deepened a debate among Chinese policy makers, government advisers, and academics about U.S. intentions and how China should respond. Many of them felt the Americans were trying to squeeze Beijing before another round of negotiations. What should Beijing do?

On September 16, a day after the *Wall Street Journal* broke the story of Trump's decision to go ahead with more tariffs, China's quandary was on full display at the Diaoyutai State Guesthouse. In one part of the complex's villas in western Beijing, a senior official publicly unloaded on Washington. In another part, senior Chinese officials quickly put together a meeting with Wall Street executives to convince them to lobby against tariffs. Beijing wanted to act tough in public while quietly maneuvering to get the Trump team to back off.

The official who made the public speech was Lou Jiwei, the

former finance minister whose bluntness earned him the nickname "Cannon Lou." Lou (pronounced "low") used a special session of the China Development Forum, a high-level policy conference held at Diaoyutai, to deliver his broadside. The United States wanted to contain China's economic rise, not simply rebalance trade relations, Lou said. "That is not going to change in the near term. But that's not going to work, either."

He then shocked many in the audience by proposing that China limit sales of materials, equipment, and other parts essential to U.S. manufacturers—known in trade circles as "export restraints"—in addition to hitting them with retaliatory tariffs. Even Apple Inc.'s China operations, which employs tens of thousands of Chinese workers to assemble iPhones, shouldn't be off-limits, he hinted to the book's coauthor Lingling in a brief chat after the speech.

Beijing so far had been fairly restrained in its retaliation, fighting Trump with the same tariff weapons that Trump had deployed against China. But Beijing had many other weapons in its arsenal; American companies operating in China could easily be held hostage. "Let's see who feels the pain first," Lou said.

Lou's influence is sometimes discounted because of his tendency to veer off script. He lost his job as head of China's national pension fund in early 2019 because he openly criticized the "Made in China 2025" plan as having "wasted taxpayers' money." But his luncheon speech at the development forum—held to mark the fortieth anniversary of Deng Xiaoping's "reform and opening-up" policy—was highly scripted. His tough talk was approved ahead of time by senior officials.

So was the behind-the-scenes maneuvering to keep negotiations on track. Inside another villa in Diaoyutai, central bank governor Yi Gang, top financial regulator Guo Shuqing, and Liao Min, the top aide to chief negotiator Liu He, held a closed-door session with a group of Wall Street executives. They wanted American banks and private equity firms to fight the tariffs.

The session was so hastily arranged that the officials didn't send out invitations to the "China-U.S. Financial Roundtable" until early September—not nearly enough time to get CEOs to commit to traveling to Beijing. Second-in-command executives attended instead. The Blackstone Group was represented by its president, Jon Gray, not Schwarzman. Goldman Sachs's newly named president, John Waldron, showed up, not then-CEO Lloyd Blankfein.

The Chinese used the meeting to talk up their plans to liberalize the financial sector. They also peppered some of their American guests privately with questions that showed how little they still understood the Trump team. Were any U.S. officials able to cut a deal with China, they wanted to know. This, despite nearly a year of evidence that Trade Representative Lighthizer had Trump's confidence on China trade, not Beijing's preferred intermediary, Treasury Secretary Mnuchin.

Liu He and his team were rightly worried that any offer Beijing made to Mnuchin, who had sent the invitation for the Washington talks, would be opposed by trade hawks led by Lighthizer and trade adviser Peter Navarro, and then turned down by President Trump. Even so, Beijing made little effort to reach out to Lighthizer—and vice versa. "They know our telephone number," one of Lighthizer's aides said at the time.

Several blocks away in the Diaoyutai complex, a third meeting was taking place. Members of the Chinese Economists 50 Forum convened to commemorate the twentieth anniversary of the think tank cofounded by Liu He, who made a brief appearance at the event. Some attendees constituted a kind of peace wing of the Chinese intelligentsia; they wanted China's economy to become more market driven. These moderates thought the U.S. trade offensive could help them further their goal of rolling back the economic power of the state and party. They urged the leadership to carry out promises Xi had made to give market forces a bigger role in the economy.

Wu Jinglian, a prominent pro-market economist, noted that private businesses in China resented expanded state control. The government needs to "build consensus through debate and then implement reforms one by one," Wu said, with Liu in the audience. Liu didn't make any remarks at the event and left after Wu's speech to catch a flight to Shanghai to attend a conference on artificial intelligence.

Others at the forum criticized Beijing's policy of retaliating against U.S. tariffs. "We shouldn't only care about gains and losses in the near term and adopt a tit-for-tat policy," said Zhang Shuguang, another liberal thinker. Deng Xiaoping, Zhang reminded the group, focused on integrating China with the rest of the world, especially the United States. "Necessary concessions should be made to resolve the disputes as soon as possible," he added.

Some of Liu's lieutenants remained and listened to the discussion, but they had more immediate questions to answer. Does Trump really want a deal? If so, should Liu still take the trip to Washington, despite Trump's additional tariffs? "That is the most difficult question at the moment," said one privately.

Shortly after the American tariff decision, on September 21, Xi Jinping convened an emergency Politburo meeting of two dozen of the nation's top officials to discuss how to deal with an increasingly hostile Trump administration. The meeting was arranged so hurriedly that three of the seven members of the group's Standing Committee couldn't attend because they were traveling. At the meeting, Xi zeroed in on the new tariffs and another battle with Washington that had caught Beijing by surprise.

Washington had slapped sanctions on a technology-development unit of the Chinese military and its director for buying Russian fighter jets and surface-to-air missiles, which the United States said violated prohibitions on Moscow for meddling in the 2016 U.S. election. China's Equipment Development Department, which focuses on advanced military technology, could no longer apply for the U.S.

export licenses needed to buy military equipment built with U.S. parts or use the U.S. financial system. Li Shangfu, head of the unit and a trusted Xi lieutenant on China's space program, was barred from conducting transactions using U.S. banks, owning property in the country, or even getting a U.S. visa.

U.S. officials said the sanctions were aimed at Moscow rather than Beijing. The Chinese leadership dismissed that explanation. They saw it as part of a U.S. plan to block China's military modernization.

The Politburo members concluded that a forceful counter was essential. China canceled Liu He's trip to Washington, suspended planned discussions with U.S. military officials, and recalled a navy chief from a visit to the United States. "There was no point in talking when the entire atmosphere was so poisonous," recalls a senior Chinese official.

A few days later, China's top diplomat used his New York meeting with senior U.S. corporate executives to vent about how Washington made it impossible for Beijing to continue the talks. "If you want to negotiate, then don't impose new tariffs," Foreign Minister Wang Yi told the group. "Wait until after the negotiations. There were very important negotiations which had a very good chance of success, because we already had consensus on many issues, and yet down came the club on our heads."

• • •

At one minute after midnight, on September 24, the United States put in place 10 percent tariffs on $200 billion of Chinese imports. Beijing immediately responded with tariffs on $60 billion of U.S. goods. Counting previous Chinese retaliatory tariffs, about 80 percent of what the United States shipped to China now faced levies, especially American agricultural exports. The only major imports China exempted were U.S. semiconductors and large commercial jetliners—products that Beijing needed and few other countries made.

Then the White House was shaken by a surprise. The stock market started to tank rather than shrug off new tariffs as it had done in the past. The Dow Jones Industrial Average fell nearly 1,000 points in the month following the September 15 news of tariffs. China's benchmark index, the Shanghai Composite Index, dropped another 100 points after declining the whole year. Analysts began to debate whether the continuing trade battle could eventually push the United States and the global economy into a recession.

At the time, most on Wall Street believed that the trade fight wasn't dealing much of an economic blow. Tariffs on $250 billion of goods were akin to a tax increase on a small portion of the $20 trillion U.S. economy.

But a minority of analysts took a different view. Seth Carpenter, the chief U.S. economist at the investment bank UBS and a former Obama Treasury official, says September 24, 2018, was the day the U.S. market started taking the trade war seriously. The impact of tariffs wasn't diffuse across the economy, he says. Tariffs targeted multinationals and other manufacturers, whose prospects greatly affected stock indices. The firms had to start planning whether to move operations out of China, at a great cost financially and in management time, and whether to slash investment at a time of great uncertainty. "The path you thought you were on was upended," he says. "Further escalation was in the cards."

Chinese economists also worried about a sharp downturn. One of the Chinese government's most prestigious think tanks, the Development Research Center, forecast that a full-bore trade war with the United States could shave as much as 1.5 percentage points off China's GDP growth rate.

Wang Yiming, deputy director of the center, warned at a fall forum that the trade war was starting to hurt many aspects of the

Chinese economy, including employment, manufacturing, and business investments, as well as exports. He worried that industrial firms were shifting production out of the country. "Go take a look at all those flights [from China] to Thailand, Malaysia, and Vietnam," Wang said. "They're all full these days."

Companies had to plan for tariffs jumping from 10 percent to 25 percent on January 1, 2019, for items essential to their operations, including industrial chemicals, computer parts, plastics, machine parts, pumps, ceramics, and metals. Increasing to 25 percent "would have a significant impact," Kelly Kramer, the chief financial officer of computer networking company Cisco Systems, told an investors' conference in the fall. While a 10 percent increase could be digested, "25 percent would be a much bigger hit and that will obviously have some impact."

U.S.-based firms started negotiating with their Chinese suppliers over who would take the brunt of the tariff hit. "We were successful to the extent there was a competition available for those goods from other suppliers," says Earl Jones, senior counsel at GE Appliances, a U.S. subsidiary of China's big appliance maker, Haier Group. Then "we could share the tariff costs."

But replacing Chinese parts suppliers—even for a Chinese-owned firm in the United States—was difficult and expensive. It required finding comparable suppliers and making sure they were dependable and could produce high-quality goods. When GE Appliances looked at buying one Chinese-made part in Mexico, the supplier there bid twice the price. The company eventually convinced the trade representative's office to waive the tariffs for that imported part.

As the economic costs became clearer, the White House and China's Zhongnanhai leadership compound tried again to pull back from the brink. Trump was facing a difficult midterm election and wanted a summit with Xi Jinping to calm market anxieties. On October 1, National Economic Council Director Larry Kudlow, who time and again tried to buck up the market with optimistic statements, went on Fox to say that the president "may perhaps" meet with Xi at a December 1 summit of the G-20 nations in Buenos Aires. "We are willing to talk if it's substantial and significant and serious," Kudlow said, making the U.S. side sound tough. But with the market tumbling, Blue-Collar Trump was giving way to Wall Street Trump. He wanted a meeting.

So did Xi, whose economy was slowing faster than authorities had anticipated. GDP growth fell to 6.5 percent in the third quarter, the weakest pace since the global financial crisis and below market expectations. While much of the slowdown was due to Beijing's campaign to reduce debt, the conflict with the United States also played a role. Industrial production, consumption, and consumer confidence all were weakening.

On October 19, the day Beijing released its economic results, China's economic mandarins launched a coordinated effort to calm jittery investors. People's Bank of China governor Yi Gang, banking and insurance regulatory chief Guo Shuqing, and then-top securities regulator Liu Shiyu all issued statements urging investors to remain calm. Guo said recent "abnormal fluctuations" in China's stock markets didn't reflect the country's economic fundamentals and stable financial system. By then, the Shanghai Composite Index had declined 25 percent since the beginning of 2018, becoming the worst performer among global benchmarks.

Shortly after the regulators' remarks, the official Xinhua News Agency published an interview with Liu He where he sought to dispel worries about the impact of the trade conflict. "Frankly, the psychological impact is bigger than the actual impact," he said. "Right now, China and the U.S. are in contact." In October, Beijing also approved sixteen Ivanka Trump trademarks, covering fashion items like sunglasses, handbags, and shoes—another sign China was getting ready to do business with the administration.

Plenty of problems remained between the two nations. Military talks were in hiatus and both sides blamed the other for a recent close encounter between their warships in the South China Sea. Vice President Mike Pence outlined a shift in U.S. strategy from engagement to confrontation with China, accusing Beijing of undermining American interests on several fronts, including meddling in U.S. elections. Beijing vehemently denied those accusations. Secretary of State Mike Pompeo exchanged testy words with China's Foreign Minister Wang Yi in Beijing, which risked complicating a planned summit meeting between Trump and North Korean leader Kim Jong Un.

On the economic front, U.S. business executives complained that they were being strong-armed into attending a Shanghai trade fair scheduled for early November. If they didn't go, Chinese officials warned them, their businesses could suffer. Beijing dismissed the claims as a "groundless accusation."

Looking for a way to get beyond the endless bickering—and ignoring his worries of just six weeks earlier about Chinese stonewalling—Trump placed a call to Xi on November 1. "What's going on?" the president asked. "Will we make a deal?" In the conversation, Trump made clear that he wanted a settlement and was probing to see if Xi felt the same way. Though the two leaders didn't discuss the specifics of a possible agreement, Xi told the president that there was a way to solve the problems, so long as the United States was willing to meet China halfway. The two leaders committed to a meeting in Buenos Aires.

Clete Willems, a White House trade adviser at the time, calls the phone call an "inflection point" in the trade battle. The two leaders tried to back away from the brink and committed to work toward a settlement.

A day later, Trump told reporters, "I think we'll make a deal," though his remarks came shortly before the midterm elections and were discounted at the time as Republican boosterism. Xinhua also carried a positive report about the discussions. It quoted Xi as saying that both sides wanted to improve U.S.-China relations and "we must work hard to turn these wishes into reality."

Soon after the leaders' phone conversation, Treasury Secretary Mnuchin resumed discussions with Vice Premier Liu. There were a host of substantive issues dividing the two nations. The United States wanted China to make a formal offer, not simply to hint at what it would do. China wanted to have talks first, before making an offer.

The two sides also didn't trust each other's leader. To the Chinese, Trump was erratic and unpredictable. Chinese officials feared he would make public, through a tweet or an off-the-cuff statement, any offer China made as a way to box in Xi, or would misrepresent what Xi said. They knew the history of China's World Trade Organization negotiations, where China's premier was wounded politically when President Clinton turned down his offer of a deal and the United States made Zhu's concessions public.

The Americans worried that the more disciplined and experienced Xi would get Trump to make commitments on issues that the president didn't understand or hadn't bothered to study. He could get ensnared in the traditional Chinese trap of endless talks that lead nowhere. Another worry: Trump might settle for Chinese purchases of soybeans and other goods, rather than fight for structural changes in China's economy. Jack-and-the-Beanstalk references were common in Washington at the time. Would the president settle for a cup of beans?

Trade Representative Lighthizer quietly worked to make sure the talks continued to focus on intellectual property protection, forced technology transfer, subsidies, and other structural issues. Ten days before the December 1 meeting in Buenos Aires, his office released an update of the Section 301 report, which accused Beijing of using cyber espionage and other techniques to steal U.S. technology. He followed that up with a statement on November 28, the day before Trump boarded Air Force One for the summit, attacking

China's "especially egregious" tariffs on U.S. car exports of 40 per-cent, which included China's retaliatory tariffs. "China's aggressive, State-directed industrial policies are causing severe harm to U.S. workers and manufacturers," the Lighthizer statement read.

Lighthizer's twin actions were aimed as much at the U.S. dele-gation to Buenos Aires as at China's: the United States won't settle easily.

• • •

The day before President Xi was to meet with his American coun-terpart in Buenos Aires, he conferred with Japanese Prime Minister Shinzo Abe. Xi told Abe that he hoped for a productive conversa-tion with Trump, but he remained defensive about China's trade practices.

While rattling off the country's major economic developments over the years, Xi said U.S. complaints about Chinese officials forc-ing American firms to share technology were unreasonable. "We don't have compulsory technology transfer in China," Xi told Abe during their November 30 discussions in the Argentine capital.

Xi wanted to try to replicate the personal rapport that the Japa-nese leader had developed with Trump and was searching for clues about what to do. When Abe visited Beijing a month earlier, in Oc-tober, he had asked Xi how he was handling the U.S.-China trade is-sues. Xi complained about Washington's unilateral actions. But the Chinese leader added: "I think I can maintain good relations with President Trump. I appreciate my personal friendship with Presi-dent Trump."

This time Xi asked about Abe's golf outings with Trump. (Xi, a soccer fan, shut down many golf courses because he viewed them as symbols of capitalist excess.)

"So how many holes have you played with President Trump?" Xi asked. "Which one of you plays better?"

"I don't want to disclose that information," Abe responded with a smile. "But President Trump is better than me."

For Trump and his entourage, Buenos Aires was a place to celebrate. On the first morning of the G-20 meeting, November 30, Mexico's president, Enrique Peña Nieto, awarded the president's son-in-law, Jared Kushner, Mexico's highest honor for a foreigner, the Order of the Aztec Eagle, for Kushner's work in helping renegotiate the North American Free Trade Agreement. He pinned a medal on Kushner's blazer at the Park Hyatt Buenos Aires, as Trump and his daughter Ivanka, Kushner's wife, looked on.

Shortly afterward, Peña Nieto, Trump, and Canadian Prime Minister Justin Trudeau lined up in front of the flags of the three nations. The leaders signed the new NAFTA accord while sitting at an ornate, French-style table. Despite Trudeau's lobbying to get the United States to remove steel and aluminum tariffs as part of the renegotiations, Trump hadn't budged. He got his deal and kept his tariffs.

Throughout the day, senior officials from China and the United States met to discuss the following night's dinner meeting between the two presidents. Chinese officials, led by Liu, said that Beijing was willing to buy vast amounts of U.S. goods—as much as an additional $1.2 trillion over six years. While the Chinese didn't guarantee that would halve the U.S. trade deficit with China, as the United States was demanding, it was an enormous sum. The United States sold $130 billion in goods to Beijing in 2017. The Chinese were saying they would boost purchases by about 30 percent a year. As noted in chapter 1, China had never managed that rate of increase over a sustained period.

The offer was couched as a "target" or "expectation," Mnuchin later said on Fox. But it was sure to please the president, who was counting on big sales to help him politically. The U.S. team, including Lighthizer, Mnuchin, and Kudlow, wanted to know what Beijing would do to meet U.S. demands on the structural issues that were at the heart of the dispute. Here Chinese officials weren't forthcoming. They spent all night crafting their response.

To give the two sides more time to prepare, Trump canceled an afternoon press conference, claiming it was out of respect for the death the day before of George H. W. Bush. As the president and his top advisers filed into the dining room at the Park Hyatt on December 1 around 6 p.m., they weren't sure what to expect. Trying to keep the mood light, Trump started to introduce his advisers arrayed on one side of a long table covered with a white tablecloth and bouquets of flowers running down the middle. "As you may know, we have had different views [on the trade fight] around this side of the table," Trump said. "There are different views around our side of the table, too," Xi replied, prompting smiles on both sides.

Then Trump explained the role the various advisers played. Lighthizer, he made clear to Xi, was now the lead negotiator—the man to see on China trade—though Mnuchin would also remain involved. "This is the guy who is going to be my negotiator," Trump said.

That simple statement ended more than a year of bitter infighting and reflected lobbying of the president by his son-in-law Kushner, whom Lighthizer had included in the NAFTA negotiations and who had become a Lighthizer partisan. The two men talked frequently to make sure they presented a united front in negotiations with Mexico and China.

Kushner also had become more jaded about Chinese intentions since his boosterism during the Mar-a-Lago summit of 2017, in part because he was tutored by Michael Pillsbury, whose *Hundred-Year Marathon*, about China's supposed plan to overtake the United States, had become required reading in the White House.

The decision also showed the quiet influence of Matt Pottinger, then the National Security Council's Asia chief, who had joined the Trump team during the transition and had the savvy to outlast three national security advisors. In September 2019, he was appointed deputy national security advisor. While neither man was trying to elbow out Mnuchin, they believed that Lighthizer had the negotiating skills and expertise to lead the talks.

The president then pointed to his super-hawk, Peter Navarro. "He's my tough guy," he told the Chinese leader. He also joked of Kushner's role. "He's the guy I blame if everything goes wrong," Trump said.

The floor turned to Xi Jinping, as the group dined on grilled sirloin with red onions, goat cheese ricotta, and dates. For forty minutes, Xi detailed the reforms Beijing planned to make, many of which would address long-standing U.S. concerns, such as market access and protection of intellectual property. Unlike other Chinese leaders, he didn't read from a detailed script, which the U.S. side took as a sign of his confidence and his personal commitment.

He told the U.S. side that he expected China to soon become the world's largest market for services. Although he didn't promise to buy an extra $1.2 trillion worth of goods and services, as his aides had sketched out earlier, it was clear to the Americans that he was counting on financial, computer, and other services for much of the import growth the Chinese promised. Before the Buenos Aires meeting, Xi had talked up China's goal of increasing imports, and China's Commerce Ministry estimated that the country would import $2.5 trillion in services globally over five years.

When Trump asked the Chinese leader whether he would also crack down on sales of addictive fentanyl, an opioid that was ravaging much of rural America, Xi quickly agreed. The same was true when the U.S. side asked whether Beijing would reconsider a merger sought by American semiconductor firm Qualcomm Inc. Beijing had dithered over the approval for so long that the deal fell apart. The Chinese side agreed to take another look if Qualcomm asked regulators. (The Americans, however, neglected to ask Qualcomm whether it still wanted the deal. Qualcomm no longer did.)

Trump and his team were impressed by Xi's daring. Chinese leaders usually leave nothing to chance when meeting an American president. Everything is scripted during days of meetings by staffers of the two nations. That wasn't Trump's style. Although Trump is briefed in advance, his closest aides don't know where he will take conversations. Xi risked rejection and embarrassment. Trump appreciated Xi's forthright presentation, as did even his most hawkish advisers.

By the end of the meeting, the United States agreed to postpone the January 1 tariff increase deadline until March 1. That gave the two sides ninety days to work out a deal. China said it would buy more agricultural goods, crack down on fentanyl sales, and help out with negotiations with North Korea over nuclear weapons. With his typical swagger, Trump told his aides after the dinner that he had no choice but to suspend heavier tariffs. When Xi comes begging, I have to give him a chance for a deal, the president said.

Around the same time, Chinese Foreign Minister Wang Yi and Commerce Vice Minister Wang Shouwen held a rare public briefing. Xi wanted to shape accounts of what the two sides had agreed upon—and make sure the American version didn't become the accepted account. Most important, he wanted to make sure he wasn't viewed as making concessions to the Americans.

Foreign Minister Wang described the summit as friendly and candid, noting that it lasted two and a half hours, longer than originally expected (a signal that Xi had been shown respect by the often arrogant Americans). Commerce Vice Minister Wang highlighted the agreement to suspend new tariffs, but made no mention of a new deadline (a signal that the Chinese had held firm about refusing to negotiate under pressure). Both Wangs also said new talks, once resumed, would focus on removing all U.S. tariffs—Xi's top priority—and Chinese retaliatory tariffs, which a White House statement didn't mention.

The Chinese officials also said they would open markets and

prevent technology theft but only in accordance with policies already approved by the government and the party. They made no mention of any U.S. requests on those issues. The coverage by China's state media, highly censored as always, was so effective that the first thing coauthor Lingling's mother said to her when she flew back to Beijing was "The Americans caved!"

Not according to Washington. Jetting back to Washington on Air Force One late on December 1, Trump was triumphant. "It's an incredible deal," he told reporters on the plane. If it works out, "it goes down as one of the largest deals ever made." After he left the reporters, he instructed Lighthizer, his newly anointed chief China negotiator, to get him an agreement. Lighthizer pushed back. The two sides aren't close yet on the issues, he said. "Well, get me a great deal then," Trump replied.

As Trump's aides worked on the U.S. press statement, Navarro sought to temper the bullishness. He had opposed postponing the tariff increase, and he feared the U.S. side was getting too giddy. An early draft of the White House statement said that if the two sides didn't reach a deal, the United States would consider increasing the tariff. That was too weak, Navarro argued. It could give the impression that Washington was backing off. The statement was rewritten to say that on March 1, "the 10 percent tariffs will be raised to 25 percent" unless there was an agreement—meaning, don't expect another reprieve.

Aside from dueling PR efforts, there were other storm clouds. At the Buenos Aires dinner, neither leader knew that Canada had arrested Meng Wanzhou, daughter of Huawei's founder, on behalf of the United States, which wanted her extradited. The United States alleged that Meng, the telecom giant's chief financial officer, had helped Huawei evade U.S. sanctions on Iran. News of her arrest produced a nationalist backlash in China and threatened once again to derail the trade negotiations. To many Chinese, the U.S.-directed action was equivalent to Beijing ordering the arrest of Ivanka Trump.

But for now, Xi instructed his lieutenants to follow through on the Buenos Aires deal, despite Meng's arrest. China pushed for her release by stepping up pressure on Ottawa, including by arresting a former Canadian diplomat. China's ambassador to Canada hinted that Beijing considered the arrest to be a reprisal. "Those who accused China of detaining some person in retaliation for the arrest of Ms. Meng should first reflect on the actions of the Canadian side," wrote Lu Shaye, in the *Globe and Mail*.

U.S. officials also sought to separate the Huawei controversy from the trade talks, though Trump suggested he would trade away the Huawei indictment if he got a good offer. "If I think it's good for what will be certainly the largest trade deal ever made, I would certainly intervene if I thought it was necessary," Trump said.

• • •

What to do about Huawei would continue to dog negotiations. But immediately after Buenos Aires, Trump couldn't have been more pleased. He had renegotiated NAFTA, as he had promised in the presidential campaign. He was pressuring Europe and Japan to cut deals. And, he thought, he had China starting to eat out of his hands. A time-out in the schoolyard battle made sense, the Americans believed.

As a goodwill gesture, China soon removed the punitive 25 percent tariffs it placed on U.S.-made cars, which Lighthizer had complained about shortly before Buenos Aires. The change promised to help Tesla Inc. and Ford Motor Company, as well as German automakers BMW AG and Daimler AG, which build sport utility vehicles in the United States for export to China.

To the president, his trade successes confirmed the importance of deploying tariffs on a massive scale. He, Lighthizer, and others believed they had proved a weapon once thought obsolete was effective for reshaping the modern economy. It was the trade equivalent of taking an old battleship out of mothballs, refitting it, and using it to bombard an adversary into submission.

"President Xi and I want this deal to happen, and it probably will," Trump tweeted on December 4. "But if not remember, I am a Tariff Man."

And with that tweet, Trump undid all the goodwill he had earned in global markets by easing off on China. The Dow Jones Industrial Average plummeted that day by nearly 800 points. The S&P 500 tumbled 3.2 percent—the second-biggest drop of the year. That was just the start of the rout. By Christmas, the Dow had lost 4,000 points, down about 16 percent.

Former National Economic Council Director Gary Cohn, who was once president of Goldman Sachs, told White House officials that the Tariff Man comment alone had cost the market 2,000 points.

Although the president regularly boasted that the tariffs didn't cost Americans anything, the overwhelming evidence showed his claims were false. Chinese suppliers didn't cut their prices for the goods they exported to the United States once Washington imposed tariffs, three leading economists found in January 2020, confirming the findings of earlier groups of academics. Tariffs added to the prices Americans paid.

Trump's constant badgering of Federal Reserve chairman Jerome "Jay" Powell to cut interest rates also played a big role in the market's decline. In his interview with the book's coauthor, Bob, shortly before Buenos Aires, Trump called the Fed a "much bigger problem than China" and hinted he might try to fire Powell—insults and threats he repeated regularly.

Uncertainty over trade and the Fed worked in tandem to batter markets. Business investment and international trade were slowing because of tariffs, and over time that was bound to reduce employment and wages and cut into consumer spending, traders feared.

Powell made it clear that he didn't have the tools to save the economy from a trade war.

Between March and December 2018, University of Chicago economist Steven Davis and two colleagues later found, trade policy was featured ten times as frequently in the media as it had been during the prior twenty years. "Trade-policy concerns went from a virtual nonfactor [in U.S. stock-market volatility] in recent decades to one of its leading sources," Davis wrote.

Trump had ignored warnings by his economic team about the market impact of trade fights. In the fall, Kevin Hassett, chairman of the White House Council of Economic Advisers, put together a chart for the president showing that tariff increases produced market declines. Hassett examined ten days when tariff news hit the market. On average, he found, stocks dropped 1.5 percent, short term. Another of his studies forecast that if the United States increased tariffs to 25 percent on $200 billion of Chinese imports, it would reduce economic growth by as much as 0.5 percentage point—a huge hit for an administration that bragged it could produce 3 percent annual growth, not the 2.2 percent that the economy had crawled under Obama.

Trump examined the data, but told his aides that a deal with China was worth the costs. Besides, he figured, the markets always rebounded.

But when the market didn't reverse course in December, Trump grew alarmed. He turned to his staff for reassurance. Kudlow treaded carefully. He told Trump there were many factors affecting the market, though he needed to be careful with his tweets. When Trump quizzed him about the market's plunge, Kudlow rattled off headlines about the decline, rather than provoke the president's fury by blaming Trump's tariff threats. Wall Street Trump had now clearly come to the fore.

"What are the benchmarks for success of the presidency?" asked Cohn, Trump's former NEC director, in a radio interview. "The stock market is the most obvious, most transparent, most talked-about-by-the-president benchmark of success."

Trump looked to his senior economic officials to buck up the market. Mnuchin made things worse. On Sunday, December 23, he tweeted that he had telephoned the heads of the nation's six largest banks, who reported they have "ample liquidity" to withstand shocks. Traders, who hadn't worried about the health of banks, fretted that perhaps they should. The S&P 500 fell 2.7 percent the following day.

A December 26 *Wall Street Journal* interview with Hassett helped ease market fears. "The president has voiced policy differences with Jay Powell, but Jay Powell's job is 100 percent safe," he said. "The president has no intention of firing Jay Powell." The Dow Jones index jumped more than 1,000 points, and Trump called Hassett to congratulate him.

A month earlier, in Buenos Aires, Trump bragged that Xi Jinping was begging him for help. Now, faced with a volatile stock market, Trump turned to Xi for help and called him on Saturday, December 29. Xinhua reported that the call showed that two sides were continuing to try to resolve their differences. Relations between the two nations are "now in a vital stage," Xinhua quoted Xi as saying.

To Trump's advisers, the call was all happy talk for the markets. Detailed negotiations hadn't begun yet; nothing had changed substantively. Nevertheless, Trump tweeted on Saturday of his conversation with Xi: "Big progress is being made!" When the markets opened on Monday, the Dow Jones average advanced 265 points.

17

PING-PONG DIPLOMACY, JANUARY 2019

Robert Lighthizer was now indisputably America's chief China negotiator. While the trade battle was on hold for now and he wanted a deal, he wasn't willing to settle cheaply.

To start, he wanted to make clear to his Chinese counterparts seated across the table from him in the Eisenhower Executive Office Building on January 30, 2019, how important the issue of enforcement was. The United States and China had decades of negotiations where Beijing pledged to open its markets fully to American businesses and ease pressure on them to hand over technology. But progress had been scant, he believed. The agreement the two sides were negotiating had to be backed up by strong enforcement—namely tariffs—to make sure any pledges were carried out.

Beijing should understand that, he said. The Chinese sage Confucius had said as much, more than two thousand years earlier. Citing a passage from Confucius's *Analects*, Lighthizer told the group: "In the past when I evaluated a person, I believed what they said. Now when I evaluate a person, I listen to them, then I see what they do." The Americans would only be satisfied, Lighthizer made clear, when they saw the Chinese do what they said they would do.

Chinese negotiators still weren't sure what to make of Lighthizer. They had studied his history as a young U.S. trade negotiator with Japan in the 1980s during his "missile man" days. Lighthizer had negotiated restrictions on imports of Japanese steel, which China thought had weakened Japan's trade-powered economy and which Beijing was determined not to repeat. They knew Lighthizer grew rich suing Chinese steel mills as a lawyer, and that he upbraided Chinese economic policies in opinion pieces and congressional testimony. They recalled his blunt talk to Xi Jinping laying out U.S. complaints about China during Trump's November 2017 visit to Beijing.

The Chinese had tried to go around him by dealing with Treasury Secretary Mnuchin, but that hadn't worked. They were stuck with Lighthizer.

On the plus side for Beijing, Lighthizer clearly had the ear of President Trump on trade. Any deal that he endorsed was more likely to be approved by a president that the Chinese viewed as fickle and unpredictable. The Americans tried to emphasize their seriousness by pairing Lighthizer with Mnuchin in talks with Vice Premier Liu He and his team.

Initially, the president was reluctant to continue to give Mnuchin a big role in the talks. Trump was angry at him for recommending Jay Powell to head the Federal Reserve, which the president believed didn't do nearly enough to support him in his trade battle. Besides, Mnuchin was a dove on China and Trump wanted a hardass negotiator.

During a contentious Oval Office meeting shortly before the Buenos Aires summit, White House economic adviser Larry Kudlow pushed to add Mnuchin over the stiff objections of trade hawk Peter Navarro. Mnuchin needed to be deeply involved in negotiations important to the global economy and had served the president well, Kudlow argued. Eventually Trump relented. "You can't have negotiations with a country like China without the Treasury secretary," Kudlow says in an interview.

The symbolism of pairing Lighthizer and Mnuchin was powerful: China was now negotiating with both the nationalist and globalist wings of the administration. The Lighthizer-Mnuchin combination could deflect criticism at home from either anti-China populists or business groups.

Although Trump officials went out of their way to disparage their predecessors, the Lighthizer-Mnuchin pairing was a repeat of Clinton White House tactics during negotiations over China's entry into the World Trade Organization. Trade Representative Charlene Barshefsky and one of her opponents on China, National Economic Council Director Gene Sperling, led the final negotiations to show Beijing that Clinton was serious about a deal.

Still, the two nations were a long way from an agreement. That was evident during an earlier January meeting in Beijing of less-senior economic officials.

The American negotiators spent the first day of the early January sessions at China's Commerce Ministry going through their demands that China stop technology theft and slash government aid to favored companies and sectors. Their Chinese peers gave little ground. The second day, the U.S. team pressed for details on the ramped-up purchases of farm goods and energy products China had said it would make. How much would China buy and when? The Chinese side balked at making specific commitments.

Mistrust of Washington ran deep in the Zhongnanhai leadership compound. If China spelled out its purchase plans, a Chinese policy maker asked at the time, "will the U.S. side keep coming back for more?"

Still both sides showed goodwill. Liu He made a brief appearance to wish the negotiators well, a courtesy that was greeted with applause by the U.S. team. Some on the Chinese side captured the moment with their Huawei smartphones and then leaked the photos to social media.

More substantively, China announced that it had approved imports of five new varieties of genetically modified crops, long sought by U.S. farmers and agribusinesses. The list of approvals included corn and soybeans produced by DowDuPont Inc., BASF, and Syngenta AG. China's stock markets surged.

There were plenty of reasons for the two sides to negotiate seriously. An increase in tariffs on $200 billion of Chinese imports had been delayed after Presidents Xi and Trump dined at the Buenos Aires G-20 meeting. They were scheduled to rise to 25 percent on March 1, a level that was sure to harm Chinese exporters and their U.S. customers.

China's economy was deteriorating faster than Chinese officials let on. Ning Jizhe, head of the National Bureau of Statistics (NBS) and also a deputy of China's economic planning agency, called a meeting with some private-sector economists at the end of 2018 and asked them how the economy was faring. One by one, they sounded alarms about the manufacturing sector, which relied on exports. New orders were plunging and managers were cutting production and delaying decisions on investment and hiring. The financial sector was also shaky, they said.

Ning listened and then implied that the economists should help put a positive spin on the situation. "Very well," he said. "We can all agree that we have confidence in the Chinese economy."

Ning's bureau also blocked the release of some statistics that showed weakness. In December, the NBS asked the southern province of Guangdong, the country's export hub, to suspend publication of a monthly indicator of regional manufacturing activity. Guangdong had published the survey since 2011, but NBS now said the province lacked permission to continue.

"The purchasing managers' survey conducted by the Guangdong Department of Industry and Information Technology was an illegal activity," the NBS said in a statement.

U.S. companies were also starting to reel as the Chinese economy weakened. In January, Caterpillar Inc. set lower-than-expected profit targets for 2019, citing faltering demands for capital goods in

China. A few months later, the company's CEO, Jim Umpleby, told analysts that trade policy uncertainty had "put a certain amount of conservatism, I think, into all of our plans for capital spending."

3M was also hit by a China slowdown. It lowered its profit outlook for 2019; about 10 percent of the industrial conglomerate's sales come from China. Ditto with General Motors, which reported that its China sales in the fourth quarter of 2018 sank 25 percent. The automaker's income from China fell to about $300 million from $500 million a year earlier.

Liu He and his delegation prepared carefully for their trip to Washington in late January, when Lighthizer was to cite Confucius. Of course, the Chinese approved five of Ivanka Trump's trademarks before they arrived, as they regularly did before big meetings with the United States. These approvals covered wedding dresses and day care centers, among other things. China no longer touted Boeing aircraft sales, as they did in the Clinton years. By early 2020, the company hadn't received a new order since October 2017, not long after the president announced the United States would go ahead with the Section 301 report. Airbus hadn't received one either.

The Chinese negotiators planned to make a new foreign investment law, discussed in chapter 14, the centerpiece of their offer to the United States of a fairer deal for American companies. Liu had pushed hard to get the law ready for approval by China's legislature in March. His efforts were applauded by U.S. business executives, but they still had plenty of criticism of the draft measure, which glossed over details and contained vague phrases that some companies thought could be used against them.

For example, a section describing the regulatory approvals needed for deals that could affect China's national security was only a few sentences long. It said China wouldn't expropriate foreign investment except under special circumstances "for the public interest"—a term that Chinese authorities could interpret to mean most anything.

The proposed law also envisioned setting up special economic zones to promote foreign investment, but didn't provide a way for companies to expand nationally. That was a throwback to the Deng Xiaoping era of the 1980s, where economic experiments were limited to a few areas before they were promoted nationwide. Now, wary of a lack of meaningful reforms in Xi's China, American officials figured the approach was aimed at delaying nationwide competition from foreigners.

Another worry: the law didn't specify how it would be enforced at the local level. Without protection from arbitrary rulings, foreign firms could remain vulnerable to pressure to transfer technology. "Our concern is that the draft is so vague and high-level," said Jacob Parker, then the Beijing-based vice president at the U.S.-China Business Council.

The draft law was hardly going to satisfy American negotiators, but for Liu it was a start. He had been able to quickly build consensus for the law within the Chinese bureaucracy. Perhaps he could also convince American negotiators that the new law could be used to address many of their concerns.

The two days of talks in Washington, January 30 and 31, didn't produce any breakthroughs—and couldn't have, given the embryonic stage of negotiations. For starters, the two sides hadn't produced a written text to serve as the basis for negotiations. Rather, the discussions began a series of meetings where the two sides would try to narrow the gaps between them.

The Chinese pledged a big increase in purchases of U.S. farm and energy products, figuring that's what President Trump wanted. They also listed plans China was devising to reduce the troubles faced by foreign investors and exporters. Then they pressed the United States to eliminate all the tariffs it had placed on Chinese goods.

The Americans responded by pushing for fundamental changes in the way China did business, including eliminating subsidies, reducing the role of state-owned businesses, and ending pressure on U.S. companies to hand over technology. (The Chinese still didn't acknowledge that they tried to strong-arm foreign firms.) And the Americans insisted on the importance of tariffs as an enforcement tool.

Still, the two sides were talking, which was bound to encourage markets in both nations. The president—Wall Street Trump for the time being—was satisfied.

At 3:43 p.m. on January 31, Liu He was ushered into the Oval Office while TV cameras broadcast the encounter, a first for the envoy. Trump opened the session by asking a member of the Chinese delegation to read a letter Liu carried from Xi Jinping, in which the Chinese leader called for "an early agreement." The letter explained why the Chinese side continued to focus on purchases despite Lighthizer's harping on structural issues. "In our last phone call," Xi wrote to Trump, "you said you wanted for China to buy more agricultural products. I have made some arrangements about which, I believe, you might have been briefed."

The Chinese leader ended the letter with a flourish aimed directly at the president's ego: "I feel we have known each other for a long time, ever since we first met," he wrote. Trump told the assembled press: "That's a beautiful letter."

Trump then lavished praise on Xi's envoy, calling Liu "one of the most respected men anywhere in the world," and six times mentioned China's pledge to buy more soybeans. Trump didn't once utter the word "structural," although attacking structural issues was the stated reason for the trade war. "That's a tremendous purchase which will take place now," Trump said of Liu's pledge to buy millions of tons of soybeans. "And our farmers are going to be very happy."

The next steps were up to the two leaders, Trump said. "I know that I'll be meeting with President Xi, maybe once and maybe twice, and it'll all seem—and it seems to be coming together." After the journalists departed, Trump didn't want to kill the feel-good buzz. The president asked everyone on his trade team to speak, except for trade hawk Peter Navarro, who was bound to raise objections. "We're having a nice meeting," the president said. "I don't want to ruin it."

For the Chinese, the meeting could hardly have gone better, aside from Trump's announcement of an early summit with Xi, which Beijing hadn't agreed to (and which never occurred). But for Lighthizer, Trump's embrace of purchases and disregard of structural issues presented a big and continuing problem: How could he convince Chinese officials that they needed to make fundamental changes in China's economy when his boss seemed uninterested in the issue and didn't pressure Beijing to change?

In a White House press briefing after the Oval Office session, Lighthizer continued to focus on forced technology transfer, intellectual property, trade secrets, and the need for enforcement—all issues that Trump had skirted. As for whether Trump should meet with Xi before the March 1 deadline for tariffs to increase, Lighthizer was cautious. "If we don't make headway between now and then," Lighthizer said, "my advice would be that we can't finish," and Trump shouldn't meet.

To amplify Lighthizer's reservations, some Trump trade officials briefed Washington allies that there had been little progress on structural issues, figuring their concerns would reach the press.

On the business side, Myron Brilliant, the U.S. Chamber of Commerce's executive vice president, spread the word. The two sides continued to differ on structural issues, he told the press later in the day, and any deal was a long way off. On the China-skeptic side, Hudson Institute's Michael Pillsbury chimed in. "Based on the Chinese cockiness that they have Mr. Trump under control from donors, I'm afraid this is Mission Impossible," he said at the time in an interview.

When outside commentators urged the United States to continue to hang tough and push China for fundamental reform, Light-hizer's staffers called to thank them, even if those doing the talking were Democrats critical of the administration. "Message management," a negotiator called it.

• • •

Over the following three months, U.S. and Chinese negotiators took turns crossing the Pacific and batting proposals back and forth, in a kind of ping-pong diplomacy. To start, the U.S. trade representative's office produced a text out of the 142 items China indicated it might negotiate. U.S. officials labeled the items green, yellow, or red, depending on whether China said they were easy, difficult, or impossible to negotiate. Then they wrote text describing the issues to be negotiated, with brackets in the text marking where there was disagreement.

As in any negotiation, officials tried to reach agreement by reducing the number of bracketed items. In a show of good faith, the Chinese accepted the American text as a basis for negotiations.

Lighthizer set the negotiating agenda, often scheduling purchases as the last item to be discussed when the two sides met. That signaled yet again that structural issues and enforcement were the heart of the dispute to him, not soybeans or energy buys. Sometimes the negotiators ran out of time before they could talk about commodity purchases.

The United States and China spent months discussing increased Chinese purchases of American semiconductors. The area seemed to be a win for both nations. The United States was the global leader in semiconductors and China needed chips for electronics manufacturing. The Obama administration had killed a number of prospective Chinese purchases of U.S. chip makers. Why not encourage the Chinese now to buy more U.S. chips rather than build their own advanced semiconductor industry, American negotiators felt.

U.S. semiconductor exports averaged about $6 billion a year. In

February, China's top economic planning agency proposed quintupling U.S. semiconductor sales to China to $200 billion over six years. In March, Beijing scaled back the offer to only doubling chip purchases. In Washington, the Chinese embassy pitched the proposal to the industry's trade association, the Semiconductor Industry Association (SIA). In China, the Ministry of Commerce and National Development and Reform Commission lobbied American semiconductor chip firms. On the U.S. side, the Commerce Department took the lead in lobbying for the deal.

But the chip industry rejected the overtures. The route American-made chips take to China is often circuitous. Semiconductors designed and manufactured in America are frequently tested and assembled into electronic components in low-wage countries like Mexico or Malaysia before being shipped to China. Those chips are counted as U.S. exports to the countries where the assembly takes place, not to China. To carry out the new purchasing proposal, U.S. firms would need to shift their assembly operations to China. Then the U.S.-produced chips would be shipped directly to China and be listed as U.S. exports to China.

The change wouldn't mean additional sales, the industry argued. Rather, U.S. companies would have to rearrange their supply chain, at great expense, build more factories in China, and shutter others elsewhere. That would make them more dependent on Beijing, which someday could decide to cut off the U.S. companies. The United States shouldn't encourage the Chinese government to take a bigger role in the semiconductor industry, industry officials said. "The Chinese must treat all U.S. companies impartially," the SIA said in a statement emailed to the U.S. trade representative's office in February.

American negotiators finally dropped the plan in March after Lighthizer talked with Sanjay Mehrotra, the CEO of memory chip maker Micron Technology. Lighthizer told Mehrotra that the president didn't understand why the chip makers objected to more sales.

"More sales are good, but we'd rather be out of it," he told Lighthizer, explaining that the industry wanted sales based on fresh demand. After the call, the Washington representatives of the big chip firms discussed the issue by conference call and reaffirmed their opposition.

"Whatever the number, the Chinese chip purchase offer is a distraction that risks deepening Chinese state influence in an environment that is otherwise market-based," said John Neuffer, the SIA's president, after the industry discussions. "The market should determine commercial success, not government fiat." Accepting defeat, a Trump administration official said Lighthizer "isn't advocating for anything the industry doesn't want."

As negotiations continued, Liu and his team lobbied in Beijing to accelerate plans to further open China's financial services and manufacturing sectors and to improve China's protection of intellectual property rights. Those changes were in China's interest, the leadership believed. Chinese negotiators also proposed having the central government monitor how local officials protect foreign patents and technology. Under the plan, American companies could report any coercion at the local level to regulators in Beijing, who would have the power to intervene.

China continued to dangle more purchases, including an order for 10 million metric tons of U.S.-grown soybeans—about one-third of what China bought from American farmers in 2017, before the trade war began. That would get Trump's attention, the negotiators figured, because it would help buck up his rural political base.

But China would only carry out those purchases if the United States dropped its tariffs. "China is making all the concessions it can," a Chinese official said. "The least the Americans can do is to cancel all the tariffs."

Lighthizer wasn't ready to move yet on tariffs. He was counting on them to enforce a deal. The two sides were planning to handle alleged violations of an accord through a series of consultations. If the disagreement couldn't be resolved at a lower level, Lighthizer and Liu, or whoever replaced them in their positions, would consult.

If they couldn't reach agreement, Lighthizer insisted, either side could levy tariffs for what it claimed was a violation of the accord. (That might sound even-handed, but only China was making pledges to change its economy and purchase more goods, so China would be the likely target for tariffs.)

Additionally, Lighthizer wanted China to agree not to retaliate if the United States reimposed tariffs. That was the only way to assure that enforcement wouldn't lead to an endless cycle of retaliation that would undermine a deal, he argued. Ultimately, U.S. negotiators understood, Beijing could always scrap the deal if it felt the United States was being unfair. Still, Lighthizer's terms were too much for Liu and the Chinese team. A no-retaliation clause would violate Chinese sovereignty, they argued. The issue remained unresolved.

"The American negotiators—they're very, very tough," said the Chinese official who complained about China having to make all the concessions.

Both sides had to worry about critics back home accusing them of weakness. On his left, Trump had to watch out for Democratic presidential candidates who looked for signs he was kowtowing. On his right, he had to placate anti-China warriors who feared he would settle too easily.

As always, he kept his eyes on Fox's Lou Dobbs as a barometer of opinion on the right. On February 22, Dobbs attacked plans by the U.S. team to label any deal with China a memorandum of understanding—trade terminology for an enforceable agreement that doesn't need congressional approval. Dobbs railed on his show that evening, incorrectly, that "an MOU isn't worth the paper it's written on. It is unenforceable." The following day, during a televised Oval Office session with Liu He, Trump attacked Lighthizer for proposing an MOU.

"The real question is, Bob, do we do a memorandum of understanding, which, frankly you could do or not do," Trump said. "I don't care if you do it or not. To me, it doesn't mean very much." The president said he wanted a "final, binding contract." After trying to explain what an MOU meant and getting nowhere with Trump, Lighthizer quickly conferred with Liu, as the cameras kept rolling. "We'll never use the term again," Lighthizer told the president, to laughter from the assembled press.

Later in the day, Lighthizer's allies tried to make sure the controversy didn't create a rift with the president, as had happened with so many other Trump advisers. They said Lighthizer regarded the presidential put-down as a simple misunderstanding. The trade representative remained in Trump's good graces.

In Beijing, hard-line sentiment was growing against the Trump administration. It was buoyed by Washington's campaign to thwart Huawei Technologies, whose commercial successes aroused enormous pride among ordinary Chinese. The Communist government had long portrayed China as a victim of years of humiliation at the hands of Western forces. Here was Beijing once again being threatened, this time by the United States—even though China had benefited greatly from its ties to the West.

Xi sought to appear unyielding. A few days before Liu left for his late February negotiating session in Washington, Xi's office approved publication of a speech the leader made six months earlier, in August 2018. Xi vowed to stay the course on China's political and legal systems. Releasing the speech then was meant to signal that Xi would resist any demands for China to, say, make judges more independent of the party so they could better enforce foreign intellectual property rights.

"We must never follow the Western path of constitutionalism, separation of powers, and judicial independence," Xi said in the speech, published by the Communist Party's influential journal *Qiushi*, or Seeking Truth.

"There is a growing call for a harder-line approach [toward the United States] in the Chinese society," said Mei Xinyu, an analyst at a think tank affiliated with China's Commerce Ministry. "The U.S. side should take such sentiment into account and shouldn't be too greedy."

The late February negotiations were so intense that officials on both sides didn't take lunch breaks and ordered takeout instead. Liu went all-American by ordering a hamburger; Lighthizer chose Chinese eggplant and chicken. By the time of the Friday, February 22 Oval office session with Liu, where Lighthizer got chewed out for proposing an MOU, Trump said he had seen sufficient progress in the negotiations to delay indefinitely the March 1 deadline for raising tariffs to 25 percent. One big win, American negotiators said, was a deal with China on how Beijing would handle currency interventions.

"We actually concluded and reached an agreement—one of the strongest agreements ever on currency," Treasury Secretary Mnuchin told the president.

"Have you discussed and reached a final agreement on currency?" Trump asked, making sure the press couldn't miss the news.

"We have on currency," Lighthizer confirmed. "But we have a lot more work to do over the next two days" as the talks extended into the weekend.

A few days later, in congressional testimony, Lighthizer said the deal involved pledges by China not to engage in competitive devaluations—meaning Beijing wouldn't intervene in markets to drive down the value of the yuan to help its exporters—and to disclose when it intervened.

But the two negotiators were hyping the progress. The Chinese never fully agreed to a currency arrangement. The issue would continue to be a sticking point in negotiations many months later.

Negotiations were going so well, said the president, that he was looking forward to a summit with President Xi, where they could wrap things up. "Probably Mar-a-Lago. Probably fairly soon, during the month of March," Trump said.

"We're planning it with your schedule, Mr. President," replied Mnuchin.

Liu He hadn't said anything about a summit before Trump spoke and didn't respond to Trump's statement. Some on the Chinese side were miffed by the presumption that a U.S. leader could decide on his own when and where a Chinese leader would meet. Still, they were pleased with the overall progress.

After journalists left the room, Trump took pictures with the Chinese delegation and told the Chinese officials that they could pick whatever picture they wanted and he would sign each of them. Lighthizer commented that he hadn't received any pictures of him with President Xi during earlier meetings. Not to worry, said Liu He, he would have the photos delivered to the U.S. team.

"Make sure to send some photos to John Bolton, too," the president joked about his hawkish national security advisor. "He's the one who's trying to destroy Russia and China."

• • •

At the beginning of March, China opened an eleven-day session of the largely ceremonial National People's Congress. Xi used the meeting, traditionally a chance for the leadership to celebrate China's growth prospects, to lay the groundwork for a potential deal with Washington.

Beijing signaled it had dropped, at least on paper, its "Made in China 2025" plan to put China at the forefront of global technology, which had spooked foreign competitors. During a nearly one-hundred-minute speech to the three thousand delegates inside the cavernous Great Hall of the People, Premier Li Keqiang didn't make any reference to the plan, which he had highlighted the prior three years.

That didn't mean that Beijing had forsworn using subsidies and other tools to help build Chinese technology, even if those policies would continue to discriminate against foreign firms. Li said the government would keep nurturing emerging industries, including advanced manufacturing, next-generation information technology, biomedicine, and electric automobiles. These were the same industries targeted by the Made in China plan.

To the Trump team, the wordplay meant that China was involved in a charade. But to the Chinese, the omission was significant. Not mentioning a plan that had been embraced by Xi Jinping was an indication Beijing was considering changes in its industrial policies. The Made in China plan had critics within the Chinese government, too, because it had led to waste and financial losses. For instance, cheap government-directed loans to battery makers had led to severe overproduction in the past few years.

Then the legislature made additional changes to the Foreign Investment Law as described earlier.

While Chinese officials pushed to make progress on a pact, they resisted American efforts to schedule a summit between the two leaders. They continued to fear that a meeting could be a disaster, given Trump's unpredictability and willingness to tweet his version of reality, even if that wasn't what the two sides agreed to. While the Buenos Aires meeting between the two leaders had gone well, Xi's advisers worried about another encounter.

When Trump abruptly broke off nuclear disarmament talks in Hanoi with North Korean leader Kim Jong Un at the end of February, officials in the Zhongnanhai were further unnerved. What if Trump threatened to walk out of a meeting with Xi Jinping unless the Chinese accepted a take-it-or-leave-it proposition? The stakes were too high for Beijing to risk such a scenario. As March slipped away with no firm date for a meeting, U.S. officials started to say the meeting could be delayed until April. Although the two sides continued to talk about a meeting, it was never scheduled.

Still, U.S. officials became convinced that a deal was near. The two sides continued to meet, including nearly daily videoconferences, and reduced the number of bracketed items in the text. The U.S. side also believed the Chinese economy was weakening rapidly, in large part because of the tariffs. "We have hurt them," White House economic adviser Kudlow claimed on CNBC on March 8. "We have them over a barrel."

Trump felt he needed a deal to buck up the economy and his chances of reelection. If the two sides agreed soon on agriculture and energy purchases, the impact would start to be felt in the early part of 2020, when the election campaign was heating up. To encourage a deal, the United States signaled it would back off on some demands that would require China to remake its economy, including a reduced role for state-owned companies and diminished use of subsidies. "We've got to be realistic that this is a one-party authoritarian system. We don't see that changing," the U.S. ambassador to Beijing, Terry Branstad, told the *Wall Street Journal* in March.

In a mid-March radio interview, Trump's former chief White House economic adviser, Gary Cohn, was blunt: "I think the U.S. is desperate right now for an agreement," he said. "The president needs a win. The only big open issue right now that he could claim as a big win—that he'd hope would have a big impact on the stock market—would be a Chinese resolution."

U.S. officials took turns expressing optimism about finishing a deal soon. On March 12, Lighthizer told the Senate Finance Committee, "Our hope is we are in the final weeks of an agreement." On April 4, Trump forecast a deal "within the next four weeks, maybe less, maybe more." On April 29, less than a week before the Chinese backed away from a deal, Mnuchin said the talks were in the "final laps."

It's clear now that the United States was misreading Beijing. What did Trump and company miss? From Xi's perspective, the price of a deal was getting too expensive, politically and economically.

Even as China was beginning to balk, Lighthizer pushed for

additional Chinese concessions, especially in high-technology fields the Chinese viewed as off-limits politically. He focused on China's restrictions on U.S. providers of cloud computing and on the flow of data across its borders.

China was one of the world's largest and fastest-growing markets for cloud computer services, which enable customers to store data, computing, and networking resources over the Internet, rather than on on-site computer servers. Alibaba Group Holding Ltd. and other domestic firms dominate the Chinese market, while foreign firms such as Microsoft and Amazon face severe restrictions.

Foreign cloud providers generally have to form joint ventures with Chinese partners, though foreign ownership of cloud firms is capped at 50 percent. In some areas such as data storage for Chinese customers, foreigners are barred outright. They usually end up licensing their technology to Chinese firms. A stringent cybersecurity law also requires cloud providers to store data in China and not move servers overseas.

For Americans, the cloud restrictions seemed deeply unfair. Chinese cloud computing companies faced no similar restrictions in the United States; they operated under the same rules as American companies.

But for the Chinese, cloud computing was a national security issue. The authoritarian government balked at changes that could loosen restrictions on the flow of data and information across borders. Ultimately, that could lead to breaches in the Great Firewall of China, they feared, and give ordinary Chinese access to information the party wanted restricted. Beijing was willing to give some ground for the sake of a deal, but not much.

On March 25, Premier Li met with about three dozen foreign CEOs attending an economic forum in Beijing. They included the heads of IBM, BMW, Daimler, Pfizer Inc., and Rio Tinto PLC, who got a chance to raise issues with the premier, though their questions were vetted by Li's office beforehand.

IBM chief executive Ginni Rometty asked whether China would start to liberalize the cloud sector. She had reason to expect a positive response. A few days earlier, Lighthizer had hinted to IBM executives that Beijing might be willing to move. He and Mnuchin were about to fly to China for another round of talks, starting March 29, and the Chinese side might want to use the premier's meeting to send a positive message.

Li said China was considering a "liberalization pilot" in one of a handful of free-trade zones in Shanghai and elsewhere around the nation. There, foreign cloud providers could own data centers in a confined area, so long as they provided "privacy protection," Li said, without defining what that term meant. He didn't offer any additional details.

The American response essentially amounted to: Huh? How would that work? How could China allow free flow of data from the operations in a small free-trade zone, but keep it separate from the rest of the country? What kind of data services could foreign firms provide in the zone? What customers could buy their services?

Even more galling, Li's proposal wasn't new. The Chinese government had floated that idea to IBM and other big U.S. tech firms as far back as 2012, but nothing had happened since. Lighthizer reported to colleagues that the offer was "half-assed."

After additional tussling, China sweetened its cloud offer during talks in Washington in early April. Liu was willing to issue more of the licenses businesses need to operate data centers in China and to lift the 50 percent equity cap that limited ownership for some foreign cloud service providers. Lighthizer consulted with U.S. tech firms about the offer.

Still not enough, industry executives responded, given all the Chinese regulations hampering foreign participation in the sector. But it was as far as the Chinese were willing to go because of opposition within the party to any technology that could be used for political liberalization.

Lighthizer tried to push China on other issues, too. He resisted eliminating tariffs. He and Mnuchin asked China to double, or maybe even triple, its plans to buy $1.2 trillion in goods from the United States over the next few years.

To the United States, this was all part of continuing negotiations. To the Chinese, it was a wake-up call. Maybe a deal on American terms wasn't worth it. What was in it for them?

On April 18, Vice Premier Hu Chunhua, who oversees foreign trade and investment and is a member of China's Politburo, told a visiting Japanese trade delegation that he wasn't sure the United States and China would reach a trade agreement anytime soon. "It's up to the United States," which was making demand after demand, Hu said.

Two weeks later, everything fell apart, as detailed in chapter 1.

Liu He hinted to Lighthizer and Mnuchin during their late April negotiating session in Beijing that his superiors weren't on board with the text. On May 3, he sent a revised version of a part of the text to Washington, reflecting the views of the top leadership. The bulk of China's concessions were crossed out and looked like "a sea of red," U.S. officials said. The Americans were enraged and Trump wanted to immediately lash out.

The most Lighthizer could do was restrain him for two days, during which the trade representative tried to figure out how he and Mnuchin had misjudged Chinese politics so badly—not realizing that it was Xi Jinping himself who killed the plan. On Sunday, May 5, President Trump announced a jump in tariffs on the $200 billion in Chinese imports to 25 percent—which he had previously delayed indefinitely—and ordered levies on everything China sold to the United States. Not long afterward, the United States hit China's most successful high-tech company, Huawei Technologies, with what seemed like a devastating blow. U.S. companies were ordered not to sell Huawei the semiconductors, software, and other components it needed unless they obtained a license that the Commerce Department rarely issued, although the ban didn't go fully into effect immediately.

The trade war, which seemed to be easing, escalated instead. The schoolyard fight metaphor only reaches so far. Both sides prepared for a long struggle. A new Cold War was taking shape.

18

BRING YOUR COMPANIES HOME, AUGUST 2019

President Trump's aggressive moves were met in Beijing with fury and puzzlement, echoing the mood in Washington.

In the Zhongnanhai leadership compound, officials were infuriated by U.S. charges that they had reneged on a deal. From their vantage point, the United States was pressing a one-sided agreement and had humiliated their chief negotiator, Liu He, by hiking tariffs when he was visiting Washington to try to repair ties. Some likened Liu's trip to the infamous "Banquet of Hongmen," an ancient Chinese tale where a general invites his rival to a feast to kill him.

As soon as Liu flew back to Beijing, President Xi called a Politburo meeting for May 13, not waiting until the end of the month, when the twenty-five-member body usually meets. The officials unanimously agreed to denounce the United States. The Politburo ordered state media to come up with forceful hit pieces targeting American hegemony. A defiant commentary aired by China Central Television two days later called out "the trade war initiated by the U.S." and declared: "Having experienced five thousand years of winds and rains, what circumstances has the Chinese nation not witnessed before?"

The Politburo also directed policy makers to prepare plans to deal with an America that tries to isolate China, reduce its trade and investment, and cut it off from new technology. Adding to Zhongnanhai's concerns were growing democracy protests in Hong Kong that started in April, which some officials believed were abetted by Washington. Another front in a new Cold War.

To prepare the populace, the Politburo also ordered two batches of party-building sessions beginning in June. In the meetings, different parts of the party, with 90 million members, were required to study the Xi Jinping Thought that concentrated on ensuring the party's leadership. Since coming to power in late 2012, Xi had sought to reinvigorate the party's "fighting spirit" by stressing the struggle between China and the United States. Over time, China's socialism would prevail over U.S. capitalism, party ideologues argued, if party members stayed united and vigilant. With stepped-up American aggression, inculcating Communist Party values became an urgent priority.

Even officials who had long admired the United States and who had used American pressure to lobby at home for economic liberalization felt betrayed. Liu He had done his best to push for reform in the fractious Chinese bureaucracy, where warring factions can block change out of their own interests.

To help forge consensus, Liu had put together a negotiating team that represented different Chinese institutional interests, including state-owned firms, financial regulators, technology industries, and the foreign policy establishment. "The Americans failed to realize how hard it had been to create a bureaucratic consensus, and to get where we were before they decided to throw it all away," says a Commerce Ministry official involved in negotiations. "It took a lot of time just to reach a consensus among ourselves."

Liu's team had painstakingly divided U.S. demands into 118 major categories, with 698 subcategories. Each subcategory had to be analyzed. "We're talking about thousands of products here," says another negotiator. In June, Beijing published an 8,300-word white paper blaming the breakdown in talks on a "U.S. breach of consensus and commitments."

The American actions had also threatened to weaken Liu at home, making it even more difficult for him to form a new consensus on reforms and purchases that might satisfy the Americans. Some officials whispered that he lacked the chops to face off with someone as tough as Robert Lighthizer.

Xi came to his defense, in classic Chinese fashion. A week after the May 13 Politburo meeting, Xi toured rural Jiangxi province, where the Communist Party's Long March of the 1930s began. Images of Liu standing by the leader's side were broadcast nationally. Without saying a word, Xi sent a powerful signal that he trusted his longtime colleague to continue to lead the battle with Washington. More than a few Chinese officials drew a contrast between the way Xi embraced his embattled lieutenant and the way Trump denigrated cabinet officers who worked for him.

In Washington, the Trump team cleared away other trade battles so they could focus on China.

On May 17, the United States delayed for six months a decision to impose 25 percent tariffs on European and Japanese cars, hoping to use the time to negotiate limits on imports. (In an astonishing finding, the Trump administration decided that imports of cars and car parts threatened U.S. national security, a ruling that especially outraged Japanese carmakers who had spent billions of dollars building plants in America.) The same day, the administration removed steel and aluminum tariffs on Mexico and Canada, after intense lobbying by Senator Chuck Grassley, an Iowa Republican who headed the Senate Finance Committee. Unless the tariffs were withdrawn, Grassley warned the president, his renegotiated NAFTA wouldn't pass the Senate. Trump, who was wedded to tariffs, finally relented.

Lifting the tariffs means a "victory with Mexico and Canada,"

Grassley later told the *Wall Street Journal*'s Will Mauldin. "It ought to give some credibility for the negotiations with China."

Less than a week later, Lighthizer met in Paris with trade ministers from the European Union and Japan to continue talks on how to confront Beijing on subsidies, state-owned enterprises, and other aspects of Chinese economic policy. For Washington, the meetings were as much about signaling to Beijing that it couldn't peel away U.S. allies, as they were about actual results.

Lighthizer's boss wasn't nearly as disciplined. On May 30, about two weeks after he lifted tariffs on Mexico, President Trump threatened Mexico with new tariffs unless it did a better job of halting migrants from crossing into the United States, as described in earlier chapters. After lobbying from Lighthizer, Treasury Secretary Mnuchin, and a slew of CEOs, Trump quickly relented.

Clearing away minor disputes to concentrate on China was a Lighthizer priority. "Going after Mexico and Canada was like going after Bulgaria in World War II," rather than Germany, Lighthizer told colleagues. "China is the threat."

• • •

President Trump regularly claimed that his tariffs were battering China and enriching the United States. "We're taking in billions and billions of dollars for the first time ever against China in the form of tariffs. I'm very happy with that," he told Fox's Maria Bartiromo in March. In early June, at a dinner in London with British royals and Prime Minister Theresa May, he boasted that Chinese retaliation helped him. "I hope China will come down hard on U.S. companies, so they can come home," Trump told the group.

But the reality was far different. When he boosted tariffs to 25 percent on $200 billion of Chinese goods in May 2019, some of his bedrock supporters suffered the most. Political pressure on him mounted and he often changed course.

When China retaliated with additional tariffs on farm goods and other products, the president sought first to take care of rural America, his firmest base of support. The administration approved a $16 billion program to reimburse soybean and other farmers for lost sales. In all, the administration committed nearly $30 billion to keep farmers happy, about as much as the United States received from China tariffs. The farmers wouldn't have needed any aid if Trump hadn't started the battle with China.

Rather than fattening Treasury's coffers, import duties were going to mollify an important political constituency. If farmers broke with Trump over the trade war, administration political tacticians worried, his political support would begin to erode. "It was a blatant vote buy," says Scott Henry, a young soybean and corn farmer in Nevada, Iowa, and helped farmers keep their losses to a minimum.

But the administration couldn't pay off everyone.

Hickory, North Carolina, the furniture-making center, was one of the earliest casualties of the massive Chinese import surge of the 1990s and early 2000s. Catawba County, which includes Hickory, was Trump country. In the 2016 presidential election, two-thirds of the voters there chose him. Nevertheless, the president's tariffs delivered another blow to the region.

Century Furniture in Hickory, which had survived Chinese competition by revamping its production and marketing, was hit twice. Its import bill for Chinese fabrics and metalwork soared because of U.S. tariffs, and its furniture exports to China plummeted because of Chinese retaliatory tariffs.

Immediately Century lost a $1.3 million order from a Chinese retailer. Over the following six months, as tariffs increased, lost sales amounted to $2 million to $2.5 million—a substantial hit for a company with $100 million in revenue. One of Century's largest Chinese customers pressed the North Carolina manufacturer to build more furniture in China to avoid tariffs. But Century balked.

Once Century taught Chinese subcontractors how to manufacture its furniture profitably, says Century's CEO, Alex Shuford III, "that will make them more competitive against us."

Without the trade war, Shuford says Century's exports would have continued to grow. "That should have been sales growth for our domestic factories," he says. "This hasn't helped Hickory. It has helped Vietnam dramatically" as well as other furniture-making nations.

MOODY'S ANALYTICS CHIEF ECONOMIST, Mark Zandi, tracked the impact of Chinese tariffs by county for this book, by examining how tariffs affected the counties' top employers. The pattern was startling. The higher the vote totals for Trump in the 2016 election, the greater the blow from Chinese levies.

Counties that voted by more than a 90 percent margin for Trump were hit four times as hard by Chinese tariffs as the average county. Those that he carried by 80 percent felt three times the impact. Conversely, counties that Hillary Clinton won by at least a 60 percent margin suffered less than the national average.

Zandi then recalculated the impact by adding in U.S. tariffs imposed on Chinese goods. While those tariffs were supposed to protect U.S. manufacturers that competed with China, they also hurt U.S. companies that depended on Chinese imports, like Century Furniture. Adding the effects of those tariffs didn't change the pattern: Trump country hurt; Clinton country was spared.

"I don't think the president could have drawn up a policy that would have done more damage to his base of voters than the trade war," Zandi says.

ECONOMISTS HAD LONG THEORIZED that businesses reacted to uncertainty by reducing investment and employment. It was a simple theory. If an executive wasn't sure whether an investment or new hire would pay off because of some uncontrollable threat, the executive would choose to hold off until there was more information to make a decision. By mid-2019, it was becoming clear that the theory was reality at businesses around the globe.

Multinational businesses had spent a quarter century building supply chains that crisscrossed the globe, with the biggest hubs in China and the United States. Now they were waiting to see how the tariff battle would play out and affect their costs.

One team of economists measured the uncertainty by scanning transcripts of investor conference calls held by nine thousand firms worldwide. They looked for words that referenced global trade wars and other uncertainties. Their index of trade risks perceived by executives, stable for more than a decade, jumped by 60 percent after the beginning of 2018. For U.S. firms it was up 43 percent.

Just as the theory predicted, business investment and hiring—crucial to economic growth—began to slow. U.S. business investment contracted in the second quarter, according to Commerce Department data, and orders by U.S. businesses for long-lasting durable goods like trucks or machine equipment also headed down. Companies weren't laying people off, but they also weren't hiring as aggressively as they had been doing in the lead-up to the trade war. By August 2019, U.S. job openings had declined 7.5 percent from their peak of the expansion reached in November 2018.

A September 2019 analysis by five Fed economists calculated that uncertainty over Trump trade policy had reduced global GDP by 0.8 percent in the first half of 2019 and could lead to a total reduction of slightly more than 1 percent through early 2020. That was a big blow to a president who had campaigned on pumping up the U.S. economic growth rate, which had been stuck near 2 percent since 2001, to 3 percent or higher. After large cuts in individual and corporate U.S. tax rates, growth had perked up in 2018, but the

chances of sustaining the higher growth rate were quickly evaporating. The trade war had become another drag on growth.

Markets reflected the corporate wariness and economic uncertainty. After the president tweeted in early May 2019 that he was
raising tariffs, the Dow Jones Industrial Average fell about 1,500
points by the end of the month. Stocks had soared after Trump's
election and continued as Congress approved his tax cuts. But the
rally had stalled as his trade confrontations heightened in 2018. Afterward, markets moved up and down on the latest tweet or news
about talks and retaliation.

Beijing also sought to make clear to the president the political
cost of continuing the battle. On June 17, state media announced
that Xi Jinping planned to make a state visit to North Korea, the
first time a Chinese leader would travel to the reclusive state in
fourteen years. North Korean leader Kim Jong Un had taken four
trips to Beijing in the previous fifteen months, mostly to consult
with Xi on how to deal with Trump. But Xi hadn't reciprocated,
despite repeated invitations from Pyongyang.

The two-day visit started on June 20 and had been planned for
some time. It was timed for the seventieth anniversary of the start
of diplomatic relations between China and North Korea. Now it
offered an opportunity for the Chinese leader to send a strong reminder to his American counterpart. China could help Trump with
his much-prized nuclear diplomacy—especially at a time when the
United States was having trouble renewing talks after the failed
summit between Trump and Kim in February—or China could undermine American plans.

Shortly after Beijing's announcement of Xi's Pyongyang trip,
Trump tweeted on June 18 that he and the Chinese leader "had a
very good telephone conversation" and the two would have "an
extended meeting" at the G-20 summit scheduled for June 28 and
June 29 in Japan. Trump once again needed a summit to calm markets. For the preceding week, he had been signaling to Xi through

televised interviews that he wanted to meet. In Trump fashion, he held out the possibility of easing sanctions on Huawei Technologies if Xi showed up and threatened more tariffs if he didn't. China subsequently confirmed the meeting. Markets rallied.

The two leaders were looking for a reprise of their summit in Buenos Aires, which had led to a truce in the trade war. That one didn't hold up. Maybe a truce this time would lead to a settlement.

• • •

Xi Jinping had plenty of reasons to seek a meeting.

The trade war had led to some 5 million lost jobs in China's industrial sector between July 2018 and May 2019, according to an analysis by China International Capital Corporation, a big state-owned investment bank. That represented 3.4 percent of the employment in mining and manufacturing, which rely heavily on international trade. The report surely understated the impact because it didn't take into account the latest tariff increase.

Beijing also worried that the trade war would prompt U.S. multinationals to shift production out of China to avoid U.S. or Chinese tariffs. The companies were big employers, as well as repositories of technological and management expertise sought by Chinese partners. China needed to create 11 million new jobs in 2019—a target announced by the central government early in the year—to ensure employment for important groups like college graduates, migrant workers, and discharged military personnel.

Meeting that target was crucial for social stability, the party believed. Signaling its concern, China's State Council, the top government body, created a committee in late May to oversee employment, headed by Vice Premier Hu Chunhua, who was in charge of foreign trade and investment.

Hu began by actively courting foreign firms. In July he spent more than two hours in a closed-door meeting listening to executives from U.S. companies including Cargill Inc., GE, Harley-Davidson

Inc., and Microsoft, along with European, Japanese, and South Korean companies.

He jotted down notes as the foreign executives took turns sharing their concerns, which ranged from possible fallout from the protracted trade war to worries about how the new foreign investment law would be enforced. Hu and other senior officials present, including those from the Commerce Ministry and the top antitrust regulator, promised a more liberal business environment and urged the foreign businesses to invest more.

China's leaders had reasons to worry about a corporate exodus. About 41 percent of the 250 respondents to a May 22, 2019 survey of U.S. companies said they had relocated or were planning to relocate manufacturing facilities outside China, reported the U.S. Chamber of Commerce in China and the U.S. Chamber of Commerce in Shanghai. That percentage was a big jump from the 11 percent when the question was first asked in 2013. Favored destinations included Southeast Asia and Mexico.

Some months later, the consulting firm Kearney estimated that about $95 billion in exports to the United States since the end of 2013 that were once produced in China now were manufactured in other low-wage nations, mainly in Mexico and Vietnam.

To figure out how likely multinationals were to decamp, a top policy advisory body to the government, the Development Research Center of the State Council, sent a survey in June to scores of foreign companies operating in China.

It laid out Beijing's growing concerns: What does your company think about the American high-tech "decoupling" strategy toward China? the questionnaire asked. How would you suggest China respond? The survey listed four answers for respondents to choose from: 1) Don't worry. The U.S. strategy is not doable. 2) Improve protection of intellectual property and the business environment. 3) Strengthen indigenous R&D. 4) Strengthen cooperation with third parties.

Beijing faced a conundrum. On the one hand, officials wanted to encourage multinationals to remain in China and expand. On the other hand, they wanted to free China as fast as possible from reliance on foreign technology, even though that would make foreign firms feel unwelcome. Policy makers figured that China's huge market would ensure enough foreign investment even if they made increasing demands of multinational companies.

Xi Jinping focused on self-reliance. He told authorities to increase funding for research institutes and to press companies to boost their R&D, especially after the United States slapped a sales ban on American technology to China's ZTE Corporation in mid-2018. Although the Trump administration later reversed the ban, the action convinced senior leaders of China's technological vulnerability. Chinese companies had long relied on American technology and suppliers for semiconductors, software, jet engines, and many other high-technology products.

Now as trade tensions with the United States deepened, officials urged Chinese companies to reduce their reliance on American suppliers if possible. In response, China's large state-owned telecom carriers barred Cisco Systems, a longtime supplier, from bidding on contracts for networking equipment. "We're being uninvited to bid. We're not being allowed to even participate anymore," Cisco CEO Chuck Robbins later told analysts. "It was a much faster decline than what we candidly expected."

Instead, the giant Chinese telephone firm, China Mobile Ltd., chose Huawei equipment. "The trade war has made Huawei the pride of China," says a senior executive at China Mobile.

Nationalist sentiment certainly played a role, but so did Huawei's increasing technological prowess. When China Mobile put out bids in 2004 for a $100 million contract, Huawei competed with a few Chinese and foreign firms. "Its products were much cheaper than, for example, Cisco's, but we told them, 'We're China Mobile. Money is not an issue for us. What we want is quality and reliability,'" the executive recalls. Cisco won that contract. "Now Huawei stands for quality and reliability, and their stuff still is cheaper than imports," the China Mobile executive says. "Why not Huawei?"

The leadership also pressed domestic companies to step up R&D. Shanghai's party secretary visited three local semiconductor companies in June and called on the chip industry to "develop an innovation chain and put more efforts in realizing technological breakthroughs." Later in the month, Miao Wei, minister of industry and information technology, instructed robotics companies in the southern Chinese city of Guangzhou to develop the technologies necessary to compete globally.

Sometimes, though, Beijing threatened tough actions on the technology front that would match the Trump administration, but wavered for fear of spooking foreign companies. After the United States sanctioned Huawei, for instance, China warned it would retaliate. If U.S. companies weren't allowed to sell to Huawei, China would block them from doing business with Chinese firms. Beijing said it would create an "unreliable entity" list and blackball companies that failed to supply Chinese firms for "noncommercial purposes."

But by early 2020, the government had yet to publish any specific companies or individuals on the list. U.S. multinationals employ more than 2 million domestic workers in China, Citigroup estimates, and Beijing didn't want to push them too hard. Chinese negotiators told visiting Americans that Beijing wouldn't proceed as long as trade talks were "going in the right direction."

• • •

On June 29, the two leaders sat down for lunch at Osaka's Imperial Hotel during a dreary stretch of rainy weather. In some ways, the summit was similar to the one in Buenos Aires. Trade tensions were mounting. The United States was threatening another round of tariffs—this time as much as 10 percent on the remaining $300 billion in Chinese imports not already covered by U.S. duties. Only the two leaders had the power to head off further clashes. Even the aides who sat in on the meeting were mainly the same, although the United States added Ivanka Trump, who looked to burnish her foreign policy credentials. The participants were arrayed on two sides of a long table.

But this time Xi didn't come prepared with a long list of reforms and concessions he was ready to make as part of a settlement. A sterner Xi addressed Trump. "Before we talk about trade, let's talk about what kind of a relationship we want," Xi told Trump at the start of the eighty-minute session. If the United States and China are partners, Xi indicated, then they should try to work toward a deal. But if the two nations see each other as enemies, there was no point in seeking an agreement because it wouldn't last.

Xi sketched what he envisioned as an optimal bilateral relationship—one based on "coordination, cooperation, and stability." In other words, if the two nations treat each other as partners, China would be willing to work with the United States on trade and other issues vexing to Washington, such as North Korea.

Trump didn't push back on Xi's vision of a bilateral relationship, although the United States preferred the term "constructive but results-oriented." Trump focused on getting Xi to guarantee outcomes, especially when it came to buying more soybeans and other goods. Twice during the meeting he raised the issue. Xi said he would consider the request to buy more, but America needed to understand that purchases must be reasonable. He wasn't going to order state-owned firms to buy goods they didn't need or cut off other nations in order to please America. Xi wouldn't make a firm commitment.

Trump pressed again, using different language: "You will buy significant amounts. That's our understanding," the president said. We will work out details, Xi replied.

The president was fixated on agriculture purchases and remained that way the rest of the year, which the Chinese side saw as weakness and a way to pressure him to back off on Huawei and to remove tariffs. For Trump, agricultural buys were important for two reasons: First, big Chinese purchases would help farmers and others in his political base, which he could tout as a win in a trade war that had stretched on for two years. Second, his trade team viewed purchases as a measure of whether Chinese would pursue a larger deal. If China wouldn't increase purchases—the simplest U.S. demand to meet—why should the United States believe Beijing would ever make difficult structural changes in its economy?

When Xi pressed the United States, in return, to free Huawei from sanctions, Trump was as encouraging but vague in his remarks as Xi had been on purchases. No firm commitments, but no firm rejection. The two sides could handle the issue separately.

During a press conference afterward, Trump claimed victory. The talks had gone so well, he said, the United States was indefinitely suspending any tariff increase. "China is going to be buying a tremendous amount of food and agricultural product, and they're going to start that very soon, almost immediately," Trump said. He lauded farmers as "great patriots" who stuck with him during the trade war.

As for Huawei, he suggested he'd go easy on the company. American firms "sell to Huawei a tremendous amount of product that goes into the various things that they make," Trump said. "And I said that that's okay, that we will keep selling that product," so long as it didn't endanger national security. Any final resolution, though, would wait until the end of the talks.

Trump went so far as to say that America and China could once again become "strategic partners," dredging up a term that hadn't been used since the Clinton administration. That was a far milder description of China than the one in his administration's National Security Strategy, which labeled China a "strategic competitor" and a "revisionist power."

Xi was also happy to claim success. According to the official Xinhua News Agency, the Chinese leader had laid out a positive vision of U.S.-China relations, saying the countries will "maintain exchanges at all levels" and work together for stability.

Despite the positive comments, some on the Chinese side worried that Trump either misinterpreted what Xi had said on farm purchases or was trying to force Beijing to accept his version. At the conclusion of the summit, Vice Foreign Minister Zheng Zeguang made a point of clarifying to the U.S. side that Xi hadn't promised increased agricultural purchases. Senior U.S. trade officials missed his warning. They said they never heard Zheng's comments or dismissed him as a junior official.

The disagreement over what Xi promised at Osaka quickly turned into another front in the battle between the two superpowers. Instead of easing tensions, the Osaka summit made them worse.

• • •

On July 4, a Chinese Commerce Ministry spokesman indicated that China wasn't in a rush to accelerate purchases—the first sign of problems ahead.

"Agricultural trade is an important topic that both sides need to discuss," said the spokesman Gao Feng, adding that China hoped "to find a solution based on equality and mutual respect"—phrasing that meant there were no firm orders yet. Shortly afterward, when some privately owned Chinese companies inquired about buying soybeans from American farmers, none of the big state-owned trading companies bothered to call U.S. suppliers about sales. Beijing wasn't budging.

To Beijing, Trump's neediness was a powerful tool to use in negotiations. They weren't going to start buying unless they could get something in return. At the top of the list was a reprieve for Huawei, which they believed Trump had promised at Osaka, but hadn't delivered.

To Washington, however, Beijing's failure to carry out farm purchases was once again viewed as acting in bad faith, similar to when China scrapped the tentative trade deal in May. Although senior trade officials acknowledge that Trump hadn't wrangled a commitment out of Xi at Osaka, they are adamant that in follow-up calls between Lighthizer, Mnuchin, and Liu, the Chinese side committed to making big purchases soon. They reported their understanding to the president, confirming his belief that the Chinese weren't living up to a deal.

A senior national security official had a darker explanation for the Chinese recalcitrance. Xi was jerking Trump around in a show of power. Between the summits in Buenos Aires and Osaka, China's state media had released a speech made by Xi shortly after he took office, where the Chinese leader talked about how Chinese socialism would prevail over American capitalism. "Xi was saying 'I won't apologize anymore for China not liberalizing economically and politically,'" the U.S. official says. "Between Buenos Aires and Osaka, Xi dropped the fig leaf."

Failing to meet Trump's expectations on agriculture, and trying to use it for leverage, was "an enormous strategic blunder," the official said. "It poisoned the well." He added China's balking on farm purchases to a list he kept of broken Chinese promises that then numbered six pages, single-spaced.

As had happened in May when talks fell apart, the two sides miscalculated their leverage and the weakness of the other side. The Chinese thought Trump was more vulnerable to political pressure than he was because he kept harping on farm goods. The Americans thought that Xi would make the concessions they wanted because he was so protective of Huawei. Both thought the other side was duplicitous.

Sometimes the two sides signaled some limited flexibility. On July 21, Xinhua reported that several Chinese firms asked U.S. companies about prices for agricultural products. They also asked the government to remove tariffs on the goods, making them cheaper to buy. But still no purchases. On the U.S. side, the trade representative's office waived tariffs on 110 Chinese industrial imports after U.S. firms argued they couldn't get the items elsewhere. But still no decision on Huawei.

Despite their misgivings, both sides hoped to make progress when U.S. and Chinese negotiators met face-to-face in China on July 30 for the first time in three months. Liu He picked the eastern coastal city of Shanghai as the venue because of the city's commercial vibe and historical resonance. During President Richard Nixon's visit to China to meet Chairman Mao in 1972, the two nations reached an agreement, called the Shanghai Communiqué, which ended more than two decades of diplomatic estrangement. In a country where symbolism underlies nearly every gesture, choosing Shanghai for the talks marked China's hope for a fresh start.

Xi Jinping also added a new face to Liu's negotiation team: Zhong Shan, the commerce minister who had worked with Xi in the eastern province of Zhejiang. Zhong's ministry would have the task of implementing any agreement Beijing signed with Washington. Getting him involved was meant to signal that China was serious about cutting a deal and carrying it out once one was reached.

But the Chinese didn't realize that Trump was stewing over what he considered China's unkept purchase promise. A Trump Twitter posting should have alerted them.

As Lighthizer and Mnuchin joined Liu and his team for dinner and informal discussions at the Fairmont Peace Hotel, a landmark on the city's riverfront, Trump unleashed. China was supposed to start buying U.S. agricultural products but it had shown "no signs that they are doing so," Trump tweeted. "My team is negotiating with them now, but they always change the deal in the end to their benefit," he added. "That is the problem with China, they just don't come through."

Liu and his team were taken aback, though some on the U.S.

side told the Chinese—incorrectly this time—that Trump's tweets were usually aimed at his U.S. audience in the run-up to the campaign season.

The following day, the teams held four hours of discussions at the Xijiao State Guest Hotel, where Nixon stayed during his visit to the city in 1972, and took a group photo. Then the U.S. officials left for the airport without speaking to reporters. The Chinese side felt the talks went well enough. Negotiations were continuing, and the two sides said they would take into account each country's legal and political situations—as if they hadn't tried to do that already.

But the Americans were disappointed. As far as they could tell, Liu didn't have any enhanced mandate to cut a deal, and the farm purchase controversy remained unresolved. The White House released an encouraging statement, calling the talks "constructive" and saying the U.S. side expected talks to continue in early September. Lighthizer approved the positive spin to boost Liu and other reformers in their domestic battles.

When Lighthizer and Mnuchin reported to Trump on August 1 that they had made scant progress, his response was volcanic. He tweeted that he would hit China with 10 percent tariffs on the remaining $300 billion of Chinese imports on September 1, starting a head-spinning month of escalation. He made the decision over the nearly unanimous opposition from his senior advisers during a two-hour discussion in the Oval Office. China hawks Lighthizer and National Security Advisor John Bolton teamed with the longtime moderates Mnuchin and Kudlow to oppose escalation, scrambling the usual lineup on China.

Lighthizer objected that the move was bound to undercut Liu and scuttle any chance for a deal. The trade representative had been urging the president for weeks not to go ahead with new tariffs. The imports left to be hit were mainly consumer goods like clothing, toys, mobile phones, and laptop computers. Higher prices could turn American shoppers against the trade war, he worried.

Lighthizer sought tariffs that were "politically sustainable," says Michael Pillsbury, the China expert who consulted regularly with the Trump trade team.

For Bolton, the United States had higher priorities than a trade fight, and new tariffs were bound to alienate allies the United States needed to oppose Iran. Only White House trade adviser Peter Navarro, who opposed almost any deal with China, backed the president.

Trump "felt very strongly that the talks were going unsatisfactorily," says Kudlow in an interview. "Coming out of Osaka he didn't see any ag buys and there were some pretty critical comments coming out of Beijing ministries." Trump also believed that China wasn't aggressively attacking fentanyl production, as Xi had pledged in the Buenos Aires summit.

A U.S. official working on the issue said, only half-jokingly, that Trump wouldn't be satisfied until the Chinese put a stack of fentanyl on a table, put some police officers next to it, took pictures, and said, "This was confiscated from a container going into the United States." Later, in early November, Chinese authorities did exactly that: nine Chinese fentanyl traffickers were convicted at a public hearing in a courtroom in northern China.

Another factor: Trump had wanted to announce big farm purchases at a reelection rally later in the day in Ohio. Now he couldn't. The Dow Jones Industrial Average fell about 500 points after he announced the new tariffs at 1:26 p.m. For once, even that didn't deter him. "Until such time as there is a deal, we'll be taxing them," he told reporters before boarding Air Force One for the rally.

• • •

With the trade battle once again worsening, an unusual combination of Kudlow, Mnuchin, and Lighthizer tried to restrain the president. The first two were free traders, so their opposition to fresh tariffs wasn't surprising. But Lighthizer proudly considered himself a China hawk and had joined the administration to confront Beijing. During 2017, he pushed a reluctant Trump to endorse the Section 301 report on Chinese intellectual property theft, which functioned as the administration's declaration of a trade war. In 2018, he fought with Mnuchin and Kudlow to impose tariffs on China as a way to force concessions.

But over time, he had come to trust Liu He and to appreciate the domestic political problems he faced. Lighthizer began to talk about how the U.S. proposals aligned with those of Chinese reformers—the same arguments that had been used by administrations dating back to Nixon and which Lighthizer had once dismissed as naive. With an agreement in sight, Lighthizer, then nearly seventy-two years old, was also thinking about his legacy as a trade negotiator. The president had instructed him to get a "great deal." Now he was ready to take the best one available.

"Anyone who thinks that one deal will change how China operates is beyond crazy," says Lighthizer in an interview.

It wasn't that Lighthizer was going soft, says his brother Jim. Rather, he realized that acting like a bad cop to China wouldn't get him a deal. "Bad cops make for the best good cops," his brother says, because they have credibility when they change.

When China's central bank, acting with approval of the top leaders, allowed the yuan to slip past 7 to the dollar on August 4, U.S. officials feared that Beijing was going to devalue its currency so much that it would offset the impact of U.S. tariffs. At 8:12 a.m. the following day, Trump tweeted that the move was "currency manipulation," which he blasted as a "major violation which will greatly weaken China over time!" By that evening, the Treasury followed up by formally naming China a currency manipulator. That was another slap in the face for China, although this one had little force. Under the law, the United States was simply required to start discussions with China over currency policy and the two sides were already talking.

Frustrated, the president started hunting for new pressure points. He considered doubling, to 50 percent, tariffs already in place on $250 billion in Chinese imports. Even the 25 percent rate was having a big impact by raising costs for U.S. companies and cutting into their investment and profits. Doubling the rates was bound to hurt more, especially since Beijing would surely retaliate with its own rate hike, which would further hurt American exporters. According to AT Kearney, U.S. exports targeted by Chinese retaliatory tariffs fell 59 percent between the third quarter of 2017—around when Trump announced the Section 301 report—and the third quarter of 2018, after initial tariffs had been put in place.

Kudlow asked Lighthizer to have lunch with the president and explain why a steep tariff increase would be counterproductive. The trade representative was convincing. Trump dropped the 50 percent rate plan, though he started talking about raising the rate by 10 percentage points to 35 percent. Then in a phone call, Lighthizer helped convince the president to limit any increase to five percentage points, or a 30 percent tariff.

Kudlow also played a direct role in keeping escalation in check. In a short interview on CNBC on August 6, he said five times that the United States wanted to keep negotiating and once that it would be "flexible" about tariffs. Then, with a Trumpian flourish, he claimed that the Chinese economy was "crumbling" so Beijing needed a deal.

Many in the administration shared that view, fed by pessimistic reports on China by Reagan-era economist Arthur Laffer, who was a close friend and compatriot of Kudlow's, and, most significant, Chinese economist Xiang Songzuo of Remin University. At a seminar for entrepreneurs in December 2018, Xiang said that the Chinese economy was growing at just 1.67 percent—or was maybe even shrinking—not expanding at 6.5 percent, as the Chinese government was then claiming. Xiang, a former chief economist at a big state-owned bank, cited an internal report from an unidentified "important institution."

Xiang called for deep reforms in the Chinese economic system and said the trade war was hurting China more than the government admitted. China's censors erased a video of his talk from the Internet after it went viral on the mainland. The Trump trade team pored over a memo with an English translation of Xiang's talk.

In an interview, Kudlow says his call for talks was approved by President Trump. "One [reason] was to signal the Chinese that we were still hoping they would come in September for negotiations" as a follow-up to Shanghai, he says. "And the second was to communicate to the markets that we wished to continue negotiations; that the door was not slammed." Wall Street Trump was once again coming to the fore.

A week later, the president made another decision that he considered a peace offering of sorts. Instead of imposing tariffs on the remaining $300 billion of Chinese goods on September 1, he delayed duties on nearly two-thirds of the goods until December 15. The decision was mainly made for domestic reasons. Best Buy and other big retailers had warned the White House that they had already signed contracts with their Chinese suppliers for Christmas deliveries. They couldn't force the Chinese to cut prices, so the American firms would bear the full cost of the tariffs. By December 15, all the Christmas orders would have been delivered, helping the retailers get through the Christmas season.

The products that the White House moved into the December 15 category included expensive consumer favorites like iPhones and laptop computers. A 10 percent price increase risked a consumer backlash, so better to postpone the tariffs. The new peace faction of Kudlow, Mnuchin, and Lighthizer backed the tariff delay. Navarro didn't, but this time Trump didn't side with him.

The president thought he deserved credit for the move from Beijing. After all, he was postponing tariffs on nearly $200 billion of goods while the two sides talked. Surely this would encourage Beijing to make the promised soybean purchases. "As usual, China said they were going to be buying 'big' from our great American farmers," he tweeted shortly after the announcement. "So far they have not done what they said. Maybe this will be different!"

But the move looked far different from Beijing. Still more Chinese goods—$120 billion worth—were being hit with tariffs, and the Americans continued to insist China make purchases that Beijing didn't think were required. Chinese officials had grievances, too. Not only had Trump failed to ease pressure on Huawei, but he was moving in the opposite direction. "Ultimately we don't want to do business with Huawei for national security reasons," the president told reporters on August 18. Trump also said it would be "much harder" to sign a trade deal if Beijing cracked down on Hong Kong protestors, reinforcing the view in Beijing that Americans were behind the protests.

Five days later, Beijing retaliated against the new tariffs, as it had warned it would do—and as it had done every time before—with fresh tariffs on $75 billion of U.S. products. Most jarring to Washington, Beijing threatened to reapply 25 percent tariffs on U.S.-made cars and car parts, starting December 15. That would affect nearly 10 percent of U.S. exports to China, hurt Ford and Tesla, and eliminate a concession China had made after the Buenos Aires summit.

Although China exempted nearly one-third of U.S. exports, including aircraft, semiconductors, and pharmaceuticals, that didn't matter to President Trump. Outraged at China's temerity, he said he would boost existing tariffs to 30 percent on October 1 from 25 percent, as he had discussed with Lighthizer. That was less than the 50 percent or 35 percent tariff rates he earlier considered, but was still an increase. He also said he would raise upcoming tariffs to 15 percent from 10 percent.

The tariffs would boost the prices for consumer goods ranging from clothing to electronics and risk a cancellation of Liu's planned September negotiating trip to Washington. But Trump wouldn't be dissuaded. He believed that China rejected his peace offerings and thought he was weak. He would show them how wrong they were.

"Our great American companies are hereby ordered to immediately start looking for an alternative to China, including bringing your companies HOME and making your products in the USA," he tweeted on August 23, the same day Beijing announced retaliation. China was already worried about losing American multinationals. Now he would really give them something to worry about.

19

NEGOTIATING A TRUCE, DECEMBER 2019–JANUARY 2020

Rather than spurring corporate executives to look again at pulling out of China, the president's tweet had them scurrying to call their Washington lawyers and lobbyists. Did the president actually have the power to force them to move out of China? Perhaps not directly, trade experts argued. But Trump had broad, untested authority under the International Emergency Economic Powers Act to block financial transactions, acquisitions, exports, imports, and many other business activities during a "national emergency." This was the law that the Treasury used to sanction terrorist groups and nations like North Korea and Iran—and which Treasury Secretary Mnuchin had refused to use in the trade war.

To make sure corporate America heard him even more clearly, the president followed up his tweet with another one citing IEEPA as the basis for his power. "Case closed!" he tweeted.

China hawks in the administration, especially those working in the Pentagon, Justice Department, and National Security Council, also sensed a firmer resolve by the president. They were especially cheered by his August 18 remarks, which he repeated on September 4, that the United States wouldn't do business with Huawei because it was a national security threat. "He killed any ambiguity with that remark" that he would use Huawei as a bargaining chip in the trade talks, asserted one senior security official, although others in the administration weren't nearly as certain.

A meeting between the National Security Council's Asia chief, Matt Pottinger, and semiconductor industry executives on September 19, 2019, demonstrated how empowered the hawks felt. Pottinger had played an important behind-the-scenes role in China policy since the presidential transition, when he helped prepare position papers for the new administration. He developed a quiet rapport with the president and, as a Mandarin speaker, often acted as a note taker for important meetings with Chinese officials. Soon after the meeting with the board of the Semiconductor Industry Association (SIA), he was named deputy national security advisor.

Pottinger felt that the United States had been complacent about the China threat before Trump took office. He told people that the foreign policy establishment in both Democratic and Republican administrations had misunderstood China in three important ways.

First, they assumed that deeper economic ties between China and the West would inevitably lead Beijing to liberalize politically and economically. That hadn't happened. Second, China experts downplayed ideology as a fundamental driver of Beijing's behavior. Under Xi, Pottinger argued, ideology was becoming as important as it was under Mao. Third, the experts believed that the Chinese Communist Party was simply interested in survival. Pottinger believed the party had global geopolitical designs.

At the SIA meeting at the Hay-Adams hotel near the White House, Pottinger stressed the administration's intention to keep up pressure on Huawei and the Chinese leadership. He warned the members, who were seated around a U-shaped set of tables, that they didn't take seriously enough the threat that Huawei products could be used for spying. Citing recent studies, he said the company was beholden to the Chinese defense establishment, if not owned by it. The executives should worry more about reducing their dependence on Huawei and less about making money supplying the company.

U.S. policy toward China over the past thirty years was "well-intentioned but naive and way too optimistic," Pottinger told them. Once China joined the WTO in 2001, he said, it stopped market reforms and became more authoritarian and intent on stealing American technology. "The conscience of everyone sitting around this table should be shocked," Pottinger said. "There are consequences when you invite the [Chinese] KGB into your networks."

In an interview afterward, Pottinger explained his thinking. U.S. technology companies should be looking for "ways to support an ecosystem for telecom infrastructure and IT infrastructure that the free world can trust instead of saying, 'We need the China market so badly that we need to deprioritize our national security,'" he says. Letting Huawei dominate global telecommunications systems "would be equivalent to Reagan and Thatcher saying [during the Cold War], 'Let's let the KGB build all our telecom networks and computer systems because they're offering such a great discount.'"

Many in the group pushed back against Pottinger's arguments. U.S. government policy toward China had become a big problem for them, executives told Pottinger. They were losing ground in China, as U.S. pressure forced Chinese companies to become more efficient and less dependent on them. The Chinese would turn to European and Japanese suppliers instead. Rather than working alone, some executives said, the Trump administration should recruit allies and deal with China multilaterally. That would get better results.

As for Huawei, the executives argued that Trump was being overly dramatic and unrealistic. Washington wouldn't be able to "kill off" Huawei and prevent Beijing from using its technology to spy. Huawei's technology was so embedded in European telecommunications networks, which are linked to American ones, they said, that blocking Huawei from the United States wouldn't end the threat.

Did China want to put them out of business? Pottinger asked the executives. "No, that's not what's happening," said the trade association's CEO, John Neuffer. "They want to replace our stuff with their stuff, but they don't want to drive us out of business. We can compete with them if we have the right policies."

• • •

While Trump's national security team was getting more assertive, his trade team was playing out a familiar pattern. Stocks, government bond yields, and commodities fell sharply on Friday, August 23, the day of Trump's "hereby ordered" tweet. The Dow Jones Industrial Average plunged 623 points, or 2.4 percent, while the yield on benchmark ten-year U.S. Treasury notes fell to its lowest level since August 2016. Both were signals of trouble ahead.

By Sunday, August 25, National Economic Council Director Larry Kudlow was on CBS's *Face the Nation*, trying to walk back what Trump had said. He claimed that the president hadn't threatened using emergency power to compel companies to leave China. (Trump did.) Was Trump thinking of using such authority? the host, Margaret Brennan, asked. "You know, I . . . I don't even want to go down that road," Kudlow replied.

The president started the following day, at a summit of the leaders of the G-7 industrial nations in Biarritz, France, by tweeting, "Talks are continuing!" Then he told reporters Chinese officials had called their U.S. counterparts and said, "Let's get back to the table" for fresh talks. But he wouldn't specify who, if anyone, had actually called. To ease the way for a deal, Trump said, maybe he'd cancel his tariff threat that had shaken the market. "I think anything is possible," the president added. For good measure, he twice called Xi Jinping "a great leader."

Chinese officials said there had been recurring talks between working-level negotiators, but not at the senior level described by Trump. "I'm not aware of that," China's Foreign Ministry spokesman

Geng Shuang told reporters when asked about the call—a polite denial of Trump's claim.

Wall Street Trump was in full swing. The election was getting closer, his ace card was the economy, and the trade imbroglio with China was the Joker that could screw up everything. The Commerce Department would soon report that third-quarter economic growth had slowed to 1.9 percent (later revised to 2.1 percent), well below Trump's goal of 3 percent growth. Business investment continued to fall as executives were uncertain how the trade battle would play out.

Markets clearly wanted a settlement—any settlement—and Trump wanted to make markets happy.

About a week later, Trump ruminated that if he hadn't taken on China, "my stock market—our stock market—would be 10,000 points higher than it is now." But he said he didn't regret the fight because "somebody had to do this. To me, this is much more important than the economy." Trump's self-reflection went only so far. His trade policies and decisions weren't at fault for markets not climbing higher, he said. "Badly run and weak companies" were at fault because they didn't adapt to tariffs, he tweeted. The Federal Reserve was, too, because it didn't cut interest rates and goose the economy, as he regularly lectured Fed chairman Jerome Powell to do.

Still, Trump was correct in arguing that China's leaders faced pressure to settle. Xi also needed a win. The year 2019 was supposed to be a time for the Chinese leader to showcase the country's seventy-year progress under Communist rule, from a dirt-poor nation torn by war to a prosperous nation striding confidently into the future. (Although, of course, the party would leave out the horrors of the Great Leap Forward, the Cultural Revolution, and Tiananmen Square.)

Instead, Xi was mired in one challenge after another. The trade war with the United States kept getting more intense and threatened to sink the economy. The unrest in Hong Kong kept building and highlighted the erosion of political freedom throughout China under Xi. The setbacks fed quiet criticism of Xi from political, business, and academic elites, who believed Xi's consolidation of power had discouraged policy debates and centralized too much power in one person. Getting a trade deal with Washington now, however narrow, could help reinforce his standing.

By early September, Washington and Beijing were ready to resume high-level negotiations, which were delayed a month until mid-October, to give the Chinese leadership time to focus on their October 1 celebration of Communist rule.

Myron Brilliant, the U.S. Chamber of Commerce's executive vice president, was among the first American business leaders to sense a shift in attitude in Beijing in favor of a deal. A business delegation he led was due to meet with Premier Li Keqiang on September 10. Given the recent escalation on both sides, Brilliant anticipated a tough message from the Chinese premier. Senior Chinese leaders had largely avoided meeting with Americans throughout the summer.

Instead, Li sought to assure the visiting Americans that China would continue to open its markets, especially the service sector, and welcome more U.S. investments. Brilliant told the premier that he would like to look at the bilateral relationship as a "glass half-full" as opposed to a "glass half-empty."

Li made a gesture of putting tea in his cup and said, emphatically: "It's more than half full."

• • •

As the October talks drew closer, China's Zhongnanhai leadership compound counted on the presidential campaign to give Beijing an edge. Officials figured that Trump would be more willing to compromise to get a deal that he could brag about on the campaign trail.

Earlier in the trade fight, the chief Chinese negotiator, Liu He, had wanted to negotiate in stages. In mid-2018, he proposed to the U.S. team that 40 percent of its demands could be met right away, while another 40 percent could be discussed over time, and the remainder would be off-limits for negotiation. American negotiators rejected what they called the 40-40-20 deal, figuring that the Chinese bid would drag out talks and avoid tough subjects. They insisted on working out a sweeping deal. Trump wanted what some officials called a grand slam, not a single.

Now Chinese officials tried again to narrow the scope of the talks. Liu and his team worked on plans to boost purchases of U.S. agricultural products, give U.S. companies greater access to China's financial market, and bolster protection of American intellectual property rights. All were offers Beijing had made previously and included reforms that Beijing realized it had to make anyway to keep its economy on track. Thornier questions, including limiting the power of state-owned enterprises, reining in subsidies, and opening the cloud computing market fully would be left to later negotiations, if then.

In exchange for the offers, Liu planned to press for some reduction in tariffs, leaving to a later date Xi Jinping's demand that all tariffs be removed. Beijing would also continue to request that President Trump lift the ban on the sale of U.S. technology to Huawei that wasn't tied to national security, which Chinese officials believed he had promised to do.

The U.S. side thought of Huawei as a kind of trump card in trade talks. Huawei depended so heavily on American chip and software suppliers that the United States ought to be able to extract big concessions from China in exchange for easing the sales ban. But over time, Huawei was growing less reliant on U.S. approval, and its value for the American side in trade talks was diminishing.

Huawei's American suppliers helped bail out the firm, even if national security officials like Pottinger wanted to kill, or at least quarantine, it. Huawei was too big to lose as a customer. In 2018,

Huawei estimated that it purchased $11 billion of goods and services from American firms, out of a procurement budget of $70 billion. U.S. industry lawyers examined the statutes authorizing the blacklist, formally called the entity list, and realized that American technology companies could legally use their overseas facilities to continue to supply Huawei with most of what it wanted.

As a result, Huawei did far better than anticipated. Shortly before the end of the year, the company reported that 2019 revenue rose 18 percent to $122 billion. In September, it introduced a new phone, the Mate 30, which contained no U.S. parts, to compete with Apple's iPhone 11. Huawei developed the components it needed internally or bought them from European firms. Four months later, the United Kingdom decided to permit Huawei to build part of its 5G network, despite furious opposition from Washington.

With business soaring, Huawei opened a three-hundred-acre R&D campus in the city of Dongguan in the spring of 2019, with more than 25,000 employees, about an hour's drive from the company's headquarters in Shenzhen. The campus consists of twelve European-style towns, including ones called Paris and Luxembourg, which are connected by a train modeled on the Shenzhen metro. "We're doing well in Europe," a Huawei executive says, explaining the design.

In an interview with the *Wall Street Journal* in November 2019, Huawei's founder Ren Zhengfei appeared unfazed by the controversy enveloping the company and invited President Trump to visit the company's new R&D campus. "I would really like to have him here," Ren said. The former military officer also appeared unyielding in face of the U.S. sanctions. "We don't expect the U.S. to remove Huawei from the entity list," he told the *Journal*. "They may as well keep us there forever because we'll be fine without them."

The company continued to receive government support. Dongguan didn't charge Huawei for the land and changed the name of the surrounding village to *Xiliubeipo* ("hillside creek" in English), from *Xiniupo* ("rhinoceros hill"), to please the firm. Shortly after the campus opened, Dongguan awarded Huawei a contract valued at 2.74 billion yuan, or $391 million, for cloud computing, databases, and other products and services. In all, the *Wall Street Journal* reported, Huawei had received as much as $75 billion in state support over the years, helping it offer low-cost financing and undercut rivals' prices by 30 percent. By contrast, Cisco collected only $44.5 million in state and federal assistance since 2000.

As speculation about a mini-deal grew in Washington, President Trump said no thanks. On September 20 he told reporters, "We are looking for a complete deal. I am not looking for a partial deal." That reflected the long-held views of his trade negotiators, who had ridiculed China's 40-40-20 offer. As far as they were concerned, China categorized most of the issues at the heart of the trade dispute into the category that couldn't be negotiated because of national security.

For instance, the two sides had spent many days discussing the closed Chinese market for cloud computing. To China, the issue was a matter of national security. As part of the narrowing of talks, China's leadership wanted to move those discussions to separate military and diplomacy dialogue between the two nations. That dialogue, set up during the early days of the Trump administration, had long been declared defunct by the United States. Betting on Trump's need for a deal, Beijing was hardening its stance on negotiations by putting cloud computing again into the off-limits category.

But by the time Liu landed in Washington, D.C., for the talks on October 10 and 11, the president and his advisers were ready to reverse course. During a week of conversations, the new coalition of Mnuchin, Lighthizer, and Kudlow mapped out a strategy for getting whatever they could from the talks and pushing off tougher issues for later. That would give the Chinese more time to work on their domestic politics and give Trump a deal he could claim as a win. It would also give the United States a reason to delay any further tariffs on consumer goods like iPhones and computers, which the trio was sure would backfire domestically.

The three talked about "segmenting" the talks, and they hit on the idea of breaking the discussions into "phases." The trio liked the term so much, that when they faced other tough issues, they joked about putting the hardest parts into "a phase two."

Kudlow broached the idea to Trump, sketching out a preliminary deal involving farm purchases and some intellectual property protection and liberalization of Chinese financial services. "No one could possibly accuse you of going soft on China," Kudlow added, mixing in the flattery that moved Trump. It worked. "I could be for that," the president said, though he wanted to see what the Chinese would actually offer.

The White House's main trade hawk, Peter Navarro, vehemently opposed any settlement along those lines, but was overruled. Trump upbraided him and told him to calm down. Asked about the incident, Navarro told *Bloomberg Businessweek* that he was "always a passionate defender of the president's deep understanding of the situation and his practical solutions." Later phases would tackle issues at the heart of the Section 301 report—that is, if the two sides ever got to the other phases.

During a dinner on October 10 between the two sides—once again at Lighthizer's favorite, the Metropolitan Club—Mnuchin tried out the idea of breaking the talks into phases. The Chinese negotiators were agreeable; it was a variation on what they were suggesting anyway.

Before Liu was ushered into the Oval Office on October 11, to meet with the president, Trump conferred with his senior trade advisers once again. "It was very clear to me the president had been briefed by Steven [Mnuchin] and Bob [Lighthizer] about phase one, and it was very clear to me the president was entirely enthusiastic about it," Kudlow says in an interview.

Then the president called in reporters to discuss the results, with Liu and U.S. negotiators by his side. Trump described the prospective deal a dozen times as "tremendous," though the particulars fell far short of that description. China would toughen its intellectual property protection and open its financial services markets more broadly than before—improvement on commitments that China had previously made. Plus, China would revamp its foreign exchange policy so it didn't devalue the currency to give a competitive edge to its exporters. Secretary Mnuchin had said eight months earlier, in February, that the two sides had reached that currency deal. Putting the best spin on the components of a partial deal, administration officials said they were trying to "harvest" parts of the agreement that fell apart in May.

What really got the president excited was what he said was China's commitment to buy as much as $50 billion of agricultural products annually, about twice what it bought before the trade war began. "I'd suggest the farmers have to go and immediately buy more land and get bigger tractors," the president boasted.

Looking to get a mention of at least some of the structural issues remaining, Trade Representative Lighthizer cited progress on resolving health regulations that China sometimes used to block purchases. But such issues were clearly secondary.

Trump said that the two sides were close to a "substantial phase-one" deal. A broader settlement, the president said, would come in later stages. The second round or third round would include such divisive issues as China's subsidies to domestic firms, reliance on state-owned industries, and cloud computing.

The two sides planned to finish the deal by mid-November when Trump and Xi were scheduled to meet at a summit of Asia-Pacific leaders. But those plans fell apart when the host, Chile, canceled the meeting because of mounting antigovernment protests in Santiago. Without a firm deadline, the talks began to flounder, even though the two sides were negotiating over a far smaller set of demands than the United States had started with.

For weeks, the two sides haggled over how sharply Washington would reduce tariffs. Once again, Chinese negotiators divided American demands into hundreds of items. They calculated that their offer covered 72 percent of what the Americans wanted, which they argued should be matched by a similar tariff reduction. No way, said Lighthizer, who wanted to keep tariffs as high as possible for future leverage. The offer was worth maybe half that, or 36 percent.

On October 31, Trump inadvertently undercut Lighthizer's position by tweeting that the deal covered 60 percent of what the United States wanted—a statement that left his negotiators dumbfounded. Still, Lighthizer held firm. He was being generous, he told Chinese negotiators. Their offer covered just 31 percent of what Trump wanted but he would give them credit for 36 percent.

Back and forth the arguments went as the real deadline drew closer. That was the December 15 deadline to assess tariffs on the rest of Chinese imports. Although Lighthizer worried that those tariffs on items like iPhones and toys would backfire and had argued against them in White House discussions, he used the threat as best he could to get Liu He to back down.

With the talks stymied around Thanksgiving, Chinese officials turned to the president's son-in-law, Jared Kushner, for counsel, as they had since the Mar-a-Lago summit between the two presidents a few months after Trump was inaugurated. Let's be realistic, Kushner told Chinese Ambassador Cui Tiankai, "there's no real way to come up with an accurate estimate of percentages," he said. "It's an arbitrary exercise."

More important was that the president was serious about going through with the last set of tariffs in a few weeks. Trump backed Lighthizer's hard-line stance. "Don't think in terms of tariff reduction," he advised Cui. "Think in terms of what will happen if you don't make a deal" and tariffs go into effect.

At the time, Lighthizer was offering only to reduce 15 percent tariffs on $120 billion worth of consumer goods to 10 percent. That left in place 25 percent tariffs on $250 billion of Chinese imports, about half what China sold to the United States, and far from Beijing's goal of having all tariffs eliminated.

But the prospective deal did have advantages from Beijing's perspective. It offered a much-needed pause in a trade battle that had harmed the Chinese economy and distracted the leadership from other priorities. The U.S. proposal also didn't touch issues that Beijing truly cared about. Beijing didn't have to change laws, cut subsidies—or even fully disclose them—or revamp the way its state-owned companies operated. China Inc. would remain fully functioning despite two years of pressure, tariffs, and endless threats by President Trump.

Chinese negotiators made one more request: cut the 15 percent tariffs to 7.5 percent instead of 10 percent on the $120 billion. Lighthizer agreed, and the two sides moved ahead toward a deal. (The math used by the negotiators was convoluted. For instance, Lighthizer wanted credit for reducing tariffs even when the United States merely scrapped tariff threats. By that math, the American offer amounted to the 36 percent reduction that Lighthizer talked about, or even 50 percent, depending on how one did the calculations. In reality, the United States cut tariffs by an insignificant amount.)

Before the two sides could announce an agreement, Peter Navarro, the White House's fiercest China hawk, tried one more time to scotch it.

Why cut tariffs at all? he argued. Weren't they working to hurt the Chinese economy? The American economy was still doing fine. On December 9, 2019, he sent a memo to people he assumed were his allies from his personal email address, which used his Ron Vara pseudonym. "Get uncertainty out of the market by announcing NO deal until after the election and ride the tariffs to victory," he wrote. His efforts went nowhere. One of the recipients leaked the letter to the *New York Times*.

Beijing wasted no time lashing out at Navarro, a China hater in its view. "Navarro, as a senior official of the U.S. government, has repeatedly used fictional characters to mislead . . . and to create a tough policy on China," a Foreign Ministry spokeswoman said at a daily press briefing the next day. "This behavior is very ridiculous and not responsible."

In one of the last White House meetings before the two sides announced a deal, Navarro continued to argue against settling, but he was isolated among Trump advisers. The president was looking for a pause to the trade war. Trump waved him off with a flick of the hand. Frustrated, Navarro dismissed his opponents. "Globalists!" he said.

On the morning of December 12, three days before a new round of tariffs was scheduled to hit $160 billion worth of Chinese imports, the two sides were getting ready to announce the mini-deal. Trump tweeted: "Getting VERY close to a BIG DEAL with China. They want it and so do we!" The latter was a rare admission by the U.S. leader that he was as hungry to settle as the Chinese.

During the day, White House officials quietly started to release details. In exchange for modest tariff reductions, China would aggressively buy more products and services, and nearly double spending on farm products from pre–trade war levels. Beijing would also once again agree to tighten intellectual property protection and open further its market for financial services.

When the book's two authors reported in the morning that Washington had considered reducing tariffs by half, which reflected some of the calculations the two sides were using, American negotiators were furious. The report got in the way of their claims that the Chinese had folded. A few days later, Lighthizer and Mnuchin issued a blistering statement slamming us by name and claiming our reporting was "totally false, untrue and baseless." *Wall Street Journal* editors stood by our reporting.

Around 4 p.m., the president called his outside China adviser,

Michael Pillsbury, to brief him on the details of the deal. Why lavish so much attention on him? Pillsbury was scheduled to go on Lou Dobbs that evening and Trump wanted to make sure he had a positive message for Dobbs's television audience. Pillsbury says Trump described the deal as a breakthrough, a term that Pillsbury used four times on the Dobbs show.

"I'm very astonished at the successfulness of these talks," Pillsbury gushed to Dobbs. The television host was wowed. "Fireworks are going off and there's great celebration," he said before a commercial break. Two weeks later, Dobbs was invited to a New Year's celebration at the president's Mar-a-Lago estate.

"The president wanted to head off the opposition and spin the news positively," says Pillsbury.

But from Beijing, silence. The following workday, none of China's state-owned media outlets or government agencies commented on the negotiations. Xi first had to approve the deal, which he did. Beijing then had to figure out how to present the agreement to avoid domestic criticism that China made too many compromises.

Nearing midnight on December 13 in Beijing, a half-dozen vice ministers held a rare press conference. Ninety minutes earlier, Trump had tweeted that the two sides had reached an "amazing deal." The ministers didn't go that far. They confirmed a deal but didn't provide details. Still, that was enough to assure Washington that Xi didn't have second thoughts and would stick with the agreement.

"It's good to have the phase-one agreement," Xi told visiting Japanese Prime Minister Shinzo Abe two days before Christmas. Abe encouraged the Chinese leader to use the deal to liberalize China's economy further. America's trade offensive against Japan in the 1980s and 1990s had helped make the Japanese economy more open, he said. But Xi sounded defensive. China had already liberalized significantly, he replied, trumpeting a World Bank survey showing that China had moved up fifteen notches in its rankings of global business environment, to number 31, during the twelve months ended on May 1, 2019.

Still, after two years of fighting, the United States and China had finally agreed to a truce in their trade war.

• • •

The ninety-page text of the agreement was released a month later, on January 15, after it was translated into Chinese and reviewed by lawyers on both sides. President Trump and Vice Premier Liu He signed the text in the East Room of the White House before hundreds of politicians and American business executives.

Essentially, the Chinese gave each of the U.S. major players what he wanted most. For the president that meant purchases; for Mnuchin it meant finally confirming that Beijing wouldn't use foreign exchange policy to benefit its exporters; for Lighthizer it meant enforcement measures.

Lighthizer and the administration's other China hawks started the trade battle mainly to end Chinese pressure on U.S. companies to hand over their technology and to stop outright theft of intellectual property. The phase-one deal included numerous pledges by China to bar such practices although Beijing didn't admit to coercion or theft. "China regards trade secret protection as a core element of optimizing the business environment," the document said. Violations could result in criminal penalties, as the United States had long demanded.

Beijing also promised to make sure that regulatory panels didn't leak American technology secrets to competitors. It had to ensure that members of the panels had no "financial interest in the result of the investigative or regulatory process." China also agreed not to "require or pressure technology transfer" from American companies seeking licenses or a bigger market.

These provisions were far more detailed than promises China had ever made. But the United States dropped its insistence that

Beijing enumerate the laws and regulations it was going to change and provide a schedule for making those changes. Beijing's rejection of American demands for legal revisions had led to the unraveling of a tentative agreement in May 2019. Now, those demands were off the table. China was no longer required, as part of the trade deal, to put in place the legal and regulatory infrastructure that Lighthizer had thought necessary. Beijing would make changes according to its own schedule.

For President Trump, the deal was about deals—Chinese purchases of farm goods and other products. From the start, he had pressed China to reduce its vast trade deficit with the United States. That was an impossible demand, given that trade deficits reflected macroeconomic factors like savings rates and currency fluctuations that no government fully controlled. But China could promise to ramp up imports, which it did.

In the agreement, China committed to buying around $40 billion of farm goods annually in 2020 and 2021, and perhaps as high as $50 billion. Overall, Beijing said it would increase exports by $200 billion during that time period compared to 2017, the year before the trade war began. Back then, China imported around $186 billion in goods and services from the United States.

The pledges seemed nearly impossible to fulfill. To hit the targets, U.S. exports would have to jump by an average of 33 percent annually, which is about three times as fast as they had grown annually since China joined the WTO in 2001. The agreement gave Beijing plenty of escape clauses. The purchases had to be made at market prices and be based on "commercial considerations." In other words, if U.S. farm prices were too high or Chinese consumer and industrial demand was too low, Beijing had legitimate reasons not to buy as much as it pledged. The coronavirus epidemic, especially, was bound to dent consumer demand.

Ning Jizhe, a top deputy at the National Development and Reform Commission, China's economic planning agency, insisted during negotiations that the purchases must reflect demand from Chinese customers—always difficult to forecast—and comply with World Trade Organization rules that forbid China from diverting orders from other countries to meet the U.S. demands. A Chinese diplomat spelled out what that meant in practice: "We can always stop the purchases if things get bad again."

The United States hoped to hold China to its promises through the deal's enforcement mechanism. Given Lighthizer's distrust of arbitration panels, the two sides agreed to settle problems during three rounds of negotiations. If the party that brought the complaint wasn't satisfied with the outcome, it could impose tariffs.

Lighthizer didn't quite get Beijing to give up its right to retaliate. But he did manage to insert a provision that would cause China to think twice about fighting back, a big concession by Beijing that was made during the end of negotiations. China would have to pull out of the deal before retaliating, which would surely reignite the trade war.

The new system "is a gigantic finger in the eye of the WTO," which relies on international arbitration panels, says Mary Lovely, a China trade expert at Syracuse University. "The decider will be the trade representative in consultation with the president."

Even so, it was uncertain whether American companies in China would be brave enough to use the system, knowing that Beijing has any number of ways to make life tough for them.

"There is a strong element of Yogi Berra's quip about déjà vu all over again," says James Green, a former Trump trade negotiator in Beijing. "The dispute resolution section will have the same problem we've always faced. U.S. companies are reluctant to become poster children for market access problems or discriminatory treatment."

In early 2020, it was far too soon to know how the system would work in practice as the coronavirus raced around the world, but trade experts were wary. Either the enforcement mechanisms would keep both parties on their best behavior, says Scott Kennedy, a China expert at the Center for Strategic and International Studies, "or it will be the way the deal comes apart."

In China, state media coverage of the agreement reflected the leadership's need to fend off any criticism that it made too many concessions and only got a small tariff reduction in return. That meant portraying the phase-one agreement as a mutually beneficial agreement negotiated by two equals. Taoran Notes, a social media account of the state-owned *Economic Daily*, which reports to the State Council, said: "There are people on both sides that are not too happy with the agreement, but it's still largely acceptable to both." That message was endorsed by Vice Premier Liu He. (Taoran Notes was the social media account that correctly predicted troubles in the negotiations in early May 2019, as mentioned in chapter 1.)

A January 16 article by the party's main publication, *People's Daily*, hinted that China could use the agreement to get Washington to back off from tightening restrictions on high-tech sales to China—probably wishful thinking given that Trump officials were lobbying firms to cut off Huawei.

"If China wants to buy a certain product from the United States but can't buy it . . . it can request consultations and invite the United States to the negotiating table," the article says. "For example, in the past, the United States imposed export controls on us in some high-tech fields, and there was no chance of negotiations. Now, with this consultation mechanism, we can initiate consultations on expanding our imports of U.S. high-tech products." The article circulated widely on Chinese social media.

* * *

For Beijing, the timing of the truce was fortuitous. Within two weeks of the signing ceremony in the White House, China was in a panic over the spreading coronavirus. Wuhan, an industrial city of 11 million people, was put under quarantine by President Xi along with much of the rest of the province of Hubei, in central China. Travel throughout the country was severely restricted and hundreds of millions of ordinary Chinese, who had expected to travel over the Chinese New Year holiday, hunkered down at home.

With stores, movie theaters, and restaurants shut, the Chinese economy was weakening and was bound to decline further. Chinese leaders also had to deal with growing resentment domestically and abroad that they had been too slow to act. But for now they didn't have to worry about economic pressure from the United States.

The spreading disease, however, quickly soured any good feeling Beijing might have had toward the Trump administration over the trade deal. State media called attention to remarks by top U.S. officials that seemed insensitive. Commerce Secretary Ross talked about how the epidemic "will help to accelerate the return of jobs to North America." China hawk Navarro expounded about the need to move supply lines out of China.

China's Foreign Ministry criticized Washington on a near-daily basis, saying it helped fan panic over the disease while the Chinese government was doing all it could to get the coronavirus under control. "The U.S. government hasn't provided any substantial assistance to us, but it was the first to evacuate personnel from its consulate in Wuhan, the first to suggest partial withdrawal of its embassy staff, and the first to impose a travel ban on Chinese travelers," a Foreign Ministry spokeswoman told reporters. "All it has done could only create and spread fear, which is a bad example."

The spokeswoman didn't mention a steady inflow of donations to authorities and charities in China from American companies—another sign of official anger. Those helping included Boeing (protective equipment), Honeywell International (medical masks and purification systems), Coca-Cola Co. (beverages), McDonald's (meals), and Celanese Corp. (protective suits), to name a few. In all, members of the U.S. Chamber of Commerce in China contributed more than $77 million in cash and in-kind donations by mid-February.

The anti-American propaganda reflected public anger at Washington, but also served to try to divert attention from Beijing's political problems at home. Xi Jinping came under rare public criticism on social media for centralizing power so much that underlings were afraid to act quickly to contain the virus. Looking to muffle criticism, Xi ordered the government to "strengthen the guidance of public opinions." Censorship was increased and the government targeted anyone seen as "smearing China." American news organizations became a ready target.

On February 19, Beijing expelled three *Journal* reporters over an opinion piece headline calling China as "the real sick man of Asia." The three journalists had nothing to do with the story or headline, which many Chinese viewed as deeply offensive. A tit-for-tat fight ensued. The administration capped the number of Chinese citizens who could work in America for Chinese media outlets. Beijing hit back by ordering U.S. journalists at the *New York Times*, the *Journal*, and the *Washington Post* to leave the country, including the book's coauthor, Lingling.

Washington and Beijing also traded accusations over the source of the pandemic. The president labeled the pandemic the "Chinese virus," and a U.S. senator speculated that the virus escaped from a Wuhan biochemical lab. Beijing officials claimed the virus might have been carried to Wuhan by visiting American military officials.

The bilateral relationship was edging toward a breaking point.

* * *

What explains President Trump's about-face on China and his willingness to accept and hype a limited settlement?

Some Trump officials say that the president had been posturing when he dismissed a partial deal earlier. Instead he wanted a quick agreement to relieve market pressure for some sort of a resolution, however limited. Then negotiators could discuss the rest of the issues under less fraught circumstances, though it is far from clear what might be accomplished.

"They are not going to stop subsidizing state-run banks and state-owned enterprises," says Kudlow. "But that doesn't mean we can't make deals along the way that might benefit both countries, which is what [Trump] was saying."

Lighthizer, Mnuchin, and others also were trying to learn the lessons of May, when they underestimated the political pressure Liu He faced back home. They sought to give him political cover and time to win over his bosses.

Lighthizer started using the term "workable dispute settlement mechanism"—the term favored by Liu to describe how the two sides would handle inevitable conflicts after a deal—rather than "enforcement." The latter suggested that Americans would play judge and jury and could reimpose tariffs (which is what Lighthizer actually envisioned). In the end, negotiators rebranded enforcement as "bilateral evaluation and dispute resolution."

All of that is surely part of the reason for Trump's turnaround, but it's not the entire story.

Steve Bannon, the former Trump strategist, says the answer is simple: impeachment. The president was looking for a way to show he could still score victories while Democrats were pursuing impeachment charges against him. Democrats had a veto on legislation, but he didn't need Congress to ink a deal with China, so he moved swiftly to get one. "It's almost psychological," he said. "He needed a win before the 2020 election."

Treasury Secretary Mnuchin rejected the impeachment explanation out of hand. "Impeachment is irrelevant," he says in an interview.

Perhaps, but the election was clearly an important motivator.

White House political advisers had been debating for months whether it was better to go into the election with a China deal, which opponents could pick apart, or with China as an unsettled issue. In the latter case, the president could argue that he was the only one tough enough to take on China, and if he didn't get a second term, his Democratic opponent was sure to cave to Beijing.

The beauty of a partial deal, his advisers said, was that it provided both a deal and an issue. Trump's former campaign manager, Corey Lewandowski, who continued to advise the White House, explained it this way: "Having a victory is always important going into an election. But you can also say, 'I got the beginning stage of a deal. If you give me four more years, you'll get so much more.' It's a way to split the baby." Privately, many of Trump's top trade officials agreed with Lewandowski's assessment.

After the two sides signed the pact, Treasury Secretary Mnuchin said that he could imagine more mini-deals before the election. Maybe a phase 2A, where the United States would remove more tariffs and Trump would have a new victory to brag about during the presidential campaign. The president said he didn't expect a full phase-two deal, which presumably would include fundamental reforms of China's economic system, until after the presidential election.

For his part, Xi Jinping appeared in no rush for a substantial follow-up deal. At the end of November 2019, he met with a group of foreign luminaries in Beijing at a Bloomberg conference, which included Secretary of State Henry Kissinger and former Treasury Secretary Hank Paulson. "China's achievements over the last seventy years show that China has followed the right path," he told the group. "In light of this progress, why should we change policies that are working?"

THE TOUGHER APPROACH TAKEN by Trump's national security team could also be a political plus, although Trump officials say that wasn't the motivation. Trump was demonstrating that the United States could confront China on national security and human rights at the same time as it sought an economic settlement. "The press has a very hard time seeing an American foreign policy that oscillates by design," Pottinger says. "There are simultaneous elements of confrontation and conciliation in the approach."

Before Liu arrived in Washington for talks in October 2019, for instance, the United States sanctioned Chinese technology companies that produced surveillance equipment used to keep a watch on Uighurs in western China. More than 1 million Uighurs had been rounded up in reeducation camps. Later in October, Vice President Pence made a speech extolling the democracy protestors in Hong Kong.

Any Democratic candidate for president could be expected to focus on such human rights issues. The actions would help Trump get ahead on the issue. "If you want to run for president, you can't be soft on China," says Bannon.

The agricultural portion of the phase-one deal was especially important for Trump. The purchases promised to be a boon to farmers, so they helped secure Trump's political base and bolster a sagging part of the economy. They also were easy for the public to understand, compared to the structural issues that revved up Lighthizer, but not the president. "It's a challenge communicating the existential threat to America's industrial future posed by China," says Jason Miller, Trump's former campaign spokesman. "That's not something Americans wake up and worry about."

Mnuchin tried to make things very simple when he appeared on Lou Dobbs in late September. (His appearance on Dobbs, who had attacked him mercilessly in the past, was itself notable.) He gave a nod to the importance of toughening intellectual property protection, but then said "farmers and fishermen are very important to the president." He soon added: "So I've become a soybean salesman." Vanished was the Mnuchin who had said a year earlier on CNBC that the fight with China was about structural issues, not soybeans. "The economy will have an impact on the election," the Treasury secretary says now, with great understatement.

To underscore that point, while the United States and China tussled to finish the mini-deal, the Kaiser Family Foundation and the *Cook Political Report* released a poll of voters in the battleground states of Michigan, Minnesota, Pennsylvania, and Wisconsin during the fall of 2019. By at least three-to-one margins in each of the states, those polled said tariffs were hurting their families, hardly the kind of news a tariff-happy administration welcomed.

The chance that the agricultural part of the deal yields anywhere near the sales that the president touted is close to nil. Purchases of some $40 billion annually were far beyond what China had spent in any one year. U.S. exports of soybeans, sorghum, pork, and other agricultural products to China peaked in 2013 at around $29 billion, falling to $24 billion in 2017 before the trade war started. Those exports further plunged to $9 billion in 2018, as Chinese retaliatory tariffs on U.S. goods kicked in.

Lu Ting, chief China economist at Nomura International, broke down the numbers: some 70 percent of China's agricultural imports from the United States before the trade war were soybeans, and 85 percent of China's soybean consumption went to feed pigs. But China's hog stock plunged a whopping 40 percent from July 2018 because of the rapid spread of the deadly African swine fever, so demand for soybeans was bound to drop. "We believe meeting this target will be quite challenging," Lu noted, before the coronavirus outbreak further sapped demand.

Commodities markets agreed with that assessment; prices for soybeans and hog futures declined after the agreement was signed even as the stock markets rallied. If markets had expected surging Chinese demand, prices would have soared.

For the 2020 presidential election, it doesn't matter whether China hits the $40 billion target. If sales increase from the shriveled level of 2018, that would give Trump something to tout. By the time anyone could tote up U.S. agricultural exports to China for 2020, Trump would either be ensconced again in the White House or tweeting from Trump Tower as a former president.

By early 2020, the trade battle looked a lot like it did at the start of the fight. The United States was relying on tariffs to compel China to keep negotiating a deal that would address the Chinese economic policies that drive American workers and companies crazy. China was fending off the United States as best it could, and looking to help its biggest companies, especially Huawei Technologies, become world-beaters. American national security officials were warning anyone who would listen about the dangers posed by a rising China.

In some surprising ways, though, the Trump administration began to resemble the Clinton administration on China trade. Trump officials, like Clinton officials before them, had come to believe that the only way to change China was to line up with reformers and try to help them with their internal battles. Chinese leaders had to believe that change was in their interest and wasn't being forced upon them from outside, officials in both administrations learned. "You can start the process of reform," says Lighthizer in an interview. "The things we're talking about are the things a reformer in China would agree to."

Washington needed another Zhu Rongji, the Chinese premier who used U.S. pressure during WTO talks to remake the Chinese economy. None was on the horizon.

Zhu had a rare combination of foresight, pragmatism, and political skills, which was lacking in the current Chinese leadership. Liu He also understood the importance of reform, but lacked the skills and power to get change made. Zhu's boss, Jiang Zemin, who was relatively hands-off on the economy, had provided strong support for Zhu's agenda. Liu's boss, Xi Jinping, had centralized power and wanted to expand the power of the state to control the economy.

Although Zhu's tenure is remembered harshly by many Chinese for the human costs of the changes—layoffs, uncertainty, rising inequality—there has been no one since who could convince, or bludgeon, the Chinese bureaucracy into accepting what was necessary for China's long-term success.

Steve Bannon says he understands why Lighthizer pushed for the deal he did, even though it left Chinese economic policies intact. "Lighthizer isn't an ideologue; he's a realist," he says. "His client wanted a deal, as good a deal as you could get." That said, Bannon calls Lighthizer a "tragic figure who gambled everything on a transformative deal and came up short."

Late in 2019, Liu He and Robert Lighthizer, opposing generals in the trade war, had a conversation that underscored the difficulty Americans face in changing Chinese behavior.

Lighthizer, a history buff, told Liu he had spent many hours studying Chinese history and society. "I know enough about China to realize that I don't have any idea of how you think about things," Lighthizer said.

"That's the beginning of wisdom," Liu replied.

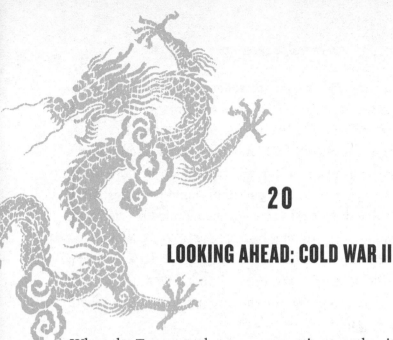

20

LOOKING AHEAD: COLD WAR II

When the Trump trade team was putting together its plans to challenge China's bid for technological dominance—and cripple it if possible—Wang Jianjun was the type of Chinese businessman Washington viewed as a threat. Wang runs a start-up called Makeblock, which makes tools for students and professionals to build robots and learn about artificial intelligence, industries that Beijing targeted in its "Made in China 2025" report, which Washington saw as China's blueprint for global expansion.

Makeblock occupies three floors of a gleaming silver high-rise owned by the Nanshan district government in the southern Chinese city of Shenzhen, which charges the company half the market rate in rent. It receives millions of dollars in government subsidies for its R&D work. A private equity fund of China International Capital Corporation, a big state-owned investment bank, is a major investor in the company.

Countless businesses like Makeblock settled in Shenzhen, China's version of Silicon Valley. Once in the shadow of neighboring Hong Kong, the former fishing village transformed into a cosmopolitan city of 13 million. In 1980, Shenzhen was designated by Deng Xiaoping as the country's first special economic zone, which gave it an enormous boost. "Time is money, efficiency is life" was the slogan that guided the city's early development.

But for all of Shenzhen's entrepreneurial spirit, the city never wandered far from the party's fold. When China's leadership was adrift following the Tiananmen Square crackdown in 1989, Deng made a trip to Shenzhen in 1992, as part of his famed southern tour, designed to energize the party to continue economic liberalization. In late 2012, days after Xi Jinping became party chief, Xi traveled to Shenzhen to show his admiration for Deng. He laid a wreath at a large bronze statue of Deng atop a hill and said: "We must stay unwavering on the road to a prosperous country and people, and there must be new pioneering."

Xi's gestures were widely interpreted in China and abroad as a signal that a new round of liberalization would follow. Instead, over time, he turned to greater state control. Today Shenzhen has a new slogan: "Follow the party, start your business."

To become a global center of innovation and manufacturing, Shenzhen offers preferential tax, funding, and other policies for entrepreneurs, along with generous grants to universities and other institutions to encourage them to team up with companies and pursue leading-edge technology.

A new university the city founded in 2012, the Southern University of Science and Technology, models its admission criteria on those of the Ivy League. It draws its faculty from the country's large pools of *hai gui*, or "sea turtles," meaning Chinese who have returned home after working overseas. They include nanotechnology scientist Limin Huang, husband of Lingling, coauthor of the book, who became an American citizen while doing research in New York.

In 2018, Shenzhen nearly doubled its funding for R&D and strategic industries, such as information technology, new energy, and materials, to 7.6 billion yuan (roughly $1.1 billion) from a year earlier. That figure doesn't count tax rebates and other forms of subsidies, so the total spending is much larger. The city government plans to further ramp up funding for years to come.

The investment has paid off. The Nanshan district, where Makeblock operates, is bustling. It is home to many big-name tech firms, like Internet giant Tencent Holdings Ltd. and commercial drone maker DJI Sciences and Technologies Ltd. The price of residential property in the area keeps heading skyward despite tightened government controls. Young programmers and software developers grab coffee at numerous Starbucks and other cafes with names like X-Life, shop at trendy boutiques for the latest gadgets, and meet up at local makerspaces to share ideas. Many of them are so absorbed in building their own businesses that they're all but oblivious to the demonstrations in Hong Kong, just a few miles away.

The impact of the American tariffs has mainly been borne by the city's traditional industrial base, which churns out low-priced products that U.S. firms can't match. Much of that production has shifted to Mexico, Vietnam, India, and elsewhere in Asia. Many vendors of selfie sticks, copycat smartphones, and other cut-rate electronics have closed in Shenzhen's huge Huaqiangbei market. In the northeastern part of the city, where migrants from the countryside toiled in sweatshop factories, a growing number of makers of low-end chemical, electronic, and machinery products have also faltered.

To make sure the trade war doesn't undermine Shenzhen's technology sector, city authorities have sought to identify what they call "choke points," or companies and industries at risk of collapse in the event they are targeted for U.S. sanctions. Those believed to be especially vulnerable could get millions of dollars in government financing to spend on R&D.

"The trade war woke us up," says Ju Xuecheng, executive chairman of the Shenzhen New Materials Association, a government-sponsored trade group, while showing off the Nanshan district to a visitor. Ju's company, which makes chemical materials for power cables, now buys components from Germany rather than America to avoid tariffs.

Wang, the studious Makeblock CEO, who is in his early thirties, benefits from government largesse, as do his Chinese competitors. American and other foreign companies usually don't get the same benefits despite complaints to the Chinese authorities.

To Wang, who has absorbed the Silicon Valley vibe of dressing in jeans, T-shirts, and sneakers, and sitting with his employees in an open-space office, government handouts are far less important than a passion for innovation. Hailing from a rural village in eastern China, Wang graduated in 2010 from the Northwestern Polytechnic University, a leading Chinese university that specializes in aeronautical and marine engineering. He rejected offers to work at state-owned firms, which promised stability but little excitement, because, as he puts it, "I don't like certainty."

Determined to start his own firm, Wang could count on an extensive network of Shenzhen manufacturers to supply the hardware he needed to build ready-to-use robotics kits. His efforts proved a hit with venture-capital investors in China and the United States. The company was valued at around $350 million in 2019. More than 50 percent of its 560 or so employees are engaged in R&D. Makeblock now generates about $30 million in annual revenue, with some 60 percent of sales from exports, mainly to Europe and Asia.

Makeblock's next big target is America. So far, the trade war hasn't hindered its U.S. expansion plans, Wang says, even though many of his products face 25 percent levies. The company is building a marketing team to promote its robotics kits to American schools. "Our biggest advantage is that we make products others can't," Wang says. Makeblock adds two lines of products a year, he adds, much faster than his American competitors. "We're not at all lagging behind in terms of innovation," Wang maintains.

• • •

If anything, the Trump trade and economic offensive reinforced Beijing's plans to make China far less dependent on American companies and their technology.

Ostensibly, Xi's government scuttled the "Made in China 2025" plan as the trade war intensified. In reality, the leadership continued to use government directives, land, tax cuts, and other forms of subsidies to get Chinese companies to shift away from foreign, especially American, technology. A new industrial policy China released in November 2019 to replace the Made in China plan still calls on the government, along with some favored companies like Huawei, to play a leading role in advancing the country's manufacturing sector by the year 2025.

Xi's self-reliance drive gained urgency in the spring of 2018, shortly after the United States banned domestic chip makers from selling to ZTE for seven years. It was a devastating blow to the Chinese telecommunications firm, which needed American semiconductors and other components to survive, and aroused much anxiety in the Zhongnanhai leadership compound. China relied too much on the United States. That had to end.

A few days after the announcement of the sanction, Xi Jinping presided over a national conference on how to increase the country's cybersecurity and information technology capabilities. He urged Chinese bureaucrats to "acutely grasp the historical opportunity" to promote breakthroughs in core technologies. It was a defiant message: rather than look at the ZTE ban as a setback, China should think of it as an opportunity. Xi reinforced that message later, even though the two nations reached a deal on ZTE that spared the company.

Shortly after the meeting, the party's Central Office, which directly reports to the top leadership, approved a major initiative, dubbed the "AnKe Project," designed to purge Chinese government agencies, telecommunications companies, and power grids of foreign hardware and software. AnKe is short for *Anquan Kekao* in Chinese, which means "secure and controllable."

Under the plan, government and infrastructure operators immediately had to allocate a certain percentage of their procurement to domestic tech providers, starting with 30 percent in 2019, an additional 50 percent in 2020, and the remaining 20 percent in 2021. It's known as the "3-5-2" rule.

Beijing had made similar efforts before, but none so sweeping. In 2013, soon after former Central Intelligence Agency employee Edward Snowden leaked classified information on the U.S. government's global surveillance programs, Beijing rolled out a campaign to encourage state companies to wean themselves off American tech providers, chiefly IBM (for its operating system), Oracle (for its database management systems), and EMC (for data storage hardware). That effort, nicknamed "De-IOE" by the U.S. tech industry for the American companies targeted, led many big Chinese banks to substitute Huawei and other domestic vendors for the American suppliers.

With the AnKe Project, Beijing plans to build a network of Chinese vendors to create and produce information technology hardware and services. By the end of 2019, more than 180 Chinese producers of computer chips, electronics, software, and other IT products and services had joined the buy-China project and were helping the government draft policy directives and carry out the plan.

Complaints by the U.S. government and trade associations went nowhere. Rather, Xi and his leadership team became more convinced to reduce Chinese dependence on American technology after the United States targeted Huawei by asking Canada to arrest its CFO and extradite her to the United States, and then sanctioning the company.

In the early summer of 2019, the leadership set up a task force to figure out how to carry out technology decoupling. Members of the group include representatives of China's economic planning agency, the ministry in charge of information technology, and the regulator overseeing big state-owned firms. The domestic semi-conductor industry, where China remains significantly behind the United States despite years of heavy spending, was set to receive additional government money, cheap bank loans, tax benefits, and other forms of support.

Even before the decoupling project, China's technology subsidies were substantial. The Information Technology and Innovation Foundation, a Washington think tank, estimates that nearly 25 percent of all R&D expenditures in China come from government subsidies to companies. To match that percentage, the United States would need to spend $86 billion more than it already does annually, ITIF says.

"Chinese authorities have been collecting data for years on the dependence of Chinese companies on American technology," says Paul Triolo, a former CIA analyst in Beijing and now an analyst specializing in global technology policy at Eurasia Group. "Now they are really pushing forward action under increased pressure from the top in the wake of U.S. policies."

• • •

Despite the January truce, two years of trade war are driving the two nations apart.

Chinese investment in the United States fell nearly 90 percent in the first half of 2019 from the comparable period in 2017 before tariffs were imposed, according to Rhodium Group, as U.S. scrutiny of Chinese investments sharpened and Beijing cracked down on lending for overseas purchases. Congress was even considering barring transit systems from buying Chinese buses and subway cars because the manufacturers received subsidies and, lawmakers feared, cameras mounted in the vehicles would transmit information to Beijing.

While U.S. investment in China held steady overall during that time, investment in China's information technology industry tailed off. American executives worried about getting snagged in national security reviews, hit with higher tariffs on imported components, and blocked from entering fast-growing Chinese industries like cloud computing.

Trade also declined, though not as precipitously. Two-way trade between the United States and China fell about 8 percent between September 2017 and September 2019, compared to 3 percent growth in the prior two years. In products targeted for tariffs, the declines were much starker. U.S. imports of those goods fell by 25 percent through the second quarter of 2019 from the year earlier, while other Chinese imports increased somewhat as buyers stockpiled items that might face levies later. Chinese imports of U.S. products hit by tariffs fell more than 60 percent. Those declines understate the impact of the trade war because the statistics generally covered periods when tariffs remained at 10 percent levels, not 25 percent.

Perhaps even more telling, attitudes of ordinary Americans toward China grew increasingly antagonistic. The percentage of Americans holding an unfavorable view of China jumped to 60 percent, according to a spring 2019 survey by the Pew Research Center. This was the highest level since Pew started asking the question in 2005. Around a quarter of Americans also named China as the country that poses the gravest threat to the United States in the future—tied with Russia as villain number one. That was twice as many who picked China as the top threat in 2007, Pew reported.

That is matched by souring attitudes in China toward America. Chinese scientists and scholars who used to admire the U.S. way of life now complain about a nation becoming increasingly inward. Wang Hongmei, a biotech scientist at the Chinese Academy of Sciences, says 40 percent of her colleagues couldn't get visas to attend events as innocuous as academic forums these days. "We're thinking about doing more conferences in Europe now," she says.

Anti-U.S. postings in China's social media also have risen, including calls to force Americans to pay more in restaurants or shops.

Many Chinese have swapped out their iPhones with Huawei smart-phones. But China's censors have sought to limit the negative comments in the media, and the United States hasn't replaced Japan as the country that truly stirs nationalist passions. When the U.S. wholesale chain Costco opened a store in Shanghai in August 2019, the store had to close early because it was inundated with Chinese shoppers.

Many in the Trump administration welcome signs that the two nations are disengaging. An America First strategy toward China means Americans need to be more wary of Beijing. If American executives better understood the threat Beijing posed, they would be less willing to invest there and less likely to have their companies' technology stolen. If U.S. pressure prompted American firms to pack up and leave China, that would weaken Beijing and slow its military and economic ascent.

The president expressed this view clearly, though with his typical hyperbole. If he hadn't become president and ramped up pressure on Beijing, he claimed repeatedly, China would already have eclipsed the United States as the world's number one economy. (Given that America's economy, measured in dollars, was about 40 percent larger than China's when Trump was inaugurated, there was no chance of that happening.)

Still, the president deserves credit for challenging the easy assumptions about China that had guided American policy since at least the Clinton administration. Economic engagement hadn't led to political liberalization, and didn't look like it would anytime soon. Xi Jinping's persecution of the Uighurs in Xinjiang was evidence of that, as was his crackdown on any independent political organization, including lawyers who argued, simply, that no one should be above the law, including the party. When China's leaders talk of rule of law, they essentially mean, "Our law, we rule."

The administration also took seriously the threats to U.S. companies in China—ranging from competition from state-owned firms to the loss of technology through outright theft or more subtle intimidation—and acted sharply to get Beijing to back down.

No less than the Western economic and political model is at stake in the competition with China. Americans and Europeans have long assumed that private enterprise coupled with democracy is the most efficient and productive form of development and would inevitably outperform any challenger. China's technological rise was doomed to peter out, the thinking went, because a lack of freedom would make it impossible for China's smart and capable scientists and engineers to innovate and take the lead in advanced technology.

Beijing now is challenging that easy assumption, with a state-led model that features bureaucratic direction, heavy censorship, and a flood of cash, combined with competition at the local level. Chinese companies compete with one another for sales, as they do in the West, though state-owned firms get a lot of help in the sectors where they compete. Local governments compete by offering incentives to lure the hottest technologies and companies. Local party leaders advance when the areas they administer adopt the central government's priorities and also grow more rapidly. It's not obvious whether America or China will prevail.

The administration has focused attention on what appears to be the inevitable moment when China's economy tops that of the United States. Economists usually point to a crossover point sometime in the 2030s, assuming China doesn't tumble into a Japan-like funk before that. With four times the population of the United States, China needs to be just slightly more than one-fourth as productive per person to become number one.

In some ways, it's remarkable that the United States has remained number one for so long, despite the population gap. China was the world's largest economy until roughly the U.S. Civil War, according to calculations by the late British economist Angus Maddison. By that time, the industrial revolution had remade the world, so technology trumped population in determining economic primacy. Now that technology has spread globally, China is determined to regain its leading position in the world.

Who's number one isn't simply bragging rights. The more powerful China's economy becomes, the more money it can pour into its military, overseas investments, and technology that can be used for repression. Other countries inevitably look to the number one economy for direction and investment. Props again to the Trump administration for alerting the West to this challenge. That lies behind the Trump team's campaign, so far unsuccessful, to halt Huawei's ability to dominate 5G telecommunications technology, which will undergird much of the global information network over the coming decade or two.

Even if Trump loses his reelection bid, his China battle has changed the relationship between the two nations for years to come, maybe even permanently, argues National Economic Council Director Larry Kudlow. "President Trump has unmasked and brought to the forefront how much China represents an economic, trade, human rights, and national security threat," Kudlow says in an interview. "That narrative is unlikely to change."

Niall Ferguson, who coined the term "Chimerica" in 2007 along with a colleague, and publicized the notion that the two nations' futures are intertwined, now thinks the coupling is dead, another casualty of the trade war. The battle "has gone from trade war to tech war to Cold War," says the Stanford University historian, and both sides benefit politically from the rift.

Having an American enemy helps Xi Jinping consolidate power and "justify his Mao-like tendencies," Ferguson says. Having a Chinese enemy gives Trump political traction, too. For Ferguson, the emergence of a new Cold War is a positive development. An external enemy will help unify fractious Americans, as the Cold War against the Soviet Union did, and it will rally Congress to spend what's needed to contain China and ultimately prevail.

"Cold War II is a good idea," he says. "The alternative is to acquiesce to Chinese superiority."

Ferguson is a favorite among conservatives, but his views may be too expansive even for the Trump administration's China hawks. U.S. Trade Representative Robert Lighthizer, the top American general in the trade war, says, "Regime change isn't in my scope. My goal is to make the economy work so we're treated fairly and we get the trade deficit down."

To try to achieve even Lighthizer's more modest goals, the United States has fired economic weapons largely left untouched since the 1930s, including the biggest tariff barrage since the Smoot-Hawley tariffs. By the end of 2019, the average U.S. tariff on Chinese goods was 21 percent, up from just 3.1 percent in 2017, calculates Chad Bown of the Peterson Institute for International Economics, a Washington, D.C., think tank. That fell slightly to 19.3 percent after the two sides reached their phase-one deal in January. The Smoot-Hawley Tariff Act in 1930 raised tariffs to 41 percent from 36 percent during an era of ultra-high duties.

Many economists argue that the Smoot-Hawley increase helped deepen the Great Depression because it led to rounds of retaliatory tariffs and the disintegration of the global trading system. Since then, the United States has led the world in reducing tariffs and liberalizing trade. Even Ronald Reagan, who used tariffs as a tool to try to pry open the Japanese market in the 1980s, paired protectionism with a big push for a new global trade deal. Trump's tactics stand alone.

While the Trump administration has been effective at recognizing the Chinese challenge, it's been woeful at conceiving, planning, and executing a strategy to deal with Beijing's further rise.

The administration could start first with a realistic appraisal of the costs of the trade war. Then it could marshal arguments to try to convince Americans that the costs are worth the fight, as president after president did when it came to the U.S. struggle with the

Soviet Union. The administration could also look for tools in addition to tariffs. Trump has replaced public persuasion with rancor and tweets.

The massive tariff hikes gave economists a fresh way to study the costs and benefits of protectionism. Academics, international institutions, and Wall Street researchers have examined the evidence and found that the costs of American tariffs are borne by Americans, as economic theory predicted, though the magnitude of the pocketbook hit varies according to the study.

A March 2019 paper by economists from the University of California, Los Angeles, UC Berkeley, Yale, and Columbia was one of the earliest reviews. The researchers studied changes in tariff levels and overall trade flows, not just with China. They concluded that the costs of U.S. tariffs to consumers outweighed the gains to companies protected from overseas competition and tariff income collected by the government, although by a fairly small margin. Their estimates of harm were on the low side because they examined a time period when the increase in tariff on Chinese imports hadn't yet reached 25 percent, and they didn't take into account the impact of tariffs on business investment.

Other studies looked at different aspects of tariffs and found bigger results. A study by economists at the Federal Reserve, Princeton, and Columbia concluded that increased tariffs in 2018 raised the wholesale price of U.S. manufactured goods by one percentage point, which was about half the annual average price increase since 1990. Broadening the perspective, researchers at the International Monetary Fund studied data from 151 countries between 1963 and 2014 where tariffs increased by at least 3.6 percentage points and reported that the duties led to reduced economic growth, more unemployment, and greater inequality.

Trying to put a specific number on the economic loss, J.P. Morgan estimated in June 2019 that China tariffs alone cost average U.S. households about $1,550 a year, which topped the $1,300 they gained from the Trump administration's tax cuts. Cummins Inc., an Indiana manufacturer of engines and power systems, reported a similar outcome, even though large manufacturers were a major beneficiary of the tax cuts. "The tax from tariffs on China has now outgrown the benefits from the tax reform act," Cummins CEO Tom Linebarger said in June 2019. After he spoke, the bulk of China tariffs jumped to 25 percent from 10 percent, adding to his company's tariff bill.

Shortly before Christmas 2019, two Fed economists surveyed the impact of all of President Trump's tariff battles on U.S. manufacturing, a sector the president had sought to nurture. The verdict: U.S. tariffs hurt far more than they helped and reduced manufacturing employment. That's because the protection afforded some industries by tariffs—steel and aluminum producers, for instance—was greatly outweighed by the many other companies hurt by the increased costs of imports and retaliatory tariffs.

From March 2018, when President Trump first threatened China with tariffs, through the end of 2019, manufacturing employment was flat while overall employment rose 4 percent.

The president's tariff strategy also did nothing to reduce the U.S. trade deficit, a major Trump goal. Through September 2019, the merchandise trade deficit with China declined by 4 percent from 2017 before the trade war began. But the overall merchandise trade deficit increased by 11 percent during the same time period.

When U.S. buyers found Chinese imports too expensive, they bought from factories in other nations, which were sometimes Chinese owned. The United Nations Conference on Trade and Development studied trade flows of more than 10,000 products shipped to the United States from China and elsewhere. In the first half of 2019, imports of tariffed goods from China fell by $35 billion from a year earlier. Of that, UNCTAD found, 63 percent were replaced by imports from elsewhere, with Taiwan as the biggest beneficiary, followed by Mexico, the European Union, and Vietnam.

• • •

For all the costs of the trade battle, little had been accomplished by early 2020, measured by the complaints in the Section 301 report and the demands the United States made of China. The $30 billion or so in tariffs collected on Chinese goods since January 2018 went to compensate farmers who lost sales in China—sales that wouldn't have been lost if there had been no trade war. The trade deficit was growing. Chinese subsidies were expanding. Chinese state-owned companies received more financing from state-owned banks even though they are less profitable than private firms. They continued to expand globally through Beijing's Belt and Road Initiative to build infrastructure across Asia, Europe, and Africa.

American companies also reported no reduction in intellectual property theft or Chinese pressure to hand over technology—the raison d'être for the trade war. President Trump reserved part of his speech to the United Nations General Assembly in September 2019 to remind Beijing that "we are seeking justice" for Micron Technology. The U.S. computer chip maker has tussled with China for years over intellectual property theft and faced threats from Chinese officials of more than $1 billion in fines, as reported in earlier chapters. Repeated lobbying from top American officials didn't spook Beijing to back off on Micron or other U.S. technology companies.

China did make some changes. Xi's government reduced tariffs for some foreign goods, although not for American merchandise hit by retaliatory duties. Beijing also promised to treat foreign businesses more fairly with a new law, and lowered the obstacles for foreigners to invest in finance, autos, and pharmaceuticals. Some of the measures, including the new foreign investment law, were in response to U.S. pressure. But in meetings with U.S. business executives, senior Chinese leaders often cast those steps as ones they would have taken anyway. They would contrast China's halting liberalization with Washington's turn to America First, to try to pry away the European Union, Japan, and other U.S. allies.

China's policy moves didn't lead to fundamental change in an economic system ruled by the ever-more-muscular hand of the Communist Party. The new investment law, for instance, still contained provisions that could lead to rules restricting foreign companies operating in China. The government was also putting in place and refining a new system of tracking company behavior, called the corporate social credit system, which deepened state control. Under the program, Chinese government agencies rate companies on about three hundred different requirements, including tax compliance, environmental protection, product quality, data transfers, prices, and licenses. Foreign firms fear that the system will be another way Beijing can discriminate against them, while claiming that it is simply administering objective criteria.

"Higher scores can mean lower tax rates, better credit conditions, easier market access, and more public procurement opportunities," the European Union Chamber of Commerce in China reported. "Lower scores lead to the opposite, and can even result in blacklisting." The corporate system is similar to the one authorities use to monitor and rate Chinese individuals, which can blacklist citizens for loans, jobs, or even air travel.

In late October 2019, Xi opened a four-day closed-door meeting of the party's 370 or so top officials, known as a plenum, by stressing the need to "modernize the state governance." But the grand-sounding slogan was just another way to emphasize the Communist party's leadership in every aspect of the Chinese society. China's state media coined a phrase, "China style of governance," to describe Xi's approach.

Xi's Beijing sometimes outmaneuvered Trump's Washington tactically during the negotiations and avoided making the hard choices the United States has demanded. But China's delay-and-parry tactics haven't made it the winner. Many of the American demands, such as eliminating subsidies and making Chinese markets substantially more open, would benefit the Chinese economy in the long run.

Partly leaders double down on central control because they believe that makes it easier to rule. But that approach will make it harder for China to rise into the ranks of wealthy countries—Xi's stated goal—and advance economically over the next quarter century as vibrantly as it did in the last. The drawbacks of the centralized approach are becoming increasingly apparent. Productivity growth has stalled as more credit flows into state companies that are far less efficient than private firms. Big investments in government-favored sectors such as electric vehicles, semiconductors, and commercial aircraft have frequently resulted in overproduction and waste, rather than meaningful breakthroughs, and bankrupted competitors in the West. That has confirmed suspicions that China is conducting economic warfare, rather than clumsily carrying out economic development.

According to a study by two veteran China experts, Scott Kennedy at the Center for Strategic and International Studies and Daniel Rosen of the Rhodium Group, China now has more than 450 electric car producers for a market of, at most, 1.8 million passenger vehicles. That translates into 4,000 vehicles per firm. That's not nearly enough sales to provide economies of scale for any producer, but the subsidies are sufficient to make it next to impossible for foreigners to compete. The report also notes that the state-owned Commercial Aircraft Corporation of China, which Beijing has hoped would become China's Boeing or Airbus, has poured close to $10 billion into developing its own C919 commercial plane. Yet the made-in-China aircraft remains years away from entering commercial service. "The C919 is the quintessential white elephant and emblematic of the reality that state preferences trump market logic in today's China," the experts noted.

The same dynamic is playing out in the semiconductor sector.

A December 2019 report by the Organisation for Economic Co-operation and Development shows that Chinese chip makers receive far more government support than international competitors. The report analyzed twenty-one of the world's largest semiconductor companies. The six American companies included Intel and Qualcomm. The four Chinese firms are Tsinghua Unigroup, Semiconductor Manufacturing International Corporation (SMIC), Hua Hong Semiconductor Ltd., and JCET Group Company.

The twenty-one companies received government support of $50 billion between 2014 and 2018, in the form of grants and government purchases of stakes in the firms. China's Tsinghua Unigroup ranked number one in the world, with government backing of more than $10 billion. Measuring government help as a percentage of company revenue, the four Chinese semiconductor companies also came out on top. That support exceeded 30 percent of the revenue of Tsinghua Unigroup and SMIC, the report said. For Intel and Qualcomm, the figure was less than 5 percent.

Despite the heavy outlays, China continues to be a big importer of computer chips, and Chinese producers haven't closed the gap with their American competitors. As Wang Zhijun, vice minister of industry and information technology, said in May 2019: "Compared with advanced international standards, China still has a considerable gap to fill in terms of the overall design, manufacturing, testing and related equipment, and raw material production of integrated circuits." The ministry pledged to increase government support to the semiconductor industry's R&D with greater tax incentives as well as more bank loans and other types of funding.

There was no mention of getting the government to back off and encourage entrepreneurs, like those in Shenzhen, to take the lead. Chinese officials don't dare to bring up the possibility of combining economic liberalization with political freedom to truly unleash the potential of the Chinese people.

With the government crackdown on dissent and public debate,

fewer Chinese are speaking up. "The theory of the 'China model' sets China as a frightening anomaly from the Western perspective, and inevitably leads to confrontation between China and the West," said Zhang Weiying, a prominent Chinese economist and a long-time advocate of free markets, in an October 2018 speech at Peking University. China's Internet censors swiftly blocked a transcript of the speech from appearing on the country's social media.

* * *

Where did the administration go wrong in the execution of its China policy? Look first at Trump's unwillingness to work with allies.

As we detail in earlier chapters, Trump used his first working day in the White House to pull out of the Trans-Pacific Partnership, a trade deal among a dozen Asia-Pacific nations. He then brawled with allies over steel and aluminum tariffs, and threatened them with car tariffs, rather than try to work together on China. As his onetime strategist Steve Bannon put it, the Trump team wanted to "flood the zone." Two years later, the colorful metaphor describes the Trump team's failure to come up with priorities and strategy.

Lighthizer rejects the criticism. He says the administration hasn't ignored allies and points to trilateral talks with Japan and Europe to devise common policies for taking on China.

Those talks have been important symbolically in showing Beijing that America's allies weren't defecting. By early 2020, after two years of meetings, the discussions were just starting to produce results. In January, the three parties agreed on the kinds of subsidies they wanted barred. Among them were industrial subsidies that kept companies afloat indefinitely even though the firms had no "credible plan" to become profitable, and subsidies to firms that couldn't get commercial loans and were deepening global over-capacity. That would apply to Chinese steel, aluminum, and glass makers, who lose money year after year, but get state loans that keep them in business and allow them to flood the global market.

The talks took so long because European nations were wary that any agreement on subsidies would be used to attack Airbus and other European government-owned companies.

A Japanese senior official described the dynamics this way: Japan and the EU are trying to convince the United States to address problems multilaterally. The United States is trying to convince Japan and the EU to tackle the tough issues they all have with China. Neither side has succeeded fully.

Next, the three partners must lobby other WTO members in Geneva to back their proposed rules. If other powerful countries join, they will turn to China and press it to accept what would then be a global standard. "The question is if we can get a critical mass of countries to go along," says EU Trade Minister Phil Hogan in an interview.

To Lighthizer, stalemate is a regular feature of multilateral approaches. "The EU has a hard time deciding, with its twenty-eight members, and Japan won't act alone," he says in an interview. "We work with allies, but we don't let them veto doing things" the United States thinks are appropriate.

Undoubtedly, recruiting allies is a tedious and tough slog. But its importance is hard to overstate. International pressure forced China to make substantial changes to join the WTO. Only after country after country—and most importantly, the United States—demanded reform as the cost of entry to the multilateral organization, did China agree. That should be a model to guide the United States now.

Trying to figure out how better to handle a trade confrontation with China, Matthew Goodman, a CSIS Asia expert who served in the Obama White House, assembled twenty-two Asia experts, including many with senior government experience, to do a war-game analysis of the conflict. They split into two groups, one playing the role of China, the other the United States.

The exercises, conducted in the spring of 2019, had limitations. The players didn't include Chinese experts; only Americans playing the role of Chinese. The scenarios they considered didn't have Trump as president, probably because the participants were so turned off by his approach. "We were trying to assume an administration that was tough on China, but one that wouldn't use the same tactics or would reconsider existing tactics," says Goodman.

The strategy sessions produced some important insights, especially the importance of gathering allies. The web of alliances created after World War II is a strength China can't match. Beijing fears being encircled by hostile nations, a weakness the United States could better exploit. "China displayed an impulse to reach out and seek partners by positioning itself as the defender of globalization and the status quo," the participants concluded. "Beijing's outreach to third countries was less about gaining allies—at which it was rarely successful—than preventing them from choosing a side in the trade war and maintaining a status quo beneficial to China."

• • •

How could the United States proceed, whether in a second Trump term or with a Democrat in the White House?

Several studies by Asia policy experts have suggested bringing what's known as a "nullification and impairment case" at the WTO. The United States and other nations it could convince to go along would sue China for behavior that is so egregious that it nullifies or impairs the benefits that they reasonably expected to receive from China joining the WTO, regardless of whether Beijing violated specific WTO rules. In layman's terms, the nations would be suing China for being a bad trade actor; the potential penalty would be massive tariffs imposed by all the nations. Plaintiffs could point to heavy subsidies, out-of-control state-owned firms, forced technology transfer, and the host of other complaints the Trump administration has named.

In 2010, Lighthizer, then a trade lawyer spurned as a protectionist, recommended bringing a case, among other actions, in congressional testimony. Attitudes toward China have hardened so much since then that an Asia Society panel in 2019 recommended the same course of action if negotiations failed, a remarkably tough stance for a pillar of the foreign policy establishment.

The upside: the case could unite U.S. allies and bring enormous pressure against China. But there is a huge downside: the United States could also lose the case or the WTO could bottle it up for years, fearful of deciding a case that could blow apart the organization. Then what?

One of the lessons of the Trump years is that unilateral action and remarkably high tariffs may hurt the global economy, but they don't derail it. The Trump team is surely right that tariffs command attention from foreign nations and are a powerful tool that the United States has long ignored. If a Democrat wins the White House, expect him or her to use tariffs for additional goals, including pressuring China and other nations over human rights, worker rights, and climate change. An early example is the law to review Beijing's handling of Hong Kong, backed by the threat of withdrawing the city's special trade status, which passed nearly unanimously. Trump endorsed it reluctantly; Democrats (and congressional Republicans) embraced it.

Multinational corporations and free traders demonize tariffs, but they have been used to enforce treaties that are symbols of multilateral harmony. The Montreal Protocol, in which nearly two hundred nations pledged to phase out production of the chemicals that were destroying the earth's protective ozone layer, was enforced by trade sanctions—tariffs—if signatories didn't comply with its provisions. The sanctions never had to be applied.

A proposal by the globalist wing of the Trump White House gives an idea of how tariff threats could be used when trying to recruit allies. Call it coercive multilateralism. When the administration was debating whether to impose tariffs across the board on steel imports, some of the Trump team's free traders pitched an alternative they called "Save Our Steel," as discussed in earlier chapters. Allies would have been warned that the United States was planning to hit them with tariffs if they didn't block imports of steel from China, which was the source of the global oversupply, or halt the transshipment of steel products into the United States.

The goal was to create a united front against China by signing up allies, but not letting endless talks fritter away the urgency to act. Trump rejected the plan because he was wary of alliance building and wanted to use tariffs immediately. But a combination of alliance building, backed by the threat of unilateral action, could be a way for a second term Trump presidency or a Democratic alternative to proceed.

A simple first step would be to rejoin the TPP, now renamed the even less felicitous Comprehensive and Progressive Agreement for Trans-Pacific Partnership, or CPTPP. The members would be sure to welcome American participation in the trade pact and would realize they needed to reconsider terms. The threat that the United States was prepared to act alone—and perhaps against some of the CPTPP members—if they didn't reach an accommodation would be a cudgel American negotiators could use. The Trump legacy should convince the parties that the Americans are serious, though the main impetus for a deal would be relief that the world's largest economy was once again reaching out for allies.

But more pressure on China isn't all that's necessary.

At the heart of the U.S.-China trade war is the fear that China will eclipse the United States technologically on its way to economic and military superiority. The United States leads in nearly every technology named in China's "Made in China 2025" report. The Trump administration hasn't coupled its trade war with a domestic program to keep the United States ahead.

China views the trade battle as its version of America's Sputnik moment—a foreign threat that requires the country to redouble its technological efforts. When the Soviet Union launched the world's first satellite in 1957, Washington panicked and then rallied. Government R&D budgets more than tripled, as a percentage of the GDP between 1957 and 1964, and remained at around that peak through 1968, as the United States mounted a manned moon mission. The United States far surpassed the Soviet Union economically and militarily.

There is no similar sense of urgency in the White House. Faced with a China challenge, the Trump administration has proposed cutting government R&D budgets year after year, even for basic science, the feedstock of technological advance. It would also eliminate programs designed to improve manufacturing technology. Congress restored many of the cuts, but government R&D still has fallen to pre-Sputnik levels, as a percentage of the economy. When asked why, Trump officials point to a big jump in corporate R&D spending as an American advantage. They also repeat the conservative mantra that pushing government R&D grants would mean picking corporate winners and losers, a Republican no-no—as if assessing tariffs on some companies but not others isn't doing precisely that.

Many studies have urged ramped-up U.S. technology spending. Several use the same terminology, calling for the government to propose "moonshots." These are Apollo-like projects so advanced that they would require inventing new technology. A White House semiconductor study finished as Barack Obama was about to leave office suggested some examples: commercial computers based on quantum physics; implantable medical devices to restore sight or hearing; a network of monitoring units to detect biological and chemical threats; or a super-detailed global weather forecasting system. More recently, a report by the Council on Foreign Relations and a Trump favorite, the hard-line National Bureau of Asian Research, picked up the call.

The Reagan administration did something similar during its tariff assault on Japan. In 1987, it put together a $500 million govern-

ment project, called Sematech, to advance the U.S. ability to manufacture semiconductors, a field that was threatened by Japanese
competitors and is now an American strength. Sematech was a joint
effort by the government and a consortium of fourteen U.S.-based
semiconductor companies. Later, foreign companies were permitted to join. The U.S. effort not only benefited American companies,
which now lead in the technology, but also ultimately helped the
global economy.

* * *

In Pella, Iowa, Vermeer Corporation had hoped for a different outcome from the trade battle. The construction equipment maker is
the kind of firm the Trump administration hoped to help when it
launched its trade offensive. Vermeer makes machinery that carves
narrow tunnels under rivers and roads and implants plastic pipes
there, which can be used to thread optical fiber cables, electricity
lines, and other wiring. Vermeer is an infrastructure company that
has long sought to expand in China, the biggest and fastest-growing
infrastructure market in the world.

It's been a struggle. In the early 1990s, Vermeer started exporting its motorized drilling machines, which generally cost about
$400,000 a piece, and initially dominated the Chinese market. But
Chinese competitors quickly adapted by copying Vermeer products
and selling simplified versions at half Vermeer's price. Vermeer's
market share tumbled. When Vermeer execs showed up at a Chinese firm that wanted Vermeer to acquire it, they saw a replica of a
Vermeer drill in the showroom.

"It was like shock and awe," says Doug Hundt, president of
Vermeer's industrial solutions unit. Patenting innovations doesn't
make sense in China because features are so quickly ripped off, he
says. To get ahead, the company must regularly innovate.

Vermeer turned down that acquisition, but started a joint venture in China in 2005 to produce and sell its machines, with some

imported items from the United States. With the slow liberalization of ownership rules, Vermeer bought out its partner in 2017 and now is the sole owner. But it faced another difficult challenge. A big state-owned firm, Xuzhou Construction Machinery Group Co. (XCMG), entered the market with subsidized prices and financing Vermeer couldn't match, and took half the market. It also dominated sales of drilling machines to China's trillion-dollar Belt and Road Initiative, making it tough for Vermeer to crack that market. After more than twenty years in the Chinese market, China accounts for just 2 percent of Vermeer's more than $1 billion in revenue.

XCMG is notorious among American companies. In 2005, Carlyle Group tried to buy 85 percent of the firm, which was then owned by a local government. It would have been the largest acquisition by a foreign investor of a controlling stake in a big Chinese state-owned company. But after another Chinese construction company publicly lobbied against the deal, warning that foreigners would monopolize the industry, Beijing intervened and found a Chinese buyer for XCMG. The company is now owned by the central government, giving it even more political clout.

Vermeer's CEO, Jason Andringa, says he had hoped the Trump offensive would curb the power of Chinese state-owned firms. "If we could make some progress with SOEs and have them compete on a level playing field, that would be great," he says.

Vermeer is as Middle America as a big corporation can be. The company was founded in 1948 by Andringa's grandfather, a farmer who liked to tinker with machinery. Paintings of the founder and his wife—Gary and Matilda Vermeer—look as if they could have been done by Norman Rockwell.

Gary Vermeer started by figuring out how to outfit his wagon with a mechanical hoist to make it easier to unload corn. His neighbors wanted one of the hoists, too, which he made in a small machine shop in his cornfields. That led to machines that cut tree stumps to ones that dug trenches and then tunnels. The company now has 3,500 employees, including 125 in China. It's still located on Gary's farmland.

The company maintains the couple's modest ranch house as a kind of tribute to midwestern values and employs four ministers as counselors. When Vermeer executives were told that the Chinese companies that copied their machinery were paying them compliments, they believed it.

So they are tempered in expressing their disappointment with how the Trump offensive has panned out. Andringa, a political conservative who voted for Trump, is a relentlessly positive person. After a tornado destroyed two Vermeer factories in July 2018, he told employees that night that the company would rebuild and "come back stronger than ever." It did.

On the trade front, he says he is pleased the United States and China eventually arranged a truce, but he says there has been no progress on the SOE front. Tariffs cost the company about $5 million in 2019, about one-quarter of what Vermeer spent on buildings and equipment, and will cost it another $5 million in 2020, he figures. The company's sourcing team spends most of its time trying to convince Chinese suppliers to share the costs of the tariff increase, rather than working on new products.

While the company thinks it won't face fresh tariffs, it is exploring ways to get around current levies. Vermeer buys steel wheels in China. If it had those wheels shipped to, say, Mexico to be manufactured into subassemblies there—the kind of work Vermeer now does in Iowa—it could avoid the China tariffs. The company doesn't want to move work out of America, but that's what the trade war is making it consider.

Andringa says the phase-one deal in January 2020 gave him confidence that he wouldn't have to pull out of China, but he isn't planning fresh investments there. "We're keeping the light on in China and maintaining our brand," he says, but that's about it.

The White House might consider that a victory—yet another

American company pulling back in China. But Andringa sees it as a loss. Despite the rough reception Vermeer has had in China, he says, the company has learned how to compete there and in other low-wage nations. Those markets don't need Vermeer's most advanced machinery, because labor is cheap and plentiful. Simplified, lower-cost products are necessary to succeed in China, the company believes, as are changes in design to keep ahead of the copycats.

Besides, China is still the largest market for the types of products Vermeer sells. Success there would strengthen the company back home and lead to more export jobs. No other country is attempting to modernize as quickly as China and has such a need for tunneling equipment.

The unwillingness of the administration to work with allies on China especially annoys Andringa, who brings up the issue repeatedly. Coordinated pressure would have been more effective in getting the changes Vermeer and other American companies sought, he says. That could have been worth the cost of the tariffs.

"Why not band with Japan, Europe, and South Korea in this fight?" Andringa asks. "I'd tell Trump, 'Why did you pick fights with our friends? Why go it alone?'"

In the first Cold War, America relied heavily on allies to share the military, political, and psychic burden of the confrontation. The winner of a new Cold War will also need allies to lead the world in the twenty-first century.

EPILOGUE

On January 15, 2020, a spring-like day in Washington D.C., President Trump and Chinese Vice Premier Liu He met at the White House to sign the phase-one deal that signaled a halt to economic hostilities between the world's two superpowers. Twenty-one years earlier, President Clinton and Chinese Premier Zhu Rongji met close by, in the rococo Old Executive Office Building, for a very different purpose. There the U.S. leader announced that trade talks had failed; a humiliated yet defiant Zhu was leaving Washington empty-handed.

The Clinton-Zhu encounter turned out to be a temporary setback. By the end of 1999, the two sides signed a deal to ease the way for China to join the World Trade Organization. That agreement transformed the Chinese economy and helped turn China into an economic juggernaut. It also cemented relations between the two nations, though cracks quickly developed and would deepen and fracture during the trade war under President Trump.

Now Trump was trying to pour fresh cement into the fissures to repair the damage. While the trade deal he was signing promised big purchases of U.S. goods and some reforms of the Chinese economy, the results were probably too little and too late to prevent the two nations from splitting further apart. The United States and China weren't quite enemies yet, but they were moving steadily in that direction. Although the trade battle was easing, the Trump administration—and Congress—were looking for ways to block China's technological and military advances. Chinese students and researchers, once welcomed in the United States, which saw immigration as a source of strength, now were treated with suspicion.

From the Chinese perspective, the United States had turned from a model to emulate, at least economically, into an adversary. The nearly two-year battle had revealed to many Chinese Washington's desire to thwart their country's ascent.

Early in the Trump administration, some among Beijing's political and business elites hoped they could use the American trade offensive to prod China to make market reforms they supported. "We talked about two old men helping push forward China's reforms. One was Deng Xiaoping," says a prominent Chinese economist who consults with the leadership. "The other was Donald Trump."

By the time both sides inked the January 15 deal, that hope had vanished. Trump was seen as just another American politician who wanted to contain China. His bullying tactics became an excuse for the Chinese leadership to double down on its state-led economic model.

The powerful forces ripping apart the relationship were palpable in the White House's ornate East Room, where hundreds of guests and press crowded to witness the signing, including the book's co-author Lingling. The president had repeatedly announced that Xi Jinping would come for the signing, which would have given the event more pizzazz. But Beijing dispatched Xi's self-effacing chief negotiator, Liu, instead. The Communist leadership wanted to shield its top man from criticism that he was giving in to U.S. pressure.

The lower-level Chinese representation didn't seem to faze Trump, who was in full P. T. Barnum mode. Instead of parading Hottentots and Zulus, as Barnum would have, the president used his Chinese guests as props. They stood behind him on a stage for nearly an hour and a half as he mugged for the cameras.

The president said he would be "going over to China in the not-too-distant future." Then he thanked more than eighty people, celebrating some, tweaking others, and making inside jokes. He called out nearly a dozen members of his administration. They were "fantastic," "incredible," "a legend," "the best guy." "Our brilliant Jared," he said of his son-in-law and adviser, Jared Kushner, who helped bridge the gap between the two sides in the final rounds of negotiations.

His shout-outs revealed much about the status of his guests. The first nonpolitician he recognized was casino magnate Sheldon Adelson, the $20 million Trump contributor, and his wife. "Tremendous supporters" and "great people," he said.

Next was his trade guru Lou Dobbs—"The great Lou Dobbs," the president said. What made him so great? Dobbs's assessment that Trump was "the greatest" of all presidents.

"I said [to Dobbs], 'Does that include Washington and Lincoln?'" Trump said, to laughter. "And he said yes. Now, I don't know if he was for real, but that's OK."

Those two came ahead of Henry Kissinger, who along with President Nixon opened China to the West. "He knows more than probably everybody in this room put together," Trump said of Kissinger. Then came Michael Pillsbury, his favorite China expert, followed by Blackstone CEO Stephen Schwarzman, another big contributor. The president teased Schwarzman for wanting a settlement so badly. "I'm surprised you're not actually sitting on the edge of the stage," Trump said.

On it went while the Chinese delegation, who all speak English, watched silently and occasionally clapped and nodded to guests. "This is a bit too much," a Chinese journalist standing in the back of the packed East Room murmured to Lingling, referring to Trump's prolonged introduction. "Show some respect."

When Liu finally got a chance to talk, almost fifty minutes into the performance, he spoke in Mandarin. Liu had spoken in English when he met Trump earlier during his negotiating trips but that had been frowned upon at home. Some in China thought he appeared humbled by the American president.

Similar criticism had been leveled against Premier Zhu two decades earlier when he met with President Clinton, though Zhu managed to save face at home by traveling across America immediately afterward and meeting with business groups. He won support for China's WTO bid with his blunt and unscripted speeches, laced with humor.

Liu first read a letter from Xi Jinping to the American president. "I will stay in close touch with you personally," the Chinese leader wrote. The letter was as significant for what it didn't say—he hadn't yet agreed to a Trump visit to China.

Then, reading from prepared remarks, Liu said he hoped the deal would improve relations, despite the big differences between the two nations.

"China has developed a political system and a model of economic development that suits its national reality," a Chinese aide translated. "This doesn't mean China and the United States cannot work together. On the contrary, our two countries share enormous common commercial interests, and we are faced with multiple challenges like terrorism, counter-narcotics, widening income gap," and other global problems. At one point during Liu's speech, the Chinese delegation in the audience showered him with applause as if to show the Chinese side was not resigned to playing second fiddle.

The president responded with Trumpian bluster. "It just doesn't get any bigger than this—not only in terms of a deal, but really in terms of what it represents," he said. "Keeping these two giant and powerful nations together in harmony is so important for the world."

Then the two men signed the ninety-page accord.

For Lingling, the event was perhaps the richest episode in her family's transformation. Just two generations earlier, her grandfather, Zhong Guang, a Communist revolutionary, had looked after Mao's health during the Long March and lived in cavelike dugouts along with the Chairman.

Zhong's sole interaction with an American was in 1936 when he met journalist Edgar Snow, who had traveled to the Communist base in Yan'an, a remote and mountainous area in northern China, to interview Mao and other party leaders. Snow's book, *Red Star Over China*, based on that experience, contrasted the spartan, disciplined lives of the Communist guerrillas with the gloom and corruption of the Nationalist government, an account that made Snow's reputation but was later seen as propaganda by a sympathetic journalist.

Years later, during the Korean War, Zhong would tell his four children, including Lingling's mother, how friendly Snow seemed to be. That's how he believed most Americans were. "The War to Resist America and Aid Korea," he said to his children, using the Chinese name for the conflict, was meant for the "American hegemony, not the American people." His only other tie to America was a Parker fountain pen given to him by Mao. After Mao's death, it was retrieved from him by party officials who wanted control of any Mao artifacts.

Zhong had a chance to see the outside world in 1946, soon after the allied victory over Japan during World War II, when the party decided to send him to the Soviet Union to study medicine. In a rare show of independence to party elders, Zhong intentionally missed his flight to Moscow. He wanted to build a New China, not study in a foreign culture.

Zhong, who died in 1973, six years after his release from the Red Guards during the Cultural Revolution, never got to see China open up to the rest of the world. He would have been astonished that his granddaughter would have benefited so greatly that she would wind up covering a momentous event from what he would have viewed as the epicenter of U.S. hegemony, the White House.

"Your grandfather would be very proud of you," Lina, Lingling's mother, told her as she returned from the signing ceremony in Washington. "You're there for history."

Two months later, Lingling found herself in a very different situation. She had to hand in her press credentials and leave the country within weeks. This is the country generations of her family helped build and which she considers her homeland.

With the coronavirus pandemic, her six-year-old son had been trapped at home with her for two months along with her mother who was recovering from pneumonia. Her father and husband were locked down elsewhere. She felt helpless and frightened about the future, but her family rallied. They collectively decided that she should return to New York and continue to write about China for the *Journal*.

Bob's experience during the signing was different. He was at the *Wall Street Journal*'s Washington office, scrambling to put together a story for the *Journal*'s website. Back in 1999, covering the Clinton-Zhu press conference was simpler. Dow Jones, the *Journal*'s parent company, had reporters whose sole responsibility was feeding the Dow Jones Newswires, which competed with Reuters and produced stories minute-by-minute. *Wall Street Journal* reporters, like Bob, had to worry only about the next day's story and filed by around 6 p.m. From the vantage point of 2020, it was a leisurely pace, though it didn't seem so at the time.

At 10:32 a.m., a colleague obtained a copy of the agreement, which was embargoed until the president signed it. That was scheduled for about 11:30 a.m., but as Trump turned the event into a spectacle, the signing slipped to 1 p.m. During this time, Bob was furiously combing through the document, scanning feeds from other reporters, and fielding phone calls from editors to try to produce a coherent and accurate story to run when the president finally stopped talking and signed the text. At one point, 160 unread emails piled up.

This was the part of journalism that most resembled manufacturing. Take a memo from one reporter, merge it with another, add some paragraphs from your own reporting, work in suggestions from editors, and produce a finished story. Not all that different in structure from how his father, Mad Mike Davis, the factory man bankrupted by Asian competition, made luggage. Only his father assembled final goods from fabric, wood, and metal, not from words.

Mike Davis would have looked at the deal skeptically, Bob was certain. He was a Democrat to his bones and would have criticized Trump politically. When he moved to Republican western Pennsylvania in the 1970s, he loved tweaking the conservatives who ran the company where he wound up working. Over drinks—there were always too many drinks—he would bait and tease them about politics.

In many ways, though, he was like the president. He was thoroughly a New Yorker. If Donald Trump was the last of the Mad Men generation, always looking for an angle or a big score, as Trump adviser Steve Bannon said, Mike Davis was close behind. He surely would have used the deal to try to nab a consulting gig to design some luggage or reconfigure a factory floor. But he would have been disappointed. Luggage production had fled to Asia. There was nothing in this partial deal that would reverse that. U.S. tariffs on components imported from China remained in place, as did Chinese tariffs on U.S. exports. The wage gap between the United States and China remained as steep as it was before the trade war began. Animosity between the two nations was steeper.

But Mike Davis would have loved the idea that his son was recording the event for the *Wall Street Journal*—writing the first draft of a powerful moment in history. He would have loved the action. He even probably would have thanked Trump, privately at least, for giving his son the opportunity to be a witness.

The trade war between the United States and China will deeply affect the lives of people in both nations. It will be studied by generations of historians. Whatever current and future readers may decide about this battle, we hope this book provides the material to understand what happened and why, and to make better, wiser judgments.

ACKNOWLEDGMENTS

This is a book by two *Wall Street Journal* reporters, whose reporting was aided enormously by the newspaper's editors and reporters. We want to thank them. They include editor in chief Matt Murray, who recognized the importance of U.S.-China relations, backed our reporting, and gave us time off to write and research the book.

In the *Journal*'s Beijing bureau, we owe special gratitude to former bureau chief Charles Hutzler, who always showed tremendous faith in our coverage and masterfully edited many of our stories for the *Journal*. Our Chinese colleagues in the bureau, notably Liyan Qi and Grace Zhu, worked round the clock chasing news even though Chinese regulations forbid them from having bylines in an American newspaper. Kersten Zhang, our long-time researcher who's the bedrock of the bureau, painstakingly helped us get the right data on the Chinese economy, spanning decades.

In the Washington, D.C., bureau, thanks to the always supportive bureau chief Paul Beckett and news editors Jathon Sapsford and John Corrigan. We particularly want to thank Jake Schlesinger, who generously shared with us his research on President Trump's trade history, and Jon Hilsenrath, who edited parts of the book and helped us with analysis. Washington, D.C., columnist Jerry Seib and

Bob's former *Wall Street Journal* coauthor David Wessel, now at the Brookings Institution, also gave us valuable advice.

We relied also on the work of other tireless *Wall Street Journal* reporters, including Kate O'Keeffe, Will Mauldin, Josh Zumbrun, Dustin Volz, Alex Leary, Chao Deng, and Yoko Kubota, among many others. Our former colleagues Peter Nicholas, now at the *Atlantic*, and Vivian Salama, now at CNN, also provided great help.

In addition, our editors in New York and Hong Kong, including Gordon Fairclough and Andrew Dowell, offered unwavering support throughout the process.

The Woodrow Wilson Center and its Kissinger Institute on China and the United States were also instrumental. Wilson provided Bob with a fellowship, a space to work, and a terrific research assistant, Amanda Oh. Amanda was dogged in ferreting out information and a pleasure to work with.

We relied on numerous officials, former officials, and China experts from both countries. The political atmosphere in both capitals is so charged these days that we decided not to list individuals who were especially helpful. Many prefer anonymity. You know who you are. We thank you.

Our reporting also relied on the work of reporters at other publications, particularly *Bloomberg News,* the *New York Times,* the *Washington Post,* the *Atlantic, Axios,* and the *Financial Times.* All of them are tough competitors.

The book also benefited greatly from a close edit by Bob's former partner at the *Susquehanna Sentinel* newspaper, Michael Millner.

This book never could have come together without the help of our agent, Rafe Sagalyn, who saw the project's potential and gave us great advice on business and writing. We are also in debt to our excellent editor, Hollis Heimbouch, and her talented crew at HarperCollins. She believed in the project, had great suggestions, and couldn't have been more encouraging.

A special thank-you to Debra Bruno, Bob's wife, who edited every word of the manuscript before we sent it to Hollis, swatted away clichés as if they were mosquitoes, and offered great insights. She also put up with two years of shop talk and grouchiness, on top of many years before that.

Finally, thank you to Gengfu, Lingling's father, who drove her around Zhejiang as part of her research for the book and was always forthcoming with critical comments about his daughter's reporting; and to Siwei, Lingling's six-year-old son, who took part in three camps in the summer of 2019 just so his mother could focus on the "big project with Bob *shushu*"—Chinese for "Uncle Bob."

Any mistakes are ours alone. Thanks to everyone.

NOTES

Introduction: Threat of War, December 2018

2 "I wouldn't say that": John Bolton interview by Gerard Baker, *Wall Street Journal* CEO Conference, Dec. 4, 2018.

Chapter I: Miscalculations, April–May 2019

17 That would only be necessary: Lingling Wei and Bob Davis, "China Hardens Trade Stance as Talks Enter New Phase," *Wall Street Journal*, May 9, 2019, https://www.wsj.com/articles/why-china-decided-to-play-hardball-in-trade-talks-11557358715.

20 $1.2 trillion in "additional purchases": Steven Mnuchin interview by Maria Bartiromo, *Mornings with Maria*, Fox Business Network, Dec. 4, 2018.

21 "read them the riot act": Larry Kudlow interview, *Squawk on the Street*, CNBC, Feb. 28, 2019.

23 stay put until further notice: Lingling Wei, Vivian Salama, Michael C. Bender, and Bob Davis, "Frustration, Miscalculation: Inside the U.S.-China Trade Impasse," *Wall Street Journal*, May 13, 2019, https://www.wsj.com/articles/frustration-miscalculation-inside-the-u-s-china-trade-impasse-11557692301.

25 "We are very clear": Wendy Wu, "China's Vice-Premier Liu He Says 'Small Setbacks' Will Not Derail Trade War Talks," *South China Morning Post*, May 11, 2019, https://www.scmp.com/news/china/diplomacy/article/3009824/chinas-vice-premier-liu-he-says-small-setbacks-will-not-derail.

27 State media labeled: "Let 'Surrender Theory' Become a Street Mouse," *Xinhua*, Jun. 8, 2019.

31 "This picture of": Nicholas R. Lardy, *The State Strikes Back* (Washington, DC: Peterson Institute for International Economics, January 2019), 2.

Chapter 2: China's Rise, 1980s and 1990s

40 Xi urged Zhejiang: *Guangming Daily*, http://cpc.people.com.cn/GB/64093
/64099/14474959.html.

41 Henry Kissinger: Andy Serwer, "Henry Kissinger: China Then and Now,"
Fortune, Sept. 8, 2011, http://fortune.com/2011/09/08/henry-kissinger
-china-then-and-now.

42 China increased per capita: "World Bank Group President Jim Yong
Kim's Remarks at the Opening Ceremony of the First China International
Import Expo," World Bank, Nov. 5, 2018, https://www.worldbank.org/en
/news/speech/2018/11/05/world-bank-group-president-jim-yong-kims
-remarks-at-the-opening-ceremony-of-the-first-china-international
-import-expo.

44 Deng signed off: *News of the Communist Party of China*, http://cpc
.people.com.cn/GB/85037/85038/7759329.html.

44 Those de facto private firms: Hong-Yi Chen, *Township and Village Enterprises* (Oxford Bibliography in Chinese Studies, 2016), https://www
.oxfordbibliographies.com/view/document/obo-9780199920082/obo
-9780199920082-0128.xml.

45 Chinese economist: Chong-en Bai, Chang-Tai Hsieh, and Zheng Song,
"Special Deals with Chinese Characteristics," National Bureau of Economic Research (May 29, 2019), https://www.nber.org/chapters/c14233.pdf.

51 "'We need to foster'": Henry M. Paulson Jr., *Dealing with China* (New
York: Twelve, 2015), 179.

Chapter 3: Taking on China, 1993

55 "forfeited moral reproof": Winston Lord, "Misguided Mission," *Washington Post*, Dec. 19, 1989, https://www.washingtonpost.com/archive/opinions
/1989/12/19/misguided-mission/961859a4-7ad0-41fa-94aa-cff3eb14
625e/.

55 "sort of the last straw": Winston Lord interview by Charles Stuart Kennedy and Nancy Bernkopf Tucker, *Association for Diplomatic Studies and
Training Foreign Affairs Oral History Project*, Initial Interview, April 28,
1998, 564.

58 stayed afterward to complain: Robert S. Greenberger, "Restraint of Trade:
Cacophony of Voices Drowns Out Message from U.S. to China," *Wall Street
Journal*, March 22, 1994.

59 went there to lose his: Greenberger, "Restraint of Trade."

59 "the Clinton coup": Michael Pillsbury, *The Hundred-Year Marathon* (New
York: St. Martin's Griffin, 2015), 91.

59 "why should China make concessions?": Lord oral history, 574.

59 "proper balance should be struck": Interview with Mack McLarty, April
2019.

60 "a 45-minute monologue": Lord oral history, 576.

60 hardly signs that China was taking seriously: Robert L. Suettinger, *Beyond Tiananmen: The Politics of U.S.-China Relations, 1989–2000* (Washington, DC: Brookings Institution, 2003). Suettinger's book is excellent in recounting Clinton's efforts to pressure China to ease up on dissidents.

61 General Electric, AT&T, and "Gold Sacks": Greenberger, "Restraint of Trade."

61 "'who they say lost China'": Warren Christopher and Strobe Talbott Oral History, UVA/Miller Center Presidential Oral Histories, April 15–16, 2002, https://millercenter.org/the-presidency/presidential-oral-histories/warren-christopher-and-strobe-talbott-oral-history.

61 "compared to publicly": Lord oral history; McLarty interview.

62 ran computer simulations: Lord oral history, 583.

62 open their meeting: Greenberger, "Restraint of Trade."

64 "door to China is open wider": Joseph Kahn, "Decision to Delink Trade, Human Rights Relieves U.S. Firms, Chinese Officials," *Wall Street Journal,* May 31, 1994.

Chapter 4: Boss Zhu Arrives, April 1999

66 "it would be an inexplicable mistake": Bill Clinton at the Mayflower Hotel, addressing the U.S. Institute for Peace, April 7, 1999, https://1997-2001.state.gov/regions/eap/990407_clinton_china.html.

68 "China can't do": Joint press conference of President Clinton and Premier Zhu Rongji, April 8, 1999, https://clintonwhitehouse4.archives.gov/WH/New/html/19990408-1109.html.

69 "Opposition within China": David Zweig, *Internationalizing China* (Ithaca, NY: Cornell University Press, 2002).

70 "Good evening": Interview with former Chinese diplomat Wang Wenyong.

70 "funny and fiercely proud": Bill Clinton, *My Life* (New York: Knopf, 2004), 793–94.

70 A series of letters: Joseph Fewsmith, "China and the WTO: The Politics Behind the Agreement," National Bureau of Asian Research, November 1999, https://www.iatp.org/sites/default/files/China_and_the_WTO_The_Politics_Behind_the_Agre.htm.

71 "President Jiang Zemin": Joint press conference of President Clinton and Premier Zhu Rongji, April 8, 1999, https://clintonwhitehouse4.archives.gov/WH/New/html/19990408-1109.html.

71 Charlene Barshefsky, now promoted: Clinton administration debates over Zhu's visit reflect the recollections of participants and their outside advisers. Coauthor Bob Davis and Helene Cooper, now at the *New York Times,* closely reported on the U.S.-China WTO negotiations at the time.

72 "The chance to get it done": Interview with Robert Rubin, February 2019.

73 " None of the groundwork": Interview with John Podesta, February 2019.

73 "I'm having trouble": Interview with Robert Cassidy, April 2019.

74 "bullet proof": Interviews with a former Chinese trade negotiator and U.S. officials.

75 "I can't imagine those words": Interview with Charlene Barshefsky, March 2019, and follow-up discussions.

76 "absolutely furious": Cassidy interview, April 2019.

76 Clinton had never intended: Helene Cooper and Bob Davis, "No Deal: Overruling Some Staff, Clinton Denies Zhu What He Came For," *Wall Street Journal,* April 9, 1999, https://www.wsj.com/articles/SB92360778 9295191805.

77 Zhu made his anger clear: Bob Drogin, "Zhu Criticizes Clinton Over Failed Trade Bid," *Los Angeles Times*, April 10, 1999, https://www.latimes .com/archives/la-xpm-1999-apr-10-mn-25940-story.html.

77 "No we're not": David E. Sanger, "How Push by China and U.S. Business Won Over Clinton," *New York Times,* April 15, 1999, https://www.nytimes .com/1999/04/15/world/how-push-by-china-and-us-business-won -over-clinton.html.

77 "I was beside myself": Interview with Robert Kapp, January 2019.

78 Clinton "didn't have enough courage": Drogin, "Zhu Criticizes Clinton."

78 "more like 99 percent": Helene Cooper and Bob Davis, "U.S., China Agree to Resume WTO Talks," *Wall Street Journal,* April 14, 1999.

79 "hard time believing it": Clinton, *My Life.*

79 "This incident": Pillsbury, *The Hundred-Year Marathon*, 95.

80 "rigged the maps": Clinton, *My Life,* 855.

80 threatened to resign: Hui Feng, *The Politics of China's Accession to the World Trade Organization* (New York: Routledge, 2012).

81 "nuclear option": Paul Blustein, *Schism* (Waterloo, Ontario: Centre for International Governance Innovation, 2019), 53.

81 Only Li Peng dissented: David Zweig, "China's Stalled 'Fifth Wave': Zhu Rongji's Reform Package of 1998–2000," *Asian Survey,* March/April 2001.

82 "Mr. Sperling said, 'no,' six times": *Speech Record of Zhu Rongji* (Beijing: People's Publishing House, 2011).

83 "we'd look weak": Barshefsky interview, March 2019.

83 "they want to sign": "Long Yongtu Recounts Details of WTO Negotiations," *21st Century Business Herald*, Nov. 22, 2011, https://news.qq.com /a/20111122/000860.htm.

84 "He wasn't acting like the negotiator": Interview with Gene Sperling, March 2019.

Chapter 5: Nailing Jell-O to the Wall, March 2000

88 "nail Jell-O to the wall": Bill Clinton speech at Paul H. Nitze School of Advanced International Studies, March 8, 2000, http://movies2.nytimes .com/library/world/asia/030900clinton-china-text.html.

88 "well along the road to democracy": Henry Rowen, "Why China Will Become a Democracy," *Hoover Digest,* Jan. 30, 1999, https://www.hoover .org/research/why-china-will-become-democracy.

89 "responsible stakeholder": Robert Zoellick keynote address to the National Committee on U.S.-China Relations, Sept. 21, 2005, https://2001 -2009.state.gov/s/d/former/zoellick/rem/53682.htm.

91 "Hey Ron, Be Kind": Helene Cooper, "Eclectic Grass-Roots Campaigns Emerge on China Trade," *Wall Street Journal,* March 13, 2000.

92 Motorola copied: Peter H. Stone, "K Street Musters for the Middle Kingdom," *National Journal,* March 25, 2000.

93 promised funding for a pipeline: Public Citizen's Global Trade Watch, "Purchasing Power," October 2000, https://www.citizen.org/wp-content /uploads/purchasingpower.pdf.

95 virtually no manufacturing job: Robert E. Lighthizer, "What Did Asian Donors Want?," *New York Times,* Feb. 25, 1997, https://www.nytimes.com /1997/02/25/opinion/what-did-asian-donors-want.html.

95 "Uncertainty would have kept": Interview with Robert Lighthizer, July 2018.

96 "sacrifice for my country": Elizabeth C. Economy, *The Third Revolution* (New York: Oxford University Press, 2018), 88.

96 "You can't coerce": Rubin interview, February 2019.

97 "The beneficiaries of the agreement": Robert Cassidy, "The Failed Expectations of U.S. Trade Policy," Institute for Policy Studies, June 4, 2008, https://ips-dc.org/the_failed_expectations_of_us_trade_policy/.

Chapter 6: China to the Rescue, 2008

102 "Let us tide over": Hu Jintao, "Tide Over Difficulties Through Concerted Efforts," Ministry of Foreign Affairs, Nov. 15, 2008, https://www.fmprc .gov.cn/mfa_eng/wjdt_665385/zyjh_665391/t524323.shtml.

102 she stressed the need to work with China: "Clinton: Chinese Human Rights Can't Interfere with Other Crises," CNN, Feb. 21, 2009, http://www .cnn.com/2009/POLITICS/02/21/clinton.china.asia/.

104 "the consequences would be catastrophic": Justin R. Pierce and Peter K. Schott," Online Appendix for the Surprisingly Swift Decline of U.S. Manufacturing Employment," *American Economic Review* 106, no. 7 (July 2016): 5, https://www.aeaweb.org/content/file?id=1634.

108 depressing prices globally: Lingling Wei, Bob Davis, and Jon Hilsenrath, "Glut of Chinese Goods Pinches Global Economy," *Wall Street Journal,* June 1, 2015, https://www.wsj.com/articles/glut-of-chinese-goods-pinches -global-economy-1433212681.

110 "He should have done more": Lingling Wei and Bob Davis, "For a Top Chinese Banker, Profits Hinder Political Rise," *Wall Street Journal,* Feb. 18, 2013, https://www.wsj.com/articles/SB10001424127887324196204578297961462046562.

111 an event called "Operation Sunday": Lingling Wei and Bob Davis, "In China, Beijing Fights Losing Battle to Rein In Factory Production," *Wall Street Journal*, July 16, 2014, https://www.wsj.com/articles/in-china-bei jing-fights-losing-battle-to-rein-in-factory-production-1405477804.

111 "a major growth slowdown or a financial crisis": Sally Chen and Joong Shik Kang, "Credit Booms—Is China Different?" IMF Working Papers, WP/18/2 (Jan. 5, 2018): 8, https://www.imf.org/en/Publications/WP /Issues/2018/01/05/Credit-Booms-Is-China-Different-45537.

112 "There are a few foreigners": Malcolm Moore, "China's 'Next Leader' in Hardline Rant," *Telegraph*, Feb. 16, 2009, https://www.telegraph.co.uk /news/worldnews/asia/china/4637039/Chinas-next-leader-in-hardline -rant.html.

Chapter 7: American Backlash, 2009

122 bullet-train makers transferred know-how: Norihiko Shirouzu, "Train Makers Rail Against China's High-Speed Designs," *Wall Street Journal*, Nov. 18, 2010, https://www.wsj.com/articles/SB10001424052748704814204575507353221141616.

122 "I am not sure": Guy Dinmore and Geoff Dyer, "Immelt Hits Out at China and Obama," *Financial Times*, July 1, 2010, https://www.ft.com/content /ed654fac-8518-11df-adfa-00144feabdc0.

124 "determined to maintain a prominent role": *China Manufacturing 2025* (Beijing: European Union Chamber of Commerce in China, 2017), 1, https:// www.europeanchamber.com.cn/en/china-manufacturing-2025.

124 one-two punch: *Made in China 2025: Global Ambitions Built on Local Protections* (Washington, DC: U.S. Chamber of Commerce, 2017), https://www .uschamber.com/report/made-china-2025-global-ambitions-built-local -protections-0.

125 demonstrated that the impact: David H. Autor, David Dorn, and Gordon H. Hanson, "The China Syndrome: Local Labor Market Effects of Import Competition in the United States," National Bureau of Economic Research (May 2012), https://www.nber.org/papers/w18054.pdf.

128 United States imposed tariffs: Chad Bown, "The 2018 U.S.-China Trade Conflict After 40 Years of Special Protection," Peterson Institute for International Economics, April 2019, 9, https://www.piie.com/publications /working-papers/2018-us-china-trade-conflict-after-40-years-special -protection.

129 "can't pussyfoot around": Barshefsky interview, March 2019.

129 "protect our financial interests": Paulson, *Dealing with China*, 248.

130 "We aren't sure": Paulson, *Dealing with China*, 240.

130 "The Chinese refused": Interview with Henry Paulson, May 2019.

132 "sets the gold standard": "Clinton Says U.S. Backs China Ties," *Gold Coast Bulletin*, Nov. 16, 2012.

133 "rape our country": Donald Trump rally, YouTube, May 2, 2016, https://www.youtube.com/watch?v=Cy9iY6CvAHU.

134 would have been enough: David Autor, David Dorn, Gordon Hanson, and Kaveh Majlesi, *The China Trade Shock, A Note on the Effect of Rising Trade Exposure on the 2016 Presidential Election*, Jan. 6, 2017, http://chinashock .info/wp-content/uploads/2016/06/2016_election_appendix.pdf.

Chapter 8: The Leaders: Trump's China; Xi's America

135 "'Listen you motherfuckers'": Trump speech, YouTube, April 29, 2011, https://www.youtube.com/watch?v=wN7KHWdyrbl.

136 "interest rates": Interview with Donald Trump, Nov. 26, 2018, https://www.wsj.com/articles/transcript-of-president-trumps-interview-with -the-wall-street-journal-1543272091.

137 "enormous amount of coverage": Jacob M. Schlesinger, "Trump Forged His Ideas on Trade in the 1980s—and Never Deviated," *Wall Street Journal,* Nov. 15, 2018, https://www.wsj.com/articles/trump-forged-his-ideas -on-trade-in-the-1980sand-never-deviated-1542304508. Schlesinger was kind enough to share his files and interviews with us for this book.

138 "the Japanese are on the move": Theodore H. White, "The Danger from Japan," *New York Times,* July 28, 1985, https://www.nytimes.com/1985/07 /28/magazine/the-danger-from-japan.html.

139 "spent a lot of time indoctrinating": Interview with Robert Lutz in Schlesinger, "Trump Forged His Ideas."

140 "threat after threat": Donald J. Trump with Dave Shiflett, *The America We Deserve* (Los Angeles: Renaissance Books, 2000), 146–49.

141 "one of the few people": Schlesinger, "Trump Forged His Ideas."

141 "It's all the same thing": Schlesinger, "Trump Forged His Ideas."

143 "planet's most efficient assassin": Peter Navarro and Greg Autry, *Death by China* (Upper Saddle River, NJ: Prentice Hall, 2011).

143 probably phony: Loren Collins, "Debunking Donald Trump's '20 Favorite Books on China,'" *Medium,* May 9, 2017, https://medium.com/@loren collins/debunking-donald-trumps-20-favorite-books-on-china-372e9 b1d4b4c.

143 "You don't need to go to China": Peter Navarro, emailed responses to questions, Dec. 5, 2019.

144 "one of the best performances of a president": Navarro emailed responses.

146 "a tough place": Interview with Wilbur Ross in Schlesinger, "Trump Forged His Ideas."

147 "The greatest dream": "Great Rejuvenation of the Chinese Nation," Xinhua, Nov. 29, 2012, http://www.chinanews.com/gn/2012/11-29/4370441.shtml.

149 Xi Jinping was dispatched: Jeremy Page, "Early Hardship Shaped Xi's Views," *Wall Street Journal,* Feb. 13, 2012, https://www.wsj.com/articles /SB10001424052970204062704577218530280697276.

155 the market had failed: Lingling Wei, "China's Xi Approaches a New Term with a Souring Taste for Markets," *Wall Street Journal,* Oct. 16, 2017, https://www.wsj.com/articles/chinas-xi-approaches-a-new-term-with-a-souring-taste-for-markets-1508173889.

156 "The Party's power": Richard McGregor, *Xi Jinping: The Backlash* (Penguin eBooks, 2019).

157 "I have the impression": Charles Hutzler, "Interview with Chinese President Xi Jinping," *Wall Street Journal,* Sept. 22, 2015, https://www.wsj.com/articles/full-transcript-interview-with-chinese-president-xi-jinping-1442894700.

157 His goal: Jeremy Page and Lingling Wei, "Xi's Power Play Foreshadows Historic Transformation of How China Is Ruled," *Wall Street Journal,* Dec. 26, 2016, https://www.wsj.com/articles/xis-power-play-foreshadows-radical-transformation-of-how-china-is-ruled-1482778917.

157 "The not-so-subtle message": Robert Zoellick, "Can America and China Be Stakeholders?" Remarks at the U.S.-China Business Council's Gala, Dec. 4, 2019.

158 "No matter how": "Several Issues on Socialism with Chinese Characteristics," *Seeking Truth,* March 31, 2019, http://www.xinhuanet.com/politics/2019-03/31/c_1124307481.htm.

Chapter 9: Flood the Zone, December 2016

161 "had some influence": Damian Paletta, Carol E. Lee, and Jeremy Page, "Donald Trump's Message Sparks Anger in China," *Wall Street Journal,* Dec. 5, 2016, https://www.wsj.com/articles/donald-trumps-message-sparks-anger-in-china-1480989202.

161 "fully explain": Interview with Stephen K. Bannon, June 2019. (We cite Bannon in the endnotes here because the quote pertained to a White House controversy in which he was a participant. We don't cite him elsewhere in the notes when he acts as an observer.)

162 "Trump is an irrational type": Bob Davis and Lingling Wei, "Chinese Finance Minister Lou Jiwei Takes Aim at Donald Trump's Trade Policies," *Wall Street Journal,* April 18, 2016, https://www.wsj.com/articles/chinese-finance-ministerlou-jiwei-takes-aim-at-donald-trumps-trade-policies-1460892988?mod=article_inline.

164 "That's how mad": Bannon interview, June 2019.

164 "They wanted to learn more": Interview with Ambassador Cui Tiankai, October 2018.

166 "very hostile": Interview with Hank Greenberg, June 2019.

168 "punched in the face": Matt Pottinger, "Mightier Than the Pen," *Wall Street Journal,* Dec. 15, 2005, https://www.wsj.com/articles/SB113461636659623128.

171 "He strongly dislikes": Koya Jibiki and Ken Moriyasu, "Abe Scores Big in 'Fairway Diplomacy' with Trump," *Nikkei Asian Review,* Feb. 16, 2017, https://asia.nikkei.com/Politics/Abe-scores-big-in-fairway-diplomacy-with-Trump.

171 With the Abe: Mark Landler, "China Learns How to Get Trump's Ear: Through Jared Kushner," *New York Times,* April 2, 2017, https://www.nytimes.com/2017/04/02/us/politics/trump-china-jared-kushner.html.

173 "not so easy": Gerard Baker, Carol E. Lee, and Michael C. Bender, "Trump Says He Offered China Better Trade Terms in Exchange for Help on North Korea," *Wall Street Journal,* April 12, 2017, https://www.wsj.com/articles/trump-says-he-offered-china-better-trade-terms-in-exchange-for-help-on-north-korea-1492027556.

174 "testified quite a bit": Interview with Wilbur Ross, October 2019.

Chapter 10: Things Fall Apart, Summer–Fall 2017

177 didn't forward the memo: Bob Woodward, *Fear: Trump in the White House* (New York: Simon & Schuster, 2018), Kindle, 142.

178 "urged their CEOs": Peter Nicholas, Paul Vieira, and Jose de Cordoba, "Why Donald Trump Decided to Back Off NAFTA Threat," *Wall Street Journal,* April 17, 2017, https://www.wsj.com/articles/trump-says-nafta-partners-persuaded-him-to-keep-u-s-in-trade-pact-1493320127.

178 "It's your base": Woodward, *Fear,* loc. 156.

181 "For the first year": Trump interview, November 26, 2018.

183 "Wilbur was delighted": Stephen A. Schwarzman, *What It Takes: Lessons in the Pursuit of Excellence* (New York: Simon & Schuster, 2019), Kindle.

184 China Investment Corporation: Lingling Wei, "Trump Trade Reboot Spurs U.S. Push by China's Sovereign-Wealth Fund," *Wall Street Journal,* May 17, 2017, https://www.wsj.com/articles/trump-trade-reboot-spurs-u-s-push-by-chinas-sovereign-wealth-fund-1495022339.

185 "The president changed his mind": Ross interview, October 2019.

187 "stop being so passive": Robert E. Lighthizer testimony before the U.S.-China Economic and Security Review Commission, June 9, 2010, 28, https://www.uscc.gov/sites/default/files/6.9.10Lighthizer.pdf.

188 "painting of me": Bob Davis, "Campaign '96: Lighthizer, Dole's Idea Man, Attempts to Derail Buchanan with Trade Issue," *Wall Street Journal,* Feb. 28, 1996.

189 "a powerful tool": Lighthizer testimony, 23.

191 "take the word 'China' out": We have independent reporting on this incident, thanks to the *Atlantic*'s Peter Nicholas, who was then with the *Wall Street Journal.* Bob Woodward in *Fear* also has an account.

192 "No, we're not going to": Lingling Wei, Jacob M. Schlesinger, Jeremy Page, and Michael C. Bender, "U.S. Rebuffs China's Charm Offensive,

Edging Closer to Trade War," *Wall Street Journal*, Nov. 19, 2017, https://www.wsj.com/articles/beyond-trump-xi-bond-white-house-looks-to-toughen-china-policy-1511124832.

193 "The deal is politically": Eva Dou, Yoko Kubota, and Trefor Moss, "Something Old, Something New: $250 Billion in U.S.-China Deals Don't Add Up," *Wall Street Journal*, Nov. 9, 2017, https://www.wsj.com/articles/trumped-up-the-250-billion-in-u-s-china-trade-deals-may-not-tally-1510227753.

195 "I told President Trump": "Remarks by President Trump and President Xi in Joint Press Statement," Nov. 9, 2017, https://www.whitehouse.gov/briefings-statements/remarks-president-trump-president-xi-china-joint-press-statement-beijing-china/.

Chapter 11: Liu He Gets a Lecture, March 2018

202 He shunned big entourages: Interview with David Loevinger, the U.S. Treasury Department's China coordinator during the first term of the Obama administration, 2018.

202 he was the "authoritative person": Lingling Wei and Jeremy Page, "Discord Between China's Top Two Leaders Spills into the Open," *Wall Street Journal*, July 22, 2016, https://www.wsj.com/articles/discord-between-chinas-top-two-leaders-spills-into-the-open-1469134110.

203 "He's not an apologist": Interview with Myron Brilliant, U.S. Chamber of Commerce's executive vice president, January 2018.

206 Chinese mills also expanded overseas: Matthew Dalton and Lingling Wei, "How China Skirts America's Antidumping Tariffs on Steel," *Wall Street Journal*, June 4, 2018, https://www.wsj.com/articles/how-china-skirts-americas-antidumping-tariffs-on-steel-1528124339.

208 wouldn't help U.S. industry: Ross interview, October 2019.

211 "We gotta make": Independent reporting on the Trump pressure on Hassett. *Axios* also had a version. Mike Allen, "1 Big Thing . . . Trump's Two-Front War: China and D.C.," *Axios*, March 22, 2018.

211 Section 301 report: *Section 301 Findings of the Investigation into China's Acts, Policies, and Practices Related to Technology Transfer, Intellectual Property, and Innovation* (Washington, DC: Office of the United States Trade Representative, 2018), https://ustr.gov/sites/default/files/Section%20301%20FINAL.PDF.

Chapter 12: American Disarray, May 2018

216 "The Treasury secretary's job": Interview with Steven Mnuchin, October 2019.

217 raised by a single mother: Leonard Bernstein, "Underdog Navarro Gets a Boost from Voter Discontent Politics," *Los Angeles Times*, April 26, 1992.

218 "The economics of protectionism": Peter Navarro, *The Policy Game: How Special Interests and Ideologues Are Stealing America* (New York: Wiley, 1984), 85.

218 "turning point": Erica Pandey and Jonathan Swan, "Peter Navarro's Journey from Globalist to Protectionist, in His Own Words," *Axios,* June 24, 2018, https://www.axios.com/peter-navarro-globalist-protectionist-china -trade-war-policy-c9822426-aa7c-4706-b1a4-3c16cab63098.html.

218 a pioneer or visionary, rather than a chameleon: Navarro emailed responses.

219 Ron Vara: Tom Bartlett, "Trump's 'China Muse' Has an Imaginary Friend," *Chronicle Review,* Oct. 15, 2019, https://www.chronicle.com/interactives /20191015-navarro.

219 "a whimsical device": Navarro emailed responses.

220 "I take great offense": Mnuchin interview, October 2019.

224 "This cut-off company's": "ZTE Corporation Document Submitted for Ratification (Review) Form," Aug. 25, 2011, posted by the Commerce Department's Bureau of Industry and Security, https://www.bis.doc.gov /index.php/documents/about-bis/newsroom/1438-report-regarding -english/file.

Chapter 13: A Buying Mission, June 2018

231 "I tend not to give up": Mnuchin interview, October 2019.

234 "All we get to do": Ross interview, October 2019.

235 "The president's view": Mnuchin interview, October 2019.

246 When the trade stuff hit": William Mauldin, "Trump's Tariffs Find Friends in Minnesota's North, Foes in South," *Wall Street Journal,* July 18, 2018, https://www.wsj.com/articles/trumps-tariffs-find-friends-in-minnesotas -north-foes-in-south-1531906201.

Chapter 14: The Complaint: Chinese Arm-Twisting

250 antitrust investigators showed up: Lingling Wei and Bob Davis, "How China Systematically Pries Technology from U.S. Companies," *Wall Street Journal,* Sept. 26, 2018, https://www.wsj.com/articles/how-china-sys tematically-pries-technology-from-u-s-companies-1537972066.

252 "should bravely employ": Shepard Goldfein and James Keite, "Chinese Antitrust Enforcement and the U.S.: An Uncertain Path," *New York Law Journal,* Aug. 22, 2016.

255 "Why do you only": "Deng Xiaoping Approves Auto Joint Ventures," *Guang'an Daily,* April 19, 2018, http://cpc.people.com.cn/n1/2018/0419 /c69113-29936354.html.

256 "diffuses beyond the confines": Kun Jiang, Wolfgang Keller, Larry D. Qiu, and William Ridley, "International Joint Ventures and Internal vs.

External Technology Transfer: Evidence from China," National Bureau of Economic Research, October 2019, https://www.nber.org/papers/w24 455.pdf.

257 hardly the first country: Bob Davis and David Wessel, *Prosperity* (New York: Times Business, 1998), 259.

259 "the only way to achieve growth in China": "GE China CEO Says China Will Remain Most Relevant Growth Market," Xinhua, Nov. 8, 2017, http://www.chinadaily.com.cn/business/2017-11/08/content_34271935.htm.

259 "GE was a concern": Interview with Senator John Cornyn, September 2019.

267 Commerce secretary Ross was convinced: Ross interview, October 2019.

Chapter 15: Old Friends No More, September 2018

273 "The mood has shifted": Michael Martina, "U.S. Firms No Longer 'Positive Anchor' for Beijing Ties: AmCham in China," Reuters, April 17, 2019, https://www.reuters.com/article/us-usa-trade-china/u-s-firms-no-lon ger-positive-anchor-for-beijing-ties-amcham-in-china-idUSKCN1RT0CA.

274 Beijing increasingly subsidized state-connected firms: Anne Harrison, Marshall Meyer, Peichun Wang, Linda Zhao, and Minyuan Zhao, "Can a Tiger Change Its Stripes? Reform of Chinese State-Owned Enterprises in the Penumbra of the State," National Bureau of Economic Research, January 2019, http://papers.nber.org/tmp/60993-w25475.pdf.

276 hand-delivered a letter: Kate O'Keeffe, Aruna Viswanatha, and Cezary Podkul, "China's Pursuit of Fugitive Businessman Guo Wengui Kicks Off Manhattan Caper Worthy of Spy Thriller," *Wall Street Journal*, Oct. 22, 2017, https://www.wsj.com/articles/chinas-hunt-for-guo-wengui-a-fugitive -businessman-kicks-off-manhattan-caper-worthy-of-spy-thriller-15087 17977.

276 double agent: Aruna Viswanatha and Kate O'Keeffe, "Chinese Tycoon Holed Up in Manhattan Hotel Is Accused of Spying for Beijing," *Wall Street Journal*, July 22, 2019, https://www.wsj.com/articles/chinese-tycoon -holed-up-in-manhattan-hotel-is-accused-of-spying-for-beijing-1156 3810726.

279 "trying to assure": Schwarzman, *What It Takes*.

281 "days of so-called easy money": Cui interview, October 2018.

282 a "white list": Trefor Moss, "Power Play: How China-Owned Volvo Avoids Beijing's Battery Rules," *Wall Street Journal*, May 17, 2018, https://www.wsj .com/articles/power-play-how-china-owned-volvo-avoids-beijings-bat tery-rules-1526551937.

Chapter 16: Couples Therapy, Fall 2018

292 "I disagreed with him": Trump interview, November 2018.

294 CEOs to commit to traveling to Beijing: Tom Mitchell, "Beijing Sum-

mons Wall Street Bankers for Tariff Talks," *Financial Times*, Sept. 9, 2018, https://www.ft.com/content/c0034cba-b2ca-11e8-99ca-68cf89602132.

295 Xi Jinping convened an emergency Politburo meeting: Bob Davis and Lingling Wei, "'Bring Me Tariffs'—How Trump and Xi Drove Their Countries to the Brink of a Trade War," *Wall Street Journal*, Nov. 28, 2018, https://www.wsj.com/articles/bring-me-tariffshow-trump-and-xi-drove -their-countries-to-the-brink-of-a-trade-war-1543420440.

303 "target" or "expectation": Mnuchin interview, *Mornings with Maria*, Dec. 4, 2018.

308 "I would certainly intervene": Jeff Mason and Steve Holland, "Exclusive: Trump Says He Could Intervene in U.S. Case Against Huawei CFO," Reuters, Dec. 11, 2018, https://www.reuters.com/article/us-usa-trump -huawei-tech-exclusive/exclusive-trump-says-he-could-intervene-in-u-s -case-against-huawei-cfo-idUSKBN1OA2PQ.

309 prices Americans paid: Mary Amiti, Stephen J. Redding, and David E. Weinstein, "Who's Paying for the U.S. Tariffs? A Longer Term Perspective," *National Bureau of Economic Research*, Jan. 2020., http://papers.nber.org /tmp/57953-w26610.pdf.

309 "much bigger problem than China": Trump interview, November 2018.

310 "one of its leading sources": Steven J. Davis, "Trade Policy Is Upending markets—but Not Investment," *Chicago Booth Review*, March 18, 2019, https://review.chicagobooth.edu/economics/2019/article/trade-policy -upending-markets-not-investment.

311 "benchmark of success": Freakonomics radio interview with Gary Cohn, March 13, 2019, http://freakonomics.com/podcast/cohn/.

Chapter 17: Ping-Pong Diplomacy, January 2019

314 "without the Treasury secretary": Interview with Larry Kudlow, October 2019.

329 "We've got to be realistic": Lingling Wei, Jeremy Page, and Bob Davis, "U.S.-China Trade Talks Hit a Bump," *Wall Street Journal*, March 8, 2019, https://www.wsj.com/articles/u-s-china-trade-deal-isnt-imminent-am bassador-branstad-says-11552031163.

329 "the U.S. is desperate right now": Cohn, Freakonomics interview, March 2019.

Chapter 18: Bring Your Companies Home, August 2019

337 Beijing published an 8,300-word white paper: Xinhua, "China Publishes White Paper on Trade Consultations, Revealing U.S. Backtracking," June 2, 2019, http://www.xinhuanet.com/english/2019-06/02/c_138110738.htm.

341 Their index of trade risks: Tarek A. Hassan, Stephan Hollander, Laurence van Lent, and Ahmed Tahoun, "Firm-Level Political Risk: Measurement

and Effects," National Bureau of Economic Research, June 2019, https://www.nber.org/papers/w24029.pdf.

341 reduced global GDP by 0.8 percent: Dario Caldara, Matteo Iacoviello, Patrick Molligo, Andrea Prestipino, and Andrea Raffo, "Does Trade Policy Uncertainty Affect Global Economic Activity?," *FEDS Notes,* Sept. 2019.

343 actively courting foreign firms: Yoko Kubota and Chao Deng, "China Faces Limited Options for Retaliating Against Latest U.S. Threat," *Wall Street Journal,* Aug. 2, 2019, https://www.wsj.com/articles/china-faces-limited-options-for-retaliating-against-latest-u-s-threat-11564750795.

345 "We're being uninvited to bid": Richard Waters, "How the Trade War Is Damaging the US Tech Industry," *Financial Times,* Aug. 16, 2019, https://www.ft.com/content/16fa93ba-bf69-11e9-b350-db00d509634e.

346 Beijing said it would create: Yoko Kubota, "China Studying Tech Companies' Exposure to U.S. Suppliers," *Wall Street Journal,* Aug. 29, 2019, https://www.wsj.com/articles/china-studying-tech-companies-exposure-to-u-s-suppliers-11567078489.

353 "the talks were going unsatisfactorily": Kudlow interview, October 2019.

354 "beyond crazy": Interview with Robert Lighthizer, September 2019.

356 "call for talks was approved": Kudlow interview, October 2019.

Chapter 19: Negotiating a Truce, December 2019–January 2020

361 "the KGB build all our telecom": Interview with Matt Pottinger, November 2019.

364 The setbacks fed quiet criticism of Xi: Chun Han Wong and Jeremy Page, "For China's Xi, the Hong Kong Crisis Is Personal," *Wall Street Journal,* Sept. 27, 2019, https://www.wsj.com/articles/for-chinas-xi-the-hong-kong-crisis-is-personal-11569613304.

364 "It's more than half full": Interview with Myron Brilliant, U.S. Chamber of Commerce executive vice president.

365 Chinese officials tried again to narrow the scope: Lingling Wei, Chao Deng, and Josh Zumbrun, "China Seeks to Narrow Trade Talks with U.S. in Bid to Break Deadlock," *Wall Street Journal,* Sept. 12, 2019, https://www.wsj.com/articles/china-seeks-to-narrow-trade-talks-with-u-s-in-bid-to-break-deadlock-11568284169.

366 from European firms: Asa Fitch and Dan Strumpf, "Huawei Manages to Make Smartphones Without American Chips," *Wall Street Journal,* Dec. 1, 2019, https://www.wsj.com/articles/huawei-manages-to-make-smartphones-without-american-chips-11575196201?mod=hp_lead_pos1.

367 $75 billion in state support: Chuin-Wei Yap, "State Support Helped Fuel Huawei's Global Rise," *Wall Street Journal,* Dec. 25, 2019, https://www.wsj.com/articles/state-support-helped-fuel-huaweis-global-rise-11577280736

368 "passionate defender": Shawn Donnan and Jenny Donard, "How Trump's

Trade War Went from Method to Madness," *Bloomberg Businessweek*, Nov. 14, 2019, https://www.bloomberg.com/news/features/2019-11-14/how-trump-s-trade-war-went-from-method-to-madness.

368 "the president had been briefed": Kudlow interview, October 2019.

370 They calculated that their offer: Bob Davis and Lingling Wei, "How the U.S. and China Settled on a Trade Deal Neither Wanted," Jan. 13, 2020, https://www.wsj.com/articles/how-the-u-s-and-china-settled-on-a-trade-deal-neither-wanted-11578931635.

370 "Think in terms of what will happen": Davis and Wei, "How the U.S. and China."

372 "Globalists!": Alex Leary, "In the Battles Over Trump's Trade Wars, Hawkish Adviser Navarro Endures," *Wall Street Journal,* Dec. 21, 2019, https://www.wsj.com/articles/in-the-battles-over-trumps-trade-wars-hawkish-adviser-navarro-endures-11576943074.

373 "It's good": Davis and Wei, "How the U.S. and China."

374 China had already: World Bank, "Doing Business 2020," Oct. 24, 2019, https://www.doingbusiness.org.

379 Xi Jinping came under: Lingling Wei and Chao Deng, "China's Coronavirus Response Is Questioned: 'Everyone Was Blindly Optimistic,'" *Wall Street Journal*, Jan. 24, 2020, https://www.wsj.com/articles/china-contends-with-questions-over-response-to-viral-outbreak-11579825832.

379 Looking to muffle: Lingling Wei, "China Strains to Stamp Out Coronavirus Criticisms at Home," *Wall Street Journal*, Jan. 28, 2020, https://www.wsj.com/articles/china-strains-to-stamp-out-coronavirus-criticisms-at-home-11580207403.

379 On February 19: *Wall Street Journal*, "China Expels Three *Wall Street Journal* Reporters," Feb. 19, 2020, https://www.wsj.com/articles/china-expels-three-wall-street-journal-reporters-11582100355.

380 "not going to stop subsidizing state-run": Kudlow interview, October 2019.

380 "Impeachment is irrelevant": Mnuchin interview, October 2019.

382 "The press has a very hard time": Pottinger interview, November 2019.

383 "an impact on the election": Mnuchin interview, October 2019.

383 close to nil: Chao Deng and Lingling Wei, "China Emerges with Wins from U.S. Trade Truce," *Wall Street Journal*, Oct. 12, 2019, https://www.wsj.com/articles/china-emerges-with-wins-from-u-s-trade-truce-11570912439?mod=searchresults&page=1&pos=10&mod=article_inline.

384 "You can start the process of reform": Lighthizer interview, September 2019.

Chapter 20: Looking Ahead: Cold War II

394 fell by 25 percent: Alessandro Nicita, "Trade and Trade Diversion Effects of United States Tariffs on China," United Nations Conference on Trade

and Development, Research Paper No. 37, November 2019, 5, https://unc tad.org/en/PublicationsLibrary/ser-rp-2019d9_en.pdf.

394 fell more than 60 percent: Patrick Van den Bossche, Brooks Levering, and Yuri Castano, "U.S. Trade Policy and Reshoring: The Real Impact of America's New Trade Policies," A. T. Kearney, 2019, 8, https://www.at kearney.com/operations-performance-transformation/us-reshoring-index.

394 China as the top threat: Laura Silver, Kat Devlin, and Christine Huang, "U.S. Views of China Turn Sharply Negative Amid Trade Tensions," Pew Research Center Global Attitudes & Trends, Aug. 13, 2019, https://www .pewresearch.org/global/2019/08/13/u-s-views-of-china-turn-sharply -negative-amid-trade-tensions/.

397 "President Trump has unmasked": Kudlow interview, October 2019.

398 "Regime change": Lighthizer interview, September 2019.

399 outweighed the gains: Pablo D. Fajgelbaum, Pinelopi K. Goldberg, Patrick J. Kennedy, and Amit K. Khandelwal, "The Return to Protectionism," National Bureau of Economic Research, October 2019, https://www.nber .org/papers/w25638.pdf.

399 raised the wholesale price: Mary Amiti, Stephen J. Redding, and David Weinstein, "The Impact of the 2018 Trade War on U.S. Prices and Welfare," National Bureau of Economic Research, March 2019, https://www .nber.org/papers/w25672.pdf.

399 data from 151 countries: Davide Furceri, Swarnali A. Hannan, Jonathan D. Ostry, and Andrew K. Rose, "Macroeconomic Consequences of Tariffs," IMF Working Paper, January 2019, https://www.imf.org/en/Publications /WP/Issues/2019/01/15/Macroeconomic-Consequences-of-Tariffs-46469.

399 cost average U.S. households: Dubravko Lakos-Bujas, "Trading Tariffs and Playing with Fire," JP Morgan Equity Strategy and Quantitative Research, June 7, 2019.

400 U.S. tariffs hurt far more than they helped: Aaron Flaaen and Justin Pierce, "Disentangling the Effects of the 2018–2019 Tariffs on a Globally Connected U.S. Manufacturing Sector," *Finance and Economics Discussion Series 2019-086, Federal Reserve System,* Dec. 23, 2019, 3, https://www .federalreserve.gov/econres/feds/files/2019086pap.pdf.

400 63 percent were replaced by imports from elsewhere: Nicita, "Trade Diversion," 11.

402 "Lower scores lead to the opposite": "The Digital Hand: How China's Corporate Social Credit System Conditions Market Actors," European Chamber of Commerce in China, Aug. 28, 2019, 1, https://www.european chamber.com.cn/en/publications-archive/709/The_Digital_Hand_How _China_s_Corporate_Social_Credit_System_Conditions_Market_Actors.

402 The corporate system is similar: Josh Chin and Gillian Wong, "China's New Tool for Social Control: A Credit Rating for Everything," *Wall Street*

Journal, Nov. 28, 2016, https://www.wsj.com/articles/chinas-new-tool-for-social-control-a-credit-rating-for-everything-1480351590.

403 According to a study: Scott Kennedy and Daniel H. Rosen, "Market Metrics: A Fact-Based Approach to the Chinese Economic Challenge," CSIS, Oct. 10, 2019, https://www.csis.org/analysis/market-metrics-fact-based-approach-chinese-economic-challenge.

404 Chinese chip makers receive far more government support: "Measuring Distortions in International Markets: The Semiconductor Value Chain," OECD Trade Policy Papers, No. 234, December 2019, http://dx.doi.org/10.1787/8fe4491d-en.

406 "we don't let them veto doing things": Lighthizer interview, September 2019.

407 "Beijing's outreach to third countries": Matthew P. Goodman, William Alan Reinsch, and Scott Kennedy, "Beyond the Brink," Center for Strategic & International Studies, September 2019, 62, https://www.csis.org/analysis/beyond-brink-escalation-and-conflict-us-china-economic-relations.

410 "moonshots": Initially recommended at the end of the Obama administration in "Ensuring Long-Term U.S. Leadership in Semiconductors," President's Council of Advisors on Science and Technology, January 2017, https://obamawhitehouse.archives.gov/sites/default/files/microsites/ostp/PCAST/pcast_ensuring_long-term_us_leadership_in_semiconductors.pdf. More recently picked up in "Innovation and National Security: Keeping Our Edge," Council on Foreign Relations, September 2019, https://www.cfr.org/report/keeping-our-edge/. Also in Charles W. Boustany Jr. and Aaron L. Friedberg, "Partial Disengagement: A New U.S. Strategy for Economic Competition with China," National Bureau of Asian Research, November 2019, https://www.nbr.org/wp-content/uploads/pdfs/publications/sr82_china-task-force-report-final.pdf.

INDEX

Xi Jinping (*continued*), overseas
capital courted by, 50–51; phase-
one deal and (2020), 369, 373–74,
415–16, 418, 420–21; phase-two
deal's prospects and, 381; presiding
over Zhejiang province, 37–38,
39–41, 50–51, 150–51, 351; removal
of all tariffs demanded by, 15, 365,
371; retaliatory acts of, 28; rise to
power of, 16, 150, 151–53, 157, 193–94,
397; self-reliance drive (decoupling
project) of, 391–92; state investment
under, 31, 151, 155, 273; strategy
of, for dealing with hostile Trump
administration, 295–96; Trump's
presidential campaign as viewed by,
162; Trump's relationship with, 145,
169–70, 171, 172, 194–95, 243, 302,
362 (*see also* Mar-a-Lago summit);
Trump's snub of Liu He answered
by, 222–23; United States first
visited by, 156–57; ZTE and,
225–26
Xi Jinping Thought, 336
Xi Zhongxun, 40, 43–44, 149
Xiang Songzuo, 355–56
Xinhua News Agency, 143, 259, 299,
300–301, 311, 349, 350
Xinjiang, 33, 64, 395
Xu Shanda, 101
Xuzhou Construction Machinery
Group Co. (XCMG), 412

Yang Jiechi, 163–64, 199–200
Yang Weimin, 241
Yao Ming, 193
Yi Gang, 293, 299
Yu Jianhua, 195
yuan. *See* currency, Chinese
Yugoslavia, U.S.-led bombing
campaigns in, 71, 78–81
Yum China Holdings Inc., 64

Zandi, Mark, 340
Zhang Shuguang, 295
Zhang Weiying, 405
Zhangjiagang Glory Chemical Industry
Company, 250–52
Zhao Leji, 17
Zhejiang province, 37–51; Fengqiao
experience and, 40–41; foreign
direct investments in, 50–51, 150–51;
private entrepreneurs in, 45–50;
wealthy population of, 41; Xi's years
presiding over, 37–38, 39–41, 50–51,
150–51, 351
Zhejiang Wanfeng Alloy Wheel
Company, 48
Zheng Zeguang, 349
Zhong Guang (originally Zhong
Fuchang), 5–6, 419–20
Zhong Shan, 48, 351
Zhou Enlai, 61, 75
Zhou Xiaochuan, 103, 104
Zhou Yongkang, 152
Zhu Chenghu, 241–42
Zhu Guangyao, 192, 195
Zhu Rongji, 65–69, 79, 103, 105, 384–85;
barnstorming tour across America of,
78; China's entry into WTO and, 11,
65–69, 71, 72, 73–85, 87, 105, 128–29,
202, 415, 418, 420; Clinton's failed
talks with, 66, 73–78, 301, 415, 418;
economic strategy of, 67–68; purged
during Cultural Revolution, 67
zhua da fang xiao ("grabbing the big ones
and letting the small ones go"), 68
Ziang Songzuo, 355
Zoellick, Robert, 89, 129, 157
ZTE Corporation, 225–26, 227, 228,
246, 267, 345, 391; as bargaining chip
in trade battle, 225–26; cybersecurity
and, 225–26, 391; U.S. sanctions
against, 221, 223–24, 391
Zuckerberg, Mark, 141

ABOUT THE AUTHORS

Bob Davis

Bob Davis has been covering international economics for the *Wall Street Journal* since the early 1990s when his Washington, D.C., bureau chief, Al Hunt, assigned him to cover "international competitiveness," whatever that was. Pretty quickly that turned into a focus on trade and globalization, especially U.S.-China relations.

Davis covered President Clinton's negotiations with Chinese Premier Zhu Rongji in 1998 over China's entry into the World Trade Organization. After that, he was Brussels bureau chief from 2001 to 2002, Latin America bureau chief from 2004 to 2007, and China economics correspondent based in Beijing from 2011 to 2014. For the past three years, he has focused on the Washington, D.C., part of President Trump's China trade war, while Lingling Wei handled the China part.

Along the way, he won a Raymond Clapper Award for Washington reporting in 2000 for his coverage of Clinton's China deal. He was also part of *Wall Street Journal* teams that won the Pulitzer Prize for international reporting in 1999 for coverage of the Asian and Russian financial crisis, and the Overseas Press Club award in 2005 for Latin American coverage.

In 2014, he and his wife, Debra Bruno, wrote an e-book about their China experiences, *Beijing from A-to-Z*. In 1998, he coauthored a book with David Wessel on the future of the American economy, called *Prosperity*, which *Business Week* named one of the year's ten best business books.

He began his journalism career in 1975 when he founded an alternative newspaper in Oneonta, New York, *The Susquehanna Sentinel*, and a newspaper printing business.

Lingling Wei

Lingling Wei is a senior China correspondent at the *Wall Street Journal*. That's the job she wanted since she first went into journalism in the 1990s, an era of greater openness of China to the world.

She learned about Bob Woodward and Carl Bernstein from visiting Fulbright scholars at her university, Shanghai's Fudan University. A new Center for American Studies at Fudan allowed her access to the *Journal*, the *New York Times*, and other American publications. Her subsequent work at a government-owned newspaper strengthened her desire to write stories reflecting real news and the interests of the people.

After she earned a master's degree in journalism from New York University in 2000, Wei started work at *Dow Jones Newswires*. Her coverage there of the U.S. housing crisis won her a Society of American Business Editors and Writers award in 2007. Wei joined the *Journal* in New York in 2008 to cover real estate.

In 2011, Wei, a newly minted U.S. citizen then, got her dream job: she became a China correspondent for the *Journal*. That's also when she started to work with Bob Davis, who helped her become a more ambitious journalist. Her coverage includes China's massive debt problems, tightened state control over the economy, and, most recently, the U.S.-China trade war.

Wei is featured in the *Journal*'s "Face of Real News" campaign aimed at celebrating quality journalism. She was a finalist at the

Society of Publishers in Asia for its 2017 Journalist of the Year award and was cited by the Overseas Press Club in 2016 for best international business reporting. She and Davis were part of a *Wall Street Journal* team that won a New York Press Club award in 2019 for coverage of "Trump's Trade Turmoil."